The
James Bond phenomenon

A critical reader
Second edition

Edited by

Christoph Lindner

Manchester University Press

Manchester and New York

distributed in the United States exclusively by Palgrave Macmillan

First edition published 2003 by Manchester University Press

This edition published 2009 by Manchester University Press
Oxford Road, Manchester M13 9NR, UK
and Room 400, 175 Fifth Avenue, New York, NY 10010, USA

Distributed in the United States exclusively by
Palgrave Macmillan, 175 Fifth Avenue, New York,
NY 10010, USA

Distributed in Canada exclusively by
UBC Press, University of British Columbia, 2029 West Mall,
Vancouver, BC, Canada V6T 1Z2

British Library Cataloguing-in-Publication Data
A catalogue record for this book is available from the British Library

Library of Congress Cataloging-in-Publication Data applied for

ISBN   978 0 7190 8095 1 *paperback*

This edition first published 2009

Typeset in 10/12 Minion Pro
by Servis Filmsetting Ltd, Stockport, Cheshire

Printed in Great Britain
by MPG Books Group, UK

Contents

Preface to the second edition

It is the nature of any book on James Bond to be out of date almost as soon as it is published. The world of 007 shifts and changes so quickly that any attempt to stabilise our understanding of the Bond phenomenon is, by necessity, provisional – at least so long as 007 continues to thrive across the range of our popular media (and there is no end of that in sight). For many fans and scholars, the dynamic between change and continuity that has always characterised the world of 007 is both the attraction and the frustration of Bond. All too aware of this tension, I conceived this book as a work in progress, one that would be updated periodically alongside the very cultural phenomenon it tracks. The question, therefore, was never whether to update this book, but rather when to start doing it. With the release of *Casino Royale* in 2006, which marks not only the launch of yet another cycle of Bond films but also a self-conscious rebooting of the 007 character and series, the time seemed right for a second edition.

In selecting new material to include, however, I consciously resisted the temptation to overemphasise the emergent Daniel Craig era, since it is still too soon to tell how this latest cycle of Bond films will play out, and also how these films will affect our reading of the 007 series as a whole. But as you will have noticed, Craig's image does grace the book's front cover, and this in itself is a loaded (and potentially controversial) statement. What the new chapters in this edition therefore offer is a balance between analysis of the 'new 007' and attention to other aspects of the Bond phenomenon that have been variously overlooked or under-examined. These include Bond's multi-faceted relationship with *Playboy* magazine, the cultural politics of Bond's erotic orientalism, and the relatively recent mega-boom in 007 video gaming. Combined with an updated Bond chronology, bibliography, and introduction, this new edition seeks not just to extend our working understanding of the Bond phenomenon, but in the process to highlight the importance of periodically reassessing the slippery cultural icon that is Agent 007.

Christoph Lindner

List of figures

List of contributors

Cynthia Baron is an Associate Professor in the Department of Theatre and Film and an affiliated faculty in the American Culture and Women's Studies Programs at Bowling Green State University. She is co-author of *Reframing Screen Performance: Analyzing Acting as a Component of Film* (2008) and co-editor of *More Than a Method: Trends and Traditions in Contemporary Film Performance* (2004).

Tony Bennett is Professor of Sociology at The Open University. He has published widely in the fields of sociology, cultural studies, and cultural history. Books include (with Michael Emmison and John Frow) *Accounting for Tastes: Australian Everyday Cultures* (1999), *Culture: A Reformer's Science* (1998), and *The Birth of the Museum: History, Theory, Politics* (1995).

Christine Bold is Professor of English at the University of Guelph, Canada. She is the author of *Selling the Wild West: Popular Western Fiction, 1860 to 1960* (1987), *The WPA Guides: Mapping America* (1999), *Writers, Plumbers, and Anarchists: The WPA Writers' Project in Massachusetts* (2006), and co-author of *Remembering Women Murdered by Men: Memorials across Canada* (2006). Currently, she is editing *U.S. Popular Print Culture, 1860–1920* for the Oxford History of Popular Print Culture series.

Tara Brabazon is Professor of Media at the University of Brighton. She is the author of eight books, including *Tracking the Jack: A Retracing of the Antipodes* (2000), *Ladies Who Lunge: Essays on Difficult Women* (2002), *Digital Hemlock: Internet Education and the Poisoning of Teaching* (2002), *From Revolution to Revelation: Generation X, Popular Memory and Cultural Studies* (2005), and *Playing on the Periphery: Sport, Memory and Identity* (2006). She is a wide-ranging writer and commentator on media education, popular memory, popular culture, and cultural studies.

James Chapman is Professor of Film at the University of Leicester. He has research interests in British cinema history, film and society, and the history of popular culture. He is the author of *Licence To Thrill: A Cultural History of the James Bond Films* (1999), *Saints and Avengers: British Adventure Series of the 1960s* (2002), *Past and Present: National Identity and the British Historical Film* (2005), and *Inside the Tardis: The Worlds of Doctor Who – A Cultural History* (2006).

Michael Denning is Professor of American Studies and English at Yale University. He is author of *The Cultural Front: The Laboring of American Culture in the Twentieth Century* (1997), *Mechanic Accents: Dime Novels and Working Class Culture in America* (1987), and *Cover Stories: Narrative and Ideology in the British Spy Thriller* (1987).

Umberto Eco is a novelist and Professor of Semiotics at the University of Bologna. His many contributions to literary theory and intellectual culture include *A Theory of Semiotics* (1976), *The Role of the Reader* (1979), *Semiotics and the Philosophy of Language* (1984), and more recently *The Search for the Perfect Language* (1995) and *Belief or Nonbelief* (2000). His critically acclaimed novels include *The Name of the Rose* (1980), *Foucault's Pendulum* (1988), and *The Island of the Day Before* (1995).

Ajay Gehlawat is Assistant Professor of Theatre and Film in the Hutchins School of Liberal Studies at Sonoma State University. His research and teaching interests include South Asian media, Third World Cinema, popular culture, and postcolonial studies. He is the author of, most recently, 'The Bollywood Song and Dance, or Making a Culinary Theatre from Dung-Cakes and Dust' (*Quarterly Review of Film and Video*, 2006). He has published articles on numerous topics, including Marilyn Monroe and Arthur Miller, Woody Allen, and media pedagogy. Currently he is preparing a manuscript on theories of Bollywood and global spectatorship.

Stefan Hall is an instructor in the Department of Theatre & Film at Bowling Green State University and teaches courses in Introduction to Film and History of Film. He is currently completing his PhD in the Critical Studies in Film, Media, and Culture track of the American Culture Studies program at BGSU. His dissertation, *You've Seen the Movie, Now Play the Game: Recoding the Cinematic in Digital Media and Virtual Culture*, examines the relationship between film and video games.

Claire Hines is Senior Lecturer in Film and Television Studies at Southampton Solent University. Her research and teaching interests include sexual repre-sentation, gender studies, and queer cinema. She has contributed articles to (with Pam Cook) *Fashioning Film Stars* (BFI, 2005), *Falling in Love Again: The Contemporary Romantic Comedy* (I.B Tauris, 2008) and *Peep Shows: Essays in Cult Visual Erotica* (Wallflower, forthcoming). She is currently co-editing a collection of essays on the hardcore screen, titled *Hard to Swallow* (Wallflower, forthcoming), and working on a book that explores the relationship between James Bond and *Playboy*.

Elisabeth Ladenson is author of *Dirt for Art's Sake: Books on Trial from Madame Bovary to Lolita* (2006), and *Proust's Lesbianism* (1999). She teaches French and comparative literature at Columbia University and is general editor of the journal *Romantic Review*.

Jim Leach is a Professor in the Department of Communications, Popular Culture and Film at Brock University in St Catharines, Ontario. His research and teaching interests include Canadian cinema, British cinema, popular cinema, and film and cultural theory. He is the author of *A Possible Cinema: The Films of Alain Tanner* (1984), *Claude Jutra: Filmmaker* (1999), *British Film* (2004), and *Film in Canada* (2006).

Christoph Lindner is Professor of English Literature at the University of Amsterdam. He is the author of *Fictions of Commodity Culture: From the Victorian to the Postmodern* (2003), and editor of *Urban Space and Cityscapes* (2006) and *Revisioning 007* (2009). He has also published articles and essays on a wide range of topics, including vertical New York, contemporary British cinema, Conrad and urban decay, and the afterlife of the Twin Towers. He is currently completing an interdisciplinary book on literature, urbanism, and the visual arts in New York City.

Toby Miller is Professor of English, Sociology, and Women's Studies at the University of California, Riverside. He is the author and editor of over 20 books, including *The Well-Tempered Self: Citizenship, Culture, and the Postmodern Subject* (1993), *Contemporary Australian Television* (with Stuart Cunningham, 1994), *The Avengers* (1997), *Technologies of Truth: Cultural Citizenship and the Popular Media* (1998), *Popular Culture and Everyday Life* (with Alec McHoul, 1998), *A Companion to Film Theory* (edited with Robert Stam, 1999), *Film and Theory: An Anthology* (edited with Robert Stam, 2000), *A Companion to Cultural Studies* (edited, 2001), *Critical Cultural Policy Studies: A Reader* (edited with Justin Lewis, 2003), and *Cultural Citizenship* (2007).

Linda Racioppi is Professor of Comparative Cultures and Politics and International Relations in James Madison College at Michigan State University. She has written *Soviet Policy toward South Asia since 1970* (1994) and, with Katherine See, *Women's Activism in Contemporary Russia* (1997), as well as articles and chapters on gender, women's mobilization, nationalism, ethnic conflict, and conflict resolution. Together with Colleen Tremonte, she has published articles on interdisciplinarity and on film and international politics; they are currently working on a book manuscript on film, gender, and nationalism.

Jeff Smith is a Professor in the Department of Communication Arts at the University of Wisconsin-Madison. His work has appeared in *Cinema Journal* and *The Velvet Light Trap*, and he has contributed essays to such anthologies as *Soundtrack Available: Essays on Film and Popular Music* (2001), *Controlling Hollywood: Censorship and Regulation in the Studio Era* (1999), *Titanic:*

Anatomy of a Blockbuster (1999), *Passionate Views: Film, Cognition and Emotion* (1999), and *Post-Theory: Reconstructing Film Studies* (1996). He is the author of *The Sounds of Commerce: Marketing Popular Film Music* (1998), and is currently working on a metacritical study of Hollywood cinema during the blacklist period.

Paul Stock is a journalist in Sydney. He has also tutored in sociology and cultural studies and worked as a reference librarian at universities across Australia. His research interests include popular memory and history, simulation and parody, and British post-war cultural history, all of which have found a convenient home in the study of 007.

Colleen M. Tremonte is Associate Professor of Comparative Cultures and Politics and Humanities, Culture and Writing in James Madison College at Michigan State University, and a Fellow in the Carnegie Academy for the Scholarship of Teaching and Learning. She has published articles on film, metaphor, and genre, and on visual culture and pedagogy, including 'Film, Classical Rhetoric and Visual Literacy' and '*Metropolis* Redux: Visual Metaphor and the Urbanscape'. Together with Linda Racioppi, she has published articles on interdisciplinarity and on film and international politics; they are currently working on a book manuscript on film, gender, and nationalism.

Martin Willis is Reader in English Literature at the University of Glamorgan and Co-Director of the Glamorgan Research Centre for Literature, Arts and Science (RCLAS). He has published widely within the field of literature and science, including a recent monograph, *Mesmerists, Monsters and Machines* (Kent State University Press) and two collections of essays, *Victorian Literary Mesmerism* (ed. with Catherine Wynne, Rodopi) and *Repositioning Victorian Sciences* (ed. with David Clifford, Elisabeth Wadge and Alex Warwick, Anthem).

Janet Woollacott has published widely on culture, politics, and mass media. Her many books include *Bond and Beyond: The Political Career of a Popular Hero* (with Tony Bennett, 1987), *Politics, Ideology and Popular Culture* (with Tony Bennett and Alan Clarke, 1982), *Mass Communication and Society* (with James Curran and Michael Gurevitch, 1979), and *Social Relationships in Art* (1976).

Acknowledgements

For financial support in preparing the first edition of this book, I am grateful to the University of Wales, Aberystwyth. A generous research grant from this institution made it possible to add William Slocombe to the 007 team. His outstanding editorial assistance proved to be invaluable. In preparing the second edition of this book, I was greatly assisted by Will Scheibel at Northern Illinois University, and I am indebted to him not just for his meticulous hard work but also for bringing his extensive knowledge of film history and popular culture to the project. A visiting fellowship at Indiana University's Lilly Library made it possible to consult original archival material related to Fleming's writing and Bond's early screen existence, and I wish to thank the library staff at the Lilly for their hospitality and help. On a personal note, I would like to dedicate this book to Graham and Sebastian Moss. On a public note, I would like to dedicate this book to 007 fans everywhere.

Christoph Lindner

Copyright acknowledgements

Cynthia Baron, 'Doctor No: Bonding Britishness to Racial Sovereignty', *Spectator: USC Journal of Film and Television Criticism* 14.2 (1994), reprinted by permission of the author and the journal.

Tony Bennett and Janet Woollacott, 'The Moments of Bond', in *Bond and Beyond: The Political Career of a Popular Hero* (Macmillan, 1987; Routledge US, 1987), reprinted by permission of Palgrave Macmillan and Routledge Inc, part of the Taylor and Francis Group.

Christine Bold, '"Under the very skirts of Britannia": Re-Reading Women in the James Bond Novels', *Queens Quarterly* 100.2 (1993), reprinted by permission of the author.

Tara Brabazon, 'Britain's Last Line of Defence: Miss Moneypenny and the Desperations of Filmic Feminism', in *Ladies who Lunge: Celebrating Difficult Women* (University of New South Wales Press, 2002, distributed in the UK by Eurospan London), also published in *Women's Studies International Forum*, 22.5 (1999), pp. 489–96, reprinted by permission of the author, UNSW Press, and Elsevier Science.

James Chapman, 'A License to Thrill', in *Licence to Thrill: A Cultural History of the James Bond Films* (I.B. Tauris, 1999), reprinted by permission of the author and I. B. Tauris.

Michael Denning, 'Licensed to Look', in *Cover Stories: Narrative and Ideology in the British Spy Thriller* (Routledge, 1987), reprinted by permission of the author.

Umberto Eco, 'Narrative Structures in Fleming', in *The Role of the Reader: Explorations in the Semiotics of Texts* (Indiana University Press, 1979), reprinted by permission of Indiana University Press.

Toby Miller, 'James Bond's Penis', in *Masculinity: Bodies, Movies, Culture*, ed. by Peter Lehman (Routledge, 2001), reprinted by permission of the author and Routledge Inc., part of the Taylor and Francis Group.

Jeff Smith, 'Creating a Bond Market: Selling John Barry's Soundtracks and Theme Songs', in *The Sounds of Commerce: Marketing Popular Film Music* (© Columbia University Press, 1998), reprinted by permission of the author and Columbia University Press.

Paul Stock, 'Dial "M" for Metonym: Universal Exports, M's Office Space and Empire', *National Identities* 2.1 (2000), reprinted by permission of the author and Taylor and Francis (www.tandf.co.uk/journals).

Janet Woollacott, 'The James Bond Films: Conditions of Production', in *British Cinema History*, ed. by James Curran and Vincent Porter (Weidenfeld and Nicolson, 1983), reprinted by permission of the author.

Select Bond chronology

1953   Ian Fleming, *Casino Royale*
1954   Ian Fleming, *Live and Let Die*
1955   Ian Fleming, *Moonraker*
1956   Ian Fleming, *Diamonds Are Forever*
1957   Ian Fleming, *From Russia, With Love*
1958   Ian Fleming, *Dr No*
1959   Ian Fleming, *Goldfinger*
1960   Ian Fleming, *For Your Eyes Only*
1961   Ian Fleming, *Thunderball*
1962   Ian Fleming, *The Spy Who Loved Me*
         Dr No (Dir. Terence Young; Sean Connery as Bond)
1963   Ian Fleming, *On Her Majesty's Secret Service*
         From Russia With Love (Dir. Terence Young; Sean Connery as Bond)
1964   Ian Fleming, *You Only Live Twice*
         Goldfinger (Dir. Guy Hamilton; Sean Connery as Bond)
1965   Ian Fleming, *The Man With The Golden Gun*
         Thunderball (Dir. Terence Young; Sean Connery as Bond)
1966   Ian Fleming, *Octopussy*
1967   *You Only Live Twice* (Dir. Lewis Gilbert; Sean Connery as Bond)
         Casino Royale (Dir. John Huston *et al.*; David Niven as Bond)
1968   Kingsley Amis (as Robert Markham), *Colonel Sun*
1969   *On Her Majesty's Secret Service* (Dir. Peter Hunt; George Lazenby as Bond)
1971   *Diamonds Are Forever* (Dir. Guy Hamilton; Sean Connery as Bond)
1973   *Live and Let Die* (Dir. Guy Hamilton; Roger Moore as Bond)
1974   *The Man With The Golden Gun* (Dir. Guy Hamilton; Roger Moore as Bond)
1977   *The Spy Who Loved Me* (Dir. Lewis Gilbert; Roger Moore as Bond)
         Christopher Wood, *James Bond, The Spy Who Loved Me*

1979 *Moonraker* (Dir. Lewis Gilbert; Roger Moore as Bond)
      Christopher Wood, *James Bond and Moonraker*
1981 John Gardner, *Licence Renewed*
      For Your Eyes Only (Dir. John Glen; Roger Moore as Bond)
1982 John Gardner, *For Special Services*
1983 John Gardner, *Icebreaker*
      Octopussy (Dir. John Glen; Roger Moore as Bond)
      Never Say Never Again (Dir. Irvin Kershner; Sean Connery as Bond)
1984 John Gardner, *Role of Honour*
1985 *A View to A Kill* (Dir. John Glen; Timothy Dalton as Bond)
1986 John Gardner, *Nobody Lives Forever*
1987 John Gardner, *No Deals, Mr Bond*
      The Living Daylights (Dir. John Glen; Timothy Dalton as Bond)
1988 John Gardner, *Scorpius*
1989 *Licence to Kill* (Dir. John Glen; Timothy Dalton as Bond)
      John Gardner, *Licence to Kill*
1990 John Gardner, *Brokenclaw*
1991 John Gardner, *The Man From Barbarossa*
1992 John Gardner, *Death is Forever*
1993 John Gardner, *Never Send Flowers*
1994 John Gardner, *Sea Fire*
1995 *GoldenEye* (Dir. Martin Campbell; Pierce Brosnan as Bond)
      John Gardner, *GoldenEye*
1996 John Gardner, *Cold*
1997 Raymond Benson, *Zero Minus Ten*
      Tomorrow Never Dies (Dir. Roger Spottiswoode; Pierce Brosnan as Bond)
      Raymond Benson, *Tomorrow Never Dies*
1998 Raymond Benson, *The Facts of Death*
1999 Raymond Benson, *High Time To Kill*
      The World Is Not Enough (Dir. Michael Apted; Pierce Brosnan as Bond)
      Raymond Benson, *The World Is Not Enough*
2000 Raymond Benson, *Doubleshot*
2001 Raymond Benson, *Never Dream of Dying*
2002 Raymond Benson, *The Man With the Red Tattoo*
      Die Another Day (Dir. Lee Tamahori; Pierce Brosnan as Bond)
      Raymond Benson, *Die Another Day*
2006 *Casino Royale* (Dir. Martin Campbell; Daniel Craig as Bond)
2008 Sebastian Faulks, *Devil May Care*
      Quantum of Solace (Dir. Marc Forster; Daniel Craig as Bond)

Christoph Lindner

Introduction

Mr Kiss Kiss Bang Bang

The name is Bond, James Bond. He is a popular hero, an icon of adventure, a guru of male style, an emblem of glamour, a champion of consumerism, the last word in gadgetry and, as his popular nickname 'Mr Kiss Kiss Bang Bang' spells out, a loaded symbol of sex and violence. He is the central character in one of the best-selling series of popular novels in literary history, and the hero of the most successful and enduring cycle of films ever produced. His critics accuse him of racism, sexism, and snobbery. His fans see him as cultured, seductive, and discerning. He is Agent 007, licensed to kill.

First appearing with the publication of Ian Fleming's *Casino Royale* in 1953 and crossing over to the big screen with the film adaptation of *Dr No* in 1962, James Bond emerged at a turning point in British post-war history, a moment of profound cultural change that saw Britain's decline as a superpower and its reinvention as a swinging mecca for music, fashion, shopping, and youth culture. As a fictional character who perpetuated British fantasies of global influence while simultaneously glamorising an affluent lifestyle based on brand-name consumerism, exotic travel, and sexual conquest, Bond perfectly captured the spirit of the moment. Ever since, the Bond novels and films have remained at the forefront of popular culture, continuously modernising the 007 formula to reflect – and often anticipate – changing social attitudes, major developments in world politics, and shifting trends in popular fiction and cinema culture.

Clearly, there is much more to James Bond than cheap thrills, fast cars, and beautiful women. But what exactly can the Bond saga tell us about Western culture's fears and anxieties over the course of the past fifty years? Where does fantasy end and ideology begin in the sensational world of 007? Engaging with such questions, this book cuts across disciplinary boundaries to explain, assess, and explore the mass-mediated spectacle we call 'the James Bond phenomenon'. It collects together a lively and diverse body of criticism on the Bond novels, the Bond films, and their tangled relationship with popular culture and mass media. The essays are drawn from the fields of literary, film, media, music, and cultural studies, ranging from early interpretations of the Bond novels by prominent thinkers like Umberto Eco to new, innovative readings of the Bond films by leading cultural critics.

Together, the essays survey the full breadth of the Bondian world, from Ian Fleming to Daniel Craig and beyond. They locate the Bond phenomenon within its historical, political, and social contexts from the Cold War period onwards. And they offer analysis informed by an array of theoretical perspectives including structuralism, Marxism, feminism, post-colonialism, and psychoanalysis. Most importantly, the essays demonstrate that there is much more to Mr Kiss Kiss Bang Bang than comic book sex and violence – that understanding how and why the James Bond phenomenon exists contributes to a wider understanding of our recent cultural history.

The essays are organised into three broad sections: 'Reading 007', 'Screening 007', and 'Re-thinking 007'. So a quick word about the organisation of the material. When dealing with the James Bond phenomenon it is tempting to overemphasise the importance of the films. This is not to say that the Bond films have not played the largest part in creating and sustaining Bondmania for the last several decades. Rather, the point is that the James Bond phenomenon lives (as it has always done) so much in the 'now' that it tends to obscure its own history – a long and sinuous history that not only stretches back to the Golden Age of British cinema but also begins in another medium altogether. Accordingly, this book attempts to strike a delicate balance between giving the films the full attention they are due, while also examining the Bond phenomenon in terms of its roots in popular fiction and its transition from there to the big screen and, more recently, the digital world of video gaming. The essays in the section 'Reading 007' focus mainly on Ian Fleming's novels. Those in 'Screening 007' concentrate on the Bond films. 'Rethinking 007' contains essays that consciously re-think, revisit, or re-read the Bond corpus. What unites the essays in this book is that each makes a contribution to a larger understanding of the James Bond phenomenon – some by looking more at the novels, others by looking more at the films, but all by keeping a sharp eye on the bigger 007 picture.

Reading 007

'The fast car, the correct recipe for a vodka martini, a dinner and a bridge game at Blade's, the brand names of superior toilet articles, the seductively ill-parted hair of a pretty girl.'[1] This is what the novelist Anthony Burgess remembers most about the James Bond novels. These playful comments may be reductive and even somewhat trivialising, but Burgess does nonetheless identify some of the key ingredients of the Bond formula originally developed by Ian Fleming in his novels and later refined in the films. As many critics have noted, it is a formula of excess that blends together consumerism, tourism, and elitism with chauvinism, sexism, and voyeurism. But why exactly did this particular formula take a worldwide reading public by storm in the 1950s? How can we account for the continuing appeal of Fleming's 007 novels fifty years later? What is Fleming's legacy to the popular genre of secret agent fiction? Was the creator of James Bond a glorified hack or an underrated literary whiz? These are just some of the questions addressed by the five essays grouped together in the opening section 'Reading 007'.

In the first essay, 'The Moments of Bond', Tony Bennett and Janet Woollacott survey the scope and reach of James Bond's career as a popular hero from the 1950s onwards. In the process, they examine the cult presence that the figure of Bond has exerted in post-war British culture, arguing that the Bond 'texts' not only articulate a broad range of cultural and ideological concerns, but do so in different ways at different moments in time. The staggering success of Fleming's 007 novels and their later film adaptations is linked to the status of Bond himself as a 'mobile signifier', a floating cultural icon who is continually reconfigured and repositioned in the face of social change.

Umberto Eco's essay, 'Narrative Structures in Fleming', takes us from the broad exploration of the Bond phenomenon provided by Bennett and Woollacott to a detailed analysis of Fleming's narrative. Eco is among the first critics to have thought seriously and carefully about the James Bond novels. In this seminal essay from the 1960s, Eco reads Fleming through the lens of structuralism in order to tease out a set of binary oppositions – such as Bond/Villain, Duty/Sacrifice, and Love/Death – that underscore and animate the 007 narratives. His structural analysis finds that, from *Casino Royale* through *Goldfinger* to *The Man With the Golden Gun*, the

Bond texts are governed by a set of rules determining the organisation of the plots and the 'moves' of the characters as in a game of chess. Eco further concludes that Fleming's writing is a 'tongue-in-cheek *bricolage*' of various popular literary forms, including fairy tale, science fiction, and adventure narrative. 'Narrative Structures in Fleming' has had a profound impact on Bond criticism – not least because it was instrumental in establishing James Bond as a 'valid' area of study in academic circles. For Bond critics since the 1960s, such as those featured in this book, Eco's essay has been a common point of reference, a frequent point of departure, and even an occasional site of contestation.

Michael Denning's essay 'Licensed to Look' locates Fleming's 007 novels in the larger context of twentieth-century British spy writing. Reading Fleming's work from a Marxist point of view, Denning argues that the Bond novels are complicit in the racist and sexist cultural politics of the late 1950s and early 1960s. Along the way, Denning explains Fleming's 007 thrillers as an historically specific variation of the imperial spy novel that, like the novels of Len Deighton and John le Carré, belongs to the era of Cold War politics and an emerging 'society of the spectacle'. For Denning, consumerism and tourism are the post-war cultural codes that the Bond texts register and ultimately reinforce.

As Umberto Eco and Michael Denning both point out, the Bond novels share many of the formal and thematic concerns of classic detective narrative. My essay argues that because Fleming locates his writing within the broader context of Cold War ideology and post-war geopolitics, the Bond novels also mark a departure from a transatlantic tradition of detective writing. Specifically, I propose that the 007 series registers a shift in the cultural understanding of crime that, in the immediate wake of World War II, came to include crimes against humanity. The discussion examines how this shift generates new ideological imperatives for the detective – a figure now reconfigured as the secret agent, licensed to kill.

In the final essay in this section, Claire Hines examines the multi-faceted relationship between James Bond and *Playboy* magazine, which was launched the same year as Fleming's first Bond novel in 1953, and which has regularly featured 007 throughout its publishing history. Addressing the significance of this long-standing association between Bond and *Playboy*, Hines examines the ways in which 007 was originally inserted into *Playboy*'s ideology of sexual liberation and hedonistic consumerism, providing readers with an ideal model of the fantasy image the men's lifestyle magazine sought to represent. Hines' persuasive argument is that the relationship between Bond and *Playboy* is far more central than most critics realise to an understanding of 007's function as a popular male fantasy figure in the 1960s and beyond.

Screening 007

In a newspaper review of the 1999 Bond film, *The World Is Not Enough*, Andrew Collins perceptively notes that '007 doesn't die, he just regenerates.'[2] The essays in the section 'Screening 007' examine some of the key cinematic moments of Bond from the edgy films of the early 1960s through to today's slickly packaged blockbusters. In the process, they show how and why the 007 films are successful not only in regenerating their social relevance and popular appeal, but also in sustaining the cultural mythology that has come to define the figure of James Bond. From Sean Connery's tuxedo to Roger Moore's Union Jack parachute, from Ursula Andress's bikini to Daniel Craig's swimming trunks, and from cocktails with Dr No to sandwiches in Q's laboratory, these essays examine the memorable scenes, defining moments, and turning points of Bond's extended screen existence.

The first essay in this section is taken from the conclusion to James Chapman's landmark study, *License to Thrill: A Cultural History of the James Bond Films*. In this concise yet astute chapter from his 1999 book, Chapman seeks to account for the commercial success and longevity of the James Bond films by looking beyond box-office receipts to questions of film culture more widely. In particular, Chapman argues that one of the main reasons the Bond films have remained at the forefront of popular cinema for so long is because they have consistently achieved a balance between repetition and variation – a balance that allows the films to satisfy audience expectations while simultaneously responding to new trends and developments in society.

Janet Woollacott's essay explores some of the theoretical problems associated with discussions of film productions in relation to a particular case: the making of the 1977 Bond film, *The Spy Who Loved Me*. Drawing on Pierre Macherey's thinking about the relationship between ideology and cultural production, Woollacott argues that Bond films like *The Spy* highlight the importance of rethinking the conventional assumption that the ideological position of a film is somehow separate and distinct from that of its makers. Her examination of the conditions of production involved in *The Spy* reveals the ideological tensions that preoccupied the production team and the way in which these were reconfigured during the making of the film. Woollacott concludes that understanding how the Bond films were made informs our understanding of how ideological discourses such as patriotism or sexism are mediated and transformed.

The James Bond theme music is an indispensable ingredient of the 007 film formula. Jeff Smith's essay reveals the fascinating history behind the Bond theme, the accompanying title songs, and their place in popular film music. Along the way, Smith examines the working relationship between the composer John Barry and the Hollywood producers Harry Saltzman and 'Cubby' Broccoli. He offers analysis of the extra-textual function of the 007 music scores and argues for the importance of the Bond theme in selling 007 to the public. Informing Smith's discussion is Theodor Adorno's idea that popular music forms are inextricably linked to economic and social considerations.

The cinema release of *Dr No* in 1962 saw James Bond successfully cross over from fiction to film. Cynthia Baron's essay examines how this transition to the big screen affected the political and ideological concerns of the 007 formula, and in particular the representation of race, ethnicity, and nationhood. The essay argues from the perspective of post-colonial theory that *Dr No* not only draws on the discourse of Orientalism to mobilise notions of British racial sovereignty, but in the process highlights aspects of modern British identity that emerged in opposition to colonial constructions of the 'other'.

Martin Willis's essay focuses on Bond's screen outings in the Pierce Brosnan era. For Willis, Brosnan's portrayal of Bond in *GoldenEye*, *Tomorrow Never Dies*, and *The World Is Not Enough* simultaneously refreshes Bond's place in contemporary culture and reconnects him with the Bond of the 1960s. The discussion begins by exploring the importance of technology in redefining James Bond's role at the turn of the millennium, before arguing that Brosnan's Bond possesses an expertise and knowledge of techno/cyber culture never before encountered in the 007 saga. The effect is to shift the emphasis of the 007 arena of conflict from the physical to the informational. In the process, Brosnan's Bond reconstitutes the importance of gadgetry and communications technology in the 007 series, and turns the 1990s films away from the low-tech pastiche of the Dalton and Moore eras and back to the moments of technological innovation characterising Connery's original Bond.

In 'Body Politics and *Casino Royale*', Colleen Tremonte and Linda Racioppi consider Daniel Craig's first cinematic sortie as Bond. Focusing on issues of gender and international security, they argue that, in the post-9/11 world, Bond must confront new inscriptions of masculinist ideology and gender politics, particularly in the new globalised capital-ist security environment. What Tremonte and Racioppi find particularly striking is the way *Casino Royale* deploys a gender politics that relies on an unprecedented hypermasculinity to meet international security threats that are now centred on global terrorism, nationalist struggles, and global finance. As their analysis reveals, a key locus of these gender politics is the body of Daniel Craig/Bond, which is used throughout *Casino Royale* to reinforce the role of masculinity in nationalistic dis-courses of 'homeland' security.

Re-thinking 007

The final section, 'Re-thinking 007', is the largest in the book. One of the reasons for this is that re-thinking the Bond phenomenon is a concern that has come to dominate Bond criticism in recent years. After all, James Bond is anything but a stable cultural signifier, and keeping tabs on this agent of cultural change requires both constant scrutiny and regular revi-sion. In other words, Bond criticism today remains as alive and alert to change as the Bond phenomenon itself. What distinguishes the essays in this section is that, as a group, they bring to light new features of the Bondian world, offer revitalised readings of the classic Bond canon, and subject both Bond and his entourage to new, innovative critiques. In short, this section delivers a fresh and often surprising look at the world of 007 from Pussy Galore's heterophobia to James Bond's penis and beyond.

In the first essay in this section, Christine Bold takes us back to the original Bond novels, and argues that Fleming's writing is not the harm-less escapism it affects to be. Through a close feminist reading of the Bond novels that rethinks Bennett, Woollacott, and Denning's work on the subject, Bold reveals the novels' serious preoccupation with pre-serving a particular order of political, sexual, and racial propriety. Her conclusion is that Bond's most dangerous adversary turns out to be the female reader.

Few critics have analysed the representation of lesbians in the 007 series, and yet this aspect of the Bond phenomenon clearly merits more critical attention. Elisabeth Ladenson's essay examines the representation and cultural significance of Pussy Galore – one of the most memorable female characters in the 007 ensemble – in order to bring into focus some of the key issues at stake in the treatment of gender and sexuality in the James Bond series. Read alongside other lesbian characters from the

007 series as well as Bond himself, Pussy Galore emerges in Ladenson's discussion as an embodiment of the many tensions that underscore the place of lesbians in popular culture.

Tara Brabazon's essay takes us from Pussy Galore to Miss Moneypenny, and so from one extreme and outrageous representation of female identity in the James Bond series to yet another. Brabazon's interest in 'the superspy's secretary' derives from a larger interest in monitoring the confluences of feminism and popular culture. She argues that, by following the on-screen career of Miss Moneypenny, we are able to trace the often ambivalent and sometimes contradictory impact of feminism not only on the Bond series itself but also on popular culture more widely. The discussion follows the many changes to Moneypenny's gendered 'ideological configuration' from the 1950s onwards, scrutinising her office flirtations with Bond from the Sean Connery years through to the Pierce Brosnan era.

Paul Stock's essay on the Bond films stays with the theme of office politics, but shifts the focus from a peripheral female character to a peripheral male one: M – 007's boss and the head of the British secret service. Through a close reading of M's office furniture and décor as it changes over the span of the Bond films, Stock argues that M's office not only functions as a metonym for England, but also represents a unique space in which to analyse the relationship between M and 007 and, through them, the relationship between ideology and iconography, nation and empire, and even capital and commodity. Stock places particular importance on M's 'gender reassignment' in the 1995 film *GoldenEye*, and finds that the transition from a male to a female M registers a much larger shift in the attitude of the Bond films towards issues of gender and power.

In 'Kamasutra Bond-ing', Ajay Gehlawat draws on the work of postcolonial thinkers Edward Said, Frantz Fanon, and Gayatri Spivak to chart the Orientalist logic underlying the Bond series. Focusing on the racial and sexual dynamics of the 1983 Roger Moore film *Octopussy*, Gehlawat not only examines 007's transnational libido and manipulation of Orientalist discourse, but in the process seeks to understand how the Bond narrative travels globally and, in particular, how it has been received in India, where much of the story of *Octopussy* is set. Gehlawat concludes by placing Bond's erotic Orientalism in the broader context of recent developments in global cinema culture and the Bollywood star system.

In his provocatively titled essay, 'James Bond's Penis', Toby Miller directs his attention to a part of James Bond that has yet to receive close critical scrutiny. Moving between the 007 novels and films, Miller shows that Bond's relationship with his penis is not as confident and comfortable as we might think. He notes that in Fleming's novels, where Bond remains largely ambivalent towards sex, Bond's penis represents a source of insecurity and a threat of loss of control. In the films, by contrast, Bond is highly sexual and explicitly sexualised. Miller considers this shift in its historical, political, and economic contexts. Drawing on recent thinking about masculinity and culture, and analysing classic screen moments such as the 'laser-castration' scene in *Goldfinger*, Miller argues that the male body in the 007 series represents both a site and a source of cultural anxiety.

The resonance of the Bond films with the terrorist attacks of September 11 2001 is the subject of Jim Leach's essay. In 'Bond in the 1990s – and Beyond?', Leach notes that the last three Bond films of the twentieth century, those starring Pierce Brosnan, breathed new life into the Bond phenomenon at a time when, according to a publicity release for *GoldenEye*, 'the world has changed'. While the comment, as Leach explains, was a reference to the dismantling of the Berlin Wall, a televised event that symbolised the end of the Cold War, the same words were widely used after the terrorist attacks of September 11. Leach argues that the televised images of mass destruction that emerged from the attacks simultaneously reduced Bondian fantasies of control to insignificance and uncannily resembled the images and plots of the Bond films. Following these thoughts, Leach explores interrelated questions of politics and technology in *GoldenEye*, *Tomorrow Never Dies*, and *The World is Not Enough*. In so doing, he considers the future of the Bond phenomenon in a hyperreal world where the distinction between the real and the imaginary has become increasingly blurred.

The final essay in the book addresses an increasingly popular and commercially significant part of the James Bond phenomenon. In 'Shaken, Stirred, Pixellated', Stefan Hall offers the first sustained critical analysis of the history and evolution of James Bond video games, beginning with the earliest adaptations for the Atari game system in the early 1980s and moving through the rise of home computer gaming to modern console releases in the 1990s. Carefully attuned to issues of genre, narrative structure, and aesthetics, Hall explores the many different (and sometimes disastrous) ways in which the video game industry has co-opted 007 over the last three decades, moving towards ever more technologically and aesthetically sophisticated recreations of the Bondian film world.

A nasty habit of surviving

One of the few memorable lines from the 1983 Roger Moore film *Octopussy* belongs to the villain, Kamal Khan, when he says to Bond: 'You have a nasty habit of surviving'. In many ways, this line sums up the message delivered by the essays in this book. Love him or loathe him, James Bond is here to stay. Alongside Sherlock Holmes, Mickey Mouse, and Superman, he remains one of the most famous fictional characters and firmly established cultural icons in the world.

The question is why James Bond – in all his many formations and incarnations – has proved so popular for so long? Together, the essays in this book go a long way towards answering that difficult question. Their readings, interpretations, analyses, explanations, definitions, and theorisations offer a wide range of ways to understand and think about the resilient cultural phenomenon that is James Bond. James Chapman begins his book on the 007 films by asking 'why should we take James Bond seriously?'[3] The reply from this book is that, given his entrenched position at the very core of contemporary popular culture, we can no longer afford *not* to take James Bond seriously.

Notes

1 Anthony Burgess, introduction to Coronet Books' editions of Ian Fleming's James Bond novels, 1988.
2 Andrew Collins, 'I spy, the new 007', *The Guardian*, 25 July 1999, p. 47.
3 James Chapman, *Licence to Thrill: A Cultural History of the James Bond Films* (New York: Columbia University Press, 2000), p. 1.

Part I

Reading 007

Tony Bennett and Janet Woollacott

The moments of Bond

Ian Fleming always maintained that he wrote *Casino Royale* in order to take his mind off his impending marriage, as an amusing diversion rather than a determined attempt to become a best-selling writer. Similarly, when, towards the end of his life, Fleming tried to categorise his work, he argued that 'while thrillers may not be literature with a capital L, it is possible to write what I can best describe as "Thrillers designed to be read as literature"', and cited, as his models in this respect, Raymond Chandler, Dashiell Hammett, Eric Ambler, and Graham Greene.[1] Although it is clear Fleming always kept a weather-eye on the market for popular fiction, this does not seem to have been the market he had primarily in view when he first started writing. Indeed, he was somewhat surprised when it became clear that the Bond novels appealed to a wider readership than he had anticipated. In a letter to CBS in 1957, he wrote:

> In hard covers my books are written for and appeal principally to an 'A' readership but they have all been reprinted in paperbacks both in England and America and it appears that the 'B' and 'C' classes find them equally readable, although one might have thought that the sophistication of the background and detail would be outside their experience and in part incomprehensible.[2]

That Jonathan Cape, Fleming's publishers, envisaged a similar readership is evident from the jacket designs they commissioned. Such designs constitute one of the primary means whereby literary texts are inserted into available aesthetic and marketing categories; they aim both to solicit a particular readership and, in establishing a set of intertextual associations, to locate reading within a particular cultural framework. The jacket designs for the first hardback editions of the early Bond novels thus

typically consisted of a collection of objects associated with either espionage or luxurious living, or both, and connoted the category of superior
quality, 'literary' spy fiction. Furthermore, the evidence from the reviews
in the literary weeklies and monthlies of the period suggests that this is
precisely how they were initially regarded and read by their intended
public. Such reviews both addressed and sought to produce a 'knowing
reader' who, in being familiar with or informed, by the reviewer, of the
series of literary and mythic allusions deployed in the novels, would be
able to read and appreciate them as flirtatious, culturally knowing parodies of the spy-thriller genre. They thus functioned as 'critical legitima-
tors', making the Bond novels permissibly readable in discounting their
evident chauvinism, racism, and sexism. The 'knowing reader', aware that
Fleming was writing tongue-in-cheek, would not, it was implied, be
adversely affected by these aspects of the novels to the degree that he/she
(but mainly he) would appreciate their purely formal role in parodying,
by means of excess, the earlier imperialist spy-thrillers of such writers as
John Buchan and Cyril McNeile.

Installed ambiguously between the aesthetic and marketing categories
of 'literature' and 'popular fiction', the Bond novels thus initially reached
only a limited readership, largely restricted to the metropolitan literary
intelligentsia. Even so, they sold quite well. The first imprint of *Casino
Royale* (4,750 copies), published in April 1953, had sold out by May of the
same year and the title sold more than 8,000 copies on its second imprint
in 1954. *Live and Let Die*, published in 1954, sold more than 9,000 copies
in its first year of publication. Conceived as 'literary' sales, of course, such
figures were more than respectable, but they were relatively small beer in
relation to the market for popular fiction. Nor, initially, did the novels
make much headway outside Britain. *Casino Royale* was turned down by
three publishers in America on the grounds that it was too British for the
American market and, when it was eventually published there by
Macmillan, sold less than 4,000 copies.[3] However, there were signs of
interest in Bond from American television. CBS paid Fleming $1,000 for
the right to produce an hour-long television adaptation of *Casino Royale*
and, later (1956–57), Fleming was asked to write a script for NBC. (In the
event, this was not used, although it subsequently formed the basis for the
plot of *Dr No*.) There were also signs of an awakening interest in the film
industry when, in 1954, Sir Alexander Korda asked to see an advance copy
of *Live and Let Die*. However, it is only in retrospect that these overtures
seem portentous of greater things to come. By 1955, when Fleming had
added a third title – *Moonraker* – to the list, the novels had been printed

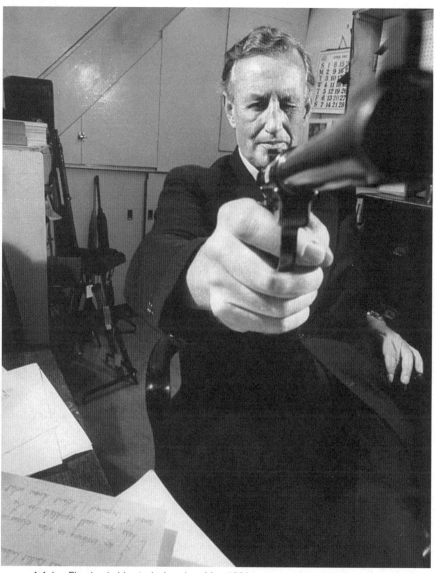

1.1 Ian Fleming in his study, London, May 1962

only in hardback editions, none had sold more than 12,000 copies in Britain, and Fleming's total earnings from sales were less than £2,000. According to Pearson, Fleming's biographer, Fleming had decided, by mid-1955, that his financial return from the Bond novels no longer justified the time and effort he put into them. He accordingly conceived *From Russia, With Love* as his last Bond novel, determining to kill his hero off on the last page.

A political hero for the middle classes

The first turning point in both the degree and social reach of Bond's popularity came in 1957. Pan had published a paperback edition of *Casino Royale* in 1955, adding *Moonraker* in 1956, pushing the British sales for the Bond novels in those years up to 41,000 and 58,000 respectively (see Table 1). It was 1957, however, that witnessed the first stage in the transformation of Bond from a character within a set of fictional texts into a household name. This was chiefly attributable to the serialisation of *From Russia, With Love* in the *Daily Express* and, later in the same year, to the *Daily Express*'s publication of a daily strip-cartoon of Bond. The *Daily Express* also subsequently organised a competition in which readers were asked to choose, from a specified range, the actor they felt best suited to play the part of Bond on the screen. The effects of the *Daily Express*'s promotion of Bond on the sales of the Bond novels are easily discernible. Sales in Britain rose from 58,000 in 1956 to 72,000 in 1957, 105,000 in 1958 and 237,000 in 1959. This, then, was the first moment in the history of Bond as a popular hero, but a moment still characterised by a limited and socially restricted popular appeal. Although no detailed research has been done that would establish the point conclusively, it is reasonable to assume an approximate fit between the readership of the Bond novels and that of the *Daily Express* and similar papers; that is, a predominately lower middle-class readership. It is, accordingly, in relation to the concerns of this class that the functioning of the figure of Bond in this period must be assessed.

Unsurprisingly, perhaps, the network of cultural and ideological concerns Bond served to condense and articulate in the late 1950s centred most closely on the relations between East and West, relations which had become particularly tense as a consequence of Russia's invasion of Hungary in 1956. Bond, that is to say, functioned first and foremost, although not exclusively, as a Cold War hero, an exemplary representative of the virtues of Western capitalism triumphing over the evils of Eastern communism. Except for *Diamonds Are Forever*, the villain in all the novels

Table 1 Fleming's Bond novels: British paperback sales, 1955–77 (000s)

Title	1955	1956	1957	1958	1959	1960	1961	1962	1963	1964	1965	1966	1967	1968	1969	1970	1971	1972	1973	1974	1975	1976	1977	Total by title
Casino Royale (April 1955)*	41	15	15	22	35	40	81	145	399	593	472	158	177	9	20	20	15	16	30	7	13	19	29	2371
Moonraker (Oct. 1956)		43	7		60	48	87	136	439	604	474	158	47	16	14	21	14	31	25	17	20	11	10	2282
Live and Let Die (Oct. 1957)			50	15	40	35	82	137	447	618	476	159	51	8	24	22	10	O/P	240	14	22	16	1	2467
Diamonds Are Forever (Feb. 1960)				68	22	45	92	142	426	592	471	146	43	24	15	14	77	72	15	26	22	13	8	2333
From Russia, With Love (April 1959)					80	40	82	145	642	600	457	149	42	20	7	33	9	33	30	17	9	14	5	2414
Dr No						115	85	232	437	530	476	134	36	19	9	15	15	31	30	3	20	12	8	2207
Goldfinger (Feb. 1960)							161	152	429	964	564	111	35	12	10	17	O/P	41	26	14	19	13	14	2582
For Your Eyes Only (May 1961)								226	441	615	480	152	49	2	28	22	8	32	16	20	22	12	13	2138
Thunderball (May 1963)									808	617	809	201	26	17	21	15	10	44	21	11	8	13	14	2635
On Her Majesty's Secret Service (Sept. 1964)										125	1794	16	39	30	117	20	20	13	25	23	24	12	9	2267
You Only Live Twice (July 1965)											309	908	178	15	9	18	5	44	23	19	23	12	16	1579
The Man With The Golden Gun (July 1966)												273	485	68	48	48	4	44	24	16	131	11	16	1168
The Spy Who Loved Me (May 1967)													517	57	33	57	61	21	19	20	22	0.5	O/P	807.5
Octopussy (July 1967)													79	362	34	40	10	17	26	16	10	6	13	613
Annual total	41	58	72	105	237	323	670	1315	4468	5858	6782	2565	1804	659	389	362	258	439	550	223	365	164.5	156	Overall total 27863.5

O/P = Out of print   * Denotes first publication in paperback   Details supplied by Pan Books Ltd

Fleming wrote in the 1950s is either directly in the service of the Soviet Union – Le Chiffre in *Casino Royale*, and Red Grant in *From Russia, With Love* for example – or indirectly in its employ, as is the case with *Dr No*. In all cases, the villain's conspiracy constitutes a threat to the peace and security of the 'Free World', usually as represented by Britain or the United States. In frustrating the villain's conspiracy, Bond effects an ide-ologically loaded imaginary resolution of the real historical contradic-tions of the period, a resolution in which all the values associated with Bond and, thereby, the West – notably, freedom and individualism – gain ascendancy over those associated with the villain and, thereby, commu-nist Russia, such as totalitarianism and bureaucratic rigidity.

This is not to suggest that these aspects of the relations between Bond and the villain constitute the only source of narrative tension in the novels of this period. But these were the aspects of the novels that were most clearly and explicitly foregrounded in the broader functioning of the figure of Bond. It is no accident, for example, that the *Daily Express* should have chosen *From Russia, With Love* to introduce Bond to a broader public since, of all Fleming's novels, this is the one in which Cold War tensions are most massively present, saturating the narrative from beginning to end. Moreover, this is the only one of Fleming's novels bear-ing an author's preface in which Fleming sought to locate reading within a horizon of realist expectations, to instruct the reader that the novel was not entirely fictional:

> Not that it matters, but a great deal of the background to this story is accurate.
>
> SMERSH, a contraction of Smiert Spionam – Death to Spies – exists and remains today the most secret department of the Soviet government. At the beginning of 1956, when this book was written, the strength of SMERSH at home and abroad was about 40,000 and General Grubozaboyschikov was its chief. My description of his appearance is correct.
>
> Today the headquarters of SMERSH are where, in Chapter 4, I have placed them – at No. 13 Sretenka Ulitsa, Moscow. The Conference Room is faithfully described and the Intelligence chiefs who meet around the table are real officials who are frequently summoned to that room for purposes similar to those I have recounted.

However, Bond also functioned, in this period, as a site for the elabora-tion – or, more accurately, re-elaboration – of a mythic conception of nationhood. Again, it is no accident that Bond's fame began to spread, to any significant degree, in 1957. In the aftermath of the national humiliation of the Suez fiasco, Bond constituted a figure around which, imaginarily, the real trials and vicissitudes of history could be halted and put into reverse. As, above all, a pre-eminently English hero, single-handedly saving the Western world from threatening catastrophe, Bond embodied the imaginary possibility that England might once again be placed at the centre of world affairs during a period when its world-power status was visibly and rapidly declining. An imaginary outlet for a historically blocked jingoism, Bond thus furnished a point of cultural reference in relation to which a chauvinism well and truly on its uppers could be reconstituted and symbolically refurbished. At the same time, of course, Bond's appeal consisted partly in the ways in which the organisation of the novels enabled questions of nation to be transposed on to those of sexuality.

In short, during the first phase of his career as a popular hero, the way in which the figure of Bond was constructed and made to stand in relation to the ideological preoccupations of the period enabled Bond to function primarily as a political and sexual hero for the lower middle classes. Yet, paradoxically, it was also during this period that Bond first became a subject for 'public concern' as evidenced by the development of a 'moralising criticism' concerned, as is ever the case, with the effects the Bond novels might have on 'other people'. Rather than, as had earlier been the case, aiming to produce a 'knowing reader' inoculated against the potentially adverse effects of the Bond novels, the purpose of this moralising criticism was to protect the 'untutored reader' from undue harm. Paul Johnson's attack on the 'sex, sadism and snobbery' of the Bond novels in the *New Statesman* is probably the most famous critical reaction of this type.[4] However, an article by Bernard Bergonzi in *The Twentieth Century* accusing Fleming of gratuitous sex and violence and of falling short of the moral and literary standards set by John Buchan and Raymond Chandler also proved influential.[5]

A hero of modernisation

Although a significant cultural presence by the end of the 1950s, the social basis of Bond's popular appeal remained limited. Moreover, he was virtually unknown outside Britain. The cycle of Bond films released in the early 1960s – starting, with *Dr No*, in 1962 – both significantly broadened the social basis of Bond's popular appeal in Britain and extended the horizons of his popularity internationally. At the same time, together with other constructions of Bond characteristic of the period, they contributed to the transformation of the figure of Bond – not, however, a total transformation so much as an ideological remodelling. The various ideological and cultural elements out of which the figure of Bond had earlier been constructed were, so to speak, dismantled and separated from one another in order to be reassembled in a new configuration which pointed, ideologically and culturally, in a number of new and different directions.

By comparison with the Bond novels, the Bond films were instantly and have remained quite spectacularly successful in terms of box office receipts, their rate of profitability, and the size and composition of the audience they have reached. This was achieved, at least initially, without much assistance from the financial backers of *Dr No*, who did not expect the film to be more than an average earner. Accordingly, very little was spent promoting the film in America; indeed, it was premiered in the Midwest rather than New York. *Dr No* also had to make its way in the marketplace against what were, initially, either lukewarm or, at worst, savagely hostile critical reactions, such as that of Ian Cameron: '*Dr No*: no, no. Too inept to be as pernicious as it might have been. Costly gloss flawed by an insidious economy on girls. Superannuated Rank starlet tries to act sexy. Grotesque.'[6]

The figures tell a different story. By 1976, *Dr No* had earned global profits in excess of $22 million. *From Russia With Love* grossed takings of $460,000 during the first week of its release in New York in 1963. *Goldfinger* became the fastest money-maker in the history of cinema, grossing $10,374,807 in fourteen weeks of its release in the USA and Canada in 1964. *Thunderball*, released in 1965, had grossed takings of $45 million by 1971 and, in the same year, *Diamonds Are Forever* earned $15.6 million during the first twelve days of its release. And, of course, in the film industry, nothing succeeds like success. Cubby Broccoli and Harry Saltzman, co-producers of the early Bond films, had some difficulty in capitalising the production of *Dr No*. In the end, they had to settle for a production budget of $950,000 and for only a little more than $1 million in financing *From Russia With Love*. *Thunderball*, by contrast, cost $6.6 million; *On Her Majesty's Secret Service*, $8 million; *Diamonds Are Forever*, $7.2 million, whilst *The Spy Who Loved Me* was budgeted at $13 million.

Nor can the cultural impact of the films be measured solely in terms of their own commercial success. They totally transformed the market for the novels, too, as an exemplary tale by Harry Saltzman testifies: 'The *Dr No* book had sold virtually nothing when we made the film. Then I went to Pan and suggested they print an extra 500,000 copies. They laughed at me. And, do you know, in the next seven months, they sold one and a half million copies.'[7]

The more general pattern of the influence of the films on paperback sales in Britain is clearly discernible. As might be expected, Table 1 shows a close connection between the release dates of particular films and the peak point in the sales graph for the individual novels on which those films were based. The release of *From Russia With Love* in 1963 saw the British sales for that title peak at 642,000 in the same year; the release of *Goldfinger* in 1964 pushed the sales for that title up to their peak of 964,000, and so on. However, the relationship is not entirely that of a one-to-one correlation. The peak of the sales graph for *Live and Let Die* – 618,000 – is reached in 1964, for example, and whilst the release of the film of that title in 1973 lifted sales from their previously flagging level of 10,000 to 20,000 annually to 240,000, this was well below their earlier peak and, just as important, this level of sales was not sustained for any appreciable period (only 14,000 copies were sold in 1974). The story is much the same for *Diamonds Are Forever* with sales peaking at 592,000 in 1964, falling to around 15,000 annually in the late 1960s to rise to 77,000 on the release of the film in 1971, and maintaining that level for a couple of years before falling back to the sales levels of the late 1960s.

Indeed, it can be seen from Table 1 that the peak point in the sales graph for each title occurs sometime in the period between 1963 and 1966. Equally important, the table shows a marked lift in the sales for all the Bond novels over the period 1962 (1,315,000) to 1967 (1,804,000), a lift that was especially pronounced in 1963, 1964, and 1965 with sales in those years of 4,468,000, 5,858,000, and 6,782,000 respectively. It was precisely during this period that the first cycle of Bond films – those starring Sean Connery before his replacement in the part by George Lazenby – appeared. Released on more or less an annual basis – *Dr No* in 1962, *From Russia With Love* in 1963, *Goldfinger* in 1964, *Thunderball* in 1965, and *You Only Live Twice* in 1967 – it is clear that the effect of the films in this period was to revivify the market for the Bond novels *as a whole*. It was as an *integrated set*, rather than as individual titles, that the Bond novels sold over this period. Subsequently, by contrast, the release of new Bond films has resulted in increased sales only for the individual titles from which they were derived. For example, in 1973, sales increased only for *Live and Let Die*; the sales for most of the other Bond novels actually fell significantly from their 1972 level.

Apart from themselves directly recruiting an international audience, the films had similar effects on the sales of the Bond novels in other countries. In France, Bond was virtually unknown until the release of *Dr No*. Two of the novels had been published in translation but sales had proved so sluggish that the publishers, Plon, had decided against issuing any of the remaining titles. In 1964, however, 480,000 copies of the Bond novels were sold in France; *France Soir* serialised *Dr No*; *Elle* made Bond its male hero for the summer season and, in 1965, sales of the novels were topping the 2 million mark. Similarly, in Italy, where the novels had been published in translation since 1958, the release of *Dr No* occasioned such a spate of Italian films exploiting the 007 trademark that United Artists had to threaten legal action for breach of copyright. In Denmark and Sweden, the *Daily Express* strip-cartoons of Bond were published in comic book form; a strip-cartoon of Bond even appeared in Yugoslavia.[8] Perhaps the most distinctive development in America was the appropriation of Bond by *Playboy* which, in 1963, 1964, and 1965 respectively, serialised *On Her Majesty's Secret Service*, *You Only Live Twice*, and *The Man With The Golden Gun*, all within a month or so of their initial publication in hardback editions. At the same time, *Playboy* also instituted, as a regular feature, photo-articles of 'The Girls of James Bond' type as did magazines like *Penthouse* and, in Britain, *Mayfair*. Finally, the early 1960s also witnessed, for the first time, the significantly widespread use of the figure of Bond in advertising and commodity design.[9]

The most significant changes in the cultural and ideological currency of Bond during this period are attributable to the effects of the films, particularly to the way they transformed the plot elements of the novels and subtly modified the characterisation of Bond. However, the use of Bond as a figure in advertising and commodity design tended to work alongside the films, modifying the associations Bond served to orchestrate so as to place him at the centre of a significantly reorganised set of ideological and cultural concerns. Three changes stand to the fore.

First, the figure of Bond was detached from the ideological co-ordinates of the Cold War period and adjusted to the prevailing climate of détente. In part, this change is attributable to Fleming himself. Beginning with *Thunderball* (1961), Fleming abandoned the SMERSH formula of his earlier novels, in which Bond is pitted against a representative of the Soviet Union or a villain in some way in the service of the Soviet Union, and wrote all his subsequent novels, except for *The Man With The Golden Gun* (1965), in the SPECTRE formula. In these novels – *Thunderball*, *On Her Majesty's Secret Service* (1963), and *You Only Live Twice* (1964) – Bond's mission involves him in a contest with SPECTRE – the Special Executive for Counter-Intelligence, Terror, Revenge and Extortion. Headed by the mad but diabolically clever Ernst Stavro Blofeld, SPECTRE is an international criminal organisation, an assembly of freelance villains, which seeks to exploit the fragility of the relations between East and West, holding one or the other or sometimes both to ransom, for the purpose of private gain. Typically, the threat which Bond thus averts in these novels is that Blofeld's machinations, in sowing the seeds of misunderstanding between Russia and the West, might result in a global conflagration.

Whilst Fleming thus provided the means by which Bond was attuned to the ideological climate prevailing in the period of détente, the primary impetus for this ideological readjustment came from the requirements of the film industry. *Thunderball* itself was developed from a film script Fleming had written in cooperation with Kevin McClory and Jack Wittingham and thus constituted the first reshaping of Bond undertaken in response to the pressures of the film industry which has consistently, although only in a relative sense, 'de-politicised' Bond in the interests, as Cubby Broccoli put it, of giving the Bond films 'legs worldwide'.[10] Thus, from the very first, Broccoli and Saltzman eschewed the SMERSH formula in favour of the SPECTRE formula, adapting those novels written to the former – even *From Russia, With Love* – so as to adjust them to the latter. That Fleming continued to write to this formula is, of course, attributable to the fact that, after the success of the film of *Dr No*, he wrote with a different public in mind and in anticipation that his novels would ultimately be transformed into films.

Secondly, Bond's functioning in relation to ideologies of nation and nationhood was also significantly modified. This was, in part, a consequence of the ways in which the relations between Bond and M were represented, with Bond being increasingly distinguished from and constructed in opposition to the films' portrayal of M as a fuddy-duddy Establishment figure. More generally, however, it was attributable to the associations established by Bond's incarnation, in this period, in the concrete form of Connery/Bond – the visual signifier through which the figure of Bond was most widely circulated. Whereas, in the late 1950s, Bond had supplied a point of reference in relation to which the clock of the nation had been put imaginarily into reverse, recalling a brighter past, the Bond of the early to mid-1960s functioned as the condensed expression of a new style and image of Englishness around which the clock of the nation was made to run imaginarily ahead of itself, a pointer to a brighter and better future. More particularly, in the context of 'swinging Britain', Bond provided a mythic encapsulation of the then prominent ideological themes of classlessness and modernity, a key cultural marker of the claim that Britain had escaped the blinkered, class-bound perspectives of its traditional ruling elites and was in the process of being thoroughly modernised as a result of the implementation of a new, meritocratic style of cultural and political leadership, middle-class and professional rather than aristocratic and amateur.

Finally, and as perhaps the most crucial addition to Bond's signifying currency in this period, the figure of Bond and, closely related, the figure of 'the Bond girl', a new construction, constituted key sites for the elaboration of a (relatively) new set of gender identities. This aspect of Bond was closely related to his functioning as a representative of a modernising Britain. Between them, Bond and 'the Bond girl' embodied a modernisation of sexuality, representatives of norms of masculinity and femininity that were 'swinging free' from the constraints of the past. If Bond thus embodied male sexuality that was freed from the constraints and hypocrisy of gentlemanly chivalry, a point of departure from the restraint, a-sexuality, or repressed sexuality of the traditional English aristocratic hero, 'the Bond girl' – tailored to suit Bond's needs – was likewise represented as the subject of a free and independent sexuality, liberated from the constraints of family, marriage, and domesticity. The image of 'the Bond girl' thus constituted a model of adjustment, a condensation of the attributes of femininity appropriate to the requirements of the new norms of male sexuality represented by Bond.

This aspect of Bond's functioning was perhaps most clearly evident in his use in advertising and commodity design, not just in Britain but internationally. Typically, in such contexts, the figure of Bond served as an ideological shorthand for the appropriate image of masculinity in relation to which feminine sexual identities were to be constructed – as in a French lipstick advertised as 'a good Bond for the lips' or an Australian brand of women's lingerie marketed under the slogan 'Become fit for James Bond'.[11] In this respect, to borrow loosely from Jacques Lacan, the figure of Bond provided a *point de capiton* within the ideological construction of gender relations and identities.[12] In a period that experienced a considerable cultural redefinition, a flux and fluidity, of gender identities, the figure of Bond furnished a point of anchorage in relation to which the sliding of meaning that had been introduced into the ideological ordering of gender relations, while not halted, was moved on and pinned down to a new set of ideological coordinates.

The early to mid-1960s, then, constituted the second significant moment in Bond's career as a popular hero. Indeed, to adopt the hyperbole of Bond's publicity writers, it constitutes *the* moment of Bond. In comparison with both the late 1950s and the periodic resurgence of interest in Bond prompted by the release of each new Bond film in the 1970s

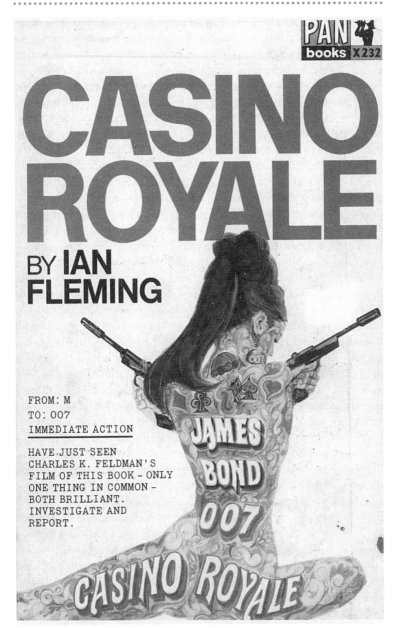

1.2 1967 Pan paperback cover of *Casino Royale*

and 1980s, the impact of Bond in this period was a peculiarly concentrated one. Except for 1966, the films were released on an annual basis
from 1962 to 1967; 22,792,000 copies of the Bond novels were sold in
Britain between these years compared with the 1,506,000 copies sold
between 1955 and 1961 and the 3,565,500 copies sold between 1968 and
1977; and, in advertising and commodity design, the figure of Bond was
omnipresent. Furthermore, the social reach of Bond's popularity had
been significantly expanded. No longer a cult figure for the metropolitan
intelligentsia or, less exclusively, a political hero for the middle classes, the
figure of Bond functioned as a popular icon in ways which cut significantly, if also unevenly and contradictorily, across class, generation,
gender, and national divisions.

Apart from being the period in which Bond's popularity manifestly
peaked, the early 1960s can also be counted as the moment of Bond in the
sense that his popularity was unrivalled by that of any other cultural
figure. Indeed, this was true for the greater part of the 1960s when, in its
taken-for-grantedness, the figure of Bond supplied an established point
of reference to which a wide range of cultural practices referred themselves in order to establish their own cultural location and identity. Most
obviously, Bond functioned as either an explicit or an implied point of
reference for the rival spy-thrillers which flooded the bookstalls, the
cinema and the television screens, in both Britain and America –
the novels of Len Deighton and the films derived from them, *The Man
from U.N.C.L.E.*, *The Avengers*, and so on. Each of these either directly
negotiated its own specific cultural space and sphere of ideological action
within the region of the spy-thriller, or had such a space negotiated for it
by the critics, through the construction of relationships of similarity
to/difference from Bond. Deighton's hero (anonymous in the novels,
portrayed as Harry Palmer in the films) was thus both likened to and
distinguished from Bond – like him (a British secret agent), yet also
significantly unlike him (a working-class anti-hero).

Nor was the operation of this system of references restricted to the cultural region of the spy-thriller. In the same period, when Jon Pertwee
played the title role, the producers of *Doctor Who* adapted the series to a
'science fiction James Bond formula' specifically in order to 'co-opt the
success of the "Swinging Sixties" and the world-wide marketing of "liberated" affluence via Carnaby Street and Biba'.[13] The significance of this is
not that such comparisons were made (a fairly common occurrence in
popular fiction) but that, where they were, it was always Bond who furnished the point of comparison. Other fictional heroes were likened
to/distinguished from Bond, rarely the other way round.[14]

Bond as ritual

By the mid-1960s, all the cultural and ideological elements out of which the figure of Bond had been constructed were well and truly in place; Bond's currency was established. The distinguishing characteristic of the third moment in Bond's career as a popular hero – roughly, from the 1970s onwards – consists in its selective and strategic activation of that currency together with the more episodic and ritualistic nature of Bond's popularity.

The point has already been made that, in the 1970s, the Bond films – released every two years rather than annually – had a more discrete impact on novel sales, promoting them only as individual titles rather than as an integrated set. Perhaps more important, the ideological and cultural concerns to which the figure of Bond resonated had become somewhat less vital, assessed in relation to the changing configuration of British popular culture as a whole. The spin-offs from the Bond films and the use of Bond-derived motifs in advertising remained legion, but the markets aimed at had changed significantly. In the 1960s, the Bond image and Bond products were closely associated with constructions of sexuality and nationhood. The dominant sponsored products of the 1970s, by contrast, were technological – such as Rolex watches – whereas most spin-offs were designed for children: Corgi cars, helicopters, and rockets; Airfix kits of Moonraker; Action Man-type dolls of Bond and Jaws, and so on. As a popular hero, and the more so as the decade progressed, Bond thus markedly descended the age scale. In the 1960s, the audience for the Bond films had consisted, in the main, of adolescents and young adults. By the time *Moonraker* was released in 1979, the audience consisted mainly of parents with pre-adolescent children. At the time of writing, local cinemas book the Bond films for the school holidays alongside or as an alternative to Disney films, while Bond imagery is now used to advertise peanuts and instant whip.

Not only did Bond's popularity become more episodic, an isolated occurrence every two years; it also became more routinised, a more or less institutionalised ritual, especially when, after 1975, the transmission of a Bond film by ITV on Christmas Day established a regular place for Bond in the 'way of life' of the British people. This is not to suggest that Bond was no longer popular but rather that the nature and periodicity of his popularity, the time rhythms to which it conformed, had been significantly reorganised. Bond thus operated as a 'dormant signifier', inactive most of the time but capable of being periodically reactivated, albeit in a fairly ritualised manner, with the release of each new Bond film, only to

be put back on ice again pending the publicity build-up to the next film
– or the next Christmas.

Paralleling these changes, the range of cultural and ideological concerns Bond served to articulate was subject to a considerable contraction
during the 1970s. In effect, it was really only in relation to ideologies of
gender and sexuality that the figure of Bond retained any significant
degree of ideological potency. While all the films produced in the period
continued to use the SPECTRE formula, their relation to that formula
became increasingly parodic and self-mocking, instances of a *paraded*
fantastic. Similarly, rather than articulating any new image of nation and
nationhood, Bond functioned more as a negative site in relation to which
earlier conceptions of Englishness – including those represented by Bond
in the earlier phases of his career – were parodied and debunked, punctured so as to release laughter, by means of carrying them to excess. The
most significant change associated with the films of this period, however,
consisted in a shift in the centre of narrative interest, increasingly pronounced as the 1970s progressed, away from the relations between Bond
and the villain towards the relations between Bond and 'the Bond girl'.
Usually portrayed as 'excessively' independent – a fellow professional who
works alongside Bond, threatening to best him in the traditionally masculine preserve of espionage work, as does Anya in *The Spy Who Loved Me*
– the destiny of 'the Bond girl' in the films of this period is to meet her
come-uppance in her encounter with Bond. The main ideological work
thus accomplished in the unfolding of the narrative is that of a 'putting-
back-into-place' of women who carry their independence and liberation
'too far' or into 'inappropriate' fields of activity. Of course, similar tensions were worked through in the narratives of the earlier films as well as
in the novels, but they were usually subordinated to and worked into the
relations between Bond and the villain rather than, as in the films of the
late 1970s, the other way round. This shift in narrative organisation
clearly constituted a response – in truth, somewhat nervous and uncertain – to the Women's Liberation movement, fictitiously rolling-back the
advances of feminism to restore an imaginarily more secure phallocentric
conception of gender relations.

Finally, Bond no longer occupied centre-stage within the reorganised
system of intertextual relations which characterised the popular culture
of the period. Rather than supplying the centre around which such intertextual references were coordinated, the cultural space within which the
figure of Bond operated was incessantly renegotiated by referring it to
new tendencies and developments within popular culture, especially the

cinema. The films of this period are thus characterised by what can perhaps best be termed a double referential structure. Playing on popular memory by referring to the earlier Bond films and to the more general figure of Bond associated with the 1960s, essentially by means of parody, they also selectively activated the established currency of Bond and, in so doing, reorganised its cultural associations by referring it to more influential genres within the contemporary cinema – to police fiction movies in *The Man With The Golden Gun*, for example, or to science fiction spectaculars in *Moonraker*. It was only by being thus constantly transformed that Bond was kept culturally alive.

The pattern of increasing use of parody and dependence on other popular films was reversed in the 1980s after *Moonraker* (1979). *For Your Eyes Only* (1981) showed a clear attempt to activate some lapsed and inactive parts of the Bond mythology. In terms of production this meant abandoning Christopher Wood, who had scripted *The Spy Who Loved Me* and *Moonraker*, and returning to Richard Maibaum, who had scripted many of the earlier Bond films. Textually, *For Your Eyes Only* abandoned comic parody, for the greater part, to concentrate on a 'straight' Bond adventure story organised around the Cold War. Some critics welcomed the absence of parody and the return to a 'human Bond'. Steven Rubin argues that 'the fact that Roger Moore was consistently beaten up and endangered, indicated to critics and public alike that the era of the automaton Bond was ending'.[15] He suggests that the summer of 1981 was a period of 'joyous celebration' for Bond fans because of this. Interestingly and unusually, however, *For Your Eyes Only* makes direct references to the British government of the time. The minister in charge of Bond is represented as in fear of Thatcher ('She'll have our guts for garters'), while Thatcher herself is the subject of comic parody which the film otherwise largely eschews. In a typical Bondian contradiction, Thatcher's views of the Cold War are incorporated into the plot of the film, but Thatcher is the object of the Bondian sexual joke; to be found, at the end of the film, in the kitchen, that 'rightful place' for womanhood. Thatcher thanks Bond for his services to his country, but as Bond abandons his radio watch for a midnight swim with the current Bond girl, a parrot takes his place uttering the words, 'Give us a kiss, give us a kiss.' Thatcher coyly pats her hair, clearly flattered by the thought.

Both *Octopussy* and *Never Say Never Again*, produced respectively by Broccoli and Kevin McLory and in opposition to one another, relocate Bond in the political concerns of the 1980s where he is reactivated as a Cold War hero, but also takes to spying in the Middle East. In the pre-credit sequences of both *Octopussy* and *Never Say Never Again*, Bond appears to be engaged in a South American caper, clad in *Never Say Never Again* like a member of the SAS, although this proves to be a training exercise. There are other noticeable shifts in emphasis from the Bond of *The Spy* and the 1970s. *Never Say Never Again* boasts a novel villainess for the Bond films, a beautiful and murderous member of SPECTRE whom Bond kills in an unusually powerful explosion from a fountain pen, engineered by the unhappy Q who, although suffering like England from cuts and contraction, is still capable of producing violent phallic solutions. The traditional narrative by which Bond puts attractive women back in their place *sexually* but reserves violence and killing for the villain is reworked to deal violently and finally with those women who cannot be conquered sexually.

Although Bond had dealt with major women villains before (Rosa Klebb in *From Russia, With Love* and Irma Bunt in *On Her Majesty's Secret Service*) they had always been characterised by extreme ugliness and sexual deviance or, in the films, had usually played a very minor part in the plot. The most notable exception to this in the novels is the part of Vesper Lynd in *Casino Royale*, a part in which the roles of 'the girl' and villainess are complexly fused. *Never Say Never Again* breaks with both these earlier models. Moreover, the villainess here is to be killed partly because she has attempted to kill Bond and has killed his girl assistant, but also because, as she holds Bond at gunpoint, she demands an acknowledgement that she has conquered him sexually. Bond is supposed to write a note in proof of this. Instead he fires his fountain pen/gun at her. A tiny dart hits her and there is a reaction shot of her incredulous laughter at Bond's response before the resounding explosion. Both the image of the villainess (aggressive, dark, sexual, vampish) and her 'punishment' seem to resort to earlier traditions in British and American cinema narratives, as does the image of 'the Bond girl' in this case (fair, frightened, and clinging).

It is clear, of course, that these developments have been, in part, prompted by the changed political conditions of the 1980s. The increasing centrality of Cold War rhetoric in the discourse of Reaganism and Thatcherism; the return, in the wake of the Falklands' Crisis, of 'the nation', in its most atavistic forms, to the centre of political life; the attempt to roll back feminism and, with it, women to their 'proper place', in the home: these developments have combined to lend to the Bond films a much harder and sharper political edge than they had in the 1970s.

A mobile signifier

To summarise, our purpose in this chapter has been to single out a number of distinct moments in the history of Bond, first as a cult phenomenon for the intelligentsia, and, subsequently, as a popular hero. In doing so, we have sought to indicate the respects in which the figure of Bond has changed between these various moments, the different sets of ideological and cultural concerns that figure has served to coordinate, and the ways in which the ideological and cultural components of which it has been comprised have been mixed in different combinations at different points in time. It can thus be seen that the figure of Bond has been differently constructed at different moments in the Bond phenomenon. 'James Bond' has been a variable and mobile signifier rather than one that can be fixed as unitary and constant in its signifying functions and effects.

To some extent, of course, such changes are the product of new additions to the 'texts of Bond'. The Bond of the late 1950s was primarily a literary phenomenon whereas, in the 1960s, the figure of Bond was a compound product operating in the relationships between Fleming's novels, the films derived from them, advertisements, commodities, and the like. However, it would be mistaken to regard such additions as simply expanding the 'texts of Bond' without, at the same time, reorganising that set of texts and, accordingly, modifying the signifying function and value of the individual texts within it. We have seen, for example, that a mass readership for the novels was produced by the films. Yet it is unlikely that the films produced that readership without, at the same time, organising it, predisposing readers to read the novels in certain ways, privileging some of their aspects at the expense of others, and so on. It will therefore repay our attention to look more closely at the various 'texts of Bond' and at the ways in which the relations between them have been reclassified and reordered. For such considerations have an important bearing on the ways in which the novels and the films have been interpreted and received – and, thereby, have been actually culturally active – at different moments in Bond's career as a popular hero.

Notes

1 Ian Fleming, 'How to Write a Thriller', *Books and Bookmen*, May 1963, 14.
2 Quoted in John Pearson, *The Life of Ian Fleming* (London: Jonathan Cape, 1966), p. 299.
3 It subsequently did rather better when published by the American Popular Library under the title *Too Hot to Handle*.

4   See Paul Johnson, 'Sex, Snobbery and Sadism', *New Statesman*, 5 April 1958, 430–2.

5   See Bernard Bergonzi, 'The Case of Mr Fleming', *The Twentieth Century*, March 1958, 220–8.

6   Ian Cameron, *Spectator*, 12 October 1962.

7   Quoted in L. Murray and R. Eglin, 'The Gilt-edged Bond', *Business Observer*, 16 January 1972.

8   For a summary and illustrations of Bond's various strip-cartoon incarnations, see *The Illustrated James Bond 007* (New York: James Bond 007 Fan Club, 1981).

9   See, for details, L. Tornabuoni, 'A Popular Phenomenon', in *The Bond Affair*, ed. by O. Del Buono and U. Eco (London: Macdonald, 1966), pp. 13–34.

10 Quoted in *The Hollywood Reporter*, 31 December 1971.

11 See Drew Moniot, 'James Bond and America in the Sixties: An Investigation of Formula Film in Popular Culture', *Journal of the University Film Association*, 28.3 (1976), 25–35.

12 According to Lacan, the arbitrary relationship of signifier to signified – the fact that the relationship of signifier to signified is engendered only via the relationship of one signifier to another – opens up the possibility of an infinite sliding of meaning in which the signifier glides over the signified, slipping into adjacent signifiers, rather than becoming attached to it. Lacan argues that this is avoided by the functioning of certain privileged signifiers – *points de capiton* – which button down the system of language around certain crucial coordinating signifiers. These furnish fixed anchoring points of meaning in relation to which the potentially infinite circulation of meaning within language can be stopped and the meaning of each signifier 'buttonholed' by pinning it down – not to its signified, but by referring it to the central coordinating signifier through which its relationship to other signifiers, and hence to its signified, is organised. According to Lacan, the Symbolic Father and the concept of the phallus function, within the context of the castration complex, as such *points de capiton*; points of anchorage in relation to which sexed identities are constructed, subject positions within language assumed and signifiers clasped to their signifieds through the relations of similarity and difference which mark their position in relation to such *points de capiton*. (For further elaboration of this concept, see A. Wilden, 'Lacan and the Discourse of the Other', in Jacques Lacan, *The Language of the Self: The Function of Language in Psychoanalysis* (New York: Delta Books, 1968), pp. 237–49, pp. 270–84). Although the analogy is not intended as a strict one, Bond's functioning as a *point de capiton* within British popular culture is closely related to the way in which the figure of Bond has been phallicly coded.

13 See John Tulloch and Manuel Alvarado, *Doctor Who: The Unfolding Text* (London: Macmillan, 1983), p. 99.

14 Bruce Merry has thus noted the widespread use of references to Bond in con-
    temporary spy-thrillers, usually as a means of advancing their claims to real-
    ism by disassociating themselves from Bondian fantasy. References to Bond
    function in this way in Frederick Forsyth's *The Day of the Jackal*, Len
    Deighton's *Funeral in Berlin*, and Desmond Bagley's *Running Blind* and *The
    Freedom Trap*. Merry also notes the way in which M supplies the implied
    point of reference in relation to which the control figure is constructed in the
    novels of Deighton and le Carré. See Bruce Merry, *Anatomy of the Spy Thriller*
    (Dublin: Gill and Macmillan, 1977), pp. 64–5, pp. 135–9, pp. 142–3, pp.
    159–60. Mention should also be made of the exceedingly wide range of Bond
    parodies. Examples from the cinema in the mid-1960s include *Our Man Flint*
    (1967), starring James Coburn, Woody Allen's *Casino Royale* (1967), and *The
    Intelligence Men* (1966), starring Morecambe and Wise. For details of literary
    parodies, see Iain Campbell, 'Not Quite Like James Bond', in *Ian Fleming: A
    Catalogue of a Collection* (Oxford: Comersgate, 1978), section 24.
15 Steven Rubin, *The James Bond Films* (Norwalk: Arlington House, 1981),
    p. 187.

Umberto Eco

Narrative structures in Fleming

In 1953 Ian Fleming published *Casino Royale*, the first novel in the 007 series. Being a first work, it is subject to the then literary influence, and in the 1950s, a period which had abandoned the traditional detective story in favour of the hard-boiled novel, it was impossible to ignore the presence of Mickey Spillane.

To Spillane *Casino Royale* owes, beyond doubt, at least two characteristic elements. First, the girl Vesper Lynd, who arouses the confident love of Bond, is in the end revealed as an enemy agent. In a novel by Spillane the hero would have killed her, whereas in Fleming's the woman has the grace to commit suicide; but Bond's reaction has the Spillane characteristic of transforming love into hatred and tenderness into ferocity: 'The bitch is dead, now', Bond telephones to his London office, and so ends his romance.

Second, Bond is obsessed by an image: that of a Japanese expert in codes whom he killed in cold blood on the thirty-sixth floor of the RCA building at Rockefeller Center with a bullet shot from a window of the fortieth floor of the skyscraper opposite. By an analogy that is surely not accidental, Mike Hammer seems to be haunted by the memory of a small Japanese he killed in the jungle during the war, though with greater emotive participation (Bond's homicide, authorised officially by the double zero, is more ascetic and bureaucratic). The memory of the Japanese is the beginning of the undoubted nervous disorders of Mike Hammer (his sadomasochism and his suspected impotence); the memory of his first homicide could have been the origin of the neurosis of James Bond, except that, within the ambit of *Casino Royale*, either the character or his author solves the problem by non-therapeutic means: Fleming excludes neurosis from the narrative possibilities. This decision was to influence the structure of the following eleven novels by Fleming and presumably forms the basis for their success.

After helping to blow up two Bulgarians who had tried to get rid of him, after suffering torture in the form of a cruel abuse of his testicles, after enjoying the elimination of Le Chiffre by a Soviet agent, having received from him a cut on the hand, cold-bloodedly carved while he was conscious, and after risking his love life, Bond, relaxing during his well-earned convalescence in a hospital bed, confides a chilling doubt to his French colleague, Mathis. Have they been fighting for a just cause? Le Chiffre, who had financed Communist spies among the French workers – was he not 'serving a wonderful purpose, a really vital purpose, perhaps the best and highest purpose of all'? The difference between good and evil – is it really something neat, recognisable, as the hagiography of counterespionage would like us to believe? At this point Bond is ripe for the crisis, for the salutary recognition of universal ambiguity, and he sets off along the route traversed by the protagonist of le Carré. But at the very moment he questions himself about the appearance of the devil and, sympathising with the Enemy, is inclined to recognise him as a 'lost brother', Bond is treated to a salve from Mathis:

> When you get back to London you will find there are other Le Chiffres seeking to destroy you and your friends and your country. M will tell you about them. And now that you have seen a really evil man, you will know how evil they can be and you will go after them to destroy them in order to protect yourself and the people you love. You know what they look like now and what they can do to people . . . Surround yourself with human beings, my dear James. They are easier to fight for than principles . . . But don't let me down and become human yourself. We would lose such a wonderful machine.

With this lapidary phrase Fleming defines the character of James Bond for the novels to come. From *Casino Royale* there remains the scar on his cheek, the slightly cruel smile, the taste for good food, and a number of subsidiary characteristics minutely documented in the course of this first volume; but, persuaded by Mathis's words, Bond is to abandon the treacherous life of moral meditation and of psychological anger, with all the neurotic dangers that they entail. Bond ceases to be a subject for psychiatry and remains at the most a physiological object (except for a return to psychic diseases in the last, untypical novel in the series, *The Man With The Golden Gun*), a magnificent machine, as the author and the public, as well as Mathis, wish. From that moment Bond does not meditate upon truth and justice, upon life and death, except in rare moments of boredom, usually in the bar of an airport but always in the form of a casual daydream, never allowing himself to be infected by doubt (at least in the novels; he does indulge in such intimate luxuries in the short stories).

From the psychological point of view, the conversion has taken place quite suddenly, on the basis of four conventional phrases pronounced by Mathis, but the conversion should not be justified on a psychological level. In the last pages of *Casino Royale*, Fleming, in fact, renounces all psychology as the motive of narrative and decides to transfer characters and situations to the level of an objective structural strategy. Without knowing it Fleming makes a choice familiar to many contemporary disciplines: he passes from the psychological method to the formalistic one.

In *Casino Royale* there are already all the elements for the building of a machine that functions basically on a set of precise units governed by rigorous combinational rules. The presence of those rules explains and determines the success of the '007 saga' – a success of which, singularly, has been due both to the mass consensus and to the appreciation of more sophisticated readers. I intend here to examine in detail this narrative machine in order to identify the reasons for its success.

The opposition of characters and of values

The novels of Fleming seem to be built on a series of oppositions which allow a limited number of permutations and interactions. These dichotomies constitute invariant features around which minor couples rotate as free variants. I have singled out fourteen couples, four of which are opposing characters, the others being opposing values, variously personified by the four basic characters:

1 Bond–M;
2 Bond–Villain;
3 Villain–Woman;
4 Woman–Bond;
5 Free World–Soviet Union;
6 Great Britain–Non-Anglo-Saxon Countries;
7 Duty–Sacrifice;
8 Cupidity–Ideals;
9 Love–Death;
10 Chance–Planning;
11 Luxury–Discomfort;

12 Excess–Moderation;
13 Perversion–Innocence;
14 Loyalty–Disloyalty.

These pairs do not represent 'vague' elements but 'simple' ones that are immediate and universal, and, if we consider the range of each pair, we see that the variants allowed in fact include all the narrative devices of Fleming.

Bond–M is a dominated–dominant relationship which characterises from the beginning the limits and possibilities of the character of Bond and sets events moving. Psychological and psychoanalytical interpretations of Bond's attitude towards M have been discussed in particular by Kingsley Amis. The fact is that, even in terms of pure fictional functions, M represents to Bond the one who has a global view of the events, hence his superiority over the 'hero' who depends upon him and who sets out on his various missions in conditions of inferiority to the omniscient chief. Frequently, his chief sends Bond into adventures the upshot of which he had discounted from the start. Bond is thus often the victim of a trick – and it does not matter whether things happen to him beyond the cool calculations of M. The tutelage under which M holds Bond – obliged against his will to visit a doctor, to undergo a nature cure (*Thunderball*), to change his gun (*Dr No*) – makes so much the more insidious and imperious his chief's authority. We can, therefore, see that M represents certain other values such as Duty, Country, and Method. If Bond is the hero, hence in possession of exceptional qualities, M represents Measure, excepted perhaps as a national virtue. But Bond is not so exceptional as a hasty reading of the books (or the spectacular interpretation which films give of the books) might make one think. Fleming always affirmed that he had thought of Bond as an absolutely ordinary person, and it is in contrast with M that the real stature of 007 emerges, endowed with physical attributes, with courage and fast reflexes, but possessing neither these nor other qualities in excess. It is, rather, a certain moral force, an obstinate fidelity to the job – at the command of M, always present as a warning – that allows him to overcome superhuman ordeals without exercising any superhuman faculty.

The Bond–M relationship presupposes a psychological ambivalence, a reciprocal love-hate. At the beginning of *The Man With The Golden Gun*, Bond, emerging from a lengthy amnesia and having been conditioned by the Soviets, tries a kind of ritual parricide by shooting at M with a cyanide pistol; the gesture loosens a long-standing series of narrative tensions which are aggravated every time M and Bond find themselves face to face.

Started by M on the road to Duty (at all costs), Bond enters into conflict with the Villain. The opposition brings into play diverse values, some of which are only variants of the basic couples listed above. Bond represents Beauty and Virility as opposed to the Villain, who often appears monstrous and sexually impotent. The monstrosity of the Villain is a constant point, but to emphasise it we must here introduce a methodological notion which will also apply in examining the other couples. Among the variants we must consider also the existence of vicarious characters whose functions are understood only if they are seen as 'variations' of one of the principal personages, some of whose characteristics they carry on. The vicarious roles function usually for the Woman and for the Villain; one can see as variations of M certain collaborators of Bond – for example, Mathis in *Casino Royale*, who preaches Duty in the appropriate M manner (albeit with a cynical and Gallic air).

As to the characteristics of the Villain, let us consider them in order. In *Casino Royale* Le Chiffre is pallid and smooth, with a crop of red hair, an almost feminine mouth, false teeth of expensive quality, small ears with large lobes, and hairy hands. He never smiles. In *Live and Let Die* Mr Big, a Haitian, has a head that resembles a football, twice the normal size and almost spherical. 'The skin was grey-black, taut and shining like the face of a week-old corpse in the river. It was hairless, except for some grey-brown fluff above the ears. There were no eyebrows and no eyelashes and the eyes were extraordinarily far apart so that one could not focus on them both, but only on one at a time . . . They were animal eyes, not human, and they seemed to blaze.' His gums are pale pink.

In *Diamonds Are Forever* the Villain appears in three different, vicarious roles. Two are Jack and Seraffimo Spang, the first of whom has a humped back and red hair ('Bond did not remember having seen a red-haired hunchback before'), eyes which might have been borrowed from a taxidermist, big ears with rather exaggerated lobes, dry red lips, and an almost total absence of neck. Seraffimo has a face the colour of ivory, black puckered eyebrows, a bush of shaggy hair, and jutting, ruthless jaws; if it is added that Seraffimo used to pass his days in a Spectreville of the Old West dressed in black leather chaps embellished with silver spurs, pistols with ivory butts, a black belt and ammunition – also that he used to drive a train of 1870 vintage furnished with a Victorian carriage – the picture is complete. The third vicarious figure is Senor Winter, who travels with a label on his suitcase which reads 'My blood group is F' and who is really a killer in the pay of the Spangs. Senor Winter is a gross and sweating individual, with a wart on his hand, a placid visage, and protruding eyes.

In *Moonraker* Hugo Drax is six feet tall, with 'exceptional broad' shoulders, a large and square head, and red hair. The right half of his face is shiny and wrinkled from unsuccessful plastic surgery, the right eye different from and larger than the left and 'painfully bloodshot'. He has heavy moustaches, whiskers to the lobes of his ears, and patches of hair on his cheekbones: the moustaches concealed with scant success a prognathous upper jaw and a marked protrusion of his upper teeth. The backs of his hands are covered with reddish hair. Altogether he evokes the idea of a ringmaster at the circus.

In *From Russia, With Love*, the Villain generates three vicarious figures. Red Grant, the professional murderer in the pay of SMERSH, has short, sandy-coloured eyelashes; colourless, opaque blue eyes; a small, cruel mouth; innumerable freckles on his milk-white skin; and deep, wide pores. Colonel Grubozaboyschikov, head of SMERSH, has a narrow and sharp face; round eyes like two polished marbles, weighed down by two flabby pouches; a broad, grim mouth; and a shaven skull. Finally, Rosa Klebb, with the humid, pallid lip stained with nicotine, the raucous voice, flat and devoid of emotion, is five-feet-four, with no curves, dumpy arms, short neck, too sturdy ankles, and grey hair gathered in a tight 'obscene' bun. She has shiny, yellow-brown eyes, wears thick glasses, and has a sharp nose with large nostrils that is powdered white. 'The wet trap of a mouth, that went on opening and shutting as if it was operated by wire under the chin' completes the appearance of a sexually neuter person.

In *From Russia, With Love*, there occurs a variant that is discernible only in a few other novels. There enters also upon the scene a strongly drawn being who has many of the moral qualities of the Villain, but uses them in the end for good, or at least fights on the side of Bond. An example is Darko Kerim, the Turkish agent in *From Russia, With Love*. Analogous to him are Tiger Tanaka, the head of the Japanese secret service in *You Only Live Twice*, Draco in *On Her Majesty's Secret Service*, Enrico Columbo in 'Risico' (a story in *For Your Eyes Only*), and – partially – Quarrel in *Dr No*. They are at the same time representative of the Villain and of M, and we shall call them 'ambiguous representatives'. With these Bond always stands in a kind of competitive alliance: he likes them and hates them at the same time, he uses them and admires them, he dominates them and is their slave.

In *Dr No* the Villain, besides his great height, is characterised by the lack of hands, which are replaced by two metal pincers. His shaved head has the appearance of a reversed raindrop; his skin is clear, without wrinkles; the cheekbones are as smooth as fine ivory; his eyebrows are dark as though painted on; his eyes are without eyelashes and look 'like the mouths of two small revolvers'; his nose is thin and ends very close to his mouth, which shows only cruelty and authority.

In *Goldfinger* the eponymous character is a textbook monster – that is, he is characterised by a lack of proportion: 'He was short, no more than five feet tall, and on top of the thick body and blunt, peasant legs was set, almost directly into the shoulders, a huge and it seemed exactly round head. It was as if Goldfinger had been put together with bits of other peoples bodies. Nothing seemed to belong.' His vicarious figure is that of the Korean, Oddjob, who, with fingers like spatulas and fingertips like solid bone, could smash the wooden balustrade of a staircase with a karate blow.

In *Thunderball* there appears for the first time Ernst Stavro Blofeld, who crops up again in *On Her Majesty's Secret Service* and in *You Only Live Twice*, where in the end he dies. As his vicarious incarnations we have in *Thunderball* Count Lippe and Emilio Largo: both are handsome and personable, however vulgar and cruel, and their monstrosity is purely mental. In *On Her Majesty's Secret Service* there appear Irma Blunt, the *longamanus* of Blofeld, a distant reincarnation of Rosa Klebb, and a series of Villains in outline who perish tragically, killed by an avalanche or by a train. In *You Only Live Twice*, the primary role is resumed by Blofeld, already described in *Thunderball*: a childlike gaze from eyes that resemble two deep pools, surrounded 'like the eyes of Mussolini' by clear whites, eyes having the symmetry and silken black lashes that recall the eyes of a doll; a mouth like a badly healed wound under a heavy squat nose; altogether an expression of hypocrisy, tyranny, and cruelty, on a Shakespearean level. Blofeld weighs twenty stone. As we learn in *On Her Majesty's Secret Service*, he lacks earlobes. His hair is a wiry, black crew cut.

To make more constant the Bond–Villain relationship, there is also a racial quality common to all Villains, along with other characteristics. The Villain is born in an ethnic area that stretches from Central Europe to the Slav countries and the Mediterranean basin: usually he is of mixed blood and his origins are complex and obscure. He is asexual or homosexual, or at any rate is not sexually normal. He has exceptional inventive and organisational qualities which help him acquire immense wealth and by means of which he usually works to help Russia: to this end he conceives a plan of fantastic character and dimensions, worked out to the smallest detail, intended to create serious difficulties either for England or for the Free World in general. Gathered in the figure of the Villain, in fact, the negative values which we have distinguished in some pairs of opposites, the Soviet Union and other non-Anglo-Saxon countries (the racial convention blames particularly the Jews, the Germans, the Slavs, and the Italians, always depicted as half-breeds), Cupidity elevated to the dignity of paranoia, Planning as technological methodology, satrapic Luxury, physical and psychical Excess, physical and moral Perversion, radical Disloyalty.

Le Chiffre, who organises the subversive movement in France, comes from a mixture of Mediterranean and Prussian or Polish strains and has Jewish blood revealed by small ears with large lobes. A gambler not basically disloyal, he still betrays his own bosses and tries to recover by criminal means money lost in gambling. He is a masochist (at least so the Secret Service dossier proclaims). He has brought a great chain of brothels, but has lost his patrimony by his exalted manner of living.

Mr Big is a black man who enjoys with Solitaire an ambiguous relationship of exploitation (he has not yet acquired her favours). He helps the Soviet by means of his powerful criminal organisation founded on the voodoo cult, finds and sells in the United States treasure hidden in the seventeenth century, controls various rackets, and is prepared to ruin the American economy by introducing, through the black market, large quantities of rare coins.

Hugo Drax displays indefinite nationality – he is English by adoption – but in fact he is German. He holds control of columbite, a material indispensable to the construction of reactors, and gives to the British crown the means of building a most powerful rocket. He plans, however, first to make the rocket fall, when tested atomically on London, and then to flee to Russia (equation: Communist-Nazi). He frequents clubs of high class and is passionately fond of bridge, but only enjoys cheating. His hysteria does not permit one to suspect any sexual activity worthy of note.

Of the secondary characters in *From Russia, With Love*, the chief are from the Soviet Union and, in working for the Communist cause, enjoy comforts and power: Rosa Klebb, sexually neuter, 'might enjoy the act physically, but the instrument was of no importance'; Red Grant, a werewolf who kills for pleasure, lives splendidly at the expense of the Soviet government in a villa with a swimming pool. The science-fiction plot consists of the plan to lure Bond into a complicated trap, using for bait a woman and an instrument for coding and decoding ciphers, and then to kill and checkmate the English counterspy.

Dr No is a Chinese-German half-breed who works for Russia. He shows no definite sexual tendencies (having in his power Honeychile, he plans to have her torn to pieces by the crabs of Crab Key). He has a flourishing guano industry and plans to cause guided missiles launched by the Americans to deviate from their course. In the past he has built up his fortune by robbing the criminal organisation of which he had been elected cashier. He lives, on his island, in a palace of fabulous pomp.

Goldfinger has a probable Baltic origin, but also has Jewish blood. He lives splendidly from commerce and from smuggling gold, by means of which he finances Communist plots in Europe. He plans the theft of gold from Fort Knox (not its radioactivation, as the film indicates) and, to overcome the final barrier, sets up an atomic attack on a NATO installation and tries to poison the water of Fort Knox. He does not have a sexual relationship with the woman he dominates, but limits himself to the acquisition of gold. He cheats at cards by using expensive devices such as binoculars and radios; he cheats to make money, even though he is fabulously rich and always travels with a stock of gold in his luggage.

Blofeld is of a Polish father and a Greek mother. He exploits his position as a telegraph clerk to start in Poland a flourishing trade in secret information and becomes chief of the most extensive independent organisation for espionage, blackmail, rapine, and extortion. Indeed, with Blofeld Russia ceases to be the constant enemy – because of the general international relaxation of tension – and the part of the malevolent organisation assumed by SPECTRE has all the characteristics of SMERSH, including the employment of Slav–Latin–German elements, the use of torture, the elimination of traitors, and the sworn enmity to all the powers of the Free World. Of the science-fiction plans of Blofeld, that of *Thunderball* is to steal from NATO two atomic bombs and with these to blackmail England and America; that of *On Her Majesty's Secret Service* envisages the training in a mountain clinic of girls with suitable allergies to condition them to spread a mortal virus intended to ruin the agriculture and livestock of the United Kingdom; and in *You Only Live Twice*, Blofeld, affected by murderous mania, organises a fantastic suicidal garden near the coast of Japan, which attracts legions of heirs of the Kamikaze who are bent on poisoning themselves with exotic, refined, and lethal plants, thus doing grave and complex harm to the human patrimony of Japanese democracy. Blofeld's tendency toward satrapic pomp shows itself in the kind of life he leads in the mountain of Piz Gloria and, more particularly, on the island of Kyashu, where he lives in medieval tyranny and passes through his *hortus deliciarum* clad in metal armour. Previously Blofeld showed himself to be ambitious of honours (he aspired to be known as the Count of Blenville), a master of planning, and organising genius, as treacherous as needs be, and sexually impotent – he lived in a marriage with Irma Blofeld, also asexual and hence repulsive. To quote Tiger Tanaka, Blofeld 'is a devil who has taken human form'.

Only the evil characters of *Diamonds Are Forever* have no connections with Russia. In a certain sense the international gangsterism of the Spangs appears to be an earlier version of SPECTRE. For the rest, Jack and Seraffimo possess all the characteristics of the canon.

To the typical qualities of the Villain are opposed the Bond characteristics, particularly Loyalty to the Service, Anglo-Saxon Moderation opposed to the excess of the half-breeds, the selection of Discomfort and the acceptance of Sacrifice opposed to the ostentatious Luxury of the enemy, the genial improvisation (Chance) opposed to the cold Planning which it defeats, the sense of an Ideal opposed to Cupidity (Bond in various cases wins from the Villain in gambling, but as a rule returns the enormous winnings to the Service or to the girl of the moment). Some oppositions function not only in the Bond–Villain relationship but also in the behaviour of Bond. Thus Bond is normally loyal but does not disdain overcoming a cheating enemy by a deceitful trick and blackmailing him (see *Moonraker* or *Goldfinger*). Even Excess and Moderation, Chance and Planning are opposed in the acts and decisions of Bond. Duty and Sacrifice appear as elements of internal debate each time Bond knows he must prevent the plan of the Villain at risk to his life, and in those cases the patriotic ideal (Great Britain and the Free World) takes the upper hand. He calls also on the racist need to show the superiority of the Briton. Also opposed in Bond are Luxury (the choice of good food, care in dressing, preference for sumptuous hotels, love of the gambling table, invention of cocktails, and so on) and Discomfort (Bond is always ready to abandon the easy life – even when it appears in the guise of a Woman who offers herself – to face a new aspect of Discomfort, the acutest point of which is torture).

We have discussed the Bond–Villain dichotomy at length because in fact it embodies all the characteristics of the opposition between Eros and Thanatos, the principle of pleasure and the principle of reality, culminating in the moment of torture (in *Casino Royale* explicitly theorised as a sort of erotic relationship between the torture and the tortured). This opposition is perfected in the relationship between the Villain and the Woman; Vesper is tyrannised and blackmailed by the Soviets, and therefore by Le Chiffre; Solitaire is the slave of Mr Big; Tiffany Case is dominated by the Spangs; Tatiana is the slave of Rosa Klebb and of the Soviet government in general; Jill and Tilly Masterson are dominated, to different degrees, by Goldfinger, and Pussy Galore works under his orders; Domino Vitali is subservient to the wishes of Blofeld through the vicarious figure of Emilio Largo; the English girls of Piz Gloria are under the hypnotic control of Blofeld and the virginal surveillance of Irma Blunt; Honeychile, wandering pure and untroubled on the shores of his cursed island, has a purely symbolic relationship with the power of Dr No, except that at the end Dr No offers her naked body to the crabs (she has been dominated by the Villain through the vicarious effort of the brutal Mander and has justly punished Mander by causing a scorpion to kill him, anticipating the revenge of No – who had recourse to crabs); and, finally, Kissy Suzuki lives on her island in the shade of the cursed castle of Blofeld, suffering a purely allegorical domination shared by the population of the place. In an intermediate position is Gala Brand, who is an agent of the Service but who becomes the secretary of Hugo Drax and establishes a relationship of submission to him. In most cases the Villain–Woman relationship culminates in the torture the woman undergoes along with Bond; here the Love–Death pair functions also, in the sense of a more intimate erotic union of the two through their common ordeal.

Dominated by the Villain, however, Fleming's woman has already been previously conditioned to domination, life for her having assumed the role of the villain. The general scheme is (i) the girl is beautiful and good; (ii) she has been made frigid and unhappy by severe trials suffered in adolescence; (iii) this has conditioned her to the service of the Villain; (iv) through meeting Bond she appreciates her positive human chances; (v) Bond possesses her but in the end loses her. This curriculum is common to Vesper, Solitaire, Tiffany, Tatiana, Honeychile, and Domino; rather vague as for Gala; equally shared by the three vicarious women of *Goldfinger* (Jill, Tilly, and Pussy); more diffuse and uncertain for the group of girls on Piz Gloria; Kissy Suzuki's unhappiness is the result of a Hollywoodian experience which has made her chary of life and of men.

In every case Bond loses the woman, either by her own will or by that of another. Thus, in the moment in which the Woman solves the opposition to the Villain by entering with Bond in a purifying-purified, saving-saved relationship, she returns to the domination of the negative. Every woman displays an internal combat between the couple Perversion-Purity (sometimes external, as is the relationship of Rosa Klebb and Tatiana) which makes her similar to the Richardsonian persecuted virgin. The bearer of purity, notwithstanding and despite her perversion, eager to alternate lust with torture, she would appear likely to resolve the contrast between the privileged race and the non-Anglo-Saxon half-breed, since she often belongs to an ethnically inferior breed; but insofar as the erotic relationship always ends with a form of death, real or symbolic, Bond resumes willy-nilly his purity as an Anglo-Saxon bachelor. The race remains uncontaminated.

A Manichean ideology

The novels of Fleming have been vicariously accused of McCarthyism, Fascism, the cult of excess and violence, racism, and so on. It is difficult, after the analysis we have carried out, to maintain that Fleming is not inclined to consider the British superior to all Oriental or Mediterranean races or that Fleming does not profess heartfelt anti-Communism. Yet it is significant that he ceased to identify the wicked with Russia as soon as international opinion rendered Russia less menacing according to the general opinion. It is significant also that, while he is introducing the gang of Mr Big, Fleming is profuse in his acknowledgement of the new African nations and of their contribution to contemporary civilisation; when the Villain is supposed to have Jewish blood, Fleming is always fairly unexplicit; he never shows more than a cautious, middle-class chauvinism. Thus arises the suspicion that our author does not characterise his creations in such and such a manner as a result of ideological opinion but purely for rhetorical purposes. By 'rhetoric' I mean an art of persuasion which relies on *endoxa*, that is, on the common opinions shared by the majority of readers.

Fleming is, in other words, cynically building an effective narrative apparatus. To do so he decides to rely upon the most secure and universal principles and puts into play precisely those archetypal elements that have proved successful in fairy tales. Let us recall for a moment the pairs of oppositional characters; M is the King and Bond is the Knight entrusted with a mission; Bond is the Knight and the Villain is the Dragon; that Lady and Villain stand for Beauty and the Beast; Bond restores the Lady to the fullness of spirit and to her senses – he is the Prince who rescues Sleeping Beauty; between the Free World and the Soviet Union, England and the non-Anglo-Saxon countries is realised the primitive epic relationship between the Privileged Race and the Lower Race, between White and Black, Good and Bad. Fleming is a racist in the sense that any artist is one if, to represent the devil, he depicts him with oblique eyes; in the sense that a nurse is one who, wishing to frighten children with the bogeyman, suggests that he is black. It is singular that Fleming should be anti-Communist with the same lack of discrimination as he is anti-Nazi and anti-German. It isn't that in one case he is reactionary and in the other democratic. He is simply Manichean for operative reasons: he sees the world as made up of good and evil forces in conflict.

Fleming seeks elementary oppositions; to personify primitive and universal forces, he had recourse to popular standards. In a time of international tensions, popular notions of 'wicked Communism' exist beside those of the unpunished Nazi criminal. Fleming uses them both in a sweeping, uncritical manner.

At the most, he tempers his choice with irony, but the irony is completely masked and is revealed only through incredible exaggeration. In *From Russia, With Love*, the Soviet men are so monstrous, so improbably evil that it seems impossible to take them seriously. And yet, in his brief preface, Fleming insists that all the narrated atrocities are absolutely true. He has chosen the path of fable, and fable must be taken as truthful if it is not to become a satirical fairy tale. The author seems almost to write his books for a two-fold reading public, those who take them as gospel truth and those who see their humour. In order to work as ambiguous texts, however, they must appear authentic, credible, ingenious, and plainly aggressive. A man who chooses to write in this way is neither a Fascist nor a racist; he is only a cynic, an expert in tale engineering.

If Fleming is a reactionary at all, it is not because he identifies the figure of 'evil' with a Russian or a Jew. He is reactionary because he makes use of stock figures. The very use of such figures (the Manichean dichotomy, seeing things in black and white) is always dogmatic and intolerant – in short, reactionary – whereas he who avoids set figures, who recognises nuances and distinctions and who admits contradictions is democratic. Fleming is conservative as, basically, the fable – any fable – is conservative; his is the static, inherent, dogmatic conservatism of fairy tales and myths, which transmit an elementary wisdom, constructed and communicated by a simple play of light and shade, by indisputable archetypes which do not permit critical distinction. If Fleming is a 'Fascist', he is so because of his inability to pass from mythology to reason.

The very names of Fleming's protagonists suggest the mythological nature of the stories by fixing in an image or in a pun the character from the start, without any possibility of conversion or change. The wicked man lives by gambling? He will be called Le Chiffre. He is working for the Reds? He will be called Red – and Grant if he works for money, duly granted. A Korean professional killer by unusual means will be Oddjob. One obsessed with gold is Auric Goldfinger. A wicked man is called No. Perhaps the half-lacerated face of Hugo Drax will be conjured up by the incisive onomatopoeia of his name. Beautiful, transparent, telepathic

Solitaire evokes the coldness of the diamond. Chic and interested in diamonds, Tiffany Case recalls the leading jewellers in New York and the beauty case of the mannequin. Ingenuity is suggested by the very name of Honeychile; sensual shamelessness, by that of Pussy Galore. A pawn in a dark game? Such is Domino. A tender Japanese lover, quintessence of the Orient? Such is Kissy Suzuki. We pass over such women of less interest as Mary Goodnight or Miss Trueblood. And if the name Bond has chosen, as Fleming affirms, almost by chance, to give the character an absolutely common appearance, then it would be by chance, but also by guidance, that this model of style and success evokes the luxuries of Bond Street or treasury bonds.

By now it is clear how the novels of Fleming have attained such a wide success: they build up a network of elementary associations to achieve something original and profound. Fleming also pleases the sophisticated readers who here distinguish, with a feeling of aesthetic pleasure, the purity of the primitive epic impudently and maliciously translated into current terms and who applaud in Fleming the cultured man, whom they recognise as one of themselves, naturally the most clever and broadminded.

Such praise Fleming might merit if he did not develop a second facet much more cunning: the game of stylistic oppositions, by virtue of which the sophisticated reader, detecting the fairy-tale mechanism, feels himself a malicious accomplice of the author, only to become a victim for he is led on to detect stylistic inventions where there is, on the contrary – as will be shown – a clever montage of *déjà vu*.

Literary techniques

Fleming 'writes well', in the most banal but honest meaning of the term. He has a rhythm, a polish, a certain sensuous feeling for words. That is not to say that Fleming is an artist; yet he writes with art.

Translation may betray him. The beginning of the Italian version of *Goldfinger* – 'James Bond stava seduto nella sala d'aspetto dell'aeroporto di Miami. Aveva già bevuto due bourbon doppi ed ora rifletteva sulla vita e sulla morte' (James Bond was seated in the departure lounge of Miami Airport. He had already drunk two double bourbons and was now thinking about life and death) – is not the same as 'James Bond, with two double bourbons inside him, sat in the final departure lounge and thought about life and death'. In the English phrase there is only one sentence, an elegant display of *concinnitas*. There is nothing more to say. Fleming maintains this standard.

He tells stories that are violent and unlikely. But there are ways and ways of doing so. In *One Lonely Night* Mickey Spillane describes a massacre carried out by Mike Hammer:

> They heard my scream and the awful roar of the gun and the slugs stuttering and whining and it was the last they heard. They went down as they tried to run and felt their legs going out from under them. I saw the general's head jerk and shudder before he slid to the floor, rolling over and over. The guy from the subway tried to stop the bullets with his hand but just didn't seem able to make it and joined the general on the floor.

When Fleming describes the death of Le Chiffre in *Casino Royale*, we meet a technique that is undoubtedly more subtle:

> There was a sharp 'phut', no louder than a bubble of air escaping from a tube of toothpaste. No other noise at all, and suddenly Le Chiffre had grown another eye, a third eye on a level with the other two, right where the thick nose started to jut out below the forehead. It was a small black eye, without eyelashes or eyebrows. For a second the three eyes looked out across the room and then the whole face seemed to slip and go down on one knee. The two outer eyes turned trembling up towards the ceiling.

There is more shame, more reticence, more respect than in the uneducated outburst of Spillane; but there is also a more baroque feeling for the image, a total adaptation of the image without emotional comment, and a use of words that designate things with accuracy. It is not that Fleming renounces explosions of Grand Guignol; he even excels in them and scatters them through his novels. But when he orchestrates the macabre on a wide screen, even here he reveals much more literary venom than Spillane possesses.

Consider the death scene of Mr Big in *Live and Let Die*. Bond and Solitaire, tied by a long rope to the bandit's ship, have been dragged behind in order to be torn to pieces on the coral rocks in the bay. In the end the ship, shrewdly mined by Bond a few hours earlier, blows up, and the two victims, now safe, witness the miserable end of Mr Big, shipwrecked and devoured by barracuda:

> It was a large head and a veil of blood streamed down over the face from a wound in the great bald skull . . . Bond could see the teeth showing in a rictus of agony and frenzied endeavour. Blood half veiled the eyes that Bond knew would be bulging in their sockets. He could almost hear the great diseased heart thumping under the grey-black skin . . . The Big Man came on. His shoulders were naked, his clothes stripped off him by the explosion, Bond supposed, but the black silk tie had remained and it showed around the thick neck and streamed behind the head like a Chinaman's pigtail. A

splash of water cleared some blood away from the eyes. They were wide open, staring madly towards Bond. They held no appeal for help, only a fixed glare of physical exertion. Even as Bond looked into them, now only ten yards away, they suddenly shut and the great face contorted into a grimace of pain. 'Aaarh', said the distorted mouth. Both arms stopped flailing the water and the head went under and came up again. A cloud of blood welled up and darkened the sea. Two six-foot thin brown shadows backed out of the cloud and then dashed back into it. The body in the water jerked sideways. Half of the Big Man's arm came out of the water. It had no hand, no wrist, no wrist-watch. But the great turnip head, the drawn-back mouth full of white teeth almost splitting it in half, was still alive . . . The head floated back to the surface. The mouth was closed. The yellow eyes seemed still to look at Bond. Then the shark's snout came right out of the water and it drove in towards the head, the lower curved jaw open so that light glinted on the teeth. There was a horrible grunting scrunch and a great swirl of water. Then silence.

This parade of the terrifying has precedents in the eighteenth and nineteenth centuries: the final carnage, preceded by torture and painful imprisonment (preferably with a virgin), is pure Gothic. The passage quoted here is abridged; Mr Big suffers even more agonies. In the same manner Lewis's *Monk* was dying for several days with his own lacerated body lying on a steep cliff. But the Gothic terrors of Fleming are described with physical precision, a detailing by images, and for the most part by images of things. The absence of the watch on the wrist bitten off by the shark is not just an example of macabre sarcasm; it is an emphasis on the essential by the inessential, typical of the *école du regard*.

And here let us introduce a further opposition which affects not so much the structure of the plot as that of Fleming's style: the distinction between a narrative incorporating wicked and violent acts and a narrative that proceeds by trifling acts seen with disillusioned eyes.

What is surprising in Fleming is the minute and leisurely concentration with which he pursues for page after page descriptions of articles, landscapes, and events apparently inessential to the course of the story and, conversely, the feverish brevity with which he covers in a few paragraphs the most unexpected and improbable actions. A typical example is to be found in *Goldfinger*, with two long pages dedicated to a casual meditation on a Mexican murder, fifteen pages dedicated to a game of golf, and twenty-five pages occupied with a long car trip across France as against the four or five pages which cover the arrival at Fort Knox of a false hospital train and the *coup de théâtre* which culminates in the failure of Goldfinger's plan and the death of Tilly Masterson.

2.1 Bond (Sean Connery) and Goldfinger (Gert Frobe) playing golf in *Goldfinger*

In *Thunderball* a quarter of the volume is occupied by descriptions of the naturalist cures Bond undergoes in a clinic, though the events that occur there do not justify lingering over the details of diets, massage, and Turkish baths. The most disconcerting passage is perhaps that in which Domino Vitali, after having told Bond her life-story in the bar of the Casino, monopolises five pages to describe, with great detail, the box of Player's cigarettes. The passage in *Thunderball* is an interruption, and it does not seem necessary to characterise the dreaming spirit of Domino by depicting in such an abundance of nuances her tendency to purposeless 'phenomenology'.

It is also 'purposeless' to introduce diamond smuggling in South Africa in *Diamonds Are Forever* by opening with the description of a scorpion, as though seen through a magnifying glass, enlarged to the size of some prehistoric monster, as the protagonist in a story of life and death at animal level, interrupted by the sudden appearance of a human being who crushes the scorpion. Then the action of the book begins, as though what has gone before represents only the titles, cleverly presented, of a film which then proceeds in a different manner.

And even more typical of this technique of the aimless glance is the beginning of *From Russia, With Love*, where we have a whole page of virtuosity exercised upon the body, death-like in its immobility, of a man lying by the side of a swimming pool being explored pore by pore, hair by hair, by a blue and green dragonfly. As soon as the author has infused the scene with a subtle sense of death, the man moves and frightens away the dragonfly. The man moves because he is alive and is about to be massaged. The fact that lying on the ground he seems dead has no relevance to the purpose of the narrative that follows.

Fleming abounds in such passages of high technical skill which makes us see what he is describing, with a relish for the inessential, and which the narrative mechanism of the plot not only does not require but actually rejects. When the story reaches its fundamental action, the technique of the aimless glance is decisively abandoned. The moments of descriptive reflection, particularly attractive because they are sustained by polished and effective language, seem to sustain the poles of Luxury and Planning, whereas those of rash action express the moments of Discomfort and of Chance.

Thus the opposition of the two techniques (or the technique of this opposition of styles) is not accidental. If Fleming's technique were to interrupt the suspense of vital action, such as frogmen swimming towards a mortal challenge, to linger over descriptions of submarine fauna and coral formations, it would be like the ingenuous technique of Salgari, who is capable of abandoning his heroes when they stumble over a great root of Sequoia during their pursuit in order to describe the origins, properties, and distribution of the Sequoia on the North American continent.

In Fleming, the digression, instead of resembling a passage from an encyclopaedia badly rendered, takes on a twofold shape: first, it is rarely a description of the unusual – such as occurs in Salgari and in Verne – but a description of the already known; second, it occurs not as encyclopaedic information but as literary suggestion, displayed in order to get a sort of literary promotion. Let us examine these two points, because they reveal the secret of Fleming's stylistic technique.

Fleming does not describe the Sequoia that the reader has never had a chance to see. He describes a game of canasta, an ordinary motor car, the control panel of an airplane, a railway carriage, the menu of a restaurant, the box of a brand of cigarettes available at any tobacconist's. Fleming describes in a few words an assault on Fort Knox because he knows that none of his readers will ever have occasion to rob Fort Knox; he expands in explaining the gusto with which a steering wheel or a golf club can be gripped because these are acts that each of us has accomplished, may accomplish, or would like to accomplish. Fleming takes times to convey the familiar with photographic accuracy because it is with the familiar that he can solicit our capacity for information. We identify not with the one who steals an atom bomb but with one who steers a luxurious motor launch; not with the one who explodes a rocket but with the one who accomplishes a lengthy ski descent; not with the one who smuggles diamonds but with the one who orders a dinner in a restaurant in Paris. Our credulity is solicited, blandished, directed to the region of possible and desirable things. Here the narration is realistic, the attention to detail intense; for the rest, so far as the unlikely is concerned, a few pages and an implicit wink of the eye suffice. No one has to believe them.

And again, the pleasure of reading is given not by the incredible and the unknown but by the obvious and the usual. It is undeniable that Fleming, in exploiting the obvious, uses a verbal strategy of a rare kind, but this strategy makes us fond of redundancy, not of information. The language performs the same function as do the plots. The greatest pleasure arises not from excitement but from relief.

The minute descriptions constitute, not encyclopaedic information, but literary evocation. Indubitably, if an underwater swimmer swims towards his death and I glimpse above him a milky and calm sea and vague shapes of phosphorescent fish which swim by him, his act is inscribed within the framework of an ambiguous and eternal indifferent Nature which evokes a kind of profound and moral conflict. Usually Journalism, when a diver is devoured by the shark, says that, and it is enough. If someone embellishes this death with three pages of description of coral, is not that Literature?

This technique – sometimes identified as Midcult or as Kitsch – here finds one of its most efficacious manifestations – we might say the least irritating, as a result of the ease and skill with which its operation is conducted, if it were not that this artifice forces one to praise in the works of Fleming not the shrewd elaboration of the different stories but a literary phenomenon.

Literature as collage

Hence Fleming composes elementary and violent plots, played against fabulous opposition, with a technique of novels 'for the masses'. Frequently he describes women and scenery, marine depths and motorcars with a literary technique of reportage, bordering closely upon Kitsch and sometimes failing badly. He blends his narrative elements with an unstable montage, alternating Grand Guignol and *nouveau roman*, with such broadmindedness in the choice of material as to be numbered, for good or for ill, if not among the inventors, at least among the cleverest exploiters of an experimental technique. It is very difficult when reading these novels, after their initial diverting impact has passed, to perceive to what extent Fleming simulates literature by pretending to write literature and to what extent he creates literary fireworks with cynical, mocking relish by montage.

Fleming is more literate than he gives one to understand. He begins Chapter 19 of *Casino Royale* with 'You are about to awake when you dream that you are dreaming'. It is a familiar idea, but it is also a phrase of Novalis. The long meeting of diabolical Russians who are planning the damnation of Bond in the opening chapter of *From Russia, With Love* reminds one of *Faust*'s prologue in the Hell.

We might think that such influences, part of the reading of well-bred gentlemen, may have worked in the mind of the author without emerging into consciousness. Probably Fleming remained bound to a nineteenth-century world, of which his militaristic and nationalistic ideology, his racist colonialism, and his Victorian isolationism are all hereditary traits. His love of travelling, by grand hotels and luxury trains, is completely of *la belle époque*. The very archetype of the train, of the journey on the Orient

Express (where love and death await him), derives from Tolstoy by way of Dekobra to Cendrars. His women, as has been said, are Richardsonian Clarissas who correspond to the archetype brought to light by Fiedler (see *Love and Death in the American Novel*).

But what is more, there is the taste for the exotic, which is not contemporary, even if the islands of Dream are reached by jet. In *You Only Live Twice*, we have a garden of tortures which is very closely related to that of Mirbeau in which the plants are described in a detailed inventory that implies something like the *Traité des poisons* by Orfila, reached possibly by way of the mediation of Huysmans in *Là-bas*. But *You Only Live Twice*, in its exotic exaltation (three quarters of the book is dedicated to an almost mystical initiation to the Orient), in its habit of quoting from ancient poets recalls also the morbid curiosity with which Judith Gauthier, in 1869, introduced the reader to the discovery of China in *Le dragon impérial*. And if the comparison appears farfetched – well, then, let us remember that Ko-Li-Tsin, Gauthier's revolutionary poet, escapes from the prisons of Peking by clinging to a kite and that Bond escapes from the infamous castle of Blofeld by clinging to a balloon. It is true that Bond hung onto the balloon remembering having seen Douglas Fairbanks do so, but Fleming is undoubtedly more cultured than his character is. It is not a matter of seeking out analogies and of suggesting that there is in the ambiguous and evil atmosphere of Piz Gloria an echo of Mann's magic mountain: sanatoria are in the mountains and in the mountains it is cold. It is not a question of seeing in Honyechile, who appears to Bond from the foam of the sea, Anadiomene, the bird-like girl of Joyce: two bare legs bathed by the waves are the same everywhere. But sometimes the analogies do not only concern the psychological atmosphere. They are structural analogies. Thus it happens that 'Quantum of Solace', one of the stories in *For Your Eyes Only*, presents Bond sitting upon a chintz sofa of the governor of the Bahamas and listening to the governor tell, after a lengthy and rambling preamble, in an atmosphere of rarefied discomfort, the long and apparently inconsistent story of an adulterous woman and a vindictive husband, a story without blood and without dramatic action, a story of personal and private actions, after the telling of which Bond feels himself strangely upset and inclined to see his own dangerous activities as infinitely less romantic and intense than the events of certain private and commonplace lives. Now, the structure of this tale, the technique of description and the introduction of characters, the disproportion between the preamble and the story, the inconsistency of the story, and the effect it produces – all recall strangely the habitual course of many stories by Barbey d'Aurevilly. And we may also recall that the idea of a human body covered by gold appears in Dmitri Merezkowskij (except that in this case the culprit is not Goldfinger but Leonardo da Vinci).

It may be that Fleming had not pursued such varied and sophisticated reading, and in that case one must only assume that, bound by education and psychological make-up to the world of today, he copied solutions without being aware of them, reinventing devices that he had smelled in the air. But the most likely theory is that, with the same effective cynicism with which he constructed his plots according to archetypal oppositions, he decided that the paths of invention, for the readers of our century, can return to those of the great nineteenth-century *feuilleton*, that as against the homely normality – I do not say of Hercule Poirot but, rather, of Sam Spade and Michael Shayne, priests of an urbane and foreseeable violence – he revised the fantasy and the technique that had made Rocambole and Rouletabille, Fantomas and Fu Manchu famous.

However, we are not here concerned with a psychological interpretation of Fleming as an individual but with an analysis of the structure of his text, the relationship between the literary inheritance and the crude chronicle, between nineteenth-century tradition and science fiction, between adventurous excitement and hypnosis, fused together to produce an unstable patchwork, a tongue-in-cheek *bricolage*, which often hides its ready-made nature by presenting itself as literary invention. To the extent to which it permits a disenchanted reading, the work of Fleming represents a successful means of leisure, the result of skilful craftsmanship. To the extent that it provides to anyone the thrill of poetic emotion, it is the last *avatar* of Kitsch; to the extent that it provokes elementary psychological reactions in which ironic detachment is absent, it is only a more subtle, but no less mystifying, example of soap opera.

Since the decoding of a message cannot be established by its author, but depends upon the concrete circumstances of reception, it is difficult to guess what Fleming is or will be for his readers. When an act of communication provokes a response in public opinion, the definitive verification will take place not within the ambit of the book but in that of the society that reads it.

Michael Denning

Licensed to look:
James Bond and the
heroism of consumption

Thrillers of the spectacle

With James Bond, the spy thriller enters its moment of greatest popularity. Whereas earlier we found espionage themes coming to dominate the thriller generally, we now see the espionage thriller coming to dominate the entire field of popular fiction. Tales of spies are no longer one part of popular culture; they are at its centre. James Bond transcended the novels and films which brought him to life, and joined that small group of fictional characters who are known by many who never read or saw the 'original' texts – figures like Robinson Crusoe and Sherlock Holmes. But this presence of Bond in the popular imagination is itself only one part of the presence of espionage in the culture of the late 1950s and early 1960s: spy stories proliferated in novels, on film, and on TV; in the daily newspapers, the sensational cases of George Blake and Kim Philby marked the spy fever of the 1960s. Christopher Booker, in a history of the period's culture, writes:

> The curious way in which the Bond phenomenon had become a shadow to the history of the age, had been given a further twist in March 1961 when an American magazine had revealed that one of the most fervent Bond readers was President Kennedy. Partly aided by this revelation, in 1961 and 1962, the sales of Bond books on both sides of the Atlantic had soared. Now, by the end of 1962, with the arrival of new authors such as Len Deighton (north London) and John le Carré (Oxford early 50s), a Foreign Office official, 'spy literature', like satire, seemed to be turning into an industry. It was also in November 1962, that with the arrival of James Bond on the screen, played by the former Carnaby Street model and Royal Court actor Sean Connery (Glasgow), the record-breaking *Dr No* marked the beginning of a turn in British cinema away from 'Northern Realism' and indeed 'naturalism' of any

kind towards an altogether more colourful and sensational kind of fantasy. The real explanation for this new popularity of spy stories, in fact, was not so much that they were a reflection of the increase in real life spying, as a more subtle reflection of the *Zeitgeist*.[1]

Though the *Zeitgeist* is easier to invoke than to define, the spy novel is in a sense the war novel of the Cold War, the cover story of an era of decolonisation and, particularly after the *débâcle* at Suez in 1956, the definitive loss of Britain's role as a world power. This flowering of the spy thriller and, in particular, of Ian Fleming's James Bond tales, will be the subject of this chapter.

Ian Fleming's first novel about James Bond, *Casino Royale*, was published in 1953; twelve more novels and the two collections of short stories were published by 1965. But the moment of Bond does not really begin until the publication of *Casino Royale* in Pan paperback in 1956, and the serialisation of *From Russia, With Love* in the *Daily Express* in 1957; after which the sales of the Bond books took off, reaching a peak in 1964 and 1965 in the wake of the release of the first Bond films. For it was the Bond books that brought the American paperback revolution to Britain. 'They were', John Sutherland writes, 'a breakthrough comparable in some ways to Lane's, thirty years earlier', that is, to Allen Lane's Penguins. Pan claimed that ten of the first eighteen million-sellers in Britain were Bond novels.[2]

And just as this qualitative leap in the mode of production of popular fiction must be marked off from the fiction that preceded it, so there is also a discontinuity between the spy thrillers of the first half of the century and this new expansion of the thriller – a discontinuity that ought not be effaced by the conventions of literary histories of the genre. For no formal account of the genre's progress explains the Bond books and their enormous popularity. Surely the logic of increasing verisimilitude, the sense that each new breakthrough in the spy novel marks a more convincing code of realism, does not account for Fleming's fantastic tales, despite his skill at using the reality-effect in details, a skill that led Kingsley Amis to define that device as the 'Fleming effect'.[3] Rather what is remarkable is the way that the earlier spy thriller had spent much of its force; both Greene and Ambler had largely given up the spy thriller by the late 1940s, and they were to return to the genre in the 1960s because of the new centrality accorded it by the work of Fleming, le Carré, and Deighton.

So how are we to account for this new thriller, and how describe its constituents? The obvious place to begin would be with the figure of James Bond himself, particularly in light of the way that he managed to transcend his textual embodiment and join Sherlock Holmes as a major character in the popular imagination. The difficulty lies in the variety of James Bonds there are. Some critics find him essentially a continuation of the tradition of snobbery with violence, an all too familiar aristocratic clubman with an even greater degree of sadism thrown in. Others see him as a modern and modernising hero, the 'perfect pipe-dream figure for organisation man', as Julian Symons put it.[4] Some see him as a 'cold warrior', a racist and a sexist; others stress the moments when he seems to parody these. Is he really an amateur out defending the realm, an updated Richard Hannay (after all, Hannay's amateur status did not preclude his working for the government), or is he the consummate professional, totally subordinate to the service? Is his amateurism maintained by his game-like attitude toward his missions and his sense of improvisation, or does his training and competence together with his lack of developed self-consciousness put him firmly in the camp of the professional, doing a job? Or, to put it another way, is he really an upper-class clubman, trained in the public school ethic, or is he an Americanised 'classless' moderniser, bringing 'the white heat of technology' to the spy thriller? Is he a superhero, or is he, as Ian Fleming thought, absolutely ordinary?

No doubt readers will answer these questions in part through their sense of the character, their after-image of the tales, and in part by citing pieces of evidence, kernels of character, the attributes mentioned in one place or another that build the narrative illusion which is 'a character'. So an Amis will point out that Bond is not really an aristocrat because he never drinks port or sherry. The point is that each set of attributes can be countered with another; Bond is a contested figure who has been accented in a number of ways. Indeed, the story of the casting for the film Bond illustrates this well: Fleming himself preferred David Niven, a figure who had played upper-class characters. However, after the choice of Sean Connery, Fleming remarked, 'Not quite the idea I had of Bond, but he would be if I wrote the books over again.'[5] Connery was meant to give more of a 'man of the people' image to Bond, and Christopher Booker argues that Connery's Bond was part of a 'new class' of image producers that dominated the culture of the late 1950s and early 1960s, mixing lower-class origins with media affluence and consumerism. The later casting of Roger Moore as Bond returned the character to an older, more class-ridden paradigm since Moore was strongly identified with his television portrayal of the gentleman outlaw of the 1930s, the Saint.

But the contest over Bond's public image was already a part of the novels. In *From Russia, With Love*, the 1957 tale which I will examine in some detail in this chapter, the point of the Russian plot is to kill Bond 'WITH IGNOMINY'. They wish to humiliate and destroy not only the man but the image, the myth which is important to the British secret service. The strength of the British, we are told, 'lies in the myth – the myth of Scotland Yard, of Sherlock Holmes, of the Secret Service . . . this myth is a hindrance which it would be good to set aside . . . Have they no one who is a hero to the organisation? Someone who is admired and whose ignominious destruction would cause dismay? Myths are built on heroic deeds and heroic people. Have they no such men?' The answer, of course, is: 'There is a man called Bond.'[6]

The plot to destroy Bond's image itself employs that image: the Russians convince the British secret service that one of their women agents has fallen in love with a photograph of Bond. The manifest absurdity of this plot is explained away by Bond's superior, M, who invokes a 'common' behaviour in a society of images: 'Suppose you happened to be a film star instead of being in this particular trade. You'd get daft letters from girls all over the world stuffed with Heaven knows what sort of rot about not being able to live without you and so on. Here's a silly girl doing a secretary's job in Moscow . . . And she gets what I believe they call a "crush" on this picture [of Bond], just as secretaries all over the world get crushes on these dreadful faces in the magazines.' Therefore Bond's job is to behave like the image: 'It is with an image she has fallen in love. Behave like that image.'[7]

In a way, our relation to Bond as readers is not far removed from that of Tatiana Romanova, investing our own energies in a mere image. This has two different effects. First, and less significantly, it means that Bond is something of a cipher which can be invested with a variety of content. But, more importantly, these different investments do not seem to distort an original Bond, for the effect of the Bond image is to efface its origins. Bond is a character of the present, not one with a particular class history, or regional rootedness. He is not a type, and we feel the self-mocking humour when, at one point in *The Man With The Golden Gun*, Bond claims that 'EYE AM A SCOTTISH PEASANT AND EYE WILL ALWAYS FEEL AT HOME BEING A SCOTTISH PEASANT.'[8]

Here we do find his link with that new class that Booker speaks of: though they are not so much a class as themselves avatars of a particular image of affluence, fashion, modernity, and classlessness. These 'New Aristocrats' were creators of images: Booker cites pop singers (The Beatles, Mick Jagger), photographers (David Bailey), interior decorators, spy novelists (Deighton), actors (Michael Caine, Connery), and fashion designers. Though they may have come from working-class, lower-middle-class, and northern backgrounds, the effect of the aristocracy of images was to efface their origins: the jacket notes on Len Deighton's novels which variously claim that he is the son of a chauffeur or the son of the Governor General of the Windward Islands, which have him educated at either the Royal College of Art or at Eton and Oxford, and which attribute to him a variety of jobs, are a playful example of this effacement and confusion of origins.

Nevertheless, the analogy between Bond as image and the brief reign of the 'New Aristocrats' is merely the beginning of an explanation of the cultural meaning and power of Bond: what it does is point us to the crucial term, the production and proliferation of images. In what follows I will look at the way two central aspects of the thriller, the game and the Empire, are reconstructed in the tales of Fleming in the terms of a society of the spectacle, and will then look at the meaning of the new prominence of the codes of sexuality in the Fleming thriller.

Killing time

In *The Spy Who Loved Me*, James Bond tries to explain the enterprise of spying to Vivienne Michel:

> It's nothing but a complicated game, really. But then so's international politics, diplomacy – all the trappings of nationalism and the power complex that goes on between countries. Nobody will stop playing the game. It's like the hunting instinct.[9]

In many ways this is, as we have seen, the oldest trope in the book. The figure of the Great Game for spying and international intrigue comes in a heroic version in the early thrillers of Buchan and Sapper, but it is no less present when it is unveiled as a mystification in the cynical tales of Ambler and Maugham. In Fleming, we find a new inflection: it is still a heroic and necessary game and one that Bond enjoys playing; nevertheless, it is clearly a deadly serious game, one for professionals not amateurs.

But much as the Bond thrillers draw on these older paradigms of the game and the ethic of sportsmanship and fair play, reworking them and at times parodying them, the game also takes on a new significance through the foregrounding of two sorts of game: first, the way the plot structure itself resembles a game, and second, the attention to the representation of a variety of games in the books.

The game-like nature of the Bond tales was the subject of Umberto Eco's important and influential essay on narrative structure in Fleming's novels. He argued that the novels were structured like a game with a set of rules, pieces, and conventional moves: the reader knows the rules, the pieces, and the moves – even the outcome is not a surprise – and watches the game unfold. The sequence of moves is strictly determined with only the slightest variation. And not only is the story constructed like a game but the story itself is a game, a contest, a series of what Eco calls 'play situations'.[10]

This game-like nature of the tales, which Bond himself recognises in his oft-repeated comment about his 'playing Red Indians', also makes for the formalism of the books (and indeed licenses the formalism of Eco's analysis). All existential or psychological elements are carefully excluded, as we can see if we think of neighbouring genres. The tradition of the thriller as a hunt, for example, which the Bond books resemble, usually takes the extremity of men hunting men as an example of an existential confrontation with the primitive, the instinctual, and so forth. In Geoffrey Household's *Rogue Male* (1939), for example, we see the reduction of all life to a 'kill or be killed' situation, as the hunter-hunted narrator progressively sheds all trappings of civilisation. One can see a similar process in more recent hunt tales such as Desmond Bagley's *Running Blind* (1970) or Gavin Lyall's *The Most Dangerous Game* (1964) (where the most dangerous game – in the sense of prey – is men). Bond's adventures, though similar, do not evoke this. They are, first of all, of a serial nature; far from being the exceptional reduction of civilised man to his 'true' primitive nature, his adventures are all part of the job. They are closer to that other popular formula, 'capers', which are elaborately and professionally planned operations, the accomplishment of a particularly difficult coup, as in the assassination of de Gaulle in Frederick Forsyth's *The Day of the Jackal* (1971) or the *coup d'état* in his *The Dogs of War* (1974). There is little mystery involved in these adventures; suspense reigns. Rather than the continually deferred question of whodunit, we have the continually repeated question of what happened next or even the technical question of how was it accomplished.

If this begins to explain the absence of an existential explanatory system, we can see the lack of real psychological motivation by comparing Bond to the formula of the avenger, exploited in a paradigmatic way in the stories of Mickey Spillane, stories which are often linked to those of Fleming and which had a significant influence on Fleming. By exploiting the desire for revenge, Spillane produces books which are fully as formulaic as the Bond tales but which are by no means game-like.

This game-like structure comes to a sort of narrative self-consciousness in *From Russia, With Love*. In *From Russia, With Love*, Bond's Turkish ally, Kerim, tells Bond: 'But I was not brought up to "be a sport" ...

This is not a game to me. It is a business. For you it is different. You are a gambler.' Like the Hairless Mexican in Maugham's *Ashenden*, Kerim 'hasn't had the advantages of a public-school education'. But it is his metaphor that marks the limit of the text:

> This is a billiard table. An easy, flat, green billiard table. And you have hit your white ball and it is travelling easily and quietly towards the red. The pocket is alongside. Fatally, inevitably, you are going to hit the red and the red is going into that pocket. It is the law of the billiard table, the law of the billiard room. But, outside the orbit of these things, a jet pilot has fainted and his plane is diving straight at that billiard room, or a gas main is about to explode, or lightning is about to strike. And the building collapses on top of you and on top of the billiard table. Then what has happened to that white ball that could not miss the red ball, and to the red ball that could not miss the pocket? The white ball could not miss according to the laws of the billiard table. But the laws of the billiard table are not the only laws, and the laws governing the progress of this train, and of you to your destiny, are also not the only laws in this particular game.[11]

Indeed, this sense of different levels of rules is more pronounced in *From Russia, With Love* than in most Fleming tales. Here we find a less pronounced version of the formula found in the other books: there is no game between Bond and the villain, no fantastic plot for world domination by the villain. Both the original plot – to destroy not so much Bond as the image of Bond – and the final struggle with Red Grant in the curious 'battle of the books' show a self-consciousness about the laws of Fleming's own 'billiard table'. And the ending, the quite unexpected and unrelieved death of Bond, seems to be a stepping outside of those laws. Ironically, perhaps, though *From Russia, With Love* killed off Bond, it surely didn't kill off his image: the peak of Bond's celebrity began with the serialisation of *From Russia, With Love* in the *Daily Express*. So Fleming dutifully resurrected Bond at the beginning of the next novel, *Dr No*, setting him up for new games.

However, the appearance of the game in the narrative structure is not the only aspect of the game figure that is new in the Fleming tales. So too is the extraordinary amount of space devoted to representing games and sports. One of Fleming's talents is as a sportswriter, whether he is writing about Bond's golf match with Goldfinger, the baccarat game against Le Chiffre, the bridge game against Drax, or the ski chase in *On Her Majesty's Secret Service*. In part, these are used to play out the conventions of the ethic of sportsmanship. In *Moonraker*, for example, Sir Hugo Drax is introduced as a quite extraordinary man – with one reservation: he cheats at cards. As M says, 'don't forget that cheating at cards can still smash a man. In so-called Society, it's about the only crime that can still finish you, whoever you are.'[12] Nevertheless, Bond's victory over Drax, and over Goldfinger, who cheats at golf, comes not through revealing the cheater to Society, the arbiter, but through cheating in return. After all, as Bond thinks in the course of his deception of Goldfinger, 'there was more to this than a game of golf. It was Bond's duty to win.'[13]

A second use of the games is to establish a system of national characters. National characters are in part delineated by the sorts of games that are played. So the Russians are chess players: Kronsteen in *From Russia, With Love*, the 'Wizard of Ice', is a chess master and spymaster who sees people as pawns and recalls cases as he does gambits. Bond and the British, on the other hand, are gamblers, both in the casino and in the field.

But the representation of games and sports has less to do with either the older public school ethic or the stereotypes of national character than with the new ethic of consumption and leisure. For the games Bond plays, like the liquor he drinks and the automobiles he drives, serve as a kind of guide to leisure. The sports represented are not the public school cricket pitch, nor the aristocratic blood sports and yachting, nor the working-class spectator sport of football: they are the consumer sports of golf, skiing, and casino gambling. They have the glamour of being the sports of the wealthy, the sports of the holiday on the Continent, yet are relatively free from traditional class connotations. Like Bond's vodka martinis, they are neither port nor a pint at the pub.

But though these books are themselves for killing time, they are not simply guides to consumption, 'how-to' books, rehearsals for leisure. Rather they are also redemptions of consumption, an investing of the trivial contests of the fairway with global intrigue. If, in *Goldfinger*, Fleming devotes three times as much space to the golf match as to the robbery of Fort Knox, this is surely because the detail and attention to the contest the reader can imagine not only prepares him or her for the absurdity of the Fort Knox plot, but is also a more interesting story than the Fort Knox plot. For just as the spy stories of le Carré tell tales of white-collar work, so Fleming's adventures are really tales of leisure, tales where leisure is not a packaged, commodified 'holiday', filling up a space of 'time off' from work, an acceptable moment to 'kill time', but is an adventure, a meaningful time, a time of life and death – in the words of *From Russia, With Love*, a killing time.

Thrilling cities

> All my life I have been interested in adventure and, abroad, I have enjoyed the *frisson* of leaving the wide, well-lit streets and venturing up back alleys in search of the hidden, authentic pulse of towns. It was perhaps this habit that turned me into a writer of thrillers, and by the time I made the two journeys that produced these essays, I had certainly got into the way of look-ing at people and places and things through a thriller-writer's eye. (Ian Fleming, *Thrilling Cities* (1964))

In his essay on James Bond, Tony Bennett examines the narrative codes that structure the stories and argues

> that the ideologies of sexism and imperialism are inscribed within the very form of the Bond novels . . . As the relations between Bond and the villain and between Bond and the girl develop and move toward their resolution, a series of collateral ideological tensions is thus simultaneously worked through and resolved. It is in this way that the Bond novels achieve their 'ideological effect' – the effect, figuratively speaking, of placing women back in position beneath men and putting England back on top.[14]

His account of the relation between ideologies and narrative codes is, I think, a persuasive and productive one; and his focus on the 'imperialist code' and the 'sexist code' is well taken: these are surely codes that unite larger ideological themes with the detail of the narratives of Fleming. However, the very names he gives these codes seems to elide the speci-ficity of Fleming's reconstruction of ideologies of Empire and the novelty of his construction of an ideology of sexuality. So rather than seeing the tales as a modernised version of the imperialist adventure tale, it seems to me that their clearly imperialist and racist ideologies are constructed through a narrative code of tourism; and rather than seeing the sexual codes as a 'sexist code', the repositioning of the 'girl', who is 'out-of-place sexually', in the traditional ordering of sexual difference, one can see that the 'girl' is put into place in a new ordering of the sex/gender system, through the narrative code of pornography. In both cases, I will argue in the following two sections, Bond's 'licence to kill' is less significant than his 'licence to look'.

Travel and tourism make up much of the interest and action of a Bond thriller. The final and climactic quarter of *From Russia, With Love* takes place on the fabled Orient Express; the final struggle with Goldfinger occurs aboard a BOAC airliner; and in almost all the novels some space is given to narrating Bond's travels by plane and train. Umberto Eco argues that the 'Journey' is one of the principal 'play situations' in the novel. And indeed, the representation of travelling also works in capturing the reader, a reader who is often travelling himself or herself. From the W.H. Smiths at the nineteenth-century railway station to those at the twentieth-century airport, the sale and consumption of cheap fiction has been tied to the means of transport. Bond himself exemplifies this as he reads a copy of Eric Ambler's *The Mask of Dimitrios* on the flight into Istanbul in *From Russia, With Love* and when he picks up the 'latest Raymond Chandler' for his flight in *Goldfinger*.

Furthermore, the stories have a relation to tourism in that almost all of them take place in exotic locales. Only one Bond novel, *Moonraker*, takes place primarily in Britain, in striking contrast to the clubland thrillers of Buchan, Sapper, Dornford Yates, and Leslie Charteris. In part, this is a consequence of the post-war fiction market, which, as John Sutherland has remarked, was oriented to international Anglophone sales and encouraged international settings in writers as unalike as Fleming and Graham Greene. The loss of British world economic and political hegemony was accompanied by the loss of a cultural centrality; the obverse of imaginary centrality to the world of the British agent Bond is the marginality of Britain as a place of adventure.

But tourism takes its place as a central narrative code in the Fleming novels in a deeper way by infiltrating Fleming's prose and organising the Fleming 'world system'. For the prose of the travel book and the tour guide is present in Fleming's work far beyond his own travel book, *Thrilling Cities*. In some cases, as in *Live and Let Die*, tourist guides supplant Fleming's prose entirely as the reader is treated to several pages about Haitian voodoo lifted directly from Patrick Leigh Fermor's *The Traveller's Tree*; a footnote tells us that this is 'one of the great travel books'. In other cases, as in *You Only Live Twice*, there are tedious sections of straightforward travelogue by Fleming, filling up a sketchy plot with what one chapter title aptly terms 'Instant Japan'. But even in less extreme cases, the prose of the tourist guide inflects much of these novels, often lending them their interest and a certain degree of verisimilitude. So in *From Russia, With Love* we often find passages like this one of Bond awakening in Istanbul:

> Bond got out of bed, drew back the heavy plush red curtains and leant on the iron balustrade and looked out over one of the most famous views in the world – on his right the still waters of the Golden Horn, on his left the dancing waves of the unsheltered Bosphorus, and, in between, the tumbling roofs, soaring minarets and crouching mosques of Pera. After all, his choice had been good. The view made up for many bedbugs and much discomfort.[15]

Here we find an epitome of the tourist's experience: the moment of relaxed visual contemplation from above, leaning on the balustrade; the aesthetic reduction of a social entity, the city, to a natural object, coterminous with the waves of the sea; the calculations of the tourist's economy, exchanging physical discomfort for a more 'authentic' view; and the satisfaction at having made the right exchange, having 'got' the experience, possessed the 'view'. Indeed, if we see Fleming's travel writing, like his sports writing, as the presence of the discourse of the spectacle, the discourse of consumer society, we can see how its effect is to redeem these activities of consumption, to heroise them. For the tourist is caught in a constant and inescapable dilemma: he or she is there to see, to capture the authenticity of the object in a moment of individual self-development. But he or she is caught in the fact that tourism is a mass spectacle, that he or she is only one of many tourists who have passed this way for the 'view', that, indeed, those other tourists may well be blocking the view and rendering impossible the solitary experience. This dilemma – to be superior to the 'tourists' while at once recognising one's kinship with them – is what is solved by Bond, the ideal tourist, always alone and always superior. His tourism has an ostensible purpose, though the line between tourism and spying is a fine one.

Tourism and touristic ways of seeing are not only inscribed in Fleming's prose but also organise what might be called the Fleming 'world system', a world system dependent upon Cold War and imperialist ideologies but not entirely congruent with them. For the setting of the Bond books is not entirely established either by the Cold War axis of East and West – to which England is not central – nor by the imperialist axis of British metropolis and colonial periphery. Rather it is established in large part by what Louis Turner and John Ash have termed the 'pleasure periphery', the tourist belt surrounding the industrialised world including the Mediterranean, the Caribbean, the Philippines, Hong Kong, and Indonesia.[16] Much of this world is dependent upon the neo-colonialism of the tourist industry; it stands, for Bond, as an idyllic paradise, as a more authentic culture, and as a source of threat and upheaval.

As an idyllic paradise, these locations are the settings for sports, elaborate meals, and sexual adventure. The women who are 'out-of-place sexually', 'deviant' politically or sexually in that they are in league with the villain or are lesbians, are encountered in these 'pleasure peripheries', and it is here, away from Miss Moneypenny and May, Bond's 'treasured Scottish house-keeper', that Bond is free to battle, seduce, and then retreat to London. These women, as their names indicate (Pussy Galore, Tiffany Case, Honeychile

Rider, Kissy Suzuki), are apparently outside of the British sex/gender system entirely (though we will examine this more closely in the next section); they are part of the 'view'. Here Fleming's setting is not far from the tourist advertisements of a holiday in the sun.

The second meaning of these settings invokes a more complex version of tourism, the viewing of a more vital, more authentic culture. For tourism has often meant the encounter with another, non-capitalist (or non-monopoly capitalist) mode of production with its kinship structures, its handicrafts, its street life and marketplaces. And here Bond is given a more privileged access than the average tourist. He is taken, by his secret work, into secret worlds – the Harlem of Mr Big in *Live and Let Die*, the Jamaica of Dr No, and the Istanbul of Kerim in *From Russia, With Love*. These are the environs of the grotesque Fleming villains, who are, as Eco has shown, usually of mixed blood, obscure origins, abnormal sexuality, and physical monstrosity, and work in obscure alliances with the KGB. But they are also the home of those figures that we might call, after Propp, the donors: the characters – quintessentially Kerim in *From Russia, With Love* and Quarrel in *Dr No* – with whom Bond makes indispensable alliances, alliances that allow him access to the non-Western cultures and therefore give him the strength to defeat the villain on his home territory. Darko Kerim, for example, who heads the secret service's Istanbul office, mediates England and Turkey, having a Turkish father and an English mother. His knowledge of the territory is indispensable to Bond; he serves as a kind of tour guide not only to the presence of the Russians but also to the clubs and taverns of Istanbul. The visit to a gipsy restaurant leads to a supper with the gipsies and to Bond's witnessing a fight between two gipsy women, the settling of a family affair. As Kerim says to Bond, 'It will not be for the squeamish, but it will be a remarkable affair. It is a great privilege that we may be present. You understand? We are gajos [foreigners]. You will forget your sense of proprieties? You will not interfere? They will kill you, and possibly me, if you did.'[17] This is a tourist's view beyond that of the Bosphorus, a view of an 'older', more thorough patriarchy, a fight between two women of the 'tribe' over the rights to the son, supervised by the father. It is a patriarchy that is seen in a less crude form in Kerim himself, all of whose operatives are sons. This world is seen as being surpassed – Kerim will be killed – but its secrets are needed by Bond, who has only the metaphoric institutional father, M.

But this world is also a threatening world to Bond. *Dr No* opens in Jamaica, where Fleming himself lived, and the narrator writes of the mansion that houses Kingston 'Society': 'Such stubborn retreats will not survive long in modern Jamaica. One day Queen's Club will have its windows smashed and perhaps be burned to the ground, but for the time being it is a useful place to find in a sub-tropical island – well run, well staffed and with the finest cuisine and cellar in the Caribbean.'[18] This sense of doom comes from the shadow of a real history hanging over the stories. The grotesque villains, each defeated in turn, are avatars of a more profound threat to the well-being, not only of England or the West, but of the tourist. We can mark this objectively as decolonisation, the emergence of the character of the 'Third World' as the result of protracted liberation struggles throughout Asia, Africa, and Latin America. Frantz Fanon has written that the psychic equivalent of decolonisation is the reversal of the look, the refusal to be the object of the coloniser's gaze. And this indeed is the anxiety of the tourist: as Felix Leiter, Bond's American helper, says to Bond: 'Harlem's a bit of a jungle these days. People don't go up there anymore like they used to ... One used to go to the Savoy Ballroom and watch the dancing ... Now that's all changed. Harlem doesn't like being stared at anymore.' A little later, 'Bond suddenly felt the force of what Leiter had told him. They were trespassing. They just weren't wanted.'[19] The narrative of tourism here finds its limits; Bond's licence to look is revoked.

For your eyes only

> But the new prominence of sex in the late Fifties was not just a concern with the realities of sex; even more, it was a preoccupation with the idea of sex, the image of sex; the written image, the visual image, the image that was promulgated in advertisements, in increasingly 'daring' films, in 'controversial' newspaper articles and 'frank' novels; the image purveyed by the striptease clubs and pornographic book shops that were springing up in the back streets of Soho and provincial cities; and the image that, mixed with that of violence, was responsible in the years after 1956 for the enormous boom in the sales of Ian Fleming's James Bond stories. (Christopher Booker, *The Neophiliacs* (1969))

Probably the most striking innovation of the thrillers of Ian Fleming for contemporary readers lay in their codes of sexuality. Both critics and enthusiasts of James Bond focused on his sexual adventures; they all noted that the Bond tales were the first British thrillers to make sexual encounters central to the plot and to the hero. The thrillers of Buchan, Sapper, and Ambler all avoided anything but the most fleeting accounts of sexual relations, and whatever erotic energy they had was covert or displaced into other codes, particularly into representations of violence and torture. Nevertheless, striking as this shift seemed to contemporary readers and reviewers, one wonders about its meaning. For the sexual politics of the Bond thrillers are in many ways very traditional, and the representations of sexuality are, by the conventions of the 1980s, tame. The apparent novelty of Bond was, one might conclude, another version of a persistent and recurrent masculine fantasy dressed up in the latest fashions of a consumer society. This is the view taken by Tony Bennett in his illuminating discussion of the 'sexist code' in the Bond narratives, which details how the plots work to reposition a woman who is 'out-of-place' sexually and politically into a traditional ordering of sexual difference.[20] As an example he cites Bond's view of the recent history of gender:

> Bond came to the conclusion that Tilly Masterton was one of those girls whose hormones had got mixed up. He knew the type well and thought they and their male counterparts were a direct consequence of giving votes to women and 'sex equality'. As a result of fifty years of emancipation, feminine qualities were dying out or being transferred to the males. Pansies of both sexes were everywhere, not yet completely homosexual, but confused, not knowing what they were. The result was a herd of unhappy sexual misfits – barren and full of frustrations, the women wanting to dominate and the men to be nannied. He was sorry for them, but he had no time for them.[21]

Faced with this world, Bond's mission is to 'rescue' these women, to re-establish order in the world of gender. And he has few doubts as to the nature of that order, as one sees in this passage from *Casino Royale*:

> He sighed. Women were for recreation. On a job they got in the way and fogged things up with sex and hurt feelings and all the emotional baggage they carried around. One had to look out for them and take care of them. 'Bitch', said Bond . . .[22]

Yet the very crudeness of Fleming's fantasies of male power should not obscure their historical specificity; nor should the manifest absurdity of Bond's history of gender in the twentieth century lead us to forget Bond's place in the history of gender. For *Casino Royale* (1953) takes its place alongside *Playboy* (1953) as the mark of the first mass pornography. To say this is to define pornography not simply as a depiction of male power (in which case it surely pre-dated Bond or *Playboy*) nor as any particular representation of sexuality (for the conventions of these representations change over time and the conventions of both Bond and the 1950s *Playboy* now scarcely qualify as pornographic); rather what characterises these representations and the era of mass pornography are, first, a narrative structured around the look, the voyeuristic eye, coding woman as its object, and second, a culture whose every discourse is dominated by, indeed translated into, a code of sexual signifiers.

The argument that pornography is better defined as a version of voyeurism than as a representation of sexuality is drawn in part from the fact that much of what passes as pornography is not the representation of sexual activities but the representation of women's bodies in various states of undress. Thus, as Annette Kuhn puts it, 'in an address to male spectators, the body of woman is constructed as a spectacle and the *mise en scène* of representations of women's bodies coded in various ways as both to be looked at by the spectator and, in the same process, to evoke sexual arousal in him'.[23] This line of thought owes much to Laura Mulvey's important essay which attempted to show how the classic Hollywood cinema constructs woman as an object of looking and constructs the spectator as male.[24] The conclusion that Kuhn draws, a conclusion that is central to an understanding of James Bond, is that pornography is not exceptional, not qualitatively different from other representations in the culture. Rather pornography occupies 'one point on a continuum of representations of women, a continuum along which are also situated such commonly available and highly socially visible representations as advertisements'.[25] Thus, the James Bond tales can rightly be seen as an important early form of the mass pornography that characterises the consumer society, the society of the spectacle, that emerges in Western Europe and North America in the wake of post-war reconstruction.

For Bond's pornographic imagination is structured not so much around explicit depictions of sexual acts as around Bond as voyeur, Bond as spy. We see this in the scene where Bond first encounters Honeychile Rider:

> It was a naked girl, with her back to him. She was not quite naked. She wore a broad leather belt around her waist with a hunting knife in a leather sheath at her right hip. The belt made her nakedness extraordinarily erotic. She stood not more than five yards away on the tideline looking down at something in her hand. She stood in the classical relaxed pose of the nude, all the weight on the right leg and the left knee bent and turning slightly inwards, the head to one side as she examined the things in her hand.[26]

This picture of Bond the voyeur is related, of course, to the tourist Bond; but it also structures the actions of Bond the secret agent.

If we take *From Russia, With Love* as an example, we can see how the permutations of the voyeur, of Bond's licence to look, organise a series of loosely connected, virtuoso anecdotes that make up the heart of Bond's adventures in Istanbul. Bond's first action after arriving and taking in the 'view' is to accompany Kerim through an underground tunnel in order to spy on the Russian Embassy through a periscope; it is through this periscope that he first glimpses Tatiana Romanova, the Russian filing clerk who has supposedly fallen in love with his photograph. This episode is followed by the celebrated scene, entitled 'Strong Sensations', in which Bond, together with Kerim, watches the fight between the gipsy women: 'Bond held his breath at the sight of the two glistening, naked bodies, and he could feel Kerim's body tense beside him. The ring of gipsies seemed to have come closer to the two fighters. The moon shone on the glittering eyes and there was the whisper of hot, panting breath.'[27] Since Bond is pledged, as a tourist, not to interfere with the women, this scene ends in an orgy of gunfire only tangentially related to the plot. The assassination of Krilencu follows this episode; but what is memorable here is not the assassination but its location, the 'mouth of Marilyn Monroe':

> 'Sniperscope. German model', whispered Kerim. 'Infra-red lens. Sees in the dark. Have a look at that big film advertisement over there. That face. Just below the nose. You'll see the outline of a trap door' . . . Bond rested his forearm against the door jamb and raised the tube to his right eye . . . The outline of a huge woman's face and some lettering appeared . . . Bond inched the glass down the vast pile of Marilyn Monroe's hair, and the cliff of forehead, and down the two feet of nose to the cavernous nostrils. A faint square showed in the poster. It ran from below the nose into the great alluring curve of the lips . . . Out of the mouth of the huge, shadowed poster, between the great violet lips, half open in ecstasy, the dark shape of a man emerged and hung down like a worm from the mouth of a corpse.[28]

The sight of Krilencu is dwarfed by the look of the spectacle, doubly magnified: the voyeur Bond with the Sniperscope, the pin-up as a grotesque but alluring poster. Bond only watches the assassin, Kerim; indeed, the narrator informs us that Bond has never killed in cold blood. Bond's licence to kill is here clearly less important than his licence to look.

Bond then returns to his hotel to find the compliant Tatiana Romanova, naked in his bed; but this final episode of his Istanbul adventures has an ironic twist. Rather than an explicit representation of Bond and Tatiana in bed, the spy Bond is spied upon, and the reader finds himself sharing a view with SMERSH itself:

3.1 Bond (Sean Connery) and Tatiana Romanova (Daniela Bianchi) perform for the hidden cameras in *From Russia With Love*

> Above them, and unknown to both of them, behind the gold-framed false mirror on the wall over the bed, the two photographers from SMERSH sat close together in the cramped cabinet de voyeur, as, before them, so many friends of the proprietor had sat on a honeymoon night in the state-room of the Kristal Palas. And the viewfinders gazed coldly down on the passionate arabesques the two bodies formed and broke and formed again, and the clockwork mechanism of the cine-cameras whirred softly on and on as the breath rasped out of the open mouths of the two men and the sweat of excitement trickled down their bulging faces into their cheap collars.[29]

These films are part of the Soviet plot to destroy the image of Bond.

This brief account of Bond's adventures in Istanbul shows the ways in which the presence of sexuality manifests itself in figures of looking, in spying and being spied upon. But this does not account for the historical specificity of these figures; surely, the dynamics of voyeurism pre-date the appearance of James Bond, as much as they contribute to his success. The novelty is signalled by the poster of Marilyn Monroe; the object of the gaze is not a woman but a commodified image, an image from the world of film. Thus the novelty of the Bond tales, and that of mass-produced pornography generally, is its place in the new organisation of sexuality in consumer capitalism. This takes two forms. On the one hand, one of the characteristics of consumer capitalism is, as the social theorist Herbert Marcuse pointed out, the libidinalisation of the workplace and daily life, what he termed 'repressive desublimation'.[30] In this situation, sexuality becomes the master code into which all discourses – commercial, political, philosophical, even religious – are translated. And just as a society which translated all economic, political, and philosophical discourse into a religious code found its ideological boundaries defined and contested in terms of heresy, so this consumer capitalism which relentlessly transcodes politics, religion, and philosophy into sexual terms fights its ideological battles under the sign of pornography. These battles are not, despite appearances, merely battles between the forces of 'liberation' and the forces of 'repression'. The apparent liberation of sexuality from patriarchal norms – the so-called 'sexual revolution' – is both a genuine change in sexual practices and a reconstitution of sexuality in a fetishised mode that continues to subordinate and oppress women. Nevertheless there is a kinship between the appearance of Bond and *Playboy* and the celebrated trials of *Lady Chatterley's Lover* and the works of Henry Miller. Indeed, John Sutherland tells us that the 'paperback revolution' arrived in Britain with the mass sales of the Bond books *and* the mass sales of these literary works the libraries wouldn't carry.

But the other part of the reorganisation of sexuality in consumer capitalism is tied to a shift in the sex/gender system itself, that contradictory combination of a particular sexual division of labour and certain dominant sexual ideologies. The new sex/gender system which has emerged in consumer society has yet to be named fully, but it is characterised by the expansion and industrialisation of the service sector with its largely female workforce, the creation of a sexual market less marked by the formal institutions of marriage and prostitution, and the demise of the family wage system; this has generated an ideological revolt by men against the 'breadwinner ethic', the self-organisation of women in the feminist movement, and indeed the construction of a new culture, a culture that might be figured in the names *Playboy* and *Cosmopolitan*.[31] It is in this context that the sexuality and masculinity of Bond appears: a masculinity defined by freedom from marriage, an easy familiarity with the brand names that are the accompaniments to a consumer lifestyle – cars, cigarettes, liquor – and a licence to look.

Notes

1 Christopher Booker, *The Neophiliacs: A Study in the Revolution in English Life in the 1950s and 1960s* (London: Collins, 1969), p. 179.

2 Tony Bennett, 'James Bond as Popular Hero', *U203 Popular Culture: Unit 21* (Milton Keynes: Open University Press, 1982), p. 6; John Sutherland, *Fiction and the Fiction Industry* (London: Athlone Press, 1978), p. 176.

3 Kingsley Amis, *The James Bond Dossier* (New York: New American Library, 1965), p. 111.

4 Julian Symons, *Bloody Murder* (Harmondsworth: Penguin, 1974), p. 246.

5 Quoted in Bennett, 'James Bond as Popular Hero', p. 18.

6 Ian Fleming, *From Russia, With Love* (St Albans: Triad Panther, 1977), p. 47, p. 40.

7 Fleming, *From Russia, With Love*, pp. 87–8, p. 123.

8 Ian Fleming, *The Man With The Golden Gun* (New York: New American Library, 1966), p. 157.

9 Ian Fleming, *The Spy Who Loved Me* (London: Pan Books, 1967), p. 118.

10 Umberto Eco, 'Narrative Structures in Fleming', in *The Role of the Reader: Explorations in the Semiotics of Texts* (Bloomington: Indiana University Press, 1979), pp. 144–72. Reprinted in this volume.

11 Fleming, *From Russia, With Love*, p. 169, p. 170.

12 Ian Fleming, *Moonraker* (London: Pan Books, 1956), p. 19.

13 Ian Fleming, *Goldfinger* (London: Pan Books, 1961), p. 90.

14 Bennett, 'James Bond as Popular Hero', pp. 18–20.

15 Fleming, *From Russia, With Love*, pp. 98–9.

16 Louis Turner and John Ash, *The Golden Hordes: International Tourism and the Pleasure Periphery* (London: Constable, 1975).

17 Fleming, *From Russia, With Love*, p. 126.

18 Ian Fleming, *Dr No* (London: Pan Books, 1960), pp. 5–6.

19 Fleming, *Live and Let Die*, p. 41, p. 50.

20 Bennett, 'James Bond as Popular Hero', pp. 13–4.

21 Fleming, *Goldfinger*, p. 189.

22 Ian Fleming, *Casino Royale* (London: Pan Books, 1955), p. 33.

23 Annette Kuhn, *Women's Pictures: Feminism and Cinema* (London: Routledge and Kegan Paul, 1982), p. 113.

24 Laura Mulvey, 'Visual Pleasure and Narrative Cinema', *Screen*, 16 (1975), 6–18.

25 Kuhn, *Women's Pictures*, p. 115.

26 Fleming, *Dr No*, p. 67.

27 Fleming, *From Russia, With Love*, p. 131.

28 Fleming, *From Russia, With Love*, pp. 139–40.

29 Fleming, *From Russia, With Love*, pp. 149–50.

30 Herbert Marcuse, *One-Dimensional Man* (London: Routledge and Kegan Paul, 1964), p. 56.

31 A good deal of contemporary cultural history and analysis is condensed in this account. See in particular the following work by Janice Winship: 'Advertising in Women's Magazines, 1956–1974', Centre for Contemporary Cultural Studies Occasional Paper, 59 (1980); 'Woman Becomes an Individual: Femininity and Consumption in Women's Magazines, 1954–1969', Centre for Contemporary Cultural Studies Occasional Paper, 65 (1981); 'Sexuality for Sale', in *Culture, Language, Media*, ed. by Stuart Hall *et al.* (London: Hutchinson, 1980), pp. 217–23; 'A Woman's World', in *Women's Study Group: Women Take Issue* (London: Hutchinson, 1978). Also see Barbara Ehrenreich, *The Hearts of Men* (London: Pluto Press, 1983); and Rosalind Coward, '"Sexual Liberation" and the Family', *m/f*, 1 (1978), 7–24.

4

Christoph Lindner

Criminal vision and the ideology of detection in Fleming's 007 series

WARNING: This is an Ian Fleming special – an explosive combination of danger, sex, suspense, chills, and thrills. (Cover blurb from the 1955 Signet edition of *Moonraker*)

In *Narrative and Ideology in the British Spy Thriller*, Michael Denning argues that in the late twentieth century 'tales of spies are no longer one part of popular culture; they are at its centre'.[1] Mike Myers' film, *Austin Powers: International Man of Mystery* (1997), testifies to just that. The film is an irreverent parody of just about every popular spy film and television series produced over the last forty years. But most of all, it is an outlandish spoof of the James Bond films. With the absurd character of Dr Evil, for example, Myers deliberately pokes fun at Fleming's arch-criminal, Ernst Stavro Blofeld. Dr Evil's secret lair is in turn but a loose replica of SPECTRE's spectacular Volcano base in the Bond film *You Only Live Twice* (1967). Similarly, Austin Powers' sports car, painted up like a giant British flag, represents an amalgamation of countless Bondmobiles with Roger Moore's Union Jack parachute from *The Spy Who Loved Me* (1977). Even Dr Evil's henchmen, like the character of Austin Powers himself, seem to have walked straight off a Bond set. Oddjob, who throws a lethal steel-rimmed hat around in the film *Goldfinger* (1964), becomes Random Task in *Austin Powers* and throws around a harmless shoe. These deliberate parallels with spy films in general and the Bond series in particular go on and on. In effect, *Austin Powers* relies for success on the audience's ability to spot these kinds of parallels. Its intertextual humour positively demands an audience armed with an intimate knowledge of the secret agent genre from the early Bond films onwards. In other words, the concept of the film presupposes that secret agent stories sit, just as

Denning suggests, at the very centre of contemporary popular culture. That *Austin Powers* proved a box office hit, and that audiences across the world actually *got* the jokes, confirms this exactly. James Bond's licence to kill is what gives Austin Powers his licence to shag.

But how did secret agent narrative become such an integral part of popular culture? How, in fact, did it become popular at all? In setting out to parody the underlying tropes of the secret agent story, Mike Myers is right to concentrate his humour on James Bond. For it was really with the publication of Fleming's 007 series beginning in the early 1950s that secret agent fiction first hijacked the popular imagination. Following this thought, this essay considers some of the reasons why Fleming's particular treatment of the secret agent story created a genre – and even a culture – of its own. In so doing, it looks at how Fleming conceives crime, conspiracy, and human agency, considering how that conception relates to earlier detective writing.

Murder, he wrote

In 1946 George Orwell declared the popular genre of crime-writing dead. Whodunit? World War II, according to Orwell. As he claims in his essay 'Decline of the English Murder' (1946), 'the violence of external events during the second world war has made murder seem unimportant'.[2] Orwell's point, however, was not so much to propose that after 1945 the British public had become wholly insensitive or emotionally immune to the horror of murder, but rather that murder at an individual and private level *seemed* unimportant in the aftermath of Europe's harrowing wartime experience. This posed a threat to the detective novel's cultural currency. The kinds of low-impact social crime found, for example, in the myopic world of Agatha Christie's drawing-room dramas, or even in that of Chandler's insular Hollywood, could hardly compete for public attention with emerging accounts of the Holocaust. Or so Orwell would have it. The classic crime story, he goes on to suggest, emerged 'from a stable society where the all-prevailing hypocrisy did at least ensure that crimes as serious as murder should have strong emotions behind them'.[3] Following the destabilising effects of war, such a society may well have seemed like a thing of the past in 1946.

Orwell, of course, was too quick in pronouncing such a stiff sentence. As it turned out, relative stability returned, hypocrisy survived, and along with it a public appetite for the morbid and murderous that kept classic crime writing very much alive. More than fifty years on, moreover, looking at bestseller lists, television ratings, and film revenues, it is clear to see that, across the full range of popular cultural production, detective narrative has never had it better. Still, the immediate post-war period did see in Britain a society overwhelmed by the sheer violence of its recent history, a reading public at least temporarily unimpressed by small-time foul-play. Though this shift in public attitudes failed to kill off the classic crime story quite as Orwell predicted, it did manage to launch the commercial golden-age of another kind of crime writing: secret agent fiction.

In the 1950s and 1960s, writers such as Len Deighton, John le Carré, and Ian Fleming in particular pioneered the formulaic British spy thriller to unprecedented commercial success. The mass publication of Fleming's Bond novels in Pan paperback beginning in 1956, for example, has been credited with triggering the American paperback revolution in Britain.[4] In fact, over half of the first 18 million Pan paperback sales in Britain were 007 adventures.[5] And in 1962, as the film adaptation of *Dr No* grossed record sales at the box office, Bond profitably crossed over into the most popular of popular media. Popular demand in turn led to the subsequent serialisation of the films (twenty and still counting), along with the continued serialisation of the novels until Fleming's death in 1964. In effect, the appearance of a screen version of James Bond created a circular market. The books sold film tickets while the films sold books.[6]

By the early 1960s, it seemed as if everyone was reading Fleming. *From Russia, With Love* (1957) popped up in President Kennedy's list of top ten favourite books, and even Jean-Paul Sartre, to the dismay of the French intellectual élite, was reputed to have been an avid 007 fan. Fittingly, at a time when the Soviet press office was busy denouncing Bond as the ultimate capitalist tool, Bond merchandise such as 007 action figures, board games, spy watches, and magic sets began appearing in British and American stores. Perhaps the most telling event in terms of Bond's commercial and cultural significance, however, occurred in 1965 when the soundtrack from the *Goldfinger* film became the top-selling album in the United States, knocking The Beatles from the number one spot. The first Bond novel, *Casino Royale*, was published in 1953. Less than a decade later the multi-media cultural spectacle we now call 'the James Bond phenomenon' was in full swing.

Significantly, the secret agent story was by no means a new popular genre when *Casino Royale* first hit the bookshops, any more than it was when the film of *Dr No* first hit the screens. The film industry had been churning out spy thrillers for decades, and publishers had been printing them long before that. So why, then, did the 007 series, and the British spy thriller more generally, have such a heavy impact on popular culture in the post-war decades? It is, I want to argue, in large part because Fleming, among others, developed a variation on the popular genre of detective writing that registered and responded to post-war concerns about crime, conspiracy, and human agency. In so doing, to put this back in Orwell's terms, Fleming succeeded in making murder *seem* important again.

In their treatment of crime, conspiracy, and human agency, the Bond novels adopt many of the formal and thematic trappings of the detective novel. Yet, because Fleming locates these issues within the broader context of Britain's Cold War ideology and post-war geopolitics, the Bond novels also mark a departure from a trans-Atlantic tradition in detective writing. That is, the secret agent novel as Fleming constructs it plays out at a global and ideological level what the detective novel plays out at a regional, social, and intimately private level (and here I am again thinking of work by the likes of Agatha Christie and Raymond Chandler, as well as later work by the likes John D. MacDonald, Ian Rankin, and even Dick Francis). So although both detective and secret agent narratives share a common preoccupation with crime and the people who pursue it, it is the specific character of that crime, and so that of its pursuers, which sets the two apart. In Fleming's case, the Bond novels record a shift in a cultural understanding of crime that, following the disillusioning experience of two world wars and the dawn of the atomic age, came to include crimes against humanity. This legacy of Europe's massive political upheavals in the first half of the twentieth century finds expression in the nature and scale of crime that Fleming envisions throughout the 007 series. It finds expression in what I want to call the novels' 'criminal vision'.

Criminal vision

In the Bond novel *You Only Live Twice* (1964) Blofeld's latest project, a Japanese 'death garden', leaves this impression on Bond: 'the whole demonic concept was on Blofeld's usual grand scale – the scale of a Caligula, of a Nero, of a Hitler, of any other great enemy of mankind'.[7] This comment sums up in precise terms the scale on which crime is conceived in the 007 series as a whole. Crimes in Fleming are no longer directed towards individuals or individual communities, but rather towards entire nations, whole continents, and, often, the human race itself. *Moonraker* (1955), *Thunderball* (1961), and *Dr No* all contain potentially genocidal atomic conspiracies. On a similar scale, *On Her Majesty's Secret Service* (1963) threatens biological warfare in an attempt to annihilate Britain's agricultural and livestock industries. In *Goldfinger* (1959), equally devious and devastating is Auric Goldfinger's scheme, backed by the Soviet machine, to plunder the gold reserves at Fort Knox and trigger the collapse of the global market economy. And though not all the Bond novels contain criminal plots of this destructive calibre, each offers at a very minimum some oblique though crippling stab at Western stability. In *From Russia, With Love*, for example, Soviet Intelligence chiefs reach a policy decision to undermine NATO Intelligence and confidence. Their solution, to assassinate Bond in a compromising (sexual) position. Along similar lines *Casino Royale* features Le Chiffre, a KGB paymaster who funds terrorist and subversive activities in France.

Taken together, Fleming's novels assemble a monumental portfolio of criminal conspiracies that played on British cultural anxieties of the 1950s and 60s: atomic paranoia, currency crises, the threat of communist expansion, organised crime, freelance terrorism, and even resurgent Nazism. In its humbled post-war condition, compounded by the accelerating collapse of Empire, Britain could not afford another Hitler, another Hiroshima, another sterling crash, or another Suez-style embarrassment, and these are precisely the kinds of paralysing threats to Britain and the larger Western world that Fleming's criminals conspire to deliver. As such, crime in Fleming is at once political and nihilistic, so that acts of political aggression or ideological heresy – in short, all that stands against Britain, capitalism, democracy, and cultural imperialism in general – double as trespasses against humanity.

Though the nature and scale of crime remain largely constant throughout the series, the criminals themselves come in two waves: the Soviet controlled operatives and the independent criminal masterminds. In the early Bond novels, Fleming typically casts his villains as agents who work either directly or indirectly for the Soviet government. Le Chiffre in *Casino Royale*, Mr Big in *Live and Let Die* (1954), Red Grant and Rosa Klebb in *From Russia, With Love*, Dr No, and Goldfinger, all take orders or receive funds and training from SMERSH, the KGB's assassination squad. SMERSH, as Bond learns in *Casino Royale* from one of M's top-secret briefs,

> is a conjunction of two Russian words: 'Smyert Shpionam', meaning roughly: 'Death to Spies'. . . Its task is the elimination of all forms of treachery and back-sliding within the various branches of the Soviet Secret Service and Secret Police at home and abroad. It is the most powerful and feared organization in the Soviet Union and is popularly believed never to have failed in a mission of vengeance.[8]

With Western hostility towards the Eastern bloc at an all time high in the 1950s, the Soviet government, though its Intelligence department in particular, made an easy typecast for villainy. As Lars Ole Sauerberg notes, at this time Fleming 'could paint an unaffected and wholly negative picture of the Soviet Union confident that it would be positively received'.[9] One notable exception to the early Bond villain, however, occurs in *Moonraker*'s Sir Hugo Drax, the megalomaniac German Nazi who masquerades as an English gentleman. But here again, Fleming simply exploits another British cultural antipathy of the 1950s. Germans, in the wake of World War II, made another easy and obvious target for bad press.

The second wave of Bond villains begins with the 1961 publication of *Thunderball*, in which Fleming abandons the Soviet-backed operative for the freelance criminal Goliath. It begins, in other words, with the move from SMERSH to Blofeld's brainchild: SPECTRE (Special Executive for Counterintelligence, Terrorism, Revenge, and Extortion). In the early 1960s, as the Cold War emerged from a deep-freeze and edged towards an atmosphere of detente that would see it through the 1970s, public attitudes towards the Soviet Union and its satellites softened measurably. In effect, slandering the Soviets was no longer in vogue, and Fleming had to turn elsewhere for his criminals. In a reported comment made in 1961, Fleming explains his change of tack: 'I could not see any point in going on digging at [the Russians], especially when the co-existence thing seemed to be bearing some fruit. So I closed down SMERSH and thought up SPECTRE instead.'[10] But as many critics point out, the two organisations, like their members, are fundamentally the same.

SPECTRE, as Umberto Eco notes, 'has all the characteristics of SMERSH, including . . . the use of torture, the elimination of traitors, and the sworn enmity to all the powers of the Free World'.[11] Sauerberg in turn suggests that the later Bond villain simply represents 'a toning down of the adversary's political attachment and a strengthening of his criminal and/or morbid pursuits'.[12] As an autonomous organisation, SPECTRE possesses no direct political affiliation. Yet its criminal philosophy, expressed so exactly by the acronym itself, is in perfect tune with that of SMERSH. Similarly, SPECTRE's operations match in kind those envisioned by the earlier Bond villains. For example, Blofeld's plan in *Thunderball* to blackmail the West with stolen nuclear weapons boils down to much the same scheme hatched in the earlier novel *Dr No*. And though SPECTRE lacks official government resources, its finances, technology, and task force rival those of any small nation, As such, the move to SPECTRE in the later Bond novels enables Fleming to dodge the exhausted topic of communist villainy without altering the Bond formula, down-sizing the crimes, or even radically re-thinking criminality. So whether under the umbrella of SMERSH, SPECTRE, or some other sinister organisation, each of Fleming's villains is hell-bent on crippling the West. More importantly, each commands the criminal apparatus with which to do it.

In the 007 series as a whole, then, the size and sophistication of the various criminal organisations mirror the size and sophistication of their criminal conspiracies. Nowhere, though, do the novels provide a more accurate yardstick for measuring these than in the criminal's secret base. Simply put, large-scale international crime requires an equally large-scale base of operations. It requires, in Fleming's writing, a space to accommodate not only the ranks of sub-villains, thugs, saboteurs, and assassins, but also the string of torture-chambers, holding-cells, laboratories, and nerve-centres. Dr No's Caribbean island, for example, houses 'the most valuable technical intelligence centre in the world',[13] hidden appropriately under a mountain of guano. In *On Her Majesty's Secret Service*, Blofeld builds his so-called 'clinic' on the summit of his own personal Swiss Alp. And in the next novel, *You Only Live Twice*, he sets up shop in a fortified Japanese castle. Hugo Drax's private missile complex in *Moonraker*, complete with sunken concrete bunkers, watchdogs, and a perimeter patrol, flaunts all the bells and whistles of a high-tech military installation. Bond says it best when, in *Dr No*, he describes these kinds of lavish hide-aways as 'private kingdoms – away from the beaten track, where there were no witnesses, where they could do what they liked'.[14]

Though Fleming, with his long, indulgent, and minutely detailed descriptions of these 'private kingdoms', gives a clear sense of what Bond is talking about here, the film adaptations of Fleming's work do it even better. From the beginning, but spiralling out of control from the Roger Moore years onwards, the 007 films have taken Fleming's vision of the high-tech and large-scale secret base to conceptual extremes. In the 1967 screen adaptation of *You Only Live Twice*, SPECTRE's base is relocated from the novel's Japanese castle to the hollowed-out crater of an inactive Japanese volcano. The volcano base, to name but a few of its assets, boasts an underground monorail, a helicopter pad, and launch facilities for nuclear missiles and space rockets. So sweeping and indulgently spectacular was the vision behind the volcano base that the actual set used in the film proved to be the most expensive film set ever built at the time of its production. In the 1970s, however, these cinematic visions of the secret

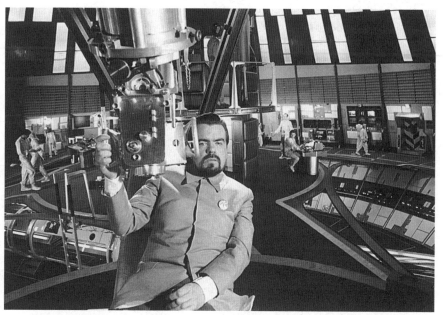

4.1 Bond villain Hugo Drax (Michael Lonsdale) inside his orbiting space station in *Moonraker*

base became increasingly outlandish and, if possible, were conceived on increasingly larger scales. In the 1977 film *The Spy Who Loved Me* (which derives only its title from the Fleming novel) the villain's base, strangely reminiscent of Nemo's *Nautilus* submarine in the film *20,000 Leagues Under the Sea* (1954), goes underwater in the fantastic shape of a submersible marine laboratory. Two years later, in the 1979 screen version of *Moonraker*, Hugo Drax's missile complex literally takes to the skies in the even more fantastic shape of an orbiting space station that makes MIR look like a Lego toy.

When it comes to secret bases, Fleming may think big but the films think even bigger. In other words, the films blow up to almost absurd proportions what the novels already exaggerate beyond credibility. As measuring sticks for gauging criminality, these cinematic visions of the secret base make the point even more bluntly and unmistakably. The message here is loud and clear: anyone with a private stockpile of nuclear weapons, a command centre hidden away under a volcano or under the sea or even out in space, and with a billboard size, illuminated map of the world behind their desk, has to be up to something magnificently sinister.

As an elaborate and expensive construction, the secret base serves as a material index that testifies to the villain's vast financial, technical, and human resources. It attests to the titanic scale of crime envisioned in the Bond series as a whole, to the series' magnified scope of criminal vision. It reconfirms in concrete terms the superlative, almost comic-strip, proportions to which Fleming inflates the issues of crime and criminality. Here, we have super-villains directing super-crimes at super-powers.

Ideology of detection

Faced in Fleming with threats such as nuclear Armageddon or biological warfare, the Western political establishment can no more afford for the novels' crimes to be made public than the Western public can afford for them to take place at all. The sheer magnitude of criminal vision accordingly moves the Bond thriller's emphasis away from detecting crime to preventing it. Similarly, the political character of crime moves the narrative away from the public exposure of criminality to its political containment. Together, then, the political crime – what doubles as criminal politics – and the scope of criminal vision give rise to a corresponding ideology of detection. In other words, they generate new imperatives for the detective that register the political and ideological status Fleming accords to crime and the criminals who commit it. For just as Fleming conceives crime and criminality in the context of Britain's Cold War ideology and post-war geopolitics, so too does he conceive the figure of the detective. The detective now becomes the secret agent.

James Bond, as secret agent, embodies a new breed of detective trained and dispatched to avert the crime against humanity and, in the process, to defuse the political crisis. That is, he embodies a new breed of detective who kills in cold blood, as the opening of *Goldfinger* makes clear:

> It was part of his profession to kill people. He had never liked doing it and when he had to kill he did it as well as he knew how and forgot about it. As a secret agent who held the rare double-O prefix – the license to kill in the secret service – it was his duty to be as cool about death as a surgeon. If it happened it happened.[15]

It is no accident, of course, that killing does happen on every job despite Bond's reluctant attitude towards it. The British government sanctions 007 to kill precisely because his assignments always do require him to kill. In *The Man With The Golden Gun* (1965), M sums it up concisely in his reading of the Scaramanga case – a case involving a hit-man/drug smuggler/all-around Soviet and Cuban crony:

> James Bond, if aimed straight at a known target – M. put in the language of Battleships – was a supremely effective firing-piece. Well, the target was there and it desperately needed destruction. Bond had accused M. of using him as a tool. Naturally. Every officer in the Service was a tool for one secret purpose or another. The problem on hand could only be solved by a killing. James Bond would not possess the Double-O prefix if he had not high talents, frequently proved, as a gunman.[16]

Killing, then, is how Bond averts the crime against humanity, how he defuses the political crisis, how he contains criminal politics. Killing is Fleming's final answer to the criminal who would topple the Free World, his paradoxically humane solution to inhumanity played out on a global scale. Accordingly, in their translation of the issue of criminality into one of ideological positioning, the Bond novels offer not a public justice, but rather a political justice served in secrecy.

More important here, however, is that Bond kills for and in the name of Britain. Which is to say that Bond kills for and in the name of what Britain represents in Fleming's writing – namely, Western capitalist imperialism. In such terms, Bond acts as a political weapon, what M simply labels a government 'tool', and what Blofeld, in *You Only Live Twice*, sardonically calls 'a blunt instrument wielded by dolts in high places'.[17] Bond fulfils the ideological function within the texts of both protecting Britain's international footing and promoting its international interests.

The Bond novels' cultural cradle now comes back into play. In the following passage from *You Only Live Twice*, Fleming comments on Britain's international standing since 1945. Tiger Tanaka, head of the Japanese Secret Service, taunts Bond:

> Now it is a sad fact that I, and many of us in positions of authority in Japan, have formed an unsatisfactory opinion about the British people since the war. You have not only lost a great Empire, you have seemed almost anxious to throw it away with both hands . . . when you apparently sought to arrest this slide into impotence at Suez, you succeeded only in stage-managing one of the most pitiful bungles in the history of the world, if not the worst.[18]

As Fleming touches upon in this passage, the 1956 Suez fiasco marks a decisive moment in Britain's post-war history. In many ways, it publicly signalled the end of Britain's international clout – a death rattle from the British Empire. As Suez made clear, in the geopolitical reshuffle that followed the end of World War II, Britain lost out to its more influential

4.2 Bond (Sean Connery) appears to defy the laws of physics as he out-manoeuvres American astronauts on a replica of the lunar surface in *Diamonds Are Forever*

wartime ally, the US. And with its Empire contracting rapidly, Britain was rapidly losing its remaining spheres of influence to what was diplomatically termed 'decolonisation'. By the 1950s, further frustrated by the US's reluctance to admit it fully into the 'atomic club', Britain had no choice but to recognise what historian Kenneth Morgan aptly calls its 'second-rate-power status'.[19]

Within the James Bond texts, Fleming plays on – and even aggravates – Britain's post-war inferiority complex and Cold War insecurity. The kinds of crime contemplated in the novels not only endanger humanity but also, and more significantly, threaten to relegate Britain right down to a third-rate power. In terms of Fleming's contemporary British readership, they represented the threat of yet another blow to an already battered national pride. Yet, by introducing the character of James Bond, Fleming goes on to alleviate those anxieties, to bolster Britain's deflated confidence. Novel after novel, Bond safeguards not just humanity itself but also Britain's reputation in the process, thereby restoring at least the façade of Britain's former super-power status.

In effect, James Bond saves everything for a country and a world that cannot save themselves. And it is precisely in this way that the 007 series, nostalgic for Empire, achieves its ideological effect – namely, the effect, as Tony Bennett argues, of 'putting England back on top'.[20] More to the point, by inscribing and coding the Bond texts with resurrected dreams of Empire and global influence reconstructed in the face of the Cold War, the arms race, and decolonisation, Fleming articulates the very ideology of detection that both drives and defines the character of James Bond.

Shaken and stirred

Fleming's manipulation of the detective genre allows for an exploration of the complex issue of crime and criminality that exceeds the generic scope of both classic and even hard-boiled detective writing. That is, in relocating the detective novel to an international and geopolitical setting, the secret agent novel adds an ideological dimension to the detective novel's largely social conception of crime, conspiracy, and human agency. The historians Richard Crockatt and Steve Smith compellingly describe the post-war division of Europe as 'a peculiarly literal translation of ideological conflict into geopolitical fact'.[21] This statement comes very close to describing one of the key elements of Fleming's writing. With post-war Europe as its narrative backdrop and symbolic centre, the 007 series can be read in turn as a peculiarly literary translation of ideological conflict into a geopolitical fiction that plays with geopolitical fact.

It is no accident, however, that the James Bond phenomenon, still with us today particularly in film, took off in the 1950s. With atrocities such as trench warfare, the Holocaust, Stalin's purges, and the dropping of atomic bombs over Japan, the first half of the twentieth century witnessed war, destruction, and genocide on an unprecedented and previously inconceivable scale. It is this string of events, culminating in the US's decision to deploy the A-bomb in 1945, that made Fleming's particular conception of large-scale crime conceivable in the first place. Moreover, it is also this same string of events which, through its heavy impact on the popular imagination, created a contemporary audience in whose collective consciousness such a form of crime would find deep resonance. By first magnifying the scope of criminal vision to include the crime against humanity, and then locating that crime politically in a post-war world order, Fleming effectively captured the popular cultural imagination with a topic that has been haunting it ever since. And if we combine this element of the Fleming formula with the fantasies of exotic women and exotic locations that have also come to define the cult of James Bond, we begin to see why, for nearly fifty years, the 007 series has been leaving its public both shaken *and* stirred.

Notes

1 Michael Denning, *Cover Stories: Narrative and Ideology in the British Spy Thriller* (London: Routledge and Kegan Paul, 1987), p. 91.
2 George Orwell, 'Decline of the English Murder', in *Decline of the English Murder and Other Essays* (London: Penguin, 1965), pp. 9–13 (p. 10).
3 Orwell, 'Decline', p. 13.
4 See Denning, *Cover Stories*, pp. 92–3.
5 See John Sutherland, *Fiction and the Fiction Industry* (London: Athlone, 1978), p. 176; Tony Bennett and Janet Woollacott, *Bond and Beyond: The Political Career of a Popular Hero* (London: Mamillan, 1987), pp. 26–7.
6 See Bennett and Woollacott's analysis of sales figures for Fleming's novels in *Bond and Beyond*, pp. 30–2.
7 Ian Fleming, *You Only Live Twice* (London: Pan Books, 1964), p. 118.
8 Ian Fleming, *Casino Royale* (London: Pan Books, 1967), p. 21.
9 Lars Ole Sauerberg, *Secret Agents in Fiction: Ian Fleming, John le Carré, and Len Deighton* (London: Macmillan, 1984), p. 160.
10 Quoted in Richard Gant, *Ian Fleming: The Man with the Golden Pen* (London: Mayflower-Dell, 1966), p. 148.
11 Umberto Eco, *The Role of the Reader: Explorations in the Semiotics of Texts* (London: Hutchinson, 1987), p. 52.
12 Sauerberg, *Secret Agents*, p. 161.
13 Ian Fleming, *Dr No* (New York: Berkley Books, 1990), p. 174.
14 Fleming, *Dr No*, p. 171.
15 Ian Fleming, *Goldfinger* (London: Pan Books, 1965), p. 7.
16 Ian Fleming, *The Man With The Golden Gun* (New York: Signet Books, 1966), p. 28.
17 Fleming, *You Only Live Twice*, p. 171.
18 Fleming, *You Only Live Twice*, p. 76.
19 Kenneth Morgan, *The People's Peace: British History 1945–1990* (Oxford: Oxford University Press, 1990), p. 158.
20 Tony Bennett, 'James Bond as Popular Hero', in *U203 Popular Culture: Unit 21* (Milton Keynes: Open University Press, 1982), p. 20.
21 Richard Crockatt and Steve Smith, *The Cold War Past and Present* (London: Allen & Unwin, 1987), p. 11.

5

Claire Hines

'Entertainment for men': uncovering the Playboy *Bond*

In honour of James Bond's forty-year-long connection with *Playboy*, the cover of the June 2000 issue asks its reader, 'Who says *Playboy* doesn't believe in long-term relationships?' It is within the context of this firmly tongue-in-cheek reference to *Playboy*'s infamous philosophy of sexual freedom and a lack of commitment to members of the opposite sex that the edition's 'James Bond File' is presented. Inside the issue, the 'Playbill' (an editorial used to introduce the magazine's monthly content to the reader) opens by outlining the strength, endurance, and interconnections that have come to define this long-term love affair:

> For forty years we've been thrilled by his ladies, his adventures and his myth. Hefner, Hugh Hefner. Oops. It's an easy mistake to make. Actually, it's Bond, James Bond. Open our hefty anniversary dossier on 007 and you'll find life lessons from Bond creator Ian Fleming, Bond girls, plenty of guns, cars and gadgets, plus a battle of the Bonds. We've even nabbed a top-secret chapter from the new Bond novel, *Doubleshot*, by Raymond Benson. For your eyes only.[1]

As both the magazine's cover and the 'Playbill' make clear, this is one anniversary that *Playboy* is keen to celebrate. In 1960, *Playboy* became the first American magazine to publish Ian Fleming's British spy adventures, when the original short story, *The Hildebrand Rarity*, appeared in the March issue.[2] The marking of this particular anniversary permits a nostalgic return to the 1960s, the decade when both 007 and *Playboy* were established as international cultural phenomena. The 'Playbill' extract also suggests a number of important connections between Bond, Fleming, Hefner, *Playboy*, and the lifestyle that together they helped to define. This is, therefore, a relationship that extends beyond the appearance of 007 in *Playboy*, to include the figures of the author, the publisher, and of course the reader who all form part of this union.

Introduced in 1953, the first issue of Hefner's *Playboy* magazine was published in the same year as Fleming's first Bond novel, *Casino Royale*. While a number of critics have previously noted this coincidence,[3] the significance of this association nevertheless remains largely unexplored. Consequently, the aim of this chapter is to examine the ways in which Bond was first taken up by *Playboy* during the 1960s, providing its readers with an ideal model of the fantasy image of hedonistic consumerism and sexual liberation that the men's lifestyle magazine sought to represent. I begin by tracing the development of *Playboy*'s connection with Fleming and 007's literary incarnation, next moving on to consider how the magazine embraced Sean Connery's cinematic Bond as uniquely expressive of its aspirational masculine ideal. In particular, I will focus on *Playboy*'s special 'James Bond Issue' of November 1965 to illustrate this alliance. The chapter then argues that the relationship between Bond and *Playboy* is central to an understanding of 007's function as a popular male fantasy figure in the 1960s and beyond.

Pen friends

The coincidence of Fleming's James Bond series and Hefner's *Playboy* beginning in the same year but on opposite sides of the Atlantic appears far less accidental when this link is understood within the cultural context of the 1950s. The 1950s, in Britain and America, is seen as a transitional period between post-war austerity and the rise of the permissive society in the 1960s.[4] According to James Chapman, the fact that Fleming's writing emerged from this transitional moment means that the content of the Bond novels both responded to and reflected its many social and cultural tensions. On the one hand, 007 still represented 'a conservative hero', whose patriotism and imperialism helped to define a nostalgic Britishness apparently untouched by recent colonial decline.[5] On the other hand, Chapman argues that Fleming was 'at some pains to portray Bond as a modern, to some extent classless, hero' whose meritocratic professionalism was a sign of consumerist-led change in Britain.[6] In this respect the character of 007 embodied an ambivalent relationship to the shifts taking place in 1950s and 1960s British society. Stylistically, Fleming's writing also captured the cultural zeitgeist, combining those 'traditional themes and archetypes' exemplified by an earlier generation of clubland heroes (such as John Buchan's Richard Hannay and Sapper's Bulldog Drummond) with 'the pace and excitement of the modern thriller'.[7] Crucially, much of this 'excitement' was generated through the Bond novels' hedonistic attitude toward women and casual sex. This, together with the use of exotic locations, violence, conspicuous consumerism, and technology, formed the ingredients for the generic formula that first Fleming's fiction and then the early Bond films were based upon.

Playboy shares a similar relationship to its original historical and cultural context. Like Fleming's Bond, Hefner's men's magazine both influenced and reflected the socio-sexual changes which happened in the post-war period. Recalling *Playboy*'s launch in the early 1950s, Hefner has characterised himself as a revolutionary whose visionary perception almost single-handedly transformed an era of 'repression and conformity'.[8] Though this rather grand claim may well be overestimating his achievements, *Playboy* did help to move further into the American mainstream the discussions of male and female sexuality that Alfred Kinsey's recently published reports had inspired. As Gretchen Edgren comments, 'The sexual revolution was being born, and if Kinsey was its researcher, Hefner would be its pamphleteer'.[9]

In terms of style, before *Playboy* the magazines that dominated the legitimate post-war men's market had placed an emphasis on the great outdoors – a setting which offered readers a brief escape from the confines of 1950s suburbia and domesticity.[10] In contrast, Hefner took his inspiration from the format originally developed by *Esquire* in the 1930s, and created *Playboy* as an upmarket men's magazine that promoted consumerism and sex as the ultimate leisure-time activities for the liberated urban male.[11] For Hefner, in April 1956, the magazine's ideal reader was 'an alert man, a man of taste, a man sensitive to pleasure, a man who – without acquiring the stigma of a voluptuary or dilettante – can live life to the hilt', a man, therefore, who already sounded very like James Bond.[12] In order to satisfy the discerning masculine tastes of its readership, *Playboy*'s regular content included features on lifestyle, quality fiction, cartoons and humour, and a nude photospread. Not only did this prove an enormously successful formula, but as I will discuss, *Playboy*'s distinctive blend of 'sex and status' also made it the right partner for 007.[13]

The transition from the 1950s to the 1960s was a crucial period for Bond's international appeal. As Tony Bennett and Janet Woollacott state, between the end of the 1950s and the beginning of the 1960s Bond went from being 'virtually unknown outside Britain', to becoming an international icon.[14] In America, even before the success of the Bond films, *Playboy*'s publication of Fleming's work played a key role in this transformation. The association between 007 and *Playboy* initially grew out of a pursuit of quality. From the magazine's beginning, Hefner had set his standards (for editorial and design) deliberately high, seeking to create an upmarket image of the 'good life' for its aspirational male readership. As several critics have noted, *Playboy*'s literary ambitions were among the most important of its defining factors.[15] By the end of the fifties the magazine had showcased fiction from such distinguished authors as Jack Kerouac, Arthur Conan Doyle, John Steinbeck, and Arthur C. Clarke. In 1960, Fleming joined this list. *Playboy*'s first mention of the author is a review of his seventh Bond novel, *Goldfinger*, recommended to readers of the October 1959 issue as 'sophisticated, tongue-in-cheek entertainment par excellence'.[16] Having admired the quality of Fleming's writing, the magazine further endorsed this positive review six months later by publishing *The Hildebrand Rarity* and cementing its relationship with 007. As mentioned earlier, *Playboy* therefore became the first American magazine to print a Bond adventure, introducing 007 to a ready-made male audience at precisely the right time.

Soon after *Playboy*'s publication of *The Hildebrand Rarity*, letters printed in 'Dear Playboy' confirm the readers' pleasure in and eager anticipation of Fleming's work. The August 1960 issue features a selection of correspondence praising what Dennis Storer of Baldwin, Kansas, judges was 'an exceptionally good suspense novelette'; and Robert Bibeau of Toronto, Ontario, demands that *Playboy* 'give us more of Commander Fleming!'[17] After this, Fleming's subsequent Bond adventures were serialised in the magazine. Starting with a three part serialisation of *On Her Majesty's Secret Service* in April, May, and June 1963, for a time *Playboy* printed a new 007 story annually. This was followed by *The Property of a Lady* in January and *You Only Live Twice* in April to June of 1964. Fleming's last full-length novel, *The Man with the Golden Gun*, was serialised over four issues from April to July of 1965, and finally the short story *Octopussy* appeared in March and April of 1966. Each of these serialisations is also accompanied by original artwork (often in an impressionistic or semi-abstract style) that depicts scenes from the Bond novels. Bennett and Woollacott observe that the fact that these paintings 'were specially commissioned for this purpose and were signed by the artist' points to *Playboy*'s desire to 'aestheticise' Fleming's writing and persona.[18] This gesture proved mutually beneficial, both confirming Fleming's literary merit and conferring on Hefner's magazine the aura of glamour and sophistication associated with 007. As one devoted *Playboy* Bond reader wrote in a letter printed in July 1965: 'It seems to me that such quality fiction does as much to substantiate the cover line "Entertainment for Men" as do such standard features as the "Playboy Forum", the interviews and the monthly centrefold.'[19]

In addition to serialising each new Bond adventure within a short time of its publication in hardback, during the early 1960s *Playboy* also cultivated a close relationship between Fleming and the magazine. This too began when *Playboy* printed *The Hildebrand Rarity* in March 1960. The issue's 'Playbill' editorial fondly recalls an 'exchange of transatlantic correspondence' in the course of which Fleming had speculated: 'I'm sure James Bond, if he were an actual person, would be a registered reader of *Playboy*.' This recommendation was followed by Fleming's first visit to Chicago and *Playboy*'s offices, when the magazine's staff arranged a special tour of their city for the much-admired 'tall, charming, Continental-suited, profoundly British, profoundly sophisticated' author of the Bond novels.[20] The visit formed part of Fleming's research for a series of articles first printed in the *Sunday Times* newspaper and later collected together into a book called *Thrilling Cities*.[21]

This meeting was the first of a number of exchanges between Fleming and *Playboy* that reveal their mutual respect, admiration, and cooperation. So, for example, when the magazine publicised the opening of a new Caribbean Playboy Club-Hotel in September 1964, Fleming's name was none too subtly dropped into a feature promoting 'Playboy in Jamaica'. In the course of this article, the reader is firstly reminded of Fleming's own Jamaican holiday home, Goldeneye, and then informed that Hefner had recently received 'a personal note from Fleming commenting on the amount of excitement Playboy's coming to Jamaica was causing.'[22] In this way, their private relationship is brought into the public sphere in order to enhance the association between *Playboy*, Fleming, and Bond. This connection also endorses the hotel where a Playboy holidaymaker might fantasise about the chance of bumping into Fleming, and possibly even Bond.

In fact, Fleming's 'close and felicitous' relationship with *Playboy* in the early 1960s still persisted from beyond the grave.[23] The 'Playboy Interview' began in 1962 and used a question and answer format to give 'an insight into the minds of leading creative and political figures of the day'.[24] Among the first interviewees were Frank Sinatra, Ingmar Bergman, Malcolm X, and Jawaharlal Nehru. Once more, Fleming joined this illustrious list. Before his death in August 1964, he granted the magazine an 'extended and exclusive' interview, which was printed posthumously in the December issue. Fleming's 'Playboy Interview' gives readers a chance to mourn the author's death, celebrate his life, and pay tribute to his 'legendary hero, 007'.[25] Having thus honoured Fleming, the magazine remained loyal to his literary creation, continuing to publish the last few remaining Bond adventures he had written.

At the same time, however, it is telling that twice in 1964, and then again in 1965, Sean Connery's face was already used as a model for the artwork that accompanied *Playboy*'s serialisations of Fleming's work. The editorial introduction to the final, two-part serialisation of *Octopussy* (also accompanied by illustrations featuring Connery as 007) in March 1966 states, 'and now, Bond returns to *Playboy* for what may be his final bow. But don't bet on it, for although Fleming has left us, James Bond – like Sherlock Holmes – lives on.'[26] This statement marks a change first suggested by the magazine's artwork, that focus had begun to shift away from Fleming as the epitome of Bondian style to Connery's popular screen incarnation of 007. And with this, *Playboy*'s love affair with James Bond entered a new phase.

Material men

The year 1965 is widely understood to represent a highpoint in James Bond's early career as a popular screen hero. Following the growing box-office success of *Dr No* (1962), *From Russia With Love* (1963), and *Goldfinger* (1964), by the mid-1960s the international phenomenon of 'Bondmania' had taken off and 007 'permeated into the wider realms of popular culture more generally.'[27] Printed in November 1965, *Playboy*'s special 'James Bond Issue' acts as both a sign and a celebration of this tremendous cultural impact. The issue features an eight page 'Playboy Interview' with 'James Bond's acerbic alter ego', Sean Connery, presenting the actor as a contemporary role model and surrogate 007 for the magazine's readers, much in the same way as Ian Fleming had been two years before. For *Playboy*, the interview with Connery clearly represented a significant coup. By this time, as the magazine notes, he had become disillusioned with his role as 007, and was 'increasingly reluctant' to talk to the press at all.[28] As a result, during the making of *Thunderball* (1965) Connery's only major interview was awarded to *Playboy*.[29] This exclusivity enabled the magazine to position itself as a confidante to the elusive Bond star, offering the reader a rare and extremely valuable insight into his, and by association 007's, character, life and style.

Bennett and Woollacott observe that during the course of Connery's *Playboy* interview a form of symbolic merging occurs. Despite Connery's early rejection of the interviewer's most obvious attempts to equate him with Bond – to which he responds angrily: 'let me straighten you out on this. The problem with interviews of this sort is to get across the fact, without breaking your arse, that one is *not* Bond, that one was functioning reasonably well *before* Bond and that one is going to function reasonably well *after* Bond' – a series of implicit links are nevertheless made between the two.[30] In the rest of the interview, Connery's discussion of his own biography, tastes, and values, is combined with reference to his attitudes towards the character of Bond. As Bennett and Woollacott point out, the characteristics of 'self-containment', 'powers of decision', and survival that Connery says he most admires in Bond are also qualities the interview reveals that he shares:

> From the time I started work at 13, I always paid my share of the rent, and the attitude at home was the prevalent one in Scotland – you make your own bed and you have to lie on it. I didn't ask for advice and I didn't get it. I had to make it on my own or not at all.[31]

Bennett and Woollacott argue that interviews like this proved influential in the 'construction of Bond/Connery as a composite figure, a unified subject, to whom there is ascribed a uniform set of values.'[32] In the case of Connery's 'Playboy Interview' I would add that this is further complicated by another, equally important, equation which can be made: between the identity and values of Bond/Connery and those fostered by the magazine and its readers.

As recognised by Connery, in the world of Bond, individual action can, and indeed repeatedly does, succeed in saving the day. Most often it is 007 alone, rather than those plans formulated and overseen by the British government, who finally overcomes the threat posed by the international criminal organisation SPECTRE in the early films of the series. For example, the importance of Bond's autonomy and ability to improvise, as well as a host of other characteristics he shares in common with *Playboy*, is clearly demonstrated in a sequence in *From Russia With Love*. This can, then, be used to understand 007's affinity with the magazine. In the film, M (Bernard Lee) sends Bond to steal a Lektor decoder from the Russian Consulate in Istanbul. Though the plot reveals that the British secret service is right to suspect that a trap lays behind the lure of the Lektor, for the majority of 007's mission the Russians are wrongly assumed to be the perpetrators of this scheme. Onboard the

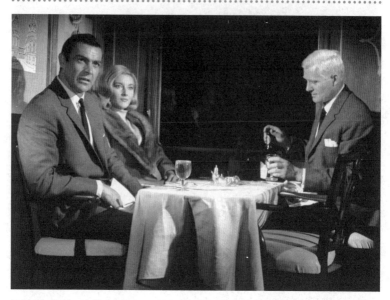

5.1 James Bond (Sean Connery), Tatiana Romanova (Daniela Bianchi) and 'Red' Grant (Robert Shaw) enjoy dinner on the Orient Express in *From Russia With Love*

Orient Express, Bond's plans to escape with the Lektor are threatened when his friend and ally Kerim Bay (Pedro Armendariz) is found dead, and instead 007 must arrange for a British agent from Station Y to meet him at Zagreb in order to assist his getaway. Unknown to Bond, the real agent is killed and replaced by trained SPECTRE assassin 'Red' Grant (Robert Shaw), who masquerades as 007's British contact 'Captain Nash'. From the film's pre-credits sequence, which sees Grant stalk and kill a Bond impersonator, the SPECTRE agent carries out his mission (which even includes shooting anyone who looks like they might be about to kill Bond during a fight that erupts at a gypsy camp) with such consummate professionalism that there might be 'serious doubts about 007's chances of survival'.[33] Bond, though, is not to be beaten, and when the two men do come face to face, Grant's masquerade and his professionalism ultimately prove no match for 007.

This is because, in addition to the ruthlessness and professional skill exhibited by Grant throughout *From Russia With Love*, Bond also displays the signature touches of style and sophistication that always signal his superiority to any antagonist. During their final confrontation, Grant initially has the advantage as he removes Bond's gun, literally bringing him to his knees and sadistically promising to ensure that his death will be 'slow and painful'. 007's response to this taunting is to coolly voice his instinctive distrust of Grant, based on an earlier warning sign. In the restaurant car, the villain had committed the unforgivable faux pas of choosing a bottle of Chianti to accompany grilled sole: Bond remarks 'red wine with fish – that should have told me something'. He follows this observation by seizing the opportunity to exploit another weakness that he has perceived in Grant's character, greed. This weakness is fatal as it enables Bond to employ the full range of his capabilities: in offering fifty gold sovereigns for a last cigarette, 007 successfully tricks Grant into opening his booby-trapped attaché case supplied by Q branch and triggering a teargas canister. After a violent struggle, Bond overpowers Grant, first stabbing him with a knife (also hidden in his briefcase), before killing him with his own garrotte. Even for the film's most casual viewer, the lessons inscribed into this scene are unmistakable: there is, of course, only one James Bond. However, some of his confidence, style, and expertise can be acquired. This is the aspirational masculine ideal that both Bond and *Playboy* trade in. The 1960s Bond films show that 007 possesses this masculine style instinctively, but perhaps if Grant had read *Playboy* (as Bond is later seen to in *On Her Majesty's Secret Service* (1969)) he may well have performed his role more convincingly.

Playboy, then, has a number of prominent features in common with the Bond films. In post-war America, the magazine advocated independent thinking and autonomy as a way for the aspiring playboy to achieve wealth and fuel consumerism. Throughout the 1960s, a regular column by 'Contributing Editor for Business and Finance' billionaire Paul Getty gives advice on career advancement and routes to 'self-made' success. In this way, *Playboy* shares with Bond/Connery an approval of the kind of 'self-reliant and competitive individualism' described in both the interview and the sequence detailed above.[34] The magazine also shares Bond's culture, love of technological gadgetry, and international adventure. The 1960s was an era that witnessed a growth in international travel. During the course of his mission in *From Russia With Love*, Bond visits a typically wide array of exotic locations, including Istanbul, Turkey; Venice, Italy; and a trip on the Orient Express. Such destinations and experiences are readily endorsed in 'Playboy's International Datebook'. Written by *Playboy*'s travel editor, Patrick Chase, from the late 1950s the 'Datebook' equipped readers with vital information on foreign travel and culture. Notably, in January 1965, Chase affirms that Istanbul's 'most scenic attractions can be seen from the Bosporus ferries.'[35] It is a recommendation which echoes 007's playful advice to Miss Moneypenny (Lois Maxwell) at the beginning of *From Russia With Love* that 'the moonlight on the Bosporus is irresistible'.

In the same way that Bond's adventures translate in the pages of *Playboy* to holidays in exotic places, his far-fetched gadgetry finds expression in the range of consumer goods and lifestyle features presented to the reader. The 1960s, as James Chapman writes, 'was a decade in which technology and technological progress came to the fore'.[36] In *From Russia With Love*, Bond receives his first gadget from Q. Issued as standard field equipment to all double-O agents, the attaché case contains an assortment of hidden, push button and spring-loaded accessories that Bond systematically puts to use, including a folding sniper's rifle with ammunition, and the gold sovereigns, knife, and magnetised talcum-powder teargas cartridge that he employs in order to defeat Grant. From *Goldfinger*, the series' growing fascination with gadgetry really took hold, so that as Connery complains in his 'Playboy Interview', by *Thunderball*, 'gimmicks' like Bond's underwater camera and jet pack had become central to the success of both 007 and the Bond films.[37] In the real world, *Playboy*'s gadgetry had to cater to a far wider spectrum of functions and pockets. At the very top end, and most akin to the Bond films' glossy fetishisation of technology, is a full-colour photo-feature on the 'Playboy Bed' in April 1965. The eight foot diameter circular bed is owned by Hefner and boasts 'the latest in mechanical innovation'. Not only is it able to rotate and vibrate 'to suit the occupant's whim', but it also has a host of gadgets built in, such as a drinks cabinet and refrigerator.[38] Meanwhile, coverage of more mass-produced, but certainly no less prized, fantasy items like the latest in televisions and hi-fi hardware are regularly presented to the *Playboy* reader as technological aids to contemporary living and field equipment for the modern male.

Gadgets, however, are not the only accessory needed to live out the *Playboy* Bond lifestyle. As the early Bond films make clear, 007 is a connoisseur with expensive tastes in cars, clothing, food, and drink. He drives a Bentley, an Aston Martin DB5, and a Rolls Royce. He dresses in black or white tuxedos, Slazenger sports wear, and custom-made, light weight suits. He eats Beluga caviar, conch chowder, and green figs with yoghurt. And he drinks vodka martinis, Turkish coffee, and Dom Perignon champagne. In this way, the film series continued a tradition instituted by Fleming, who had used references to 'leading brand names and stylish living' to create his sophisticated and aspirational fantasy hero.[39] Like the character of Bond, the names and tastes with which he is associated are always of the highest quality, at once complementing and confirming his superior style and standards. *Playboy*'s adverts and service features emphasising male fashion and leisure work in a very similar way, helping to build its image and reputation as an upmarket men's lifestyle magazine.

In particular, Thomas Wyer notes Hefner's early strategy of associating *Playboy* with adverts for the right kind of product. From the magazine's beginning, Hefner had established 'strict standards for advertising respectability', [40] filling its pages with mainstream adverts for brand named garments, alcohol, and sports cars. So, in the same year that *Goldfinger* saw Bond outfitted with a gadget-laden Aston Martin DB5, an advert for this handbuilt, British sports car features in *Playboy*'s October 1964 issue. By association, 007, Aston Martin, and *Playboy* all share the same attributes of luxury, style, and quality. For the magazine's readers, the suggestion is that these attributes can be achieved by purchasing the DB5, and with it a genuine slice of the *Playboy* Bond dream.

It is, therefore, 007's sophisticated and educated tastes, as well as his aspirational masculine image, which make him the perfect hero for *Playboy*. Significantly, as the sequence in *From Russia With Love* illustrates, style is also regarded as a matter of protocol and correct form in the early Bond films, and Grant's inappropriate wine order automatically makes 007 suspicious of him. In contrast, Bond's knowledge and choices are always impeccable, following set rules and codes of behaviour – most obviously, his martini must be 'shaken, not stirred'. Similarly, 007 doesn't just enjoy Dom Perignon, he is alert to both the temperature and the vintage of what he is consuming. Thus, in *Dr No*, he states his preference for a bottle of 1953 over the inferior 1955 vintage served by the villain, and in *Goldfinger* he teasingly tutors Jill Masterson (Shirley Eaton) in the etiquette of its consumption, saying 'my dear girl, there are some things that just aren't done, such as drinking Dom Perignon '53 above the temperature of thirty-eight degrees Fahrenheit' (which, he adds, 'is as bad as listening to The Beatles without earmuffs').

Reflecting on the Bond films' appeal to America in the 1960s, Jay McInerney has likened 007 to the '"Playboy Advisor" – that faceless feature of our favourite magazine, the man who knew how to do everything, who knew what to wear and what to say in any situation.'[41] From 1960, the 'Playboy Advisor' column responded to *Playboy* readers' requests for advice on a variety of subjects, from questions about dating and sex, to queries concerning social etiquette. For example, in September 1964, the 'Advisor' responds to a query on the correct procedure for storing and serving wine. The advice goes into detail, telling the reader that 'white sparkling wines should be served at near-freezing temperature' but not overchilled or left too long because this will 'impair flavour and bouquet'.[42] Like Bond, *Playboy* is always authoritative, often playful, and is an expert in matters of etiquette and style.

In his 1965 'Playboy Interview', Connery was asked to account for the growth in 007's international popularity. He says that 'Bond, you see, is a kind of present-day survival kit. Men would like to imitate him – or at least his success – and women are excited by him.'[43] The same thing can, of course, be said of *Playboy*, since by the mid-1960s, Hefner's magazine had emerged to become 'a handbook and a book of dreams' for young, urban males.[44] Connery's comment calls attention to the fact that, similar to *Playboy*, the Bond films emphasise male grooming, accessorisation, and style as means to achieve sexual success. Women are central to this fantasy and lifestyle, and play a vital role in mediating the affiliation between 007, *Playboy*, and their male audiences.

Female Bonding

Women in the 007 films, or 'Bond girls' as they are widely known, are integral to the formula and success of the series. Ursula Andress's emergence from the Caribbean Sea in *Dr No* represents a memorable moment in cinema history that is rehearsed in order to explain the Bond girl's traditional visual image and two-dimensional narrative role. But, for me, the apparent simplicity of this sequence masks the underlying complexity of the Bond girls and their significance. Even in these moments, Andress's Honey Ryder is more than just the decorative object that either her clinging white bikini or her punning name suggest. When approached by 007, Honey immediately pulls out a knife to defend herself, aggressively ordering him to 'stay where you are.' Like the many Bond girls that have followed, Honey is at once beautiful and resourceful, sexually available, and independent. Consequently, as Chapman points out, the Bond films are 'criticised for being overtly sexist, for presenting women as little more than disposable playthings for the dominant male hero'. At the same time, he says, publicity discourses celebrate the Bond girls as 'modern, liberated, independent women' who reflect the increased sexual liberalism of the 1960s.[45]

Playboy's representation of women has also been subject to these same debates. For all those readers who don't buy *Playboy* for its articles, each issue has a triple-page nude centrefold, named the 'Playmate of the

Month'. Additionally, there are other nude and semi-nude pictorials which feature female models and film stars. Often, like the Bond girls, *Playboy*'s Playmates are considered 'free only in the areas (bed) and respects (sexuality) that 'liberated' man required'.[46] Yet as Barbara Ehrenreich argues, even if women are a commodity in *Playboy*, this is not their only role. They are 'necessary not just to sell the magazine, but also to protect it'.[47] For, having rejected domesticity and marriage, the playboy is left open to charges of homosexuality that, it is hoped, female companionship will guard against. According to this view, liberated female sexuality is key to the presentation and performance of *Playboy*'s aggressively heterosexual masculinity, and casual sex is endorsed as a leisure activity that men and women can (and should) enjoy together.

Elsewhere, I have argued that in surrounding both 007 and *Playboy* with glamorous and desiring women, the intention is to make it clear that they are the natural focus for male lust and neutralise accusations of homosexuality.[48] The playboy might spend time and money on his clothing, accessories, and apartment, but as Ehrenreich says, women are always there 'to let you know that there [is] nothing queer about these urbane and indoor pleasures'.[49] This disavowal is particularly important when considering the relationship between James Bond and *Playboy*. Significantly, the issue that features Connery's 'Playboy Interview', also includes the magazine's first Bond girl pictorial. Over ten pages, the pictorial showcases scenes from the early Bond films alongside photographs of some of the female stars in various poses and states of undress. For example, stills taken from *Dr No* feature Ursula Andress during her appearance as Honey Ryder, next to an off-camera moment between her and Connery, and a naked shot borrowed from a previous *Playboy* issue in July 1965. Similarly, Honor Blackman is pictured in her role as Pussy Galore and also in a state of partial undress sitting on a bed of hay. Not only do these photographs celebrate the Bond girls' beauty and sexuality in a way 'that is impossible within the constraints of the requirements imposed by the family entertainment film',[50] but they also provide an alibi for *Playboy*'s worshipful relationship with 007.

In the text to accompany the November 1965 pictorial, 007 series scriptwriter Richard Maibaum puts further emphasis on women's role in the signification of Bond's sexuality. He recounts 007's relationships with the Bond girls who appear in the pictorial, rating each of his conquests in terms of her good looks and sexual challenge. Honey is ranked 'best' for her 'innocence, charm and pristine beauty', and the fact that finally she surrenders to Bond's magnetism at the end of *Dr No*. In *Goldfinger*,

007's seduction of Pussy is also graded highly, as a sexual 'tour de force' and a triumph of Bond's 'sheer masculinity' over her implied lesbianism. Maibaum admires Bond/Connery at considerable length, noting his classless accent, 'rugged' features, and 'sinewy' athletic physique. The secret agent's survival techniques, his gadgets, cars, and equipment are all well and good, but when *in extremis*, Maibaum stresses that 007's 'most potent weapon is himself'.[51] In this way, the pictorial essay echoes *Playboy*'s general policy of setting Bond/Connery up as a masculine ideal and figure of identification, but it also positions him as an object of the erotic gaze. 007 is only kept 'safe' by surrounding him with women. Like the film series' Bond girls, *Playboy*'s pictorial makes it possible for the magazine's heterosexual male readers to continue idolising 007 with their sexual identities more or less intact.

A long-term relationship

Following the special November 1965 issue, *Playboy* has maintained its close association with 007, and over the years there have been well over thirty Bond-inspired features in the magazine. During the 1970s and 1980s these mostly took the form of regular Bond girl pictorials, as *Playboy* continued to run nude photo-shoots, timed to correspond with new films in the series. Amongst others, these have included a 'Vegas Comes Up 007' pictorial on the girls of *Diamonds Are Forever* (1971), printed in the December 1971 issue; and a pictorial on the girls of *For Your Eyes Only* (1981) published in June 1981, which includes photographs of Robbin Young, winner of the Playboy/United Artists sponsored James Bond Girl contest. The July 1983 issue features a Bond girl retrospective, celebrating their importance to the series and the 'The Spy They Love to Love'. During these years it seems that only by paying tribute to 'the lovelies who made Agent 007 a legend in his home movies',[52] can *Playboy* reconcile its fascination with the spy that it too loves to love.

In 1997, after a gap that mirrors Bond's absence from the screen in the early 1990s, the magazine re-established its ties with 007. Printed in the January issue, *A Blast From the Past* is an original short Bond story written by Raymond Benson. During his tenure as the fourth official author of the 007 novels, Benson also wrote a second short story for *Playboy*, *A Midsummer Night's Doom*. Published in the magazine's forty-fifth anniversary issue in January 1999, the adventure is set in the Playboy Mansion, where 007 and Hefner meet. This story serves as added proof of the synergistic relationship between Bond and *Playboy*, as in fictionalising Hefner and setting him alongside 007, parallels are repeatedly drawn between the two.

Like any successful long-term relationship, Bond's alliance with *Playboy* has, therefore, adapted and survived through decades of social and cultural change. It is an association that has endured different 007 authors, and periodic alterations in star. Today, the *Playboy* Bond is still very much alive and kicking, and at the time of writing Playboy.com is host to a number of interactive features about 007, including information on all Bond's cars, his women, and an opportunity to investigate the contents of his desktop.[53] In a review, *Casino Royale* (2006) and Daniel Craig's new Bond are both praised for their 'retro Connery-era look'.[54] Yet again, *Playboy* returns nostalgically to the 1960s and the birth of its association with Bond. As I have shown, it is a relationship that first began with Fleming's fiction and soon extended to include the popular film series. Moreover, beyond those magazine features explicitly devoted to the secret agent, the leisure activities, accessories, advice, and attitude to women found in *Playboy*'s pages reflect a deeper union of style and tastes with 007. As the fictional embodiment of the *Playboy* lifestyle, James Bond is still offered to the reader as a masculine icon and fantasy ideal. Together, 007 and *Playboy* are a partnership that is as yet unbroken. So far, the *Playboy* Bond is the only long-term relationship that either of them is eager to sustain.

Notes

1 'Playbill', *Playboy*, June 2000, p. 3.
2 This short story later appeared in the book collection, *For Your Eyes Only*, printed in 1960.
3 For example, see Tony Bennett and Janet Woollacott, *Bond and Beyond: The Political Career of a Popular Hero* (London: Macmillan, 1987), p. 32; James Chapman, *Licence to Thrill: A Cultural History of the James Bond Films* (London: I.B. Tauris, 2000), p. 36 and Michael Denning, *Cover Stories: Narrative and Ideology in the British Spy Thriller* (London: Routledge and Kegan Paul, 1987), p. 109.
4 See Christopher Booker, *The Neophiliacs: A Case Study of the Revolution in English Life in the Fifties and Sixties* (London: Collins, 1969) and Arthur Marwick, *The Sixties: Cultural Revolution in Britain, France, Italy and the United States c.1958–1974* (Oxford: Oxford University Press, 1998).
5 James Chapman, 'Bond and Britishness', in *Ian Fleming & James Bond: The Cultural Politics of 007*, ed. by Edward P. Comentale, Stephen Watt and Skip Willman (Bloomington: Indiana University Press, 2005), p. 131.

6 Chapman, 'Bond and Britishness', p. 133.

7 Chapman, 'Bond and Britishness', p. 131.

8 Hugh M. Hefner, 'Introduction', *The Playboy Book: Fifty Years*, by Gretchen Edgren (London: Taschen, 2005), p. 7.

9 Edgren, *The Playboy Book*, p. 12.

10 See Gail Dines, 'Dirty Business: *Playboy* Magazine and the Mainstreaming of Pornography', in *Pornography: The Production and Consumption of Inequality*, by Gail Dines, Ann Russo and Bob Jensen (London: Routledge, 1998), pp. 37–63.

11 See Thomas Weyr, *Reaching for Paradise: The Playboy Vision of America* (New York: Times Books, 1978), p. 8.

12 Hugh Hefner, 'What is a Playboy?', *Playboy*, April 1956.

13 Bill Osgerby, *Playboys in Paradise: Masculinity, Youth and Leisure-style in Modern America* (Oxford: Berg, 2001), p. 122.

14 Bennett and Woollacott, *Bond and Beyond*, p. 29.

15 See Edgren, *The Playboy Book*, p. 18.

16 'Playboy After Hours', *Playboy*, October 1959, p. 19.

17 See 'Dear Playboy', *Playboy*, August 1960, p. 6.

18 Bennett and Woollacott, *Bond and Beyond*, p. 48.

19 'Dear Playboy', *Playboy*, July 1965, p. 7.

20 'Playbill', *Playboy*, March 1960, p. 1.

21 See John Pearson, *The Life of Ian Fleming* (London: Jonathan Cape, 1966), pp. 338–9.

22 'Playboy in Jamaica', *Playboy*, September 1964, p. 98, p. 176.

23 'Playbill', *Playboy*, December 1964, p. 3.

24 Osgerby, *Playboys in Paradise*, p. 137.

25 'Playboy Interview: Ian Fleming', *Playboy*, December 1964, pp. 97–106.

26 'Playbill', *Playboy*, March 1966, p. 3.

27 Chapman, *Licence to Thrill*, p. 114.

28 'Playboy Interview: Sean Connery', *Playboy*, November 1965, pp. 75–6.

29 See Bob McCabe, *Sean Connery: A Biography* (New York: Thundermouth Press, 2000), p. 53.

30 Bennett and Woollacott, *Bond and Beyond*, p. 58; 'Playboy Interview: Sean Connery', p. 78.

31 Bennett and Woollacott, *Bond and Beyond*, p. 58; 'Playboy Interview: Sean Connery', p. 81.

32 Bennett and Woollacott, *Bond and Beyond*, p. 58.

33 Jim Smith and Stephen Lavington, *Bond Films* (London: Virgin Books, 2002), p. 29.

34 Bennett and Woollacott, *Bond and Beyond*, p. 58.

35 Patrick Chase, 'Playboy's International Datebook', *Playboy*, January 1965, p. 45.

36 Chapman, *Licence to Thrill*, p. 116.

37 'Playboy Interview: Sean Connery', p. 78.

38 'The Playboy Bed', *Playboy*, April 1965, pp. 88–9, p. 184.

39 Andrew Lycett, *Ian Fleming* (London: Weidenfeld & Nicolson, 1995), p. 222.

40 Weyr, *Reaching for Paradise*, p. 31.

41 Jay McInerney, 'How James Bond Saved America—And Me' in *Dressed to Kill: James Bond The Suited Hero* by Jay McInerney, Nick Foulkes, Neil Norman and Nick Sullivan (Paris: Flammarion, 1996), p. 36.

42 'The Playboy Advisor', *Playboy*, September 1964, p. 59.

43 'Playboy Interview: Sean Connery', p. 79.

44 Hefner, 'Introduction', *The Playboy Book*, p. 8.

45 Chapman, *Licence to Thrill*, p. 117.

46 Bennett and Woollacott, *Bond and Beyond*, p. 241.

47 Barbara Ehrenreich, *The Hearts of Men: American Dreams and the Flight from Commitment* (Bristol: Pluto Press, 1983), p. 51.

48 See Pam Cook and Claire Hines, 'Sean Connery *Is* James Bond': Re-Fashioning British Masculinity in the 1960s', in *Fashioning Film Stars: Dress, Culture, Identity*, ed. by Rachel Moseley (London: BFI, 2005), pp. 147–59.

49 Ehrenreich, *The Hearts of Men*, p. 51.

50 Bennett and Woollacott, *Bond and Beyond*, p. 246.

51 Richard Maibaum, 'James Bond's Girls', *Playboy*, November 1965, pp. 132–41, p. 144, pp. 205–6.

52 'The Spy They Love To Love', *Playboy*, July 1983, pp. 86–93.

53 See 'Bond, James Bond', *Playboy Online* <http://www.playboy.com/arts-entertainment/features/james-bond-index/index.html> [accessed 4 January 2007].

54 Rob Walton, '*Casino Royale*', *Playboy Online*, <http://www.playboy.com/arts-entertainment/reviews/movies/casino-royale/> [accessed 4 January 2007].

Part II

Screening 007

6

James Chapman

A licence to thrill

It is difficult to draw any conclusions about the place of the Bond movies in cinema history and film culture while the series itself is still on-going. Only when the series ends, when the cycle is complete, will it be possible to arrive at a conclusive assessment of its overall historical and cultural significance. What I offer here, therefore, are not definitive conclusions about the Bond series, but rather some observations on its history so far. 'To be continued . . .', as the legend goes.

It is surely no exaggeration to suggest that the Bond films have been the most popular and enduring series in motion picture history. That the Bond series is still on-going is perhaps the most extraordinary facet of its extraordinary history. The very longevity of the series is quite remarkable. For over thirty-five years, a time span which represents roughly a third of the entire history of the cinema and half the period since the introduction of talking pictures in the late 1920s, the Bond films have been one of the constants of the film industry: ever present, ever familiar, ever popular with audiences around the world. The continuing popular appeal of the films is enough to confound those critics who assert that James Bond has had his day and should be pensioned off to a retirement home for secret agents and superheroes. Ever since the early 1970s, when the Bond series was already ten years old, there has been a constant undercurrent of criticism to the effect that Bond himself is a complete anachronism, and that the longer the films continue the more derivative and depressingly formulaic they become. As an ideological and cultural construct, James Bond has long since outlived his historical moment. To quote, for example, one 1990s commentator:

> But then times have changed, and James Bond was of his time – a time when Britain (and British Intelligence) held a certain position in the world. A time

when Johnny Foreigner knew his place. A time when beautiful women from other countries existed primarily to be seduced, and the phrase 'sex tourism' held no dark overtones. A time when an obsessive interest in guns and hardware seemed a logical outlet for an adult male brain.

Read Ian Fleming's books today, and they seem terribly snobbish, silly and dated. The sun has set for good on Fleming's heyday, the era that produced James Bond. Now let it set on the old boy's films, too.[1]

Such a comment, however, merely highlights the gulf between the critical and popular reception of the films, for whereas many commentators are ready to consign Bond to the dustbin of history, his screen adventures continue to find a large and enthusiastic audience.

So why have the Bond films proved so popular? Various reasons have been advanced to explain their success. For the film industry's own discourse, exemplified by the trade press, the answer is simply that the Bond movies provide those qualities of 'entertainment' and 'escapism' that audiences want. While this is undoubtedly true, however, it explains little. Entertainment value is virtually impossible to define; most films possess it to some degree, so what is it about the entertainment provided by the Bond films that makes them stand out? According to Cubby Broccoli, the films' appeal has been due in large measure to their production values. 'The success of James Bond has always depended upon the values we put up there on the screen', he said in his autobiography. 'People may argue about the relative merits of the Bond films, but few would deny that they reveal the highest production values and technical skill.'[2] For John Brosnan, it is the visual qualities of the films that stand out and explain their popularity with audiences around the world:

The most obvious answer is that they are pure cinema in the sense that they are highly visual films depending on lots of fast-paced action and sheer spectacle. This assures them of a large international audience because they are able to bypass language and cultural barriers and appeal directly to people of various nationalities and age groups, in the same way as did the slapstick comedies of the silent era and the cartoon films of Disney (two film genres that the Bonds have grown increasingly to resemble of late).[3]

According to this argument, it is the style of the films which accounts for their success. Brosnan attributes to the Bond films a universal filmic language that transcends national and cultural boundaries. The Bond films, in this sense, represent the continued existence of a 'cinema of attractions' based on visual spectacle rather than narrative or characterisation. The 'cinema of attractions' – a term originally applied to the study of early

cinema before the emergence of the narrative feature film – is exemplified, variously, in the 'trick' films of Georges Méliès, in the cliff-hanger
serial melodramas of the silent era, in the Cinema-Scope and Cinerama
epics of the 1950s, and, more recently, in the high-tech special-effects
blockbusters of George Lucas, Steven Spielberg, and others.

Simply attributing the success of the Bond films to their qualities of
visual spectacle and 'pure cinema', however, does not explain why they
have sustained their popularity over such a long period. Other popular
films which foreground style and spectacle over narrative, such as the
Superman and Indiana Jones series, have rarely been sustained beyond
three or four instalments. The Bond films, however, have been consistently successful since the 1960s, winning the approval of several genera-
tions of audiences. Many of the cinema-goers who flocked to see
GoldenEye and *Tomorrow Never Dies* in the late 1990s would not even have
been born when *Dr No* and *From Russia With Love* were released in the
early 1960s. That the Bond films should have sustained their popularity in
this way suggests they have successfully negotiated changes in film culture
over the period during which the series has been active. The impact of the
first Bond movies, especially in Britain, was due largely to the way in
which they offered a particular style and pattern of entertainment that
was completely unlike anything else in popular cinema at the time, but the
same can hardly be true of the more recent films which are part of a film
culture in which the high-tech action thriller, which the Bond series itself
in large measure spawned, is one of the most prolific genres.

The pivotal historical period of the Bond series was the 1960s. This was
the period when the distinctive formula and style of the films were
forged, and when the phenomenon of 'Bondmania' was at its height. The
Bond films embodied certain aspects of the 'cultural revolution': the new
vitality of British popular culture, the prominence of science and technology, and the increasing permissiveness in sexual attitudes and behaviour. As *Screen International* observed upon the thirty-fifth anniversary of
the series: '*Dr No* instantly tapped the 60s' feel-good *zeitgeist*, parlaying a
$1m. budget into a worldwide gross of $60m. and launching the most
successful franchise in box-office history.'[4] This quotation illustrates,
albeit probably unintentionally, one of the contradictions of the Bond
series. On the one hand the success of the early films is attributed to the
way in which they reflected the mood of the 1960s, whereas on the other
hand the films have continued to be successful long beyond that particular historical moment. If the 1960s Bond films struck a chord because
they seemed so modern and new, in subsequent decades the films have

6.1 1963 film poster for *From Russia With Love*

become institutionalised, a biennial ritual in which familiarity breeds
the contempt of critics but the loyalty of audiences. For Bennett and
Woollacott, writing in the mid-1980s, Bond 'is now, more than anything
else, a trademark which, having established a certain degree of brand loyalty among certain sections of the cinema-going public, remains a viable
investment in the film industry'.[5]

As genre films, the Bond movies have to find the right balance between
repetition and variation, between continuity and change, so that they can
simultaneously provide the sort of entertainment pattern which audiences
expect while at the same time providing new thrills, new set pieces, new
variations on old situations. On the one hand the narrative formula of the
Bond series remains constant. Audiences have come to expect the familiar
situations such as Bond's briefing by M, his visit to Q's workshop to collect
his equipment, or alternatively Q equipping him in the field, the seduction
of the girl, and the scene where the villain reveals his grand design to Bond
before leaving him in a bizarre and elaborately improbable death-scenario,
from which he escapes, and so on. It is surely no coincidence that those

films which have deviated furthest from the usual narrative conventions, such as *On Her Majesty's Secret Service* (unhappy ending) and *Licence To Kill* (non-secret service storyline), have been the least successful. But the Bond formula also extends beyond narrative conventions. Ingredients such as the opening gun barrel motif, the visually inventive title sequences and the 'James Bond Theme' have become institutionalised to such an extent that, without them, a Bond film would not feel like a Bond film at all.

On the other hand, however, the Bond series is in a process of constant renewal. The films have remained at the forefront of popular cinema because the producers have followed a strategy of continually modernising the formula. Thus the conflicts must be updated, the technology must remain on the cutting edge of what is scientifically feasible, and the jokes must be suitably topical to strike a chord with audiences. In this way the Bond films have responded to changes in the film industry, film culture, and society at large, keeping apace of changing tastes and popular attitudes. Their conspiracy plots have reflected changes in the international political situation, from Cold War to détente and back again, before relocating themselves in the 'new world' of the 1990s, while the slight modifications made in some of the later films of the relationship between Bond and the girl may be seen as a response (albeit a fairly limited one) to the greater prominence and confidence of women in society since the 1960s. The periodic changes of star, furthermore, enable Bond to remain a contemporary hero whose age remains roughly the same even as the world around him changes.

The character of Bond remains the most constant element of the films. It is to the eternal credit of the film-makers that they have resisted the attempts of American studio executives to cast a big Hollywood star as James Bond and have instead remained loyal to a group of actors who, if not all British themselves (they include an Australian and an Irishman), have nevertheless been capable of playing Bond as British. The Britishness of Bond has been central to the ideology of national identity which the films project; it also serves as a means of differentiating Bond from the all-American action heroes incarnated by the likes of Mel Gibson, Bruce Willis, and Sylvester Stallone.

In the view of film critic and Bond fan Giles Whittell, the Bond films have thrived for so long 'as realisations of wild adolescent fantasies about sex, gadgetry, invincibility and what it means to be British'.[6] According to this line of argument, the Bond films work in much the same way as the original Ian Fleming books, creating a fantasy world of beautiful women, easy sex, and consumer affluence, and, moreover, one in which the decline of British power never took place. The sexist and patriotic values of the Bond films, therefore, rather than being criticised for their lack of political correctness, should be seen as the essential ingredients which make the Bond films so distinctive. Certainly the foregrounding of patriotic motifs – so brilliantly exemplified in the Union Jack parachute jump of *The Spy Who Loved Me* – has played an important role in the Bond series, though, as the analysis of individual films has shown, the patriotic code has not been asserted with equal stridency in all the films, some of which do allude to Britain's decline.

One recent commentator, however, has offered a reading of the films which detaches Bond completely from his British roots. In his book *American Dreamtime*, Lee Drummond reacts against those critics who have seen Bond as an essentially British ideological construct and claims him instead for American popular culture. 'The *story of Bond*, his *geste* or *saga*, has become fully incorporated into the larger, ongoing *story of America*, the Dreamtime chronicle of that rich, gimmicky and bizarre land that is less a place than a state of mind', Drummond writes. The essence of his argument is that the Bond films were the first truly international media phenomenon of the modern age:

> If there were any question about assigning the story of Bond to an American Dreamtime, it would lie in the *universality* of Bond's appeal, and not in a parochial Britishness that . . . others have insisted on ascribing to him. For Bond's career has paralleled, and impelled, the process of media saturation of the planet made possible by post-war technology and the booming sixties. When movie theatres went up and began showing Western films to the burgeoning urban populations of Manila, Jakarta, Lima, Rio de Janeiro, Mexico City, and points north, east, south, and west, James Bond became a star attraction, perhaps the very first truly global media sensation. Enormous differences in language, social background, and cultural values melted away in the cerebral furnace of the theatre showing a Bond movie, reduced in many instances to the lowest common denominator: Bond was the 'kiss, kiss, bang, bang' loved by Third World audiences and immortalized in Pauline Kael's book title. Luke Skywalker, Indiana Jones, E.T., Sue Ellen and J. R. Ewing, Rocky and Rambo – these and other international media sensations would follow Bond into those dingy Third World theatres, some with their wooden benches and dirty floors, and into the sleepy towns with their public television sets. But it was Bond who showed the way, and it is Bond who remains at or near the pinnacle of world-wide popularity.[7]

Drummond's book, as this extract illustrates, is an impressionistic discussion of the role of popular movies in American culture. While it throws up occasional points of interest, it is, nevertheless, methodologically flawed and intellectually shallow. Drummond marginalises the motifs of British-ness which are drawn so explicitly in the films; nor does he locate them in relation to the British generic and cultural contexts from which the char-acter of James Bond originally came. His disavowal of the Britishness of the Bond films perhaps has something to do with the fact that of all the popular cultural icons which he cites, Bond is the only one which does not originate in America itself. The twentieth century, after all, has been one dominated by America, not only politically but also in the spread of mass culture. If the Britishness of the Bond films were to be emphasised, it would prove an exception to the rule of American cultural imperialism, the Coca-Colonisation of global culture. For the American critic, it seems, James Bond is just too successful to be considered as anything other than a product of American popular culture.

What the Bond films present is an image of Britishness carefully pack-aged for the international market. Bond is a modern, virile, classless char-acter who combines the suave sophistication of the traditional British gentleman-hero with the toughness and sexual magnetism of the Holly-wood leading man. He is also very much the Englishman abroad, a pro-fessional tourist whose job (saving the world from diabolical masterminds) takes him to exotic foreign locations which are presented with all the glossy sophistication of an upmarket travel brochure. While foregrounding the Britishness of the central character, therefore, the globe-trotting travelogue narratives bring an international and cosmo-politan dimension to the films. This is one of the major differences between the Bond films and, say, the *Die Hard* or *Lethal Weapon* type of films which are usually set in one city. The only other screen hero whose adventures take him around the world is Indiana Jones, whose films are set, of course, in a comic-book past of Nazi villains and sword-wielding warriors rather than in the modern technological fantasy world of the Bond movies.

The internationalism of the Bond movies is also evident in the nature of their conspiracy plots. A crucial difference between the films and the novels is that in the films the conspiracy is rarely directed against England alone. In some films America is the main target (*Goldfinger, Diamonds Are Forever, Live and Let Die, A View To A Kill*), while in others the entire world is threatened with destruction (*You Only Live Twice, The Spy Who Loved Me, Moonraker*). In this respect Bond is an international hero who just happens to be British. The most explicit statement of Bond's role as an international Mr Fix-It comes, ironically, from one of the films made outside the official series. As Nigel Small-Fawcett (Rowan Atkinson) tells him in *Never Say Never Again*: 'M says that without you in the service he fears for the security of the civilised world.'

A fully cognitive explanation of the success of the Bond films must take into account all the reasons advanced hitherto. Indeed, it is the combination of all these elements – the production values, the visual spectacle, the pattern of repetition and variation, the Britishness and the internationalism – which accounts for the distinctive style of the Bond films. The Bond series has its own unique generic identity, as there is no other example of popular cinema which includes all these elements in precisely the same combination. While it may represent a form of film-making by numbers, as so many critics have alleged, this should not obscure the fact that the Bond formula has proved remarkably durable and consistently successful over a very substantial period of cinematic history. Moreover, there is every indication that, for the foreseeable future at least, the James Bond films are likely to go on being what they have always been, a unique and very special kind of popular cinema.

Notes

1 David Gritten, '00-Dear', *Daily Telegraph Weekend Magazine*, 12 August 1995, p. 33.
2 Albert R. Broccoli, with Donald Zec, *When the Snow Melts: The Autobiography of Cubby Broccoli* (London: Boxtree, 1998), p. 308.
3 John Brosnan, *James Bond in the Cinema* (London: Tantivy, 1981), p. 11.
4 'The Avatar of Espionage', *Screen International*, 5 December 1997, p. 21.
5 Tony Bennett and Janet Woollacott, *Bond and Beyond: The Political Career of a Popular Hero* (London: Macmillan, 1987), p. 294.
6 Giles Whittell, 'Forever shaken not stirred', *The Times*, 3 November 1995, p. 16.
7 Lee Drummond, *American Dreamtime: A Cultural Analysis of Popular Movies and Their Implications for a Science of Humanity* (London: Littlefield Adams, 1996), pp. 128–9.

Janet Woollacott

The James Bond films: conditions of production

I think that the mere fact that we were lucky to stumble upon Ian Fleming and Bond was a bit of good fortune. The rest was all hard work. (Cubby Broccoli)[1]

Accounts of film production have a certain 'built-in' fascination both for those interested in film generally and for those intellectually concerned with the products and organisation of the mass media. The story of 'what happens behind the scenes' or behind the cameras is constructed endlessly in the popular press and in academic accounts of film-making. At the same time, studies of film production, from Lillian Ross's description of the making of *The Red Badge of Courage* onwards, have occupied a space within film studies which has been conspicuous for its lack of integration with more general theoretical approaches to the mass media.[2] Why should this be? I want to explore some of the problems associated with the discussion of film productions in relation to a particular case: that of the making of the James Bond film, *The Spy Who Loved Me* (1977).

Moreover, I also want to consider some of the implications of analysing the making of *The Spy* in terms of its 'conditions of production'. I want to use the idea of *condition* here in the sense defined by Pierre Macherey: as the principle of rationality which makes works of fiction accessible to thought, rather than as a cause in the empirical sense. 'To know the conditions of a work is not to reduce the process of its production to merely the growth of a seed which contains all its future possibilities from the very beginning', Macherey argues. 'To know the conditions of a work is to define the real process of its constitution, to show how it is composed from a real diversity of elements which give it substance.'[3]

Macherey's distinctive contribution to literary theory has been to develop a particular conception of the relationship between fiction and ideology whereby literary work both organises and in a novel manner 'works over' ideological themes. The direction of Macherey's argument operates against the notion of literary works conceived of as 'created' and 'finished' products and towards the analysis of literary texts as they are inscribed in a variety of different institutional and ideological contexts. Studying a particular text does not require elevating it and isolating it from its history of productive consumption, but looking at everything about it, 'everything which has been collected on it, become attached to it – like shells on a rock by the seashore forming a whole incrustation'.[4] The production of literary work, according to Macherey's argument, is a process and a labour which transform ideologies through formal mechanisms and which are further transformed by literary criticism into a body of 'works' with a particular status and meaning. Clearly, the James Bond films do not fall easily into the arena of literary theory within which Macherey has constructed his theoretical strategy. But Macherey's ideas have some interesting implications not only for the analysis of the James Bond phenomena generally, but also for the specific area of the production of the Bond films.

There have been a number of accounts of film production which focus on the institutions within which film-making takes place, the occupational ideologies of the film-makers, and the specific day-to-day decision-making involved in the production of any one film. The Open University case study on *The Making of The Spy Who Loved Me* examines precisely these areas in its television programmes and accompanying booklet.[5] The Bond films and *The Spy* in particular were considered in the context of the British film industry and its interrelationship with Hollywood. The Bond films, it is pointed out, were made at Pinewood Studios in England in an industrial context characterised by constant financial crisis. The perennial problems of the British film industry have been the lack of a large enough home market to support stable and permanent film-making and the inroads made by large-scale and expensive American productions on British screens. The 1960s saw the increasing exploitation of cheap film-making facilities in Britain by Americans attracted by the conditions of the Eady Levy and favourable exchange rates. The first Bond film (*Dr No*, made in 1962) was produced in this way. The partnership of the Canadian, Harry Saltzman, and the American, Cubby Broccoli, bought up the film rights to all the Bond novels, with the exception of *Casino Royale*, and got financial backing from United Artists.

> Here was a series of books written by Fleming that were selling, really you know, like hot cakes and no one really had envisaged making the films. And

no distributor would put up the money for it until Arthur Krim of United Artists agreed to do it. He was primarily interested in making a film with me. For years we had talked about making films. I was making films for Columbia prior to that . . . So I flew to New York and that's where it all started and then in about forty-five minutes we had a deal. I think one of the main reasons was David Picker – who was then given the job of production. He stepped in at that time. He knew about Fleming too and he was also a James Bond aficionado. He liked the idea.[6]

The Bond films proved to be immensely profitable and United Artists continued to finance the series, even though the American involvement in the British film industry substantially decreased in the early 1970s, through major cutbacks, sales of assets and write-offs. Only in the 1980s did the Bond films cease to have a British base. *Moonraker*, for example, was made from the United States, with location work elsewhere and only the special effects produced at Pinewood.

However, the combination of a studio base at Pinewood over a number of years and the continuing success of the series ensured the development and maintenance of a team of people who worked together on the Bond films over a period of time. Although there have clearly been many changes in the members of the Bond production team, it is surprising how many people have either continued to work on the Bond films or have returned to them after working on other films. At the time of the making of *The Spy*, new members of the production team – Claude Renoir (director of photography), Christopher Wood (writer), and others – were far outnumbered by those who had worked on previous Bond films. Moreover, they experienced a conscious effort on the part of Broccoli (by this time the sole producer) and other members of his team to initiate them into the world of 'Bondian' film-making. 'Bondian' was the phrase used by Broccoli and other members of the production team to mean 'in the spirit of James Bond'. To a certain extent the term 'Bondian' was used to describe the Bond films, which were seen as a distinctive formula, a specific genre of film. As Lewis Gilbert, who directed *The Spy*, said:

Most of the things in Bond films today have kind of grown up with the picture . . . they tend to keep it into the pattern they've had all along. For instance, they have an unknown leading lady. They don't like to change all the people who are well known like 'M' and Miss Moneypenny and there's no way in which they could be changed because the public really wants to see them . . . they like the pattern, the formula. I think that part of the charm of the Bond picture [is] you know what you're going to get . . . You're not disappointed . . . You see audiences in a Bond film aren't looking for great acting – they want to be overwhelmed by physical things. Well the character of Bond, you couldn't change, of course . . . but you can change his attitude to a certain extent . . . he doesn't find this girl so easy – such a pushover as the other girls have been. And so in that sense, you can change it slightly, but it's very well laid down, the law of Bond and people want you to abide by it . . . Bond films are very very different from any other kind of film made. They've disproved every law in the cinema, they've done everything wrong and they're huge successes . . . I mean in story elements, in characterization elements, things like that – the anti-climatic bit they always have at the end which you wouldn't dare do in other pictures where they have a huge big ending and then suddenly, the film starts up again . . . Many things they do wrong, things which you would think get a laugh in a normal picture, but it's a kind of sympathetic laugh.[7]

A great deal of discussion between members of the production team of *The Spy* centred on the provision of 'Bondian effects' within the film: on the importance of the sets, the gadgets, the foreign locations, the threatening character of the villains (which must incorporate both a physical threat and an intellectual threat to the hero), Bond's relationship with the girl in the story, the jokes, and the form of the crucial pre-credits sequence. The 'formula' of the Bond film was generally understood, and to a certain extent the term 'Bondian' was used to refer to that formula. At the same time, people working on *The Spy* also used the term to refer to the process of working on a Bond picture. It was recognised and acknowledged that this was different from the process of working on other films. Claude Renoir, the cameraman, listed aspects of Bond pictures as 'a lot of people, a lot of good technicians, a lot of tricks, special effects and so on' and underlined the importance of the big budget in a Bond film, pointing out that 'it's quite rare for a French cameraman to be involved in such a big budget picture'.[8]

The importance of the big budget was stressed by many members of the production team (it is part of the 'Bondian' ethos), including Christopher Wood:

I have worked on films in which people have said to me, Chris baby, it doesn't matter. The sky's the limit. You want to shoot this in Saudi Arabia, shoot it in Saudi Arabia, we don't care, as many people as you like, just don't feel there are any constraints. So I write it and then they come back and say, well, why have we got two rooms. I mean couldn't she be his uncle and his wife at the same time. I mean, we'd save money on casting as well. With a Bond film, you do know that with anything you write, money is no restraint.[9]

Wood also acknowledged some of the frustrations of working on a Bond picture, in which slightly different conceptions of the Bondian might compete:

> I was very pleased with a sequence I had when we established Bond in the film in which we'd have a scene of the sea . . . On the raft, Bond is lying with the girl, beep, beep, beep, comes a little message. Then in his usual cursory rather boorish way, he waves her farewell leaving her sort of yelping on the raft and just steps aboard his surfboard, picks up the nearest roller, roars forward on a mind-bending shot, riding a forty-five-foot-high wave, comes straight down, up the beach, still on the board to where there's a jeep, just slips off the board . . . inside the jeep, flicks up the microphone and gets his orders . . . shoves his foot down on the jeep which raises up at a priapic angle up the side of the sand dune, just roars up into space and in about thirty seconds I thought we'd establish the persona of Bond . . . Cubby had a better idea . . . when you see Bond's entrance in the movie, it's better . . . which I now accept, but when it was first mooted I was rather sulkily rubbing my foot against the floor and thinking, 'Blast'.[10]

In the event, the pre-credits sequence in *The Spy* involved establishing the loss of British and Russian submarines and the contacting not only of Bond (acted by Roger Moore), but also of the Russian Special Agent X, who is apparently a Bond-type figure making love to a beautiful woman, but turns out to be the woman herself. Bond, similarly occupied in a chalet in the Alps, skis off to answer his call – only to be attacked by Russian agents, from whom he escapes and whom he kills during an extended chase, finally leaping off an enormous cliff, only to open his parachute, which unfolds to reveal the Union Jack. The production team were satisfied that this was an effective, 'Bondian' opening to the film.

The idea of the Bondian also percolated through to those directly involved in film production. Saul Cooper, for example, the director of publicity, argued that the only bad publicity for a Bond picture was that which 'destroys the illusion'. 'The illusion', he suggested, 'is the thing that I have learnt from Cubby Broccoli . . . that there are things that are Bondian and things that are not Bondian.' Cooper explained that 'Bondian is our own special word . . . everything that involves Bond has to be a little bigger, a little better, to be larger than life, it has to have a certain special flair.'[11] In the publicity for the film, the whole notion of the Bondian was brought into play. Journalists, for example, were invited to a 'Bondian weekend', in which they stayed at an international hotel and were served a banquet of James Bond dishes, culled from the novels. The tanker set was much publicised as the 'biggest set' in Europe. The opening of the set was a publicity event, which involved not only the participation of the bevy of beautiful, scantily-clad girls which accompanied most Bond publicity stunts, but also a visit by Harold Wilson and his introduction to Roger Moore and Barbara Bach – the new Bond girl, dressed in Russian uniform.

While the Open University case study focuses on the background in the British and American film industries of the Bond films, and of the process of making *The Spy Who Loved Me* in particular, it also offers a particular ideological reading of the Bond films, including *The Spy*:

> The film is in a sense the perfection of the SPECTRE[12] genre although SPECTRE is never mentioned inasmuch as Stromberg's ransom plan is applied indiscriminately to East and West, playing upon the tensions which subsist beneath detente. Stromberg himself being presented to us as a personification of the irrational forces which permanently threaten the delicate balance of peaceful co-existence. In this sense, particularly at this precise moment in history, Bond's adventures take on a new significance inasmuch as it is through his endeavours that the ever impending crisis which threatens the world with calamity is averted. The world is led to the brink of nuclear holocaust and back again. It is by thus effecting a purely imaginary resolution of real social contradictions, which are themselves misrepresented in the form of the fantastic and the grotesque, that the Bond films attain their ideological effect.[13]

The Spy is in effect read as a working over of contemporary ideologies around international tensions. Moreover, the pattern of coverage of the case study implicitly takes for granted the classical Marxist hierarchy of determinants. We are led as readers from the financial and economic 'determinants' of the Bond films through the institutional space within which they were made and the occupational ideologies of the filmmakers to a reading of *The Spy* as realist. It is 'the product of a camera which conceals itself', in which even moments of technological and fantastic excess in the film are conceived of as part of an ideological motif in which the viewer's disbelief is played upon, only to reinforce its suspension 'and the false consciousness which that suspension promotes'.[14]

The problems of this approach, however, are clearly evident. The Marxist base/superstructure model, with its focus on the problem of determination, has provided an implicit or explicit background for many studies of culture. Raymond Williams summarises the general proposition of Marxism in the following way:

> The whole movement of society is governed by certain dispositions of the means of production and when these dispositions – forces and relations in

a mode of production as a whole – change through the operation of their own laws and tendencies, then forms of consciousness and forms of intellectual and artistic production (forms which have their place in orthodox Marxist definition as a 'superstructure') change also. Some shift in relatively direct ways, like politics and law, some shift in distant and often indirect ways – the traditional examples are religion, philosophy and aesthetics.[15]

Although few, including Williams himself, would now accept a crude form of the base/superstructure model as an acceptable theoretical framework for the analysis of culture, problems associated with the base/superstructure notion have continued to dog the analysis of culture. In the study of film and media organisations, questions of determination frequently remain in the background, but they do to a certain extent justify the many studies of professional people and organisations concerned with the media. As Philip Elliott argues, such studies in America and Britain 'provide the basis for an analysis of the production of media culture under the conditions of democratic capitalism'.[16]

In film studies, accounts of the production process are either considered in isolation or they are organised around questions of determination. Hence, John Ellis, in his admirable analysis of Ealing Studios, contends that 'to determine the possibilities of any film, the material, technological, aesthetic and ideological determinants in its production have to be examined: only here can it be decided where a film coincides with the dominant ideology and where it diverges from it'.[17] Ellis's listing of the determinants of an Ealing text includes 'the entire history of the cinema (its system of production, distribution and exhibition)', 'the specific organisation of production' and 'the beliefs of the group controlling production'.[18] The difficulties of attempting to explain films in terms of this type of hierarchy of determinants is often simply that an examination of 'the entire history of the cinema', even of 'the specific organisation of production' and 'the beliefs of the group controlling production', tends to establish at best a series of fragmentary connections between film texts and the views of the owners or controllers of production. Ellis, for example, suggests that although the concentration of Ealing films on the lower middle class was the result of a complex of factors, the primary factor was biographical, in that the majority of the film-makers concerned were born into middle-class families, many of them strongly imbued with lower-class liberalism, 'which expressed the class interest of the emergent lower sections of the bourgeoisie'.[19] Thus Ealing is seen as the product of a generation which was 'radicalised' by the experience of the Depression and for whom the desire to show 'the people' in films was satisfied by a focus on the characters and situations of the petit bourgeoisie.

The interconnections proposed by Ellis seem less than obvious. But the implication seems to be that Ealing films, like all films, have a number of levels of determination, that they were, in effect, 'overdetermined', but that one of the crucial elements in that over-determination was the class origins and views of the group controlling production. I find some slightly worrying gaps in the analysis here. The concentration of Ealing films on lower-middle-class characters, shopkeepers, small businessmen and the like, is explained in terms of the class position and outlook of those in charge of production. The final variable area in the hierarchy of determinants seems to be 'individuality':

> This is Ealing's situation; a group of conventionally educated intellectuals, through a certain liberal radicalism, come to make films about and for 'the people', whom they think of as the lower levels of the petit bourgeoisie. Thus individuals are a vital part of the process, not as finished entities with world-views and metaphysical preoccupations, but as social beings.[20]

Unfortunately, individuality, albeit socially formed, does not seem to explain why the Ealing film-makers' class origins are 'displaced' onto the petit bourgeoisie.

In this kind of analysis, the inevitable gaps between determining factors and the films tend to be dealt with either through a designation of 'individual' activity or, in other circumstances, through an accepted and understandable lack of knowledge about the complex inter-penetration of different levels of determination, because of the absence of any detailed histories of the film industry and of the productions of different films. Edward Buscombe's interesting attempt to explore the relationship between Frank Capra's films and the ownership and control of Columbia Pictures Corporation sounds a number of warnings about categorising the relationship between films, studios, and more general social attitudes, arguing that films 'cannot be explained simply in terms of who owned the studios or in terms only of social attitudes at the time'.[21] Buscombe suggests that the history of the American film industry constitutes a kind of missing link in attempts to make connections between Hollywood films and American society. The assumption in this case is that 'many of the materials needed to forge that link are missing'.[22]

The case study on the making of *The Spy Who Loved Me* shares this familiar problem of making connections between (in this instance) the occupational ideologies and actions of the Bond production team in the process of making the film and the script of *The Spy Who Loved Me* in relation to a hierarchy of determinations. Both Stuart Hall and Dyer, in their discussion of the occupational ideologies of the film-makers, stressed the limitations of the conscious views and actions of the members of the production team. Dyer argued that the whole area of professionalism and commodity production which characterises the Bond team permits a repression of considerations of ideology. Hall suggested that Dyer's argument involved 'a species of professional unconsciousness', that 'professionalism really means being conscious about certain foreground things in order not to be conscious about some of the ideological themes'. On the one hand, Dyer's argument eschewed the notion of simple manipulation by the Bond team, but, on the other hand, it also suggested that 'you have to recognise that there is a gap between what they [the Bond production team] think they're doing and what they're actually doing'.[23] One of the difficulties of this kind of approach is precisely that the views of the Bond production team are seen to be to a large extent either irrelevant or misleading for anyone who wishes to understand the ideological meaning of the film of *The Spy Who Loved Me*. Such views have to be taken into account, but not accepted at their face value.

A number of issues seem to be involved in this placing of the views of the film-makers within the context of production studies. The first of these is undoubtedly the over-emphasis on determination. The views and practices of film-makers are conceived of as inadequate in terms of the determination of film texts. As I have suggested, they are interesting evidence, but are not to be accepted at face value, because other determining forces (technology, ownership, and so on) have not only to be taken into account but also ranked in the hierarchy of determinants. The second important assumption of such arguments is that the ideological meaning of a film can be established and that that ideological meaning is self-evidently not the meaning with which the film-makers themselves would have endowed their film. Given these premises, the realm of professional ideology inevitably becomes tinged with notions of 'false consciousness'.

I would argue that it is important to rethink this formulation of the place of production studies. Firstly, the endeavour to reinsert the script of *The Spy* into its conditions of production should not be seen in terms of the exegesis of determination, conceived of in terms of the classical Marxist hierarchy of determinants. Secondly, the script of *The Spy* has to be conceptualised as part of a group of texts, including novels, films, advertising, and other cultural forms, the ideological meaning of which cannot be 'delivered' in a 'once and for all' manner outside their conditions of production and the history of their consumption. Given these provisos, the role of professional ideologies and the labour of film production take on a rather different meaning. It becomes less necessary to take for granted that the ideological work involved in producing the Bond films takes place 'behind the backs' of the Bond production team. Rather, the opposite case could be argued. The detailed and enthusiastic discussion of the experience of working on a Bond film collected in the Open University case study provides rich material both on the production team's use and transformation of existing James Bond texts (both novels and films) and on specific ideologies, outside those texts, which they were concerned to rework in the production of *The Spy Who Loved Me*. The 'hard work' of making a Bond film is not simply a matter of anecdotal interest, nor yet another example of the organisation of the mass media and of the role of professional ideologies. An examination of the process of working on *The Spy Who Loved Me* actually informs us both about the existing ideologies with which the Bond production team were concerned and about the way in which these were transformed during the making of the film.

Clearly, a key element in the making of the later Bond films was the existence and popularity of the preceding films and novels. The early Bond films tended to follow the plots of the novels quite closely, but later films, such as *The Spy*, have taken little more than the title from Fleming's work. When Broccoli talked about his 'good fortune' in finding the Ian Fleming books, he was quite right to stress that, while this was mere luck, the development of the Bond films was 'all hard work'. Even in the making of the early Bond movies, the Bond books were not simply reproduced but were consciously worked over and changed. At the time of the making of *The Spy Who Loved Me*, while the production team were well aware of the heritage of Bond and happily referred to the Bond films as 'formula' pictures, they were also concerned to update and slightly shift the emphasis of these films. It is worth touching on some of the areas on which the Bond team could be seen to be working and which have implications for transformation of ideologies achieved in a film such as *The Spy Who Loved Me*. The three areas with which the latter part of this chapter is concerned are the attempts to de-politicise James Bond, to engage with ideas about the independence of women, and to construct and maintain comic strategy around Bond's own sexuality.

The James Bond of Fleming's novels written before the 1960s (such as *Moonraker* (1955); *From Russia, With Love* (1957); *Goldfinger* (1959)) is strategically located in the Cold War tensions of the period. 'The villain', remarks Umberto Eco of the Bond novels, is born in an ethnic area that stretches from central Europe to the Slav countries and to the Mediterranean basin; as a rule he is of mixed blood and his origins are complex and obscure; he is asexual or homosexual, or at any rate is not sexually normal; he has exceptional inventive and organisational qualities which help him acquire immense wealth and by means of which he usually works to help Russia; to this end he conceives a plan of fantastic character and dimensions; worked out to the smallest detail, intended to create serious difficulties either for England or for the Free World in general.[24]

The later novels to a certain extent discard the more obvious trappings of Cold War hostilities, although the films have always pitted Bond against SPECTRE. The producer of the Bond films, Cubby Broccoli, has been noted for his declaration that the Bond films are 'not political' but are good 'old fashioned entertainment'. What Broccoli seems to mean by this claim is that he has shown a constant desire to play down the overtly anti-Soviet views of Fleming's Bond. By the time of the making of *The Spy*, the tenth James Bond film, the plot portrays Russia as being under threat. The villain, Stromberg, threatens East and West alike with nuclear destruction, and East/West relations become a matter of the sexual and professional subordination to the West's best agent (Bond) of Russia's 'Special Agent', X (Anya).

This type of de-politicisation of the Bond myth was put vigorously into effect by the production team, with a view to 'up-dating Bond' and, possibly, serving commercial interests. Members of the Russian Embassy were invited to the opening of the tanker set at Pinewood – to which Harold Wilson, as I have mentioned, was also invited. Roger Moore and Barbara Bach were conspicuously posed together hand in hand, for publicity purposes. The production team liked to characterise the Bond films as a 'circus', as 'entertainment' in which the villain or villains have to offer both an intellectual threat and a physical threat to Bond, but there is a real sense in which the specific political threat embodied in the villain in the Fleming books was consciously and systematically eradicated. In a Bond film, the typical villain, and Stromberg in *The Spy Who Loved Me* is no exception, intends not merely to threaten a particular country or the Western world, but to 'destroy the world'. Stromberg is, in effect, represented as a madman, a villain who threatens to destroy the existing world in order to build another one under his control under the sea. The general nuclear threat is tied here to irrational desires for change. At the same time, however, Stromberg's character takes on the quality of parody in the 'larger than life' excesses of Bond villainy. Stromberg's assistant, whose enormous size and steel teeth constitute the main physical threat to Bond, was conceived of comically as a parody of other films. Broccoli, Wood and Michael Wilson (the assistant to the producer) saw the development of the character of 'Jaws' in terms of an elaborated joke. 'Jaws', for example, reverses popular assumptions about sharks: he kills a shark by biting it.

A crucial and important part of the Bond myth has always centred around sexuality. Indeed, the elaborate sexual coding of the novels ties together Bond's relationship to M, to the villain and to the women.[25] Women in the Bond films have always been conceived in terms of male desire and pleasure. When Ursula Andress, as Honeychile Rider, clad in a bikini and with knife in hand, walked out of the sea in *Dr No*, the visual image of the Bond woman was resoundingly established. The scenes in which Honey makes her appearance as a latter-day Venus could be read as a textbook illustration of scophophilic pleasure, whereby the manipulation of 'looks' in the film establishes the woman as the object of sexual desire both for the hero and for the audience. The Bond films generally would seem, on one level, to conform to Laura Mulvey's analysis of scophophilic pleasure in Hollywood films. Mulvey's argument suggests that, in such films, a particular regime of pleasure is established through the 'looks' of the hero and the audience. While women are represented as erotic spectacle, the audience is led to identify with the male hero, the active performer.[26]

The Bond films also took over and reworked the motifs of the books in which the sexual subordination of the 'Bond women' plays an important part in reordering the narrative disturbances which is the task of the hero. In the books, the Bond girl is not simply the bland but desirable and sexual creature who emerges from other peoples' reworkings of the Bond myth.[27] Rather, Bond's girls have some initial claim to independence. There are no clinging romantic heroines in the Bond novels. But the narrative pattern of the Bond novels establishes the women as in some manner sexually and ideologically 'out of place'; too aggressive (Vesper Lynd in *Casino Royale*), frigid (Gala Brand in *Moonraker*), damaged by rape (Tiffany Case in *Diamonds Are Forever* and Honeychile Rider in *Dr No*), or lesbian (Tilly Masterton and Pussy Galore in *Goldfinger*). Such women are 'out of place' in relation to men, as represented by Bond, and are likely, therefore, also to be in the service of the villain. Such a girl represents a challenge to the traditional sexual order, and Bond's answer is that of 'putting her back into place beneath him (both literally and metaphorically)'.[28] In so doing, he also pulls her into the cause of 'right', removing her from an alliance with the villain and recruiting and attaching her to his task and views.

The early Bond films contained distinct echoes of these themes of the novels, although the sexual ambiguity of the Bond girls tended to be underplayed. The lesbianism of Tilly Masterton and Pussy Galore in the film of *Goldfinger* is muted to the point that only a 'knowing' viewer would recognise it. On the whole, the films reworked the role of the Bond girls in terms of plenitude and availability. Constant references are made to Bond's success with women by characters around him, particularly Moneypenny and Felix Leiter. The Bond formula, as understood by the production team on *The Spy*, involved a plethora of beautiful women and the repeated demonstration of Bond's mastery over them. The traditional ending of a Bond film sees Bond, having disposed of the villain and destroyed his headquarters, making love to the new Bond girl of the film, in the aftermath of violence, while the credits roll, promising his return in a new Bond film. The production team working on *The Spy* were powerfully aware of that tradition and of its importance in the Bondian formula. At the same time, they were also well aware of the importance of the women's movement and of public criticisms of Bond. The team saw clearly that Bond had to fulfil certain sexist expectations revolving around male pleasure, but they also wanted to register the impact of Women's Lib. The heroine of *The Spy Who Loved Me* is Anya, a Russian agent who is Bond's professional equal. Barbara Bach, the new Bond girl of the film, was told that this was a Bond girl with a difference:

> Well, first of all, she's a spy and a serious spy. And she's really not one of Bond's girls so to speak. She's in the film doing her own bit and she meets up with Bond and it's only almost at the end of the film that there's any kind of attraction between the two of them, other than let's say, professional competition. So it's quite different. Most of the girls in the Bond films have just been merely beautiful girls that you know have small parts and come in and go out. Anya stays from the beginning to the end.[29]

In some limited formal terms, the character of Anya was given equal status with Bond. Lewis Gilbert remarked that 'Women's Lib would be rather proud of her.'[30] Nevertheless, the Women's Lib heroine is used within the Bond formula. The pre-credits sequence includes a joke, which plays on the audience's expectations of Bond, when the problem of disappearing submarines produces the simultaneous calling of the top British and top Russian agents by their respective governments. In the Russian case, the camera pans across a palatial room to a virile young man making love to a beautiful girl. She is clearly upset that he will have to leave, but when the call to Special Agent X is made, it is she who picks up

7.1 Bond (Roger Moore) prematurely pops his cork when Agent Triple X (Barbara Bach) points her piece at him in *The Spy Who Loved Me*

the telephone and identifies herself. Anya is set up as a challenge to Bond, but one to be subordinated by Bond in the characteristic development of the Bond narrative, in the visual spectacle focused on the Bond girl in the film and in the publicity for the film.

The production team were well aware of the ambiguities attached to the use of this type of heroine and their willingness to exploit a particular notion of Women's Lib was predicated on the assumption that it would reinforce the exploits of James Bond. The exploitation was both conscious and, at one level, quite cynical. Anya was conceived as the Russian and female equivalent of Bond, but she was also intended to succumb to him in the course of the film. Outside the role of Anya in the plot, Broccoli was not prepared to hire a more experienced actress for the part. Barbara Bach was selected for the following reasons:

> She's a very beautiful girl. She's comparatively unknown which I think brings a certain freshness to a Bond film. We have explored getting various well known ladies, high priced ladies, to bring in, but in my humble opinion, there's no lady today who contributes that much success, if she's high priced or otherwise, unless we like what she does. I don't think there's any

actress today that can support a picture box office wise with the possible exception of Barbra Streisand . . . But the price doesn't distinguish the girl in our film from the success of a Bond picture. I mean we've explored a certain lady in Hollywood who commands a 500,000 dollar wage . . . and that blew her right out of the box for me because she'd contribute no more than Barbara Bach will.[31]

This view of what a Bond girl must contribute was given a particular edge in discussions about publicity for the film. Barbara Bach had worked as a fashion model and wanted to avoid the 'cheesecake' image of much accepted 'Bond girl' publicity. While members of the production team were, on the one hand, anxious to create a more interesting heroine, they were also, on the other hand, concerned to fulfil people's expectations of the traditional Bond girl. Saul Cooper, for example, had clear ideas about what a Bond girl had to be: 'A Bond girl is part of the whole dream world that Bond creates. She is a woman of fantastic sexual allure and promise, just as Bond is every man's dream of suddenly being able to spring into action.'[32] Inevitably, there were some clashes over this view of the Bond girl:

> You have the traditional Bond girl image, which involves having the girl photographed in a bikini, in a bathing suit. This was something that took a certain amount of hassling with Barbara at the beginning. But it was something that was absolutely required because a Bond girl must, at some point, be seen within the Bond mould.[33]

The Bondian formula, as the production team were well aware, was likely to be *strengthened* by the creation of a Bond girl whose challenge to Bond was more contemporary and more direct, and seen to be more relevant. Barbara Bach's description of Bond, quoted in *Time* magazine, as 'a male chauvinist pig', centred on the themes which the Bond team wanted to introduce in relation to the Bondian formula.

At the same time, questions of sexuality are not just linked to the displayed charms of the Bond girls in the films. Bond's sexuality is the crucial route into the 'formula' in which the girls are sexually subordinated by the hero. Bond's sexuality has been much discussed by film-makers in the past. Sean Connery, for example, was originally chosen to play Bond by Saltzman and Broccoli because 'He looked like he had balls.'[34] This aspect of the Bond films has been one which has clearly shifted over the years, partly in relation to specific performances of Bond. Roger Moore's James Bond has always had a more flippant and jokey style, particularly in relation to Bond's sexual prowess. Moreover, Bond's physical presence on the screen has increasingly come to be associated with his mastery of and use of technology. Whereas it was usual for the Bond of the novels to begin his adventures with an interview with M, it was much more necessary to the Bond films that Bond also sees Q and the recurring joke of Q's elaborate workshop, full of gadgets which would be used in the film. For the production team, concerned to establish Bond as 'family' entertainment, the hero's sexuality has been conceived of in terms both of his joking conquest of beautiful women and of the technological extensions of his role. In writing the script, Christopher Wood turned to his own children to establish what was attractive about Bond and, in response to their replies, reworked the car chase (used to great effect in *Goldfinger*), in which Bond's car is equipped with every kind of weaponry. In *The Spy*, Bond drives into the sea in his efforts to escape pursuit, equipped with a Lotus which converts into a submarine and which does battle with the villains under water. But this physical mastery of technology and nature is constantly punctured by the comic strategy of the film. After an underwater battle, Bond and Anya drive from the waves, before the startled glances of the holiday-makers on a nearby beach, and Bond casually and ostentatiously removes a small fish from the car, comically underlining the technological feat which he has just performed.

The Bond team made a conscious effort to avoid what they considered to be overt sexuality and excessive violence, largely because they wanted to win the widest possible audience for *The Spy* and partly because they perceived that the Bond films are particularly attractive to children. Their main concern was with visual style and the creation of plausible but impossible technological gadgets. Hence, the most detailed discussions took place about the development of sets and gadgets and the use of these in the action sequences, or 'bumps', in the film. But the sting in the tail of this almost obsessive concern with technology – displayed by many members of the production team, from Broccoli downwards – was that this concern was set up only to be comically deflated. Michael Wilson, the assistant to the producer, pointed out that the one-line jokes for which Bond is famous were part of a well worked out strategy. An exciting action sequence, involving some technological excess, has to be followed by a joke, both to release the audience's tension, aroused by the action, and to mitigate the considerable demands that Bond films make on the audience in terms of suspension of disbelief. Scenes which members of the team felt were worked out satisfactorily almost always followed the pattern described by Christopher Wood:

> I can remember one instance in a place in the script . . . I'd developed the idea of having a motorcycle combination – a sidecar and a motorcycle. The

motorcycle sidecar breaks away and becomes a rocket which chases Bond when he's in a car. Now the way I had written it at that stage, Bond took evasive action and drove off the road, the sidecar exploded against a wall, blew a big hole in the wall and that was the end of the sequence. Now somebody in the art department thought out the idea . . . why shouldn't the sidecar hit another vehicle . . . that made me think . . . and we investigated it hitting another vehicle or how could you build something extra into hitting a vehicle, other than just a blinding flash and bits of explosive material blowing all over the place, suppose we made that vehicle something unusual . . . a vehicle that was carrying a load of feather mattresses so that when you explode the vehicle, voom, instead of just a big bang, you get a big bang and millions and millions of feathers.[35]

The effect consciously sought is that of a parody of the 'super-hero'. The strategy of *The Spy* involved a constant comic rupturing of the illusion of the reality of the fiction – a comic rupturing which has been traditionally focused on the relationship between Bond and technology, but which was also mobilised increasingly in *The Spy* in relation to women. The film ends with Bond and Anya being rescued from Stromberg's escape capsule in the sea. This traditional ending for a Bond film is capped by Bond's flippant answer to M's inquiry about what he has been doing: 'Keeping the British end up.'

Clearly, within the bounds of a single chapter, it has only been possible to indicate very briefly some of the ideological processes at work in the making of a Bond film. I have suggested, however, that questions of determination have dominated attempts to relate production studies to the meanings of specific films to the detriment of understanding the relationship between particular films or groups of films and other texts in wider and more far-reaching ideological frameworks. I do not wish to imply that all questions of determination are irrelevant to an understanding of the ideological processes involved in film-making. The organisation of the industry, financial constraints, existing conventions and genres, and the particular people involved in the making of any one film, will all necessarily constrain and order the making of films. Nevertheless, I would suggest that what happens in film production in working over existing ideological tensions and controversies and turning them into a film, is crucial to our understanding of the transformation of ideologies. To know about the conditions of production of a Bond film, it is not only important to examine current ideological discourses but also to know how a Bond film was made – that is, how those ideologies were ordered and worked upon in the film. Of course, such an analysis of the meaning of a Bond film does not exhaust its ideological currency. It is only the beginning of an examination of how ideology is mediated and continuously transformed.

Notes

1 Cubby Broccoli, interview. All the interviews cited in these notes were given in the course of work on the case study, *The Making of the Spy Who Loved Me*, ed. by Tony Bennett *et al.* (Milton Keynes: Open University, 1977), carried out by the staff of the Open University in 1976.
2 See Lillian Ross, *Picture* (London: Faber, 1998).
3 Pierre Macherey, *A Theory of Literary Production* (London: Routledge, 1978), p. 49.
4 Pierre Macherey, interview, in *Red Letters*, 5 (Summer 1977), 3–9 (p. 9).
5 See Tony Bennett *et al.*, *The Making of the Spy Who Loved Me*.
6 Broccoli, interview.
7 Lewis Gilbert, interview.
8 Claude Renoir, interview.
9 Christopher Wood, interview.
10 Wood, interview.
11 Saul Cooper, interview.
12 Special Executive for Counterintelligence, Terrorism, Revenge and Extortion: the villainous organisation, created by Fleming in his later novels, with which Bond was to contend.
13 Bennett *et al.*, *The Making of the Spy Who Loved Me*, p. 29.
14 Bennett *et al.*, *The Making of the Spy Who Loved Me*, p. 31.
15 Raymond Williams, 'Marxism, Structuralism and Literary Analysis', *New Left Review*, 129 (1981), 51–6 (p. 55).
16 Philip Elliott, 'Media Organization and Occupations; an Overview', in *Mass Communication and Society*, ed. by J. Curran, M. Guervitch and J. Woollacott (London: Arnold, 1977), pp. 142–73 (p. 143).
17 John Ellis, 'Made in Ealing', *Screen*, 16.1 (1975), p. 80.
18 Ellis, 'Made in Ealing', pp. 80–1.
19 Ellis, 'Made in Ealing', pp. 80–1.
20 Ellis, 'Made in Ealing', p. 81.
21 Edward Buscombe, 'Notes on Columbia Pictures Corporation 1924–41', *Screen*, 16.3 (1975), 65–82 (p. 82).
22 Buscombe, 'Notes on Columbia Pictures', p. 82.
23 Open University Radio Programmes 14 and 15, DE 353, 'Mass Communication and Society', 1977.
24 Umberto Eco, 'The Narrative Structures in Fleming', in *The Bond Affair*, ed. by O. Del Bueno and U. Eco (London: Macdonald, 1966), pp. 35–75 (p. 42). Reprinted in this volume.

25 See Tony Bennett, 'James Bond as Popular Hero', in *U203 Popular Culture: Unit 21* (Milton Keynes: Open University Press, 1982), pp. 5–33.

26 Laura Mulvey, 'Visual Pleasure and Narrative Cinema', *Screen*, 16 (1975), 6–18.

27 See Furio Columbo, 'Bond's Women', in *The Bond Affair*, ed. by O. Del Bueno and U. Eco (London: Macdonald, 1966), pp. 86–102.

28 Bennett, 'James Bond as Popular Hero', p. 20.

29 Barbara Bach, interview.

30 Gilbert, interview.

31 Broccoli, interview.

32 Cooper, interview.

33 Cooper, interview.

34 Alexander Walker, *Hollywood England: the British Film Industry in the Sixties* (London: Michael Joseph, 1974), p. 187.

35 Wood, interview.

Jeff Smith

Creating a Bond market: selling John Barry's soundtracks and theme songs

The commercial importance of John Barry's music for the James Bond series should not be understated. Of the eleven Bond soundtrack albums featuring Barry's work, only two, *The Man With The Golden Gun* (1974) and *The Living Daylights* (1987), failed to have any action on US trade charts. Their lacklustre showing, however, perhaps only further points up the importance that a string of more successful title-songs from other Bond films have played in the series. Over the years the Bond series has attracted such songwriters as Lionel Bart, Anthony Newley, Leslie Bricusse, Paul McCartney, and Narada Michael Walden, while songs were performed by such stars as Louis Armstrong, Carly Simon, Sheena Easton, Duran Duran, and the Pretenders. With these diverse talents at their disposal, Saltzman and Broccoli reaped the financial benefits of nine charting singles, five of which were Top Ten hits.

While many producers from the 1950s onward attempted to exploit title-songs as promotional tools, Saltzman and Broccoli innovated the notion of using pop songs as a regularised aspect of production. Earlier efforts at such cross-promotion had been piecemeal and erratic, with each film developing its own textual and extra-textual strategies of merchandising music. While these early efforts did have their share of successes, they were somewhat risky from both a commercial and aesthetic standpoint. If the producer and composer greatly misjudged audience tastes, as Stanley Kramer and Ernest Gold did with 'Waltzing Mathilda' in *On the Beach* (1959), the result was often a score that could be dramatically effective in the film itself but of very little promotional value.

To resolve the issue of audience taste, producers frequently commissioned or selected a song to be used for the credits, but which was not integrated with the film's other cues. Commissioned songwriters often understood the need for melodic hooks and clever lyrics better than film composers and thus were frequently more capable of servicing the ancillary markets that helped ameliorate a producer's risks. Since such a tune was often used only during the credit sequence, however, it had a limited chance of ingratiating itself within the collective consciousness of the audience. If a tune failed to make an impression on viewers during this small window of opportunity, then it functioned as little more than a musical announcement of the film's title.

In developing their own approach to marketing film music, Saltzman and Broccoli combined both of these strategies in a way that maximised their benefits. The frequent repetition of the 'James Bond Theme' in film after film made this signature tune synonymous with the central character. The almost Pavlovian association of music and character has been a key to the series' success in both domestic and international markets. The twangy, reverbed electric guitar and forceful brass melody transcend language barriers and serve as a simple, economical, and immediately recognisable means of promoting the character. *Variety* estimates that over half the world's population has seen a Bond film, and it is likely that virtually all of them can identify the 'James Bond Theme'.[1]

Yet by introducing new exploitable tunes with each film, Saltzman and Broccoli were able to hedge their bets by continually offering a new product to radio programmers and music vendors. With the films conceived as a series from the outset, each song became an anticipated element in a reliable promotional formula. Just as fans eagerly anticipated the display of the new Bond girl in *Playboy* pictorials, they also awaited the promotional drama concerning who will write and sing a new Bond theme.[2] By pairing the familiar 'James Bond Theme' with a new title-song, each film conformed to an implicit set of musical norms for the series in a formula that balanced conventionality and novelty, homogeneity, and variety.

The groundwork for this formula was laid in June 1961 when Saltzman and Broccoli met with United Artists' (UA) Arthur Krim to discuss a distribution deal for their nascent James Bond series. Saltzman had already secured the exclusive film rights to all but one of Ian Fleming's Bond books, but the two producers had not yet received any financial backing for their project. After a fruitless discussion with Columbia Pictures, Saltzman and Broccoli sought out UA, which subsequently agreed in principle to a regular development deal with the pair's Swiss production company, Danjaq. On April 2, 1962, the details of the agreement were finalised in a formal document that gave Saltzman and Broccoli financing for the first film in the series, *Dr No*, in exchange for UA's standard distribution fees and rights of approval over the main artistic elements of each film.[3]

Also stipulated in this basic agreement was UA's broad control over the various music rights for the Bond series. UA was granted both copyright privileges and the licensing rights for any original songs, instrumental, or background music contained in the films, and was further given the right to manufacture and sell said soundtrack in the form of records, tapes, and written transcriptions. Not only did UA receive authorisation to assign these rights to its own publishing and recording subsidiaries, but the parent company also collected two cents on every piece of sheet music sold in the US, 20 per cent of the aggregate net receipts of foreign sheet music sales, and 20 per cent of the net receipts from the sale of mechanical and synchronisation rights. Additionally, the contract provided that UA and the films' composers would share an aggregate 5 per cent royalty on records sold in the US. The remaining profits were mostly divided among UA's publishing and recording subsidiaries after each had deducted its production and distribution expenses.

For its part, Danjaq got only a small share of these music earnings but retained the power to hire composers and musicians for the films. This privilege was granted to Danjaq with the understanding that it would exercise certain powers over its music personnel. First, Danjaq was to contract composers for no more than customary royalties and provide assurance that music writers would enter into direct agreements with UA assignees. Second, Danjaq was also asked to use its rights as producer to entitle UA to the likeness, name, and biographical data of any Bond composer, performer, or cast member in the promotions of UA's music subsidiaries.[4]

At the same time that Broccoli and Saltzman's deal with UA was formalised, the pair were also finalising a licensing agreement with author Ian Fleming that would allow them to use the character's name and likeness in promoting various Bond merchandise. Fleming granted Danjaq these rights, but under a number of rather stringent conditions. For one thing, Broccoli and Saltzman were free to make licensing arrangements, but they were not to receive any payment in such deals. Fleming also stipulated that Bond's name would be used with no more than five products, and further that these products would be used only with *Dr No* and only within one year of that film's release date. Finally, concerned over the proper image of his literary creation, Fleming also specified that Bond would not be used in the promotion of toiletries such as soaps, deodorants, or laxatives.[5]

With limited opportunities for merchandise tie-ins, Saltzman and Broccoli planned to feature only the most obvious angles of the character. Given Bond's well-documented tastes in spirits and cigarettes, Saltzman and Broccoli sought tie-ins with liquor and tobacco companies, including Old Granddad, Smirnoff, Pall Mall, Players, DuMaurier, and Bond Street Tobacco. UA's publicity staff explored additional tie-ins with Gossard for bikinis, Hathaway for men's shirts, and Triumph for automobiles. Since Sean Connery was an unknown actor at the time, UA felt it was particularly important to use these tie-ins as a means of building up the actor's Bondian persona.[6]

It was soon clear, however, that these merchandising angles would play only a minor role in launching the series. Given Fleming's licensing restrictions, UA initially hoped to promote *Dr No* through publicity photos, television featurettes, and casting gimmicks. Many of UA's early suggestions were centred around Fleming himself, who was at the time the most saleable element of their commodity. Perhaps the most interesting of these ideas was the suggestion to cast Fleming in the role of M, a part that UA believed was especially suited to Fleming's authorial persona. Another idea involved arranging a visit by Fleming to Cape Canaveral and having him introduce Connery to President Kennedy and his family.[7]

After an initial flurry of promotional activity in late 1961 and early 1962, UA decided to bide its time until after *Dr No*'s London premiere. After impressive showings in Europe and the British Isles, UA once again cranked up its publicity machine for the film's US run. In March 1963, UA scheduled a national publicity tour that featured Connery and director Terence Young. As Charles Juroe, then UA's head of European production and publicity distribution, noted years later, it was decided that Bond would always be accompanied by a matched set of ladies – blonde, brunette, and redhead – who would travel with Connery throughout the tour.[8] This tour was followed by a highly publicised Western Hemisphere premiere in Kingston, Jamaica, an area that provided a number of locations for the *Dr No* shoot.

Yet such campaigns, which constitute the customary pre-release hype, are typically quite ephemeral in nature. Personal appearances and premiere parties bring newspaper notices, magazine coverage, and trade reports for a day or two, but aside from establishing name recognition, they generally do not have any lasting value as publicity measures. Merchandising can often serve as a long-term means of publicity and exploitation, but such angles were relatively limited by Danjaq's agreement with Fleming. Thus, as *Dr No*'s various promotional campaigns were developed, it became increasingly apparent that the project's music angles would play a significant role in making James Bond a household name. As earlier music tie-ins showed, hit songs and soundtrack albums could keep a film in the public eye for months and even years.

To this end, UA and Danjaq trumpeted the hiring of British songwriter Monty Norman during the latter months of 1961. Before *Dr No*, Norman was known primarily for his work on the 'French' musical *Irma La Douce* and his work as co-composer on the Terence Fisher film, *House of Fright* (1960). Still while Norman was given the task of writing the score, UA continued to have considerable input regarding the music's overall conception. As a 1962 memo indicates, UA's publicity department made very specific suggestions about music angles they wished to play up. In that meeting, UA executives made two particular requests: they recommended that a 'calypso song about the exploits of James Bond somehow be worked into the motion picture', and they recommended that a 'Scottish theme be written into the score . . . to distinguish James Bond throughout the picture'.[9] From this it seems clear that UA intended to use the music to highlight the film's exotic Jamaican setting and to play up Sean Connery's Scottish heritage.[10]

Upon examining the final product, however, UA evidently decided that Norman's score accommodated only part of this plan. According to Steven Jay Rubin, Norman visited the Jamaican location and became enamoured with calypso music. He then incorporated several calypso songs into his score, including 'Under the Mango Tree', 'Jump Up Jamaica', and an island version of 'Three Blind Mice' entitled 'Kingston Calypso'.[11] By March 1962, Charles Juroe was enthusiastically praising Norman's music in internal correspondence. Writing to fellow publicity staffer Fred Goldberg, Juroe exclaimed, 'The music for DR NO is really exciting, particularly the variation of the theme of "Three Blind Mice". I think that we have a chance for a really successful sound-track album for this film.'[12]

However, while calypso enlivened *Dr No*'s prospects on the soundtrack market, the producers experienced difficulty in getting their desired signature theme, although the exact nature of that difficulty is currently a matter of some dispute. Much of this dispute devolves on the question of John Barry's involvement in the creation of the 'James Bond Theme'. According to Norman, who received the song-writing credit and is legally considered its rightful author, the 'James Bond Theme' grew out of a tune he had written for a planned musical adaptation of V. S. Naipaul's *A House for Mr. Biswas*. After completing the theme, Norman then

8.1 John Barry and the John Barry Seven

contacted EMI producer John Burgess, who suggested hiring Barry to do the theme's orchestration. Describing the final product, Norman says:

> I worked with Barry on what I wanted: a rhythmic sustained sound for the opening four-bar figure; low octave guitar for my main melodic theme; big band for the hard riding middle section, etc. . . . John Barry did a wonderful, definitive orchestration of the Bond theme.[13]

Barry, however, tells a rather different tale.[14] In Barry's version of events, he was called in on *Dr No* by London's UA Music head, Noel Rodgers. Barry claims that the producers were dissatisfied with Norman's attempts to compose a signature theme for Bond, and had asked him to write something for the film's credit sequence. At the time, Barry was considered a valid scoring prospect based on his work for pop singer-actor Adam Faith's film *Beat Girl* (1959), and for a string of instrumental hits recorded with his group, the John Barry Seven. Working quickly, Barry adapted the twangy guitar hook of his combo tune, 'Bees Knees', and combined it with a swinging, Dizzy

Gillespie-like break. Barry says he recorded the theme a few days later with five saxes, nine brass, a solo guitar, and a rhythm section. For his efforts, Barry was paid two hundred pounds and was given the right to record the theme as a single under his Columbia Records contract. Because of their contractual obligations to Norman, though, Saltzman and Broccoli persuaded Barry to give up his song-writing credit in exchange for the promise of future employment.[15] Norman continues to receive the song-writing credit for the 'James Bond Theme' as evidenced by recent Bond films, including *GoldenEye* (1995) and *Tomorrow Never Dies* (1997).

Whether the 'James Bond Theme' was written by Norman or Barry, it gave Saltzman and Broccoli the signature tune they were seeking. Although Barry says that they had initially agreed to use it only during the main titles, the producers went back and began inserting it at several points throughout the film. The most memorable of these was the scene which introduced Bond's character. When we first see him, Bond is playing *chemin de fer* at a casino. Interestingly, director Young initially keeps Bond's face off camera. Bond's presence is signalled only through an over-the-shoulder shot showing him seated at the gaming table and through a close-up of his hands dealing cards to his opponent, an elegantly dressed Sylvia Trench (Eunice Gayson). After losing a couple of rounds to him, Sylvia remarks, 'I admire your luck Mr, er…' Young then cuts to Bond's face as he lights his cigarette and utters his famous tagline, 'Bond. James Bond.' At this point, Barry's theme sneaks in on the soundtrack and creates an indelible link between music and character.

Armed with a distinctive commercial tune, UA's publicity department nevertheless committed only a meagre $5,000 to its music advertising and exploitation budget.[16] With limited resources, UA's publicity staff chose to target radio and a burgeoning audience of teenage film patrons. Calling the 'James Bond Theme' (here identified as the *Dr No* theme) a 'very important promotional tool', UA's exploitation manual recommended targeting disc-jockeys through two strategies. First, the manual suggested that a lovely lady posing as 'Bond's woman' conduct a wider than usual tour of radio and television jocks in support of the film; second, the manual advised local theatre owners to screen *Dr No* for local disc-jockeys and hand out promotional copies of the UA single, which was set for release in April 1962. Additionally, the manual also encouraged theatre owners to play the theme in their lobbies, both before and after screenings, and at school recesses.

Based on their subsequent chart and box office performances, both the film and its music tie-ins were judged only modest successes. *Dr No* would go on to make some $22 million in domestic and foreign rentals, but much of this was made in reissues. During its initial run, the film made a mere $6 million, with only $2 million coming from domestic rentals. The soundtrack, on the other hand, offered some support for the film, but finished nowhere near UA's high expectations. Released by United Artists Records in May 1963, the *Dr No* soundtrack would only reach number 82 on *Billboard*'s charts. A UA single version of the 'James Bond Theme' fared even worse by failing to make *Billboard*'s 'Hot 100' singles chart. The only bright spot was the overseas performance of John Barry's 'James Bond Theme' as a single for Columbia. The record, which was produced as part of Barry's initial agreement with Danjaq, was released in October 1962 and peaked at number 13 on UK record charts. Still, while the music campaign achieved only nominal success, it nonetheless helped Bond achieve some measure of name recognition, and supported Saltzman and Broccoli's belief that they were on the right track.

With the next film, *From Russia with Love*, Saltzman and Broccoli developed the first of many successful singer-songwriter-composer packages for the series. Clearly the most important component of the package was songwriter Lionel Bart, who was coming off his recent success with the stage musical *Oliver!* Publicity for the film called Bart 'Britain's leading theater composer', and noted that the producers were 'fortunate' to hire him.[17] The eminent songwriter, however, was packaged with relative unknowns in the singer and composer slots. Singer Matt Monro was viewed as a rising star on the Liberty label, but had nothing comparable to Bart's credentials. Perhaps in deference to an earlier agreement, Saltzman and Broccoli also hired Barry to replace Norman as the series' featured composer. Yet even as UA touted Barry's television work for *The Human Jungle*, it was apparent that publicising him was something of a problem. Known primarily as a rock and roll instrumentalist, Barry had very few 'legitimate' song-writing or composing credits.

In March 1964, UA released the soundtrack album for *From Russia with Love* on their subsidiary record label to coincide with the film's April release. Improving on the performance of its predecessor, *Russia* reached number 28 on *Variety*'s album charts and remained there for over four months. More importantly, though, the title tune quickly became Unart Music's most recorded song. Within a month of the film's release, Bart's tune was featured in eighteen different single versions, both vocal and instrumental, and also turned up as a track on numerous albums. The heavy activity on the *Russia* music was driving UA's music publishing operations to a peak level and racking up considerable licensing fees in the process.[18]

None of these singles, however, was able to crack *Billboard*'s 'Hot 100'. To some extent, the single's poor performance was likely due to the weak placement of Monro's vocal version within the film. It is heard only twice, first as a snatch of radio music during Bond's picnic with Sylvia Trench, and then later in a more complete version over the end credits. Neither of these instances does a particularly good job of selling the song or reinforcing the film's dramatic material. In the former, the excerpt is so short that it can be easily missed; in the latter, it is easily ignored.

All the elements of the Bond musical formula finally came together with *Goldfinger* in 1964. For the first time, Saltzman and Broccoli gave Barry full musical authority over the score and made him the centrepiece of their musical 'package'. Barry would not only compose and conduct the score, he would also co-write the theme song with Leslie Bricusse and Anthony Newley. The song was written in the early months of 1964, and Newley had already recorded two versions of it two months before shooting was completed. Newley's recordings were probably considered at some point for inclusion in the film, but as Scott Shea points out, they presumably failed in some measure to capture the proper tone of the series.[19]

With the composer and songwriters in place, Saltzman and Broccoli brought in Shirley Bassey, a songstress from UA Records' stable of performers, to complete the package. Bassey turned out to be perfect 'casting' for *Goldfinger*'s title-song for a number of reasons, not the least of which was the great conviction she brought to her performance.[20] For one thing, Bassey was already a star in England and was on the verge of stateside stardom as *Goldfinger* was being produced. For Danjaq, Bassey's name recognition would help gain attention for the film during the build-up to its world premiere in London. For UA Records, on the other hand, the film would be just the thing to propel Bassey to stardom in the States. With a star in the making, Saltzman and Broccoli would not make the same mistake they had made with Monro. Bassey's performance was featured prominently during the film's famous credit sequence, which projects images from the film on the golden body of a bikini-clad woman.

Goldfinger became a huge box office smash and generated a number of hits for UA and its subsidiaries. The film set records during its initial Christmas release and went on to earn nearly $50 million in domestic and foreign rentals. The soundtrack album, released by UA Records in October 1964, eventually topped both *Billboard*'s and *Variety*'s album charts. Within five months of its release, the *Goldfinger* soundtrack had sold 400,000 copies and was certified gold for reaching the $1 million mark in total sales.[21] It was also named one of *Variety*'s Top Fifty albums of 1965.

Though its eventual sales were more modest, Bassey's single was issued in December 1964 and climbed to number 8 on the singles charts. Additionally, Unart Music further profited from the success of some copycat albums: Roland Shaw's *Themes from the James Bond Thrillers* on the London label; UA's own *Music to Read James Bond By*; and Epic Records' *Confidential Sounds for a Secret Agent*, which featured four John Barry tunes, eight originals named after Fleming's unfilmed novels, and one tune by a bass player whose real name was James Bond.[22]

Yet the success of the film and its music were only part of the story. The commercial breakthrough of *Goldfinger* created a veritable mini-industry as Bondmania swept through theatres. The total sales of all of Fleming's Bond novels grew throughout 1964 and 1965 with nearly thirteen million books sold during that two-year period. Similarly, with Fleming's death in August 1964, the floodgates opened on dozens of items of Bond merchandise. These included golf jackets, sheets, jigsaw puzzles, shoes, pyjamas, dolls, trading cards, board games, toy automobiles, lunch boxes, and alarm clocks that played the 'James Bond Theme'. By February 1966 the Licensing Corporation of America estimated that the total sales of Bond merchandise amounted to some $50 million.[23]

With the Bond merchandising machinery operating at full tilt, Saltzman and Broccoli quickly followed *Goldfinger* with *Thunderball*, their fourth Bond production in four years. Budgeted at $5.5 million, *Thunderball* was touted in publicity as 'the biggest Bond of all'. Shooting began around the time of *Goldfinger*'s initial distribution with the expectation of a Christmas 1965 release date.

Early in the production, Saltzman and Broccoli considered changing the title to *Mr Kiss Kiss Bang Bang*, a nickname by which Bond was known in Japan. Barry and Leslie Bricusse were asked to write a song for this new title, which was subsequently recorded by both Dionne Warwick and Shirley Bassey.[24] When the title reverted to *Thunderball*, however, Barry had to quickly come up with a second song to accommodate the name change. Since Bricusse was tied up with another project, Don Black was hired to draft new lyrics for Barry's melody. With two exploitable tunes in hand, Saltzman and Broccoli initially decided to use them both, Tom Jones's title tune for the opening credits and Bassey's version of 'Mr Kiss Kiss Bang Bang' over the closing credits. As *Thunderball*'s release date neared, Saltzman and Broccoli changed their minds yet again and decided to leave Bassey's number out of the film completely.

In anticipation of a *Thunderball* music bonanza, Saltzman and Broccoli renegotiated their original distribution agreement with respect to the music rights. As a 1 October 1965 contract amendment indicates, the basic structure of their original deal was maintained, but with three very significant changes. First of all, Saltzman and Broccoli were to form their own music publishing subsidiary under the laws of Switzerland. This subsidiary would operate as an 'employer for hire' with Danjaq acquiring the various music rights and subsequently assigning them to UA Music. This new arrangement entitled Danjaq to royalties from both music publishing revenues and record sales. Under the new terms, Danjaq would receive a 10 per cent aggregate royalty on records sold in the US and half of the net publishing profits. For its part, UA Music agreed to bear all the direct costs incurred in the exploitation of the music publishing rights in exchange for the reimbursement of these costs and a 10 per cent service fee deducted from the gross music publishing revenues.[25] Seven months after these changes, UA sweetened the deal by extending these arrangements to also cover non-Bonds produced by Saltzman and Broccoli.[26]

At about the same time, publicity for Barry attempted to match the composer with the series' central character. In 1966, for example, *Time* magazine described Barry as a 'swinger in the Bond mould – clothes with an Edwardian flair, fashionable Chelsea apartment, Pickwick Club, E-Type Jaguar (white, XK), E-Type wife (brunette actress, Jane Birken)'.[27] To further reinforce the parallel between Bond and Barry, the latter is photographed sitting in his Jaguar in an obvious attempt to invite comparison with 007's famous Aston Martin.

Basking in *Goldfinger's* afterglow, *Thunderball* matched its predecessor's success on record charts and surpassed it at the box office. *Thunderball* amassed nearly $55 million in total rentals and spawned both a Top Ten album and a Top 25 single. As *Thunderball* entered its foreign run, *Variety* estimated that the first four Bond films had accumulated over $100 million in total box office receipts, with Saltzman and Broccoli's share of this sum amounting to some $26 million.[28]

Due to the unprecedented international success of Bond, hundreds of imitators attempted to cash in on the spy craze. More than thirty secret agent films were released in 1966 alone, many of them made by European and British production companies. Among these were the first entries in the Matt Helm (Dean Martin) and Derek Flint (James Coburn) film series, and the second in Saltzman's Harry Palmer series for UA. The latter starred Michael Caine as a 'thinking man's Bond', and the series featured such Bond stalwarts as John Barry and director Guy Hamilton.[29] Italy contributed some of the oddest films in this espionage cycle, including *Operation Kid Brother* (1967), which starred Sean Connery's brother,

Neil, and featured Bond veterans Daniela Bianchi, Adolfo Celi, Lois Maxwell, and Bernard Lee; and a series of Bond-like westerns which de-emphasised gunplay in favour of explosive gimmickry such as gunpowder cigars and dynamite-laden sombreros.[30]

Outside the domain of cinema, the secret agent fad also began to infiltrate the television and music industries. Borrowing the character names Napoleon Solo and April Dancer from Ian Fleming, producer Norman Felton developed the Bond-inspired *The Man from U.N.C.L.E.* for MGM in 1964. The series became a major success and spawned a number of additional projects for MGM, such as the Stephanie Powers spin-off *The Girl from U.N.C.L.E.* and a group of theatrical features compiled from footage used in the series. *U.N.C.L.E.* was followed by a number of other Bond-inspired shows, including *Get Smart, The Wild, Wild West, Honey West, I Spy, The Baron,* and *Amos Burke – Secret Agent.*[31] Perhaps the weirdest Bond spin-off, however, was an album recorded by popular European jazz organist Ingfried Hoffman, who billed himself as '001'. The album, *From Twen with Love,* was produced by the Philips label and featured a number of tunes parodying the Bond persona. Beside straight versions of 'Goldfinger' and 'Thunderball' were goofy musical spoofs such as 'Yeah Dr No' and 'Vabanque in Casino Royale'.

By November 1966 many European background music companies were churning out music for commercials, industrial films, and television news programmes which was explicitly modelled on Barry's well-known Bond scores. In fact, the demand for jazzy, Bond-ish background music was so high that Mort Ascher, the head of a top background music supplier, complained that the old, straight symphony music could not even be given away.[32]

After the commercial peak of *Goldfinger* and *Thunderball,* sales of Bond songs and soundtrack albums steadily declined throughout the 1960s. Nowhere was this decline more apparent than in 1967's 'Battle of the Bonds', which pitted producer Charles Feldman's *Casino Royale* against Saltzman and Broccoli's *You Only Live Twice.* Though the latter won the battle at the box office, the former won the battle on the record charts. Burt Bacharach's *Casino Royale* soundtrack album, which featured numbers by Herb Alpert and Dusty Springfield, reached number 12 on *Variety*'s album charts and was a radio staple throughout the summer of 1967. On the other hand, the soundtrack for *You Only Live Twice,* featuring Nancy Sinatra's rendition of the title-song, never got higher than number 42 and dropped off *Variety*'s charts after only a month. Continuing this downward trend, the two Bonds that followed, *On Her Majesty's*

Secret Service (1969) and *Diamonds Are Forever* (1971), failed to match even the dubious chart performance of *Twice*.

With Connery's decisive departure from the series in 1972, Saltzman and Broccoli were once again faced with the prospect of launching a new actor as Bond. After considering Burt Reynolds, Robert Redford, and Paul Newman for the role, they settled on Roger Moore, who had previously starred in the television series *The Saint*. Once he was cast, UA began an extensive promotional campaign to sell Moore as the new Bond, and, as with the *Dr No* campaign, music would prove to play an important part in the process. With yet another unknown as Bond, it was incumbent on Saltzman and Broccoli to find a major star for the next Bond theme. If Moore could not sell the picture, then perhaps a catchy theme recorded by a major pop star could.

As the production for *Live and Let Die* (1973) was planned, Saltzman and Broccoli appeared to suffer yet another setback when Barry's commitment to another project prevented him from working on the new Bond. To make up for Barry's absence, Saltzman and Broccoli approached Paul McCartney about the prospect of working on *Live and Let Die*. In the deal that resulted from these negotiations, McCartney agreed to write the title-song, perform it with his group Wings for the credit sequence, and produce a version of it performed by the Fifth Dimension in the 'Filet of Soul' scene.[33] In exchange for his services, McCartney received a $15,000 song-writing fee and a lucrative cut of the music royalties. McCartney and UA agreed to share the copyright on the title-song and split the renewals and performance fees fifty-fifty. Additionally, McCartney was granted a 5 per cent royalty on record sales, a 75 per cent royalty on record club and direct mail sales, a 75 per cent cut of the mechanical license fees, and a commitment from UA to pay for recording and re-use costs.[34]

Though signing McCartney was undoubtedly a coup for UA and Eon Productions, his salary demands put Saltzman and Broccoli in a somewhat awkward position. With a $25,000 total music budget, McCartney's song-writing fee left only $10,000 to pay for the additional scoring, arranging, and conducting services. Clearly Saltzman and Broccoli would not be able to get a composer of Barry's stature since the standard scoring fee was somewhere between $20,000 and $25,000. With this in mind, Saltzman and Broccoli sought out former Beatles producer George Martin. Martin had had very little previous film work, but several other factors worked to his advantage. For one thing, Martin's previous work with both McCartney and UA on previous Beatles films such as *A Hard Day's Night* (1964) and *Yellow Submarine* (1968) made him seem a natural fit for *Live and Let*

Die. Moreover, Martin's work on the Bondish orchestral intro to 'Help' showed that he had a good sense of Barry's style and orchestration. The most important factor, however, was Martin's lack of film experience, which allowed UA to negotiate a lower scoring fee and stay within its music budget.

McCartney's single for *Live and Let Die* was released by Apple Records in the week of 18 June 1973, and became an immediate chart success. The song peaked at number two on *Billboard*'s 'Hot 100' singles chart and remained there for three weeks. The soundtrack album, released about the same time, did not perform quite as well for UA Records, but nevertheless made an admirable showing by cresting at number fifteen on *Billboard*'s charts. With solid record and sheet music sales and an Oscar nomination for McCartney, the Bond theme song re-established its importance both in film promotion and in shaping popular music tastes. Saltzman and Broccoli had taken a calculated risk in using their first rock and roll performer, but McCartney's reputation and enormous popularity overcame any resistance to his style.

In the films after *Live and Let Die*, Bond themes continued to have their share of hits and misses, but on balance no other film series could boast its long-term success. By the time of *The Man With The Golden Gun*, Barry and company had written enough familiar melodies that press-books recommended organising contests around radio programmes of James Bond music. Listeners would be invited to listen for Bond themes and asked to match them to film titles or stills. The wide recognition of Bond music not only made it a vital promotional tool, but also allowed it to function as a remarkably adaptable component of the Bond formula.

Notes

1 Roger Watkins, '007 Sights $2–Bil in Ducats Overall', *Variety*, 13 May 1987, p. 67.

2 Simon Smith, 'Mood Music: An Inquiry into Narrative Film Music', *Screen*, 25.3 (May–June 1984), 78.

3 See Tino Balio, *United Artists: The Company That Changed the Film Industry* (Madison: University of Wisconsin Press, 1987), pp. 253–74, for a more complete account of Saltzman and Broccoli's relationship with United Artists.

4 Distribution agreement between Danjaq and United Artists, UA Collection Addition (Box 3, file 2), Wisconsin Center for Film and Theater Research, State Historical Society Library, Madison. Subsequent citations are from this collection unless otherwise noted.

5 Letter from Ian Fleming to Danjaq, Inc., 3 April 1952 (Box 3, file 4).

6   Memorandum from Sam Kreisler to Mort Nathanson, 9 January 1962 (Box 3, file 4).

7   Kennedy was reported to be an avid reader of Fleming's novels, and in fact *Life* magazine listed *From Russia, With Love* as one of JFK's ten favourite books of all time.

8   Charles Juroe, 'Launching Sean Required Blonde, Brunette, Redhead', *Variety*, 13 May 1987, p. 58.

9   Memorandum from Sam Kreisler to Mort Nathanson, 9 January 1962 (Box 3, file 4).

10 The character of Bond was also of Scottish heritage. According to an obituary written by M in Ian Fleming's *You Only Live Twice*, Bond was born to a Scottish father, Andrew Bond, and a Swiss mother, Monique Delacroix. Yet it is extremely doubtful that the character's literary heritage had any bearing on UA's request. The character's Scottish background had never been a particularly important trait in either the novels or the films. More importantly, Fleming's 'obituary' was not published until 1964, two years after the release of *Dr No*. In fact, as Raymond Benson notes, it is more likely that Fleming invented this bit of Bond's background with Connery's film incarnation in mind. Fleming reportedly believed that Connery was too 'uncouth' when he was first cast, but changed his mind upon seeing the actor portray his character on-screen. See Raymond Benson, *The James Bond Bedside Companion* (New York: Dodd, Mead, and Co., 1984), p. 164; and Lee Pfeiffer and Philip Lisa, *The Incredible World of 007* (New York: Citadel, 1992), p. 16.

11 Steven Jay Rubin, *The James Bond Films* (New York: Arlington House, 1981), p. 18.

12 Letter from Charles Juroe to Fred Goldberg, 23 March 1962 (Box 3, file 4).

13 Monty Norman, quoted in Geoff Leonard and Pete Walker, 'John Barry and James Bond: The Making of the Music', *Film Score Monthly*, 63 (1995), 15–17 (p. 15). The article provides an excellent summary of the internecine struggles behind the composition of the Bond theme.

14 Over the past ten years, Barry has tried to reclaim authorship of the 'James Bond Theme' in published interviews. For accounts of Barry's work on *Dr No*, see Rubin, *The James Bond Films*, p. 21; Wolfgang Breyer, 'An Interview with John Barry', *Soundtrack!*, 7.25 (1988), 28–31 (p. 28); Fred Karlin and Rayburn Wright, *On the Track: A Guide to Contemporary Film Scoring* (New York: Schirmer Books, 1990), pp. 6–7; and Royal S. Brown, 'My Name is Barry . . . John Barry', *Fanfare*, 16.5 (May–June 1993), 118–25 (p. 121).

15 Though Barry's account is not corroborated by any documents in the archival resources I consulted, there is some strong circumstantial evidence to support his claim. For one thing, the theme is stylistically quite different from much of the other music of the score. This does not prove that two different men worked on the score, but Barry's claim does offer some explanation as to why such differences exist. Moreover, as Barry himself points out, Norman was

primarily known as a lyricist. Here again this does not disprove Norman's authorship, but it does support the assumption that Norman wrote the calypso songs but did not write the instrumental theme music. Finally, and importantly, Barry, of course, went on to score another eleven or so Bond films while Norman did not score another film, Bond or otherwise. If a deal had been struck by Barry and Danjaq, we would have to conclude that Saltzman and Broccoli rejected the successful composer of their first film in favour of an untried newcomer. Such a hypothesis makes little sense from a business perspective (why throw away a proven commodity?), and even less sense from an aesthetic perspective. In light of all these things, and the stylistic similarities between the 'James Bond Theme', Barry's 'Bees Knees', and his work on the later Bond films, one might conclude that Barry is indeed the composer of the signature Bond theme.

16 In part this was because the overall production budget for *Dr No* was itself relatively small, approximately $900,000.

17 Undated production summary of *From Russia with Love* (Box 3, file 6).

18 '"Russia" Booms UA Music Firm', *Variety*, 6 May 1964, p. 67.

19 Scott Shea, liner notes to *The Best of James Bond: 30th Anniversary Limited Edition*, EMI Records, 1992.

20 According to Barry, this conviction was one of the big reasons for the song's success. See Shea, *The Best of James Bond*; and 'Tunesmith Keeps in Mind the Kid on the Edge of His Seat', *Variety*, 13 May 1987, p. 66.

21 'UA Label Mines Big Sales in "Goldfinger" track', *Variety*, 10 March 1965, p. 59.

22 See 'Epic Riding "007" into Sales Groove with SESAC Deal', *Variety*, 31 March 1965, p. 53. The bass player referred to here is actually better known as Jimmy Bond.

23 '"Batman" Merchandizing Bonanza to Surpass "James Bond" Record Take', *Variety*, 23 February 1966, p. 1.

24 Shea, *The Best of James Bond*.

25 Letter from United Artists Corporation to Danjaq, SA, 1 October 1965 (Box 3, file 3).

26 UA memorandum, 30 March 1966 (Box 3, file 3).

27 'Aboard the Bondwagon', *Time*, 14 January 1966, p. 65. This linkage between composer and character has continued to the present; a May–June 1993 interview in *Fanfare* was titled, 'My Name is Barry ... John Barry' as a spoof of Bond's familiar greeting.

28 See Mike Gross, 'Record Men Roll 007's in "Thunderball" Game', *Billboard*, 4 December 1965, pp. 1–6; and 'As Fantastic As Its Sexy Sleuth, 007 Pix Rentals Hit $100,000,000', *Variety*, 12 October 1966, p. 1.

29 'Broccoli Bond Spawned Imitators', *Variety*, 13 May 1987, p. 62.

30 'Bond-Type Horse Operas in Spain', *Variety*, 14 June 1966, p. 25.

31 'Broccoli Bond Spawned Imitators', *Variety*, p. 74.

32 '"James Bond Music" Calling Tune in Today's Background Themes', *Variety*, 23 November 1966, p. 51.

33 Memorandum from Ronald Kass to Harry Saltzman (Box 3, file 10). Note that the Fifth Dimension did not end up recording the song for the film. Instead the number was performed by RCA recording artist B.J. Arnau.

34 UA Office Rushgram, 15 March 1973 (Box 3, file 10).

9

Cynthia Baron

Doctor No: *Bonding Britishness to racial sovereignty*

James Bond's legendary status as womaniser and secret agent has drawn attention to Ian Fleming's representation of sexuality and the Cold War.[1] But the Bond phenomenon discloses not only 'a reworking of images of female sexuality in line with the requirements of a "liberated" male sexuality, [and] a movement from Cold War to detente and back again', but a 'shift from an archaic to a modernised myth of nationhood' as well.[2] Thus, while 007's humour and 'masterful' style have consistently reassured the First World of its hegemonic position, and have provided a nostalgic bandage for England's wounded pride in the 'post-colonial' era, the Bond phenomenon also illuminates aspects of a 'modern' British identity that emerged in opposition to 'colonial' Others who had come to England to find a home. Bond's relationship to this 'new' identity invites us to re-examine British strategies of self-definition in the 'post-colonial' era, for 007's exploits remain steeped in the discourse of 'Orientalism' which had positioned the East as mysterious, incomprehensible, and pathologised in order to justify Western imperialism.[3]

The British sensibility that developed during the late 1950s and early 1960s was also a reaction to the older generation of 'feather-headed fuddy-duddies'. This 'modern' stance was not only important to the Bond phenomenon, but it shaped the social realism of the 'Angry Young Men' and British New Cinema, as well as the shimmering theatricalism of British Pop that helped make 'Swinging England' the centre of Western popular culture.[4] One might see the early 007 adventures as providing a transition from British New Cinema to films like *Darling* (1965) which rejected the bleakness of social realism, for Bond's espionage missions caused colourful images of the international jet-set to be *imported* into the Mother Country. But the agenda of the Bond films was quite different from other British films of the period, for 007 did not critique Britain's welfare state or class system, but instead implicitly attacked the older generation's 'liberal' complacency and inveterate mismanagement (the charge of mismanagement being tantamount to that of failing to be British). These 'blunders', in the mind of young reactionaries, were the reason that the Empire was lost, and that there had come to be a blurring of the boundary between 'trueblood' and Other.

Throughout the Bond films, 007's Cold War and sexual adventures masked the fact that Bond was an imperial hero, who provided a way for Britishness to continue to be defined in opposition to the 'dark' people of the world. Even in a film such as *Octopussy* (1983), which occurs late in the series, and which foregrounds the Cold War and anxieties about modern technology and emancipated women, Britishness is defined in terms of an absolute difference between white and non-white. For example, Bond's encounters in Britain's former colony, India, are presented as far more threatening to Bond than the mind-boggling adventures in East Germany. The opposition between Bond and the exotic world of tigers and sword-swallowers is at the base of the film's way of defining Britishness, and so the narrative ends, not after Bond has disarmed the Russian atomic bomb, but only after he has rescued Octopussy from the Khan, in a sequence that begins with Bond and Q literally flying the Mother Country's colours (they are aboard an air balloon covered by the British flag).

The film that started it all, *Dr No* (1962), illustrates the series' methods of representing British identity in a particularly forceful way, because it clearly identifies the 'British Race' with natural, undisputed ascendancy and a psychic/sexual autonomy that must be rigorously maintained. The film identifies Britishness with racial sovereignty, and 007's mission is to recreate the grounds for that sovereignty. Bond is the ultimate Orientalist, for with the spy's 'license to look' 007 polices the boundaries of Britishness, and with his 'license to kill' reactivates the power of the British Empire. Producers Harry Saltzman and Albert Broccoli chose to adapt *Dr No* because they saw the novel as being topical, and of interest to an international (i.e. American) market, for it dealt with, and provided at least a fictional excuse for, the repeated failures at Cape Canaveral.[5] Yet even before this, *Dr No* was a central text in the Bond phenomenon, for while it was the sixth Fleming novel to recount the exploits of James Bond, 'the first five adventures had met with only routine responses from newspaper and magazine critics either attracted or repelled according to personal tastes', but with the publication of *Dr No* in 1958, the 'critical hoopla about all the Bond books began to snowball'.[6]

Some would argue that *Dr No* must be seen as a parodic project, and as an ironic commentary on conventions used to represent Britishness.[7] The Fleming novels had initially occupied 'the category of superior quality, "literary" spy fiction', designed for a knowing reader who saw the novels as 'flirtatious, culturally knowing parodies of the spy-thriller genre'.[8] This original (upper-class, British) audience assumed that the novels' chauvinism, racism, and sexism could be discounted. They believed that these elements were to be considered only in terms of their 'purely formal role in parodying by means of excess, the earlier imperialist spy-thrillers of such writers as John Buchan and Cyril McNeile'.[9] But the novels and the films have allowed, and perhaps even encouraged audiences to heroicise and glamorise Bond, rather than see him as a parodic anti-hero.[10] Moments of stylistic excess do not generate a larger ideological parody of the master narratives through which the fiction structures itself, and even in its least spectacular passages, the text defines Bond through tropes of Orientalism *in an entirely unmediated way*.[11] Furthermore, every element is integral to the text's overall economy, for the overlapping narratives of colonial power, white racism, and patriarchy serve to naturalise one another. Thus, the films' parody of earlier spy-thrillers does not critique the values embedded in the genre, but instead provides a way to repackage outdated mythologies of Britain's imperial past.

A context for Dr No

In the early 1950s, Churchill could promote the idea that England was the only country which had a central part in the 'three great circles among the free nations and democracies' (with the three circles defined by England's relationship to America, Europe, and the Commonwealth).[12] But by the end of the 1960s, Britain was dependent on American military force, had been denied entrance into the European Common Market, and 'was shorn of empire except for headaches like Rhodesia and Ulster'.[13] The event that most clearly symbolised Britain's painful readjustment to a changed world was the Suez war of 1956, when Britain, in consort with the French and the Israelis, attacked the Egyptian Republic in response to Egypt nationalising the Suez Canal. The United States and the United Nations condemned the action, and the occupation ended after one week.

The break-up of the Empire began in India, Pakistan, and Ceylon in 1948. In the late 1950s, Sudan, Ghana, Malaya, and Singapore became independent, and England turned to the United Nations to resolve matters in Cyprus, as it had done a decade earlier with Palestine. Jamaica, the setting for Bond's exploits in *Dr No*, established internal self-government in 1959, and was granted independence in 1962. The withdrawal of France and Belgium from Africa in 1960 forced England to grant independence to eight former colonies on that continent. Altogether, seventeen British colonies in Africa, Asia, the Middle East, and the Caribbean became independent between 1960 and 1961. Britain redoubled its efforts to secure its influence east of Suez, particularly in oil-rich territories, until the late 1960s. But this seems to have been a last, desperate attempt to maintain a global role, for the British had to contend with the fact that between 1945 and 1960 'some 500 million people in former British dependencies became completely self-governing'.[14]

Yet a monolithic view of the 'post-colonial period' obscures the fact that in the late 1950s and early 1960s, the British were 'basking in the glory of having been the one unconquered European power, [and] of being an imperial power which had graciously condescended to grant independence to a number of her imperial possessions'.[15] In spite of the lasting effects of wartime devastation, the British 'were living in an era of unprecedented material prosperity and were in the process of being relieved of much of the remaining apparatus of social control dating from Victorian times'.[16] These factors gave rise to Britain's new 'meritocracy', and they begin to account for the emergence of 'Swinging England' as the cultural trend-setter for the entire world. During this period, the British exported not only music and fashion, but a social revolution and a new postmodern aesthetic. Thus, economic affluence and its attendant freedoms, and Britain's unfailing sense of confidence, were crucial in the formation of 'modern' Britishness.

The Fleming novels, and the Bond films produced by Saltzman and Broccoli, played a part in this transformation, for they echoed a perspective that had crystallised in John Osborne's *Look Back in Anger* (1956). The play, and later the film, reflected the mounting Liberal attack on state subsidies, for it critiqued England's rigid class structure, and assailed the 'moral bankruptcy of the welfare state'.[17] What links the Bond thrillers to the Free Cinema Movement, British New Cinema, and the work of novelists such as David Storey, John Braule, Alan Sillitoe, and Shelagh Delaney, is an anger and contempt for 'the spiritual torpor that had been induced' by situations and structures for which the older generation was responsible, and the articulation of an emerging 'modern' outlook that placed a premium on individual action.[18]

This new sensibility focused on 'style'. Bond's version of 'modern' Britishness, however, rather than being defined by individual 'style' or

Mod clothing, entailed the 'license to kill'. I believe that 007's stance represents a popular, and very troubling British response to the unprecedented immigration from the West Indies, India, and Pakistan. By the mid-1960s, 2 per cent of Britain's total population was already made up of people from the colonies. Observers point out that when the Empire crumbled, the lower class realised 'that they were at the bottom of the heap', but immigrants from the former colonies soon provided 'people they could look down on in their very own country'.[19] David Frost and Anthony Jay wryly explain that here 'the Empire, that much-abused institution, performs its last and its greatest service for the Mother Country. From Trinidad and Barbados, from India and Africa, it sends its sons to save the class system.'[20]

Doctor No

Imperialism and racism intersect in the opening moments of the film. As the title sequence ends, we begin to hear a 'Jamaican' version of 'Three Blind Mice'. The song plays over the silhouettes of three figures walking with canes, and then continues over the first live images: three (blind) black men making their way through Kingston. The sequence prepares us for an ironic twist, for the song tells us that the mice 'cut da pussy cat's tail'. But, perhaps more importantly, it also calls on racial stereotypes, and the coloniser's image of the childlike/childish 'native' in need of imperial control, for the black men are relegated to a world of children's nursery rhymes. These 'Orientalised' figures contrast sharply with the British characters we next meet; they belong to a private club who spend their afternoons engaged in gentlemanly games of strategy, exchanging witty repartee, and drinking cool cocktails served by a docile manservant. This group of Englishmen, of course, includes gentlemen of high rank: a general, and secret agent Strangways, who maintains the rigour of the Mother Country by making contact with his superiors every day at precisely the same time.

The 'proper' relation between the British and their subjects continues to exist into the next scene, as Strangways gives a few coins to the 'three blind mice' on his way to his car. But the relationship is reversed in the next instant when they turn and shoot him. The threat posed by the black men builds, for the next scene opens with a black hand opening the gate to Strangways' compound. The 'three blind mice' surround the room in which Strangways' blonde assistant, dressed in a tight white blouse, begins the radio transmission to London. Three quick pans show her point of view just as the men open fire. The novel is especially clear in the meaning of this scene, for it tells us that 'Mary Trueblood opened her mouth to scream. The man smiled broadly. Slowly, lovingly, he lifted the gun and shot her three times in and around the left breast.'[21] I would argue that the scene's overlapping rape and murder imagery establishes racial impurity as the 'real' threat to the Empire, for here, death is inextricably joined to transgressive sexual unions between white women ('true-bloods') and non-white men. This episode also establishes the threat posed by 'black hands' – an image that comes to dominate the film's representation of archvillain Dr No, who is identified with, and finally reduced to, his false black hands.

The contrast between the nascent chaos in the colony, and the stately order of the British homeland, is reconfirmed in the next scene, which opens with an image of Big Ben in the distance at dawn, then moves to the interior of the secret service agency which is 'manned' by a compliant female secretary and dozens of efficient, young white men in white shirts who follow clearly established protocol in dealing with the interrupted radio transmission. The film goes on to present the contrast between British 'trueblood' and pathologised 'dark' people in rather hyperbolic terms, for a secret service agent is sent to find Bond in his exclusive gambling club, which proudly displays a large painting of a 'thoroughbred' horse in its foyer.

Bond's arrival in Jamaica announces his role as imperial hero, and presents the island as a 'natural' site for colonial adventure. Bond demonstrates his right to rule by mastering the Orientalised Others he encounters who consist of 'sneaky' Asians and 'bungling' blacks. The difference between 007 and the 'natives' in need of imperial control is demonstrated early on, perhaps most clearly in the humorous moment of a scene where Bond is using a Geiger counter to establish the radioactivity of rock samples Strangways had been collecting. Bond examines the boat which had carried the samples, and then casually waves the device's huge white wand between his legs as he tells his intent listeners what he has found. Bond's 'phallic power' contrasts sharply with the 'native innocence' of Quarrel, the black man who had assisted Strangways, for Quarrel tells 007 he is afraid to go back to Crab Key because there is a dragon on the island. Quarrel finally agrees to take 007, but largely it seems because he cannot give Bond the directions since he plots a course by *instinct*.

Bond's exploits in Jamaica not only demonstrate the British right to rule; they also re-establish the 'proper' boundary between 'trueblood' and non-white. For example, even before going to Crab Key, 007 callously eliminates British Professor Dent, who had threatened the 'integrity' of British racial sovereignty by working for Dr No. Furthermore, throughout the adventure the power of Bond's 'secret intelligence' depends on a type of knowledge that is, like Orientalism, 'a form of paranoia'. As Edward Said explains, 'Orientalism is absolutely anatomical and enumerative, to use its vocabulary is to engage in the particularising and dividing of things Oriental into manageable parts.'[22] This is precisely 007's 'language', for as a secret agent, he is by definition engaged in watching, enumerating, and particularising, and his exploits mobilise a knowledge of the Other that exists for the sake of controlling it. Bond exemplifies the perspective of the Westerner Said describes, who surveys 'as if from a peculiarly suited vantage point the passive, seminal, feminine, even silent and supine East'.[23] Michael Denning echoes this point in saying that Bond's power lies in the spy's 'license to look'.[24] Thus, in the same way that 'the Orient is *watched*', and the European 'tours the Orient, is a watcher, never involved, always detached', 007 tours the globe in search of adventure and is 'always ready for new examples of . . . bizarre jouissance'.[25]

Like imperialist discourse itself, the 'paranoia' of *Dr No* leads to continual classification of the Other. This process is most obvious in the film's representations of racial Others, who are neatly categorised in terms of the threat represented to the British Self.[26] For example, Quarrel embodies the 'proper' relationship between British imperial power and the Other, for he exists as an appendage to the British imperialist, and is the innocent, eternally loyal servant who follows the Englishman unquestioningly. Moreover, Quarrel is a caricature, for the character stutters and drinks rum when he is afraid, and is played by John Kitzmuller, whose bulging eyes invite the character to be read as the stereotyped 'spook'.

By comparison, Dr No occupies the space of the threatening or boundary-transgressing Other, for No is a hybrid who speaks the language of power. We are given a sense of No's power when Professor Dent visits Crab Key early in the story, and we begin to see the immense scale of No's operation. Dent's 'meeting' is designed to give us the impression that No is 'all powerful', for it takes place with Dent trapped in a surreal cell, and No represented by a booming, disembodied voice. Throughout the narrative, the British try to neutralise the threat Dr No poses to 'truebloods' by always referring to the half-Chinese, half-German villain as Chinese. Similarly, when Bond and Dr No meet, 007 attempts to put a distance between himself and the half-breed by identifying No with the communist bloc. But the 'danger' to British racial sovereignty that

9.1 Dr No (Joseph Wiseman)

Dr No represents lies precisely in his rejection of categorisation, for as he tells Bond, 'east, west, just points on the compass, one side as stupid as the other'.

The magnitude of No's threat to the boundary between 'trueblood' and non-white is revealed by the fact that he is not only a half-breed, but has even double-crossed people from his 'dark' side, the Tong society. The novel conveys the threat No represents in an especially forceful way, for it tells us that No has usurped his father's place, naming himself Julius after his father, and No for his rejection of him and all authority. Similarly, the film does not simply position Dr No as the racialised Other. It also presents him as the idea gone wrong, as the site of disavowal, for No becomes the exorbitant Other in his valorisation of the criminal mind. As Dr No lectures Bond on the virtues that set the superior man apart from the vices of the herd, it becomes clear that without this pathologised representation of power, Bond's 'license to kill' would take on a very different image, for even Dr No can see that the two men have a great deal in common.

But Bond, and the film, resist the connection between the two throughout the narrative, for Bond's legitimate authority and agency must be contrasted with No's illegitimate attempt to grasp power. The film must conceal the connection between Dr No's criminality and Bond's license to kill, for Bond's exploits are supposed to demonstrate not only the existence of the British Empire, but its legitimacy as well. In their first face to face encounter, Bond plants the notion of Dr No's 'impotency' for he chides the villain, asking 'does toppling missiles make up for having no hands?' Similarly, 007 assures us that his British, 'trueblood' code of conduct would obtain in any situation, for when Dr No presents Bond with the possibility of joining SPECTRE, Bond explains that if he were to join, he would immediately revenge the deaths of Strangways and Quarrel.

The racial and imperial discourses established from the beginning of the film over-determine every aspect of the encounters between 007 and Dr No. For example, No concludes their meeting when he decides that Bond is 'just a stupid policeman', and while the comment could be damning – for Bond's status as a mere policeman is precisely what the film must disprove – the racial and imperial hierarchy already in place forecloses any possibility of No presenting a critique of 007. Similarly, racialised distinctions preserve the 'proper' relationship between Bond and No to the end, for the last image of Dr No is of his false black hands slipping into his own tank of bubbling radioactive water, a sign, it seems, of the retribution promised to any 'black hand' raised against the Empire, and of the impotency of any 'black hands' that might try to wrest control from British 'truebloods'.

'Post-colonial' imperialism

The fact that Jamaica is presented as a site where Bond's Britishness can be fully expressed reveals an important connection between the Bond figure and the heroes who populate the imperial fiction of Rider Haggard.[27] In both cases, the Englishman 'needs Africa, India or some distant Ruritania to act out the role of his destiny'.[28] The connection between Bond and Haggard's imperial heroes resides in their shared opposition to liberals who embody 'a misplaced humanism, a penchant for ease and a degenerate morality'.[29] The Haggard novels illuminate the paradox one finds in *Dr No*, namely that Bond is the lone secret agent 'who could do it all – but always on behalf of the ruling order',[30] for as Wendy Katz points out, Haggard's adventurer is also 'the traditional solitary man' whose 'devotion to Empire often involves a submergence of self'.[31] She explains that the hero's paradox becomes resolved through fate, for the Haggard hero is born to follow 'the call of his destiny', and 'the Englishman's destiny had called him to build the Empire . . . the proof of this destiny was in fact the Empire itself'.[32] For Bond, the proof of his destiny as global policeman in a post-colonial world resides in the collection of villains he must face.

The 'imperial' stance did not vanish in the post-colonial period, for its 'logic' would be echoed in the modern representations of masculinity that *Dr No* and the Bond phenomenon as a whole foreshadowed.[33] Bond's anti-democratic style, that made him ill-suited for life at home, was emblematic of the image of masculinity frequently offered by 1960s films. The image projected in the Bond films demonstrated that the modern hero 'distrusted everything but his own effectiveness'.[34] The imperial/ modern heroes were consistently positioned in opposition to the effeteness of the times: 'whether a soldier, an adventurer, or simply an embodiment of "manliness"', the hero believed that his society was getting soft or somehow straying from its course.[35] 1960s narratives often revealed the notion that the hero's strong action had actually created and now confirmed the 'established' order. In *Dr No*, the efficacy of Crown and country are a consequence rather than a cause of Bond's actions. The image of the world with Britain in control is an effect of his exploits rather than the source of his success.

The racism that pervades the 'post-colonial' Bond films and 'colonial' Haggard novels arises from the texts' method of defining the hero's image.[36] Katz explains that 'racism, sometimes understood as a cause of imperialism, ought instead to be seen as . . . a natural "consequence" of Empire'.[37] Similarly in *Dr No*, it may appear that the narrative simply reflects a bigoted mentality, but the text's racism actually serves to legitimise Bond's role as imperial policeman, and Britain's place in a post-colonial world. It seems possible to understand the film's project of British self-definition in terms of what Hannah Arendt calls 'race thinking', and there are a number of points of contact between Bond's image and what we have come to think of as indices of a fascist stance: racism, an anti-democratic mode of operation alongside a devotion to country, and the spectacle of power that arises from a license to kill.[38]

Andrea White has noted that the policeman is often emblematic of a civilised society in colonial literature.[39] Her observation points to the complex relationship between Gramsci's notion of political and civil societies, and to the fact that 007 stands at the intersection of the two realms. On the one hand, Bond, like the policeman, embodies military might in its most literal and familiar form, while at the same time, his role is essentially symbolic, presumably inviting rather than forcing compliance with the law. But if Michel Foucault is right and each successive era simply deploys a new modality of power, the modern policeman may appear to be another civil servant when he in fact embodies the structure of knowledge and power of the earlier, military age. Thus, Bond's fictional exploits of policing represent a provocative means of creating consent, for the power of Bond and every other imperial policeman resides in physical force. Yet in Bond's case, consent is actually secured by the narrative desire generated by the fiction.

Bond's role as the global policeman also illuminates the intersection between Orientalism and domestic regimes of discipline and punishment.[40] Both discourses focus on departure from the norm, with the 'delinquent' located in an entirely different world, and labelled not by reference to a specific act, but instead to a way of life.[41] The criminal and the racialised Other are positioned as exorbitant and/or in need of rehabilitation. Foucault points out that the delinquent is not outside the law, but instead is the very heart of the law.[42] Similarly, Dr No is not outside the imperial system Bond polices, but instead is the very reason for its existence.[43]

Foucault's distinctions between the significance of public executions and prisons clarify the role played by 007's relentless acts of retribution. Bond's dependence on surveillance and secrecy are related to the more 'modern' prison system, but the spectacle of his vengeance and the exercise of his license to kill bears a striking resemblance to the ceremonial punishment of old monarchical law.[44] When Bond eliminates a villain, it appears to be on behalf of society, yet its fantastic fictional expression takes the form of a right to punish that is more closely related to 'the vengeance of the sovereign'.[45] Thus, Bond's acts of retribution echo the monarch's exercise of terror, and in fact restore the power of the Empire. As Foucault explains, 'the public execution did not re-establish justice; it reactivated power'.[46]

Phantom twitchings of an amputated limb

The film *Dr No* was produced as a result of the rising popularity of the Fleming novels. This popularity can be related to Britain's declining position in the world, for 'in the aftermath of the national humiliation of the Suez fiasco, Bond constituted a figure around which, imaginarily, the real trials and vicissitudes of history could be halted and put into reverse'.[47] But *Dr No* is not simply a knee-jerk reaction to lost Empire, for the era was also a time of affluence and energy, and the Bond phenomenon 'initiated a process of reformation of more traditional fictional representation of Englishness', and facilitated an adjustment 'from one mythic conception of Englishness to another'.[48]

Dr No represents a rupture with the past, yet the film indicates a 'reluctance to abandon the notion of reviving an imperial past in a new form', for it is quite clearly engaged in preserving and justifying British privilege.[49] The discourse of Orientalism that structures the film reflects not only the concern that the global Empire was being reduced to the span of the British Isles. It also discloses an anxiety about the 'integrity' of the boundary between coloniser and colonised, which was being threatened by the unprecedented immigration of people from the former colonies. The shrinking Empire *and* the 'incursion' of the colonised into the coloniser's homeland foregrounded the problems of defining Britishness in terms of difference. Thus, in the face of lost Empire *and* lost racial homogeneity at home, *Dr No* defined Britishness as racial sovereignty, with the racial Other, and particularly the racially mixed Other, presented as the threat to British 'truebloods'.

Post-colonial theory has often addressed the lasting influence of colonialism on the colonised. It has also considered the fact that the process of producing difference between coloniser and colonised opens a space for resistance to the coloniser. Yet *Dr No* suggests that hegemonic power's instability also provides motivation for it to do whatever is necessary to occlude the gap between its 'appearance as original and authoritative and its articulation as repetition and difference'.[50] This (reactionary) project comes into view in *Dr No* precisely because the film mobilises notions of British racial sovereignty, which functions in terms of difference, yet is a 'natural' difference that transcends the vagaries of history – as long as the British maintain their psychic and sexual borders.[51]

Notes

1   See Joan Mellen, *Big, Bad Wolves: Masculinity in the American Film* (New York: Pantheon Books, 1977).

2   Tony Bennett and Janet Woollacott, *Bond and Beyond: The Political Career of a Popular Hero* (New York: Methuen, 1987), p. 281. Also see p. 21, p. 141.

3   Edward Said, *Orientalism* (New York: Vintage Books, 1979), p. 6.

4   The connection between the slick Bond films and the gritty British New Cinema films exists at least in the person of Harry Saltzman. Saltzman, who co-produced the Bond series, had produced the film version of John Osborne's *Look Back in Anger* (1959), directed by Tony Richardson, and, with Osborne and Richardson, had formed Woodfall Films (1959–63) which produced *The Entertainer* (1960), and *Saturday Night and Sunday Morning*

(1960), and *The Loneliness of the Long Distance Runner* (1962). One might also note that American-born Albert Broccoli had been producing films in England under the auspices of the British company, Warwick Films, and that until *Never Say Never Again* (1983) all of the Bond films were directed by British directors: Terence Young, Guy Hamilton, Lewis Gilbert, and Peter Hunt.

5   The producers had originally considered *Dr No* and *Thunderball* as the first Fleming novels to adapt. They went with *Dr No* when *Thunderball* ran into litigation problems.

6   Ann Boyd, *The Devil With James Bond* (Richmond: John Knox Press, 1967), p. 37.

7   For example, the novel announces its tongue-in-cheek stance in the very first sentence: 'Punctually at six o'clock the sun set with a last yellow flash behind the Blue Mountains.' (Ian Fleming, *Dr No* (New York: Signet Books, 1959), p. 7.) Similarly, the film's opening song, 'Three Blind Mice', can be taken as a self-parody.

8   Bennett and Woollacott, *Bond and Beyond*, p. 23, p. 83. In 1957, when Bond's fame began to spread, the intended audience began to express 'public concern' about the effect the novels might have on untutored readers who would not understand that Fleming was writing tongue-in-cheek. See Bennett and Woollacott, *Bond and* Beyond, p. 23, p. 29; also see Boyd, *The Devil*, p. 38.

9   Bennett and Woollacott, *Bond and Beyond*, p. 23.

10 It may be that positive values are assigned to Bond simply because he is the hero. Still, as Richard Dyer points out, 'the norm too is constructed', and it is the task of analysis to articulate how positive features of a hero are created by displacing negative features onto the Other. See Richard Dyer, 'White', *Screen*, 29.4 (1988), 44–64 (p. 44).

11 For example, the novel presents the 'proper' alignment of women in unproblematic terms. Honeychile Rider is an object for men's pleasure. She is also identified with amoral Nature, especially in opposition to Bond's civilising influence, and so becomes the site for Bond to express his Englishness. The novel presents Bond's view of helping/mastering Honey in the following way: 'it was as if some beautiful animal had attached itself to him. There would be no dropping the leash until he had solved her problems for her' (Fleming, *Dr No*, p. 102). Like all the women Bond ends up with, Honey is descended from trueblood colonisers, for her father travelled the globe, cataloguing, analysing, particularising the inchoate 'Orient'.

12 Quoted in David Reynolds, *Britannia Overruled: British Policy and World Power in the Twentieth Century* (New York: Longman, 1991), p. 202.

13 Reynolds, *Britannia Overruled*, p. 233. The fact that the era was dominated by America and the Soviet Union was made clear during the Cuban Missile Crisis when the United States squared off with the Russians without even consulting the British.

14 David Thompson, *England in the Twentieth Century* (Harmondsworth: Penguin, 1963), p. 284.

15 Arthur Marwick, *Britain in the Century of Total War* (Boston: Little Brown, 1968), p. 407.

16 Marwick, *Century of Total War*, p. 407.

17 See Marwick, *Century of Total War*, p. 429; David Cook, *A History of Narrative Film* (New York: Emory University, 1990), p. 593.

18 Cook, *A History of Narrative Film*, p. 592.

19 David Frost and Anthony Jay, *The English* (New York: Stein and Day, 1968), p. 41, p. 42.

20 Frost and Jay, *The English*, p. 42. Marwick makes a similar point in proposing that the British government's response (the Immigrant's Act of 1962 that put a ceiling on immigration, and required all immigrants to have special skills or a position waiting for them) seemed to give 'official endorsement to what a wealth of evidence was already making too plain: racial discrimination was already firmly established in the British Isles' (Marwick, *Century of Total War*, p. 442).

21 Fleming, *Dr No*, p. 13.

22 Said, *Orientalism*, p. 72.

23 Said, *Orientalism*, p. 138.

24 Michael Denning, *Cover Stories: Narrative and Ideology in the British Spy Thriller* (London: Routledge & Kegan Paul, 1987), p. 102.

25 Said, *Orientalism*, p. 103.

26 For example, the novel frames the exotic other's 'history' in Orientalised terms, giving its account according to contrasting racial histories.

27 Haggard's novels include *She, King Solomon's Mines*, and *Allan Quatermain*. The reactionary character of 007's 'modern' Britishness becomes especially clear when contrasted with the liberal critique of Empire that informs Paul Scott's *The Jewel in the Crown* (1992). *Dr No* is also different from Joseph Conrad's *Heart of Darkness*. For Conrad, 'darkness' exists in the heart of the imperialist, but for Fleming darkness exists in the colony and serves as proof that something must be done.

28 Wendy Katz, *Rider Haggard and the Fiction of Empire* (Cambridge: Cambridge University Press, 1987), p. 83. Dr No's image of 007 as a global policeman who ensures that Britain will remain in control of the world is especially clear in light of earlier adventure fiction. Bond's curious position as the imperialist without an empire can be related to the adventure genre itself, for the genre's development has been understood as a 'justification of the existence of an embattled upper class . . . and as a glorification of its deeds'. See Andrea White, *Joseph Conrad and the Adventure Tradition* (Cambridge: Cambridge University Press, 1993), p. 71.

29 Katz, *Rider Haggard*, p. 48; see also White, *Joseph Conrad*, p. 87.

30 Mellen, *Big, Bad Wolves*, p. 262.

31 Katz, *Rider Haggard*, p. 86.

32 Katz, *Rider Haggard*, p. 86.

33 Through the popularity of both the novels and the films, James Bond became the most pervasive male image in the world in the 1960s. See Mellen, *Big, Bad Wolves*, p. 249.

34 Mellen, *Big, Bad Wolves*, p. 230. Mellen draws a connection between Bond and the characters played by Clint Eastwood beginning with the Italian westerns.

35 Katz, *Rider Haggard*, p. 61.

36 *Dr No* follows the example of Haggard's fiction in its obsession with policing racial mixing. For example, *King Solomon's Mines* insists that 'the sun cannot mate with darkness nor the white with the black' (Rider Haggard, *Three Adventure Novels* (New York: Dover, 1951), p. 394).

37 Katz, *Rider Haggard*, p. 131.

38 Quoted in Katz, *Rider Haggard*, p. 25. There are differences, of course. Still, as Arendt points out, race thinking exists not only in the ideology of racial purity associated with Nazi Germany, but in the 'national sectarianism' associated with the colonisation of Australia, New Zealand, and Canada, as well.

39 See White, *Joseph Conrad*, p. 96.

40 The system of representation that Said examines under the rubric of Orientalism mirrors the discourse Foucault argues has developed from the carceral system. Said's analysis echoes Foucault's observation that power produces reality, and shares with it the view that 'structure' produces value systems. See Michel Foucault, *Discipline and Punish* (New York: Vintage Books, 1979), p. 194.

41 See Foucault, *Discipline and Punish*, p. 299, p. 286, p. 251. Similarly, the prison, like the Orientalist discourse of the Empire 'is able to isolate, to place in full light and organise [the criminal, the Other in] a relatively enclosed, but penetrable, milieu' (Foucault, *Discipline and Punish*, p. 276).

42 See Foucault, *Discipline and Punish*, p. 301.

43 Foucault also argues that in the domestic carceral system, penalties are not designed to check illegalities, but instead they exist to differentiate them (Foucault, *Discipline and Punish*, p. 272). Again, 007 does not eliminate all threats to the Empire, but instead maintains and justifies a boundary between Britishness and the Orientalised Other.

44 See Foucault, *Discipline and Punish*, p. 130.

45 Foucault, *Discipline and Punish*, p. 190.

46 Foucault, *Discipline and Punish*, p. 49.

47 Bennett and Woollacott, *Bond and Beyond*, p. 28.

48 Bennett and Woollacott, *Bond and Beyond*, p. 112, p. 113.

49 F.S. Northedge, 'Britain as a Second-Rank Power', in *Twentieth-Century Britain: National Power and Social Welfare*, ed. by Henry R. Winkler (London: New Viewpoints, 1976), pp. 242–53 (p. 248).

50 Homi Bhabha, 'Signs Taken for Wonders', in *Race, Writing, and Difference*,

ed. by Henry Louis Gates, Jr. (Chicago: University of Chicago Press, 1986), pp. 163–84 (p. 169).

51 In his discussion of the Thatcher era's Raj revisionism, Salman Rushdie has observed that there are still expressions of 'conservative ideologies in modern Britain' that invoke the power of the Empire (Salman Rushdie, 'Outside the Whale', in *Imaginary Homelands* (London: Granta Books, 1991), p. 92). He notes that the rediscovery of British-Indian fictions 'puts one in mind of the phantom twitchings of an amputated limb', with Britain posturing 'like a great power, while, in fact, its power diminishes every year' (p. 92).

Martin Willis

Hard-wear:
the millennium, technology,
and Brosnan's Bond

When Pierce Brosnan took over the role of James Bond in the mid-1990s he found himself occupying a character that was, in some respects, to be radically different from the one that had last been dusted-off at the end of the 1980s. The new Bond was to be technological rather than physical, an expert rather than the muscular vigilante played by Timothy Dalton. Pierce Brosnan returned the character, in part, to the James Bond of Sean Connery's heyday in the 1960s. Connery's Bond in films like *Dr No* (1962), *Goldfinger* (1964), and *Thunderball* (1965) was cool in his use of violence, serious about his use of technological gadgetry, and able to combine the physical, mental, and technological to great effect. Yet Brosnan's Bond departs from Connery's in fundamental ways; most particularly in the way he reflects and intervenes in contemporary technological and cultural debates. His technological mastery, his defence of the human body in the face of cybernetic threats, and his 'analysis of the network society, and of its conflictive challenges'[1] to the nation-state, make Brosnan's Bond a potent force for British interests at the end of the millennium. Bond is a key switch in an informational network that runs through the secret service alphabet from M to Q. Yet Bond can also be heralded as a saviour against millennial anxieties of technological domination. This should not shock: popular culture is often the site of contemporary social fears. Philip Lamy, for example, sees 'expressions of the millennial myth [in] ... Hollywood movies, popular music, best-selling books'.[2] Nor should it be surprising that Brosnan's Bond investigates such distinct and engaging concerns. Although many earlier critics believed Bond to be an anachronism by the 1970s, it has always been the case that the Bond films continually re-invented themselves by looking outward to the world around them. For many cultural theorists the world of the 1990s demanded scrutiny of 'the relation between knowledge/information and the system of political and corporate power'.[3] Certainly a scrutiny of the first three Bond films with Pierce Brosnan in the leading role – *GoldenEye* (1995), *Tomorrow Never Dies* (1997), and *The World Is Not Enough* (1999) – illuminates a fascinating reinvention of James Bond as a technological maestro who uses his virtuosic skills to alleviate increasingly hysterical millennial anxieties.

Audiences attending the new Bond film, *The World Is Not Enough*, on its release in November 1999 would have been schooled thoroughly in the potentially disastrous consequences of the coming millennium. Certain fin-de-millennial anxieties had taken hold in Britain and throughout the Western world. Most particularly, fears over the destructive power of computer technologies or 'cybercultures' pervaded society. Yet if audiences hoped that the fantasy world of Bond would allow them some respite from these fears they were wrong: the film directly confronted Bond with out of control millennium technologies. In the longest pre-title sequence of any Bond film to date, Pierce Brosnan (as James Bond) falls onto the sloping sides of London's Millennium Dome, tumbling out of control to the ground, fractured and in pain. The visual imagery of the Dome scene combines with the previous events of the pre-title sequence (which always work on the boundary between the film and the external world) to firmly strike home the message of millennium expectations and anxieties. The scene suggests that at risk is the stability of the British nation-state, as Bond (the state's representative) breaks his body against the national symbol of the millennium in a failed attempt to gain knowledge through technological superiority.

Throughout the 1990s – when Pierce Brosnan took over the role of Bond from Timothy Dalton – the James Bond films have negotiated a path through the cultural politics of technological millenarianism. In the 1980s and before, concluding with the non-formulaic and unsuccessful *Licence To Kill* in 1989, Bond had often seemed apocalyptic but never before so strikingly connected to fin-de-millennium anxieties. As Tony Bennett and Janet Woollacott have argued, Bond has remained at the forefront of popular film because of his 'ability to coordinate' what they describe as 'a series of ideological and cultural concerns that have been enduringly important in Britain'.[4] These ideological concerns have, since the release of *GoldenEye* in 1995, coalesced around several key questions brought about by the end of the millennium. What place is there for the human in an increasingly technological world? What power will technology wield in the future? What impact will global information and communication networks have on the continued prosperity of the nation-state?

Always taking place in a 'technological fantasy world' where 'the technology must remain on the cutting edge'[5] it is no surprise to find the Bond of the 1990s determined to 'contend with the sea changes wrought by technoculture'.[6] It is equally predictable, given the politics and temper of the Bond films, that James Bond's role is to uphold the central position of the capitalist nation-state in the face of a technoculture that threatens to dismantle it. Indeed, as this chapter will argue, *GoldenEye*, *Tomorrow Never Dies*, and *The World Is Not Enough* portray a Bond of unlimited technological ability whose expert knowledge of applied science maintains a Western stranglehold on political, economic, and cultural power in an Information Age wrought by fears of millennium catastrophe. In certain respects this parallels Sean Connery's 1960s Bond where the 'white heat' of British utilitarian technology was refracted through Bond's Cold War offensives on behalf of Britain's interests in global politics.

The technocracy of Bond

Central to Bond's power is his ability to master technology. However fantastic this expert knowledge appears, its importance to Brosnan's Bond cannot be underestimated. With the 1990s increasingly dominated by the superiority of technology Bond needed to respond to this cultural phenomenon. His proficiency acts as an antidote to the pre-eminence of technology that has, in turn, led to a belief in the inability of the human to deal with technological sophistication. Bond undercuts this growing sense of impotence most obviously in *Tomorrow Never Dies* where the Q scene introduces Bond to his new (remote-controlled) BMW car. Q's clumsy attempts to move the car result in failure, despite the fact that he, ostensibly, is the designer of the technology that permits remote control. Bond, having never before used such a device, throws the car through a series of complex manoeuvres, bringing it to a sharp halt only inches from himself and Q. Bond's immediate mastery of the technology, especially by humorous comparison with Q as the baffled boffin, serves to place the audience at ease. The contest between the technological and the human is shown to be no contest at all. Bond's aptitude reconfigures the relationship between the technological object and the 'user' of that object, privileging not the machine but the human. Q's car will serve Bond (and thereby Britain) rather than the reverse.

Moreover, the aggression that Bond brings to his manipulation of the car foreshadows his abuse of that same technology later in the film. In a pastiche of everyday car-hire procedure, Q asks Bond to provide details of insurance cover. Bond's answers make it perfectly clear that he views with some relish the opportunity to place Q's technological objects in harm's way. Q, always concerned for his inventions, concludes by pointing out that 'you have a licence to kill, 007, not to break the traffic laws'. Implicit in this neatly delivered punch-line is an acknowledgement of Bond's use of technology to transcend (or at the very least disavow) the rules of society. Technology, as Q points out, appears to place Bond above the law. Yet Bond not only uses but also abuses the technology with which he has to work. In a neat circularity, the BMW finds its way back to a car rental office later in the film. Bond, using his remote control, drives it off the top of a building and through the shop's front window. Together, the flagrant disregard for law and the flagrant destruction of the technological object highlight Bond's ambiguous relationship with technology. On the one hand, Bond acts as a symbol of control that responds to millennial fears of technological dominance. On the other, he uses technology to abnegate social responsibility. If we take Bond as a symbol of the nation-state, these apparently opposing positions are initially disconcerting.

Bennett and Woollacott argue that such shifting, ambiguous signification is part of Bond's popular appeal. That Bond is 'a figure capable of taking up and articulating quite different and even contradictory cultural and ideological values'[7] makes him continually refreshing for a film audience. Notwithstanding this astute commentary, Bond's technological excesses perform another role in the Brosnan films. There, the 'moving sign'[8] that is James Bond both reassures us that technology will not dominate society and also proves that those who would seek to exploit technology for their own advancement will come into conflict with an exploiter *par excellence*, one whose loyalties are to the nation-state rather than to individual wealth and power.

This powerful, technologically astute Bond is central to Brosnan's performance of the character as the cool professional whose job takes precedence over his private life. As Alec Trevelyan reminds Bond in *GoldenEye*, his loyalty was always to the mission, never to his friend. Yet this is only one aspect of a multifaceted Bond, belied most clearly by the manner in which Bond responds to, and is interpellated by, the key scientific figures in the films. Q – like his successor R who debuts in *Tomorrow Never Dies* – continually seeks to categorise Bond not as the professional but as the layman, the foil to his status as scientist. In each of the Q scenes,

10.1 Bond (Pierce Brosnan) and Q (Desmond Llewelyn) inspecting gadgets in *GoldenEye*

therefore, Bond is a chameleon figure who moves indiscriminately from amateur to expert to hubristic scientist. Each of these positions merits some further consideration.

When Q hands Bond the mobile phone that controls his car, points to each end in turn, and says 'speak here, listen here', or when R shows Bond how to put on a coat ('one arm in here, the other arm here'), the actors play these scenes for laughs. Indeed the choice of John Cleese as Desmond Llewelyn's replacement serves to heighten the comic identity of the government scientist in the Bond series. Yet it is less the comedy and more the assumption of Bond's ignorance that is relevant here. Q's intimate knowledge of Bond's technological expertise seems to be sidelined in favour of a hierarchical approach to scientific power. Without scientific credentials Bond can only be treated as distinctly inferior by Q, who becomes schoolmasterly and patronising in the explanation of his technological inventions.

The Q scenes place Bond within a clear system of roles and responsibilities with regard to science and technology. Bond's technological superiority, so pivotal to the success of his missions, is disregarded in this context. The laboratory of the scientist privileges creation and invention. Bond's expertise is application. It is undoubtedly this division of labour that the Q scenes attempt to represent in the background activity in which the audience can watch experimental trials go awry. These slapstick events serve as a balance to Q's superior attitude by suggesting that the application of Q's inventions should be left to the expert, Bond. Science, even applied science, is portrayed as comic, pompous, and self-inflated, and its value shifts to use and application.

Technology and the body

The gender-explicit context to the technological excesses of Brosnan's Bond is significant. At one level this is no more complex than Bond girl Natalya Simonova's disgruntled comment in *GoldenEye* that Bond and his enemies are 'like boys with toys'. For each of the five actors who have played James Bond there has always been a clear connection between technology and masculinity/sexuality. Certainly Bennett and Woollacott have argued that 'Bond's sexuality has become fetished on to machinery'.[9] Yet Brosnan's Bond differs from the others. He indulges in what has become known as 'the disappearing body',[10] where the 'masculinist dreams of body transcendence'[11] become focused on the 'phallic excesses'[12] of technological objects. Brosnan's Bond is not simply extending his sexuality through technology, he is transferring that sexuality from his own body onto the hardware itself. That Bond imbues the technology he uses with his own sexual potency serves to increase the power of that technology, and by extension the power of Bond himself. The circular network of power and control suggested by the sexualising of technology is a microcosm of the wider sphere of cyberculture in the Bond films of the 1990s. Bond is the start and endpoint of that circulating system, as he becomes the powerful, technophilic body of the nation-state. In part, this masculinist mastery of technological excess can be seen as a reaction to the feminised counters to technological power that other 1990s films provided. In both the *Alien* and *Terminator* series, for example, it is the female figure who successfully combats the science fictional monster as well as all the technological apparatus of the future. In the Bond films a more traditional, if not outright reactionary, cultural politics allies technology to male sexuality and returns power to the patriarchal British nation.

For Bond to be so physical, so body-ridden, is only to bring to the foreground yet another millennial anxiety pervading 1990s culture and society. For the West, millennial fears surrounding the increasing power and control of technology often segued into growing concerns around cyberculture. The protracted humanising of the machine in the 1980s and 1990s served to exacerbate fin-de-millennium misgivings over the cyberisation of the human body. Prosthetics, implants, and plastic surgery, among other medicalised forms of cyberculture, contributed to the notion of a human body under threat from technological advances. Gretchen Bender and Timothy Druckrey, for example, argue that 'as the system of technology expands to dominate the regulation of the external world, it also contracts and increasingly penetrates the internal world. The body is unquestionably the next frontier.'[13] Not everyone, however, was fearful of the penetrative force of technology. Some, indeed, saw the rise of cyberculture as an opportunity rather than a danger. Mike Featherstone and Roger Burrows discuss how the 'utopian discourse around computer technology'[14] at this time was 'the potential offered by computers for humans to escape the body'.[15]

For Bond and his adversaries it is technologies other than computers that allow the physical body power and freedom. For the ostensible villain of *The World Is Not Enough* technological penetration has extended the body's capacity beyond normal boundaries. Renard, his brain altered by the intrusion of a handgun bullet (an item of technology that is amongst the lowest used by 00 agents but a technology none the less), becomes the first Bond cyberbody. Compare this technological intervention with a much earlier example in *Goldfinger* where Bond awaits penetration from a laser operated by the eponymous villain. The expectation in this scene is that Bond will die, as Goldfinger tells him with relish, when his physical body meets the technological object. For Renard, however, penetration by technology brings resistance to pain and an increase in strength. The merger with the bullet at a cerebral level increases the physical possibilities of Renard's body, a cyborgian notion to which the film continually alludes. From the scalding rocks he is able to pick up with bare hands to the bullet that grazes his shoulder without causing discomfort, Renard's inhuman or ultra-human qualities are highlighted. Subtle comparisons are drawn here between the inability of Renard and other cinematic cyborgs to 'feel' – the replicants in *Blade Runner* (1982) foremost among them.

Unlike Ridley Scott's film, however, where the status of the replicants remains highly ambiguous, *The World Is Not Enough* clearly establishes Renard as the villain to Bond's hero. That the cyber-figure becomes associated with the enemies of the Western nation-state signals the Bond films' sympathy with those who express some concern over fin-de-millennium cyberculture. Brosnan's Bond, therefore, is placed in direct confrontation with the human-machine interfaces of the late 1990s, either those smart weapons that have the ability to think for themselves (such as the airborne missile fired at the arms bazaar in *The World Is Not Enough*) or the humans (like Renard or even Boris Grishenko) whose mechanical or digital accoutrements increase their power dramatically. While Brosnan's first three Bond films exacerbate cultural anxieties about cybernetics, they also attempt to ease those anxieties by showing a James Bond who takes power from the machine and hands it back to the human. Indeed, Bond defends the deserving human body from technological invasion and turns that technology back upon those seeking to overpower the symbolic body of the nation-state.

Those technologies that Bond must combat in this way normally take the form of military hardware. Bond saves first Christmas Jones and then M from bombs in *The World Is Not Enough*, Natalya Simonova from helicopter missiles and an electromagnetic pulse weapon in *GoldenEye*, and the body of the British state from nuclear disaster in all three of *GoldenEye*, *Tomorrow Never Dies*, and *The World Is Not Enough*. By the final scenes of each of these films Bond also brings the criminal masterminds to appropriate justice by using their own technologies to penetrate and destroy their physical bodies. A communication satellite fragments Alec Trevelyan, Elliott Carver is bored by his own sea-drill, and Renard is impaled by a nuclear fission rod. Such conclusive and symbolic victories subvert fin-de-millennial unease about cyberculture by destroying the criminal techno-body and leaving intact the bodies of Bond and his female counterpart. This allows the final mode of penetration – that of the sexual liaison with which Bond films invariably conclude – to be a 'natural' act of human interaction in opposition to the previously 'unnatural' acts of technological intervention.

Nevertheless, James Bond often arrives at this moment of carnal satisfaction only through a process in which he, like the criminal, has used cutting-edge technology to extend the capabilities of his physical body. But it is vital to note that while Bond might appear to indulge technology in the same way as the criminals, his use of these technologies highlights his difference from them. Bond's power comes from making technology perform for him rather than allowing it to take his place. The most immediate examples of this are the many gadgets that come as bodily accoutrements, including X-ray spectacles, an avalanche jacket, the standard issue secret service watch, and a rope belt. Each of these technological objects allows Bond to perform outside the limits of the body. In fact, some pieces of technology even allow Bond to 'double' his body, to be both present and absent at the same time, or to exist in two distinct spaces at one moment.

A simple example is the timer switch Bond attaches to a series of bombs in the pre-title sequence of *GoldenEye*. The detonation of the bomb is completed while Bond's physical body is elsewhere. In this instance, then, Bond is both near the bombs and at some distance from them. Occupying the same technological territory is the mobile phone Bond uses in *Tomorrow Never Dies*. Its ability to act as a remote control for Bond's enhanced BMW allows Bond to distract his enemies with a car chase while he escapes by other means. Once again Bond is doubled. He is both inside and outside the car at the same moment. In this instance, technology extends the human body by enabling Bond to use only a small part of that body as a substitute for the whole: the fingertips which pass across the sensitive pad of the mobile phone become the body of the car driver. Ultimately, though, this is a form of illusion. Bond appears to be in the car but is not. A technological object masks the absence of the human body. This is a significant shift in power from the cybernetic dominance preoccupying 1990s culture. Here, technology does not just supplant the body but also performs on its behalf. The result is that Bond's expertise makes malleable the very technologies that threatened to create a dystopian cyberculture at the fin-de-millennium. The terrorising of the stability of the human body is neutralised by Bond's ability to control powerful cyber-technologies.

Information and communication

It is an irony that the most powerful technologies in the 1990s Bond films are those that replicate traditional forms of intelligence-gathering. The information age (as the end of the millennium is often characterised) foregrounds information and communication technologies whose primary roles are information gathering, networking, and surveillance. The traditional remit of James Bond (from Connery's conflict with Dr No onwards) is strikingly similar. The spy must be adept at all three of these key skills to succeed in the Bondian world. Yet in Brosnan's Bond these functions are transferred from the individual to technology. For some contemporary commentators, this fin-de-millennial shift towards an 'informational'[16] society is to be applauded. Frances Cairncross, for example, believes that while 'surveillance power will be a serious potential danger to liberty'[17] it is far more likely that information and communication technology will 'be a powerful force for peace'.[18] Utopian visions of technological futures are not uncommon in millenarian thinking, but they are not the dominant view. More often critical opinion takes a pessimistic view of information and communication technologies as harbingers of greater inequality, exclusion, and differentiations of wealth and power.

For Brosnan's Bond, the world of the 1990s seems to conform to this pessimistic view. Indeed, all three of Brosnan's films depict information and communication as a key battleground between the British nation-state and global crime, usually symbolised in the more individual conflict between Bond and the criminal mastermind. This conflict rests on three foundations: surveillance, information/communication, and concealment.

Let us deal first with surveillance. Of all Brosnan's films *Tomorrow Never Dies* most clearly investigates the tropes of surveillance. Its pre-title sequence, in which Bond surveys an arms bazaar in Afghanistan, begins to construct a series of complex relationships that revolve around different types of vision. The stress in the first scenes is on the viewer: from Bond's hidden gaze at the arms sale through the gaze of British intelligence watching the events from an operations room to the gaze of the film audience who watch Bond on both the cinema screen and the screen of the operations room. Indeed, the audience is given a perspective unusual in the Bond oeuvre: a double vision that defamiliarises the cinema experience by calling attention to the methods of viewing. This is repeated later in the film when Bond drives his BMW remotely using a screen on his mobile phone to view the car's trajectory. Once again, the audience is invited to gaze as Bond gazes.

The gaze is also important to the Bond villains. In *GoldenEye*, hidden cameras – the screens for which are mounted on mobile palmtop computers – protect Alec Trevelyan's secret base. In *Tomorrow Never Dies*, Elliot Carver controls his media corporation through a series of video-links that allow him visual access to his employees. And in *The World Is Not Enough*, Renard keeps British Intelligence under almost constant surveillance through his liaison with Elektra King. Bennett and Woollacott argue that James Bond has a 'scopophilic instinct'[19] in many of the earlier (pre-Brosnan) films. By the mid-1990s this gaze has also become common to Bond's adversaries and has shifted from a simple scopophilia to a techno-scopophilia.

In the recent Bond films, a big part of the attraction of technology comes from its ability not just to survey but in the process to provide information. In *GoldenEye*, Bond's digital camera may begin by taking Xenia Onatopp's picture but it concludes by providing biographical details that a photographic representation alone could not discover. The Bond film of the 1990s becomes an arena in which information and knowledge circulate 'in a recurrent network of globally connected exchanges'.[20] For Bond, mastering the bewildering array of information flowing through the film is the key to success. Several times we witness Bond's sudden access to information providing him with the key necessary to unlock the film's remaining enigmas. Renard's knowledge of Bond's injury alerts Bond to the danger posed by Elektra King, and Natalya Simonova's knowledge of computer passwords derails Alec Trevelyan's plans for the golden eye pulse weapon. Equally, there are moments when information flows away from Bond toward his opponents: Henry Gupta gains online access to Bond's faked banking career and Boris Grishenko ensnares Natalya Simonova by email. Technologies of communication and information become the new weapons of millennial warfare. As Elliot Carver states, 'satellites are the new artillery'.

To control information and communication technologies is to control society. These technologies have always 'been closely associated with processes of social management'[21] and as they become more sophisticated they become increasingly 'central to the maintenance of political and administrative cohesion'.[22] So while it may seem that the Bondian villain is trying to play a military game (Carver's war in the South China Seas, Trevelyan's military base and Russian cold war weaponry, and Renard/Elektra's nuclear warheads) s/he is actually seeking much subtler control of society through its networks of information. In each of *GoldenEye*, *Tomorrow Never Dies*, and *The World Is Not Enough* millennial anxieties over rampant and powerful technology – weapons, gadgets, digital computer systems – permeate the film-text. The Bondian villain becomes aligned with each and all of these technologies.

Bond, by contrast, appears decidedly annexed from the military might of the nation-state. For example, in the pre-title sequence of *Tomorrow Never Dies* Bond's life is placed in danger because of, rather than despite, the help of the British navy. Too quick to make judgments, the navy fires on the arms bazaar which Bond has under surveillance. The sudden sighting of a nuclear weapon at the bazaar gives rise to an imminent disaster that Bond averts. Filled with the usual array of stunts and fast-paced action, Bond's 'mission' is little more than to save Britain from itself. Often alone, Bond works at the very boundaries of the military systems that nations have in place. As a 'secret' agent Bond cannot reveal himself as military personnel. Those scenes where Bond does appear in navy uniform are disarming to the viewer for the dressing up is actually a stripping of the cloak of secrecy upon which Bond usually relies.

For Bond to be able to combat realistically the militaristic strengths of his adversaries he must have some form of individual power that he can bring to bear in conflict situations. For all his technological expertise (and the expertise he gains through partnerships with Natalya Simonova, Wai Lin, and Christmas Jones) Bond's greatest ally in opposing the military-inspired information and communication technologies of Trevelyan, Carver and Renard/Elektra is his apparent lack of technology. In an environment where information equals power and where surveillance controls the distribution of that power, to appear low-tech is to be ignored and therefore to gain some degree of freedom. If that low-tech status is also faked then the freedom gained comes with a power that can be used to combat military superiority. This concealment of technological power is the most vital component in Brosnan's Bond, and is symbolised in the great number of hidden technological objects he uses: pens, watches, spectacles, belts, mobile phones, and so on. Once more, Brosnan's Bond makes use of hidden technologies in a manner not entirely dissimilar to Connery's Bond. Although Connery's concealment of gadgets typically leads to a personal advantage for Bond in conflicts with single individuals (as opposed to Brosnan's fight with multiple technologies), the actual concealing of gadgets is crucial to the plot and taken seriously by the characters and film-makers. By contrast, Roger Moore's gadgets are played to melodramatic and slapstick excess.

In *GoldenEye*, Moore's humorous gadgetry is parodied in Brosnan's first ever Q scene in order to stress the importance of hidden technologies to Bond in the 1990s. After a guided tour of Q Division's laboratory, Bond curiously picks up what appears to be a large baguette filled with meat and cheese. Q's immediate response is to shout, 'don't touch that'. In the pause that follows, the audience is invited to speculate on what concealed technology the innocent sandwich may contain. Explosives? Timed grenades? Short-range missiles? After the pause, Q dissolves the tension by explaining 'that's my lunch'. One effect of the scene is to turn the high-tech into low comedy. But another effect is to reinforce the idea that hidden technologies work to give power to those who know about them. Knowledge is at the core of the low/high-tech object (objects that appear as basic technologies but are actually very sophisticated). Those who can see the high-tech even when disguised as low-tech have a distinct advantage. Bond not only has power over his adversaries because of his disguised technologies, but also because he has knowledge that surveillance cannot always provide. Hidden technologies, in fact, work doubly to give Bond knowledge that only he possesses and a way of undermining the surveillance technologies (the gaze) of the criminal.

This is very clearly what occurs towards the end of Brosnan's first Bond film, *GoldenEye*. Captured by Alec Trevelyan, Bond is forced to stand in the operations room while Trevelyan arms the electromagnetic pulse weapon with which he plans to destroy the information and communication technologies of London. Boris – the film's computer expert – works at his bank of digital screens while toying with Bond's confiscated pen. This pen (a disguised grenade) is the key to the scene and, along with Bond's eyes, the central point of reference for the camera. Along with Bond, the audience is aware that the pen conceals a powerful weapon which is likely to be set off accidentally by Boris. Neither Trevelyan nor Boris is paying any attention to this apparently commonplace piece of 'old technology'. The hidden technology gives Bond a double advantage at this point. He has, firstly, knowledge unavailable to the other characters; and secondly, his gaze is directed at the correct piece of technology. While Bond remains focused on the pen, the others stare at the display screens. This allows Bond to react first when the grenade is set off and to escape from his imprisonment in Trevelyan's operations room.

Despite inferior manpower, weaponry, and support systems, Bond's use of hidden technologies always gives him an edge over his opponents. This occurs not only because the Bond formula demands that Bond be the victor but also because power resides in the flow of information and communication rather than in traditional military strengths. Indeed, power itself is hidden, internalised in informational networks that cannot be seen on satellite photographs, thermal images, or with the naked eye. Bond's hidden technologies are, in a sense, symbolic of this internalisation of power structures at the end of the millennium. The fear of unknown power residing 'within' networks to which society has little knowledge and even less access was a significant anxiety in the late 1990s. Bond's role is to challenge that fear by articulating a very different version of the story of hidden technology. In Brosnan's 007 films, the use of hidden technology actually saves the nation-state and the capitalist democracy from disaster. Concealed threats against the British nation are overcome by the concealment of technology on a 'secret' agent of that nation.

The quiet millennium

By the end of *Tomorrow Never Dies*, which was to be followed so very quickly by the end of the millennium, James Bond had made certain that the year 2000 would be ushered in without the apocalyptic disasters predicted by millenarianists. It was to be a quiet millennium in the Bondian world, despite the attempts by Alec Trevelyan, Elliot Carver, Renard, and Elektra King to have it otherwise. Brosnan's Bond had managed to maintain the status quo of British (and Western) superiority on the global economic stage. Trevelyan did not steal all the money in the City of London, Carver did not corner the Chinese market in television media, and Elektra King did not secure her monopoly on oil supplies. The nation-state was preserved and wealth remained in the hands of those friendly to the interests of Western capitalism. The credit for avoiding these power shifts disguised as millennial disasters is due to one man, James Bond, who proves himself both a saviour to the nation-state and an antidote to the collective fears brought on by a whole range of millennium bugs.

One further component of this antidote worth consideration is Brosnan's reinvention of James Bond along lines set by Connery in the 1960s. That the Bond of the millennium should revert to the Bond of the 1960s is due in some degree to the various interlinking themes – including global conflict and technological advancement – that bind the two periods together. It is also, of course, a recognition of Connery's esteemed position in the Bond canon. But the nostalgia of Brosnan's Bond for the Connery years is additionally a part of millennial culture's fascination with a pre-computerised and not yet post-nuclear world, a world most clearly articulated in filmic terms by Mike Myers' excellent Bond spoofs *Austin Powers* (1997) and *The Spy Who Shagged Me* (1999). These vastly influential Bond tributes transport the heroic spy between the swinging London of the 1960s and the global conflicts of the 1990s solely to mine comedy from the clash of cultures. Brosnan's Bond, less the self-parody of Moore and more the cultural colossus of Connery, stands a chance of being as important to the Bondian world and to contemporary film culture as its early incarnations and even its later pastiches. Will Brosnan's James Bond continue to exert cultural influence in the new millennium? Will Bond continue to investigate and contribute to the cultural politics of contemporary global capitalism? Yeah, baby.

Notes

1 Manuel Castells, *End of Millennium* (Oxford: Blackwell, 1998), p. 371.
2 Philip Lamy, 'Secularizing The Millennium: Survivalists, Militias and the New World Order', in *Millennium, Messiahs, and Mayhem: Contemporary Apocalyptic Movements*, ed. by Thomas Robbins and Susan J. Palmer (London: Routledge, 1997), pp. 93–117 (p. 114).
3 Kevin Robins and Frank Webster, *Times of the Technoculture: From the Information Society to the Virtual Life* (London: Routledge, 1999), p. 110.
4 Tony Bennett and Janet Woollacott, *Bond and Beyond: The Political Career of a Popular Hero* (London: Macmillan, 1987), p. 18.
5 James Chapman, *Licence To Thrill: A Cultural History of the James Bond Films* (London: I. B. Tauris, 2000), p. 274, p. 272.
6 Gretchen Bender and Timothy Druckrey (eds), *Culture on the Brink: Ideologies of Technology* (Seattle: Bay Press, 1994), p. 6.
7 Bennett and Woollacott, *Bond and Beyond*, p. 19.
8 Bennett and Woollacott, *Bond and Beyond*, p. 19.
9 Bennett and Woollacott, *Bond and Beyond*, p. 203.
10 Anne Balsamo, 'Forms of Technological Embodiment: Reading the Body in Contemporary Culture', in *Cyberspace, Cyberbodies, Cyberpunk: Cultures of Technological Embodiment*, ed. by Mike Featherstone and Roger Burrows (London: Sage, 1995), pp. 215–37 (p. 233).
11 Balsamo, 'Forms', p. 233.
12 Bennett and Woollacott, *Bond and Beyond*, p. 227.
13 Bender and Druckrey, *Culture on the Brink*, p. 9.
14 Featherstone and Burrows (eds), *Cyberspace, Cyberbodies, Cyberpunk*, p. 100.
15 Featherstone and Burrows (eds), *Cyberspace, Cyberbodies, Cyberpunk*, p. 100.
16 Scott Lash, *Critique of Information* (London: Sage, 2002), p. 1.
17 Frances Cairncross, *The Death of Distance* (London: Orion, 1997), p. 257.
18 Cairncross, *The Death of Distance*, p. 259.
19 Bennett and Woollacott, *Bond and Beyond*, p. 211.
20 Castells, *End of Millennium*, p. 359.
21 Robins and Webster, *Times of the Technoculture*, p. 109.
22 Robins and Webster, *Times of the Technoculture*, p. 109.

Colleen M. Tremonte and Linda Racioppi

Body politics and Casino Royale: gender and (inter)national security

Simon Winder's recent popular examination of the James Bond phenomenon roots Bond firmly in the ground of British nationalism in the
post-World War II era, when society was suffering the after-effects of a
devastating war and revisioning itself as a post-imperial actor. Winder's
examination as well as those of many other scholars tends to emphasise Bond's Britishness, even when acknowledging his position as an
internationalised operative engaged in defending the nation-state from
ominous external threats such as terrorism, weapons of mass destruction, illicit arms transfers, and intrastate conflicts.[1] During the Cold
War, dealing with such threats required the talents of a super agent who
was deeply British yet organically cosmopolitan and inherently anti-
authoritarian. But it also required a spy who was thoroughly 'manly'.
There was never any question that Bond would not only vanquish his
male enemies but that he would also dominate even the most assertive
Bond 'girl'. The masculinist ideology and binary gender order under-
girding the world of Bond paralleled those of the Cold War system
and the nationalist politics of bipolarity. Yet the Bond series has proven
to be remarkably adaptable. If Bond girls remain stunning and Bond
debonair, the characters have also responded to changing social and
political mores, as a woman heads up MI6, as Bond girls acquire new
competencies (in espionage skills, computer programming, and financial management), as Miss Moneypenny is replaced by a male assistant,
and as Bond himself exhibits some emotional vulnerability. However,
within the matrix of competing and shifting post-Cold War nationalistic discourses about global terrorism and (inter)national security,
such gender responses remain grounded in a masculinist ideology that
inscribes gender as a marker of national and cosmopolitan identities.

Such gendered identities are literally and figuratively represented through the films' body politics.

The 2006 Bond film, *Casino Royale*, is a particularly rich text in which to explore the relationship between such body politics and (inter) national security, especially when set against other post-Cold War Bond films such as *GoldenEye* (1995), *Tomorrow Never Dies* (1997), *The World Is Not Enough* (1999), and *Die Another Day* (2002). Indeed, *Casino Royale* provides both a revision to the post-Cold War series, introducing a new Bond in Daniel Craig and a grittier, slightly more realistic feel to the narrative, and a return to the series' roots as it introduces Bond before his 00 status. Film critics overwhelmingly praised Craig's interpretation of Bond as rougher, darker, and sexier than Brosnan or the previous Bonds.[2] What is most striking, however, is that this Bond film deploys a gender politics that relies on hypermasculinity to meet (inter)national security threats that are now centred on global terrorism, nationalist struggles, and global finance.[3] One of the most powerful articulations of these gender politics is what happens to Bond's body in *Casino Royale*. Throughout the film, a very taut and fit Daniel Craig/Bond is subject to (and subjects) his body to numerous physical blows, most viscerally in the on-screen torture scene. The level of violence and brutality that James – the embodiment of Britain – suffers is grizzlier than in previous post-Cold War films.[4] Throughout *Casino Royale* the vicious physicality of the assaults against Bond (and his body) is juxtaposed against a sensuous and eroticised Bondian body in many of the other scenes in the film. The hypervisibility of Bond's body – in motion, specularised, under threat – throughout *Casino Royale* helps to reinforce the role of masculinity in the international and gender orders. An analysis of the body trope more generally in *Casino Royale* reveals that gender and gender relations continue to circulate as markers of national identity and (inter)national security.

Gendering national identities in a post-Cold War world

In the post-Cold War era, nationalisms and national identities have been formed and reconstructed in the face of a hostile security environment that is populated by the dangers of emerging global terrorist networks, ethnic and religious conflicts, civil wars, failed states, economic instability and inequality, invasive technologies, and conventional, nuclear, and biological arms proliferation, among others. Such insecurities threaten states individually and severally, but they can also undermine international stability, particularly to the extent that they may jeopardise the global capitalist economy. As processes of globalisation have made international boundaries more porous and have undermined state sovereignty,[5] the expansion and intensification of international capitalism have also precipitated contrary nationalist reactions as nation-states and peoples respond to globalisation's opportunities and its disparities.[6]

Bond films, then, circulate among a range of discursive fields and practices in a globalised (in)security environment in which (nation-)states still comprise an important, if attenuated, normative framework. Within this normative framework, Bond remains very much a British national. As has been well established, Fleming created Bond as a white, upper class, well-schooled, and sophisticated figure.[7] The films construct Bond's 'Britishness' by consistently showing him to be a well-educated, multilingual, and suitably polite operative who can in fact function in elite society, even when trying to deflect his upper-class affiliation. For example, Bond knows his wine, vintage and origin; he wears clothes that are impeccably tailored; he drives a very English car, the Aston Martin; and, most obviously, he works for the British Secret Intelligence Service (MI6) in service to Her Majesty. Such markers of identity are not merely cosmetic signifiers of 'Britishness', they are also symbols of the confluence of nationalism and globalism: that is, there is no apparent contradiction between the 'national' Bond and 'cosmopolitan' or globalised Bond; his identities are mutually reinforcing, and as such, reinforce the linkage of nation-state and the international system.

Indeed, in *Casino Royale*, global security looms larger than British security: there is no direct threat at all to Britain, and so Bond's work is not just in service to Her Majesty but to the international system and by extension, to Britain. As international relations scholars would put it, contemporary states are often representative of specific 'national' interests, but they can also be accomplices in support of the international order. In this sense, powerful states act to preserve a global system that is itself a legitimator of (nation-)states. In a post-9/11 world, as SPECTRE-like threats become increasingly pervasive, Bond must embody both national and cosmopolitan ideals in order to keep Britain and the global capitalist system safe.[8]

But Britain and the West are not gender-neutral constructs. As the feminist literature has amply demonstrated, nations, states, and international systems are profoundly gendered: men control the state and international politics. They control the military and related apparatuses of (inter)national security which, as many feminist and non-feminist scholars have noted, have been closely associated with the construction and maintenance of nationalism and national identities. Thus, men are the main agents of the state and the international system of states; women, as some feminist scholarship has argued, are positioned as subordinate helpmeets and often embodied as symbols of the 'nation'.[9] This 'division of signification' parallels the components of the (nation-) state itself: both a driving force in international politics and a space (geo-political, psychic, communal) to be protected. National identities, such as Britishness, therefore have been constructed within the context of a binary gender/political order; they are differentiated for men and women and reflect and direct gender roles. Historically, men protect and defend the nation-state, if necessary sacrificing their own lives; women serve the nation through reproducing and socialising its children and support-ing militarised men who may be away from home. Even when, as Steve Niva (1998) suggests, constructions of national masculinity shift, they continue to maintain a gender binary. And even as women may break traditional gender norms by joining military and paramilitary forces, their service seldom results in a disruption of male power and control over politics and the military.

The Bond films have always interpolated the 'real world' gender order and complicated gendered national identities. After all, the gender roles which persisted across the more than forty years of Bond films are neither static nor necessarily traditional. Thus, on the one hand, as Janet Woollacott observes about the novels: sexy, assertive, and sometimes wicked Bond girls 'have some initial claim to independence. There are no clinging romantic heroines in the Bond novels'.[10] For example, the post-Cold War Brosnan films contain female characters who are clearly aligned with Bond and central to the defence of (inter)national secu-rity: the now female head of MI6; the computer programmer Natalya Simonova in *GoldenEye*; Chinese secret agent Wai Lin in *Tomorrow Never Dies*; the physicist Dr Christmas Jones in *The World Is Not Enough*; and CIA agent Jinx in *Die Another Day*. Each of these women possesses official or professional capabilities that not only help Bond defeat the enemy but that reflect contemporary gender politics. The films also contain beautiful, desirable, and competent female opponents who are necessary to advancing the plot against Britain and/or the West: Xenia Onatopp in *GoldenEye*; Elektra King in *The World Is Not Enough*; and Miranda Frost in *Die Another Day*.

On the other hand, as Woollacott goes on to note, 'the narrative pattern . . . establishes the women as in some manner sexually and ideologically "out of place"; too aggressive . . . "out of place" in relation to men, as represented by Bond ... Such a girl represents a challenge to the traditional sexual order, and Bond's answer is that of "putting her back into place beneath him (both literally and metaphorically)".'[11] In the post-Cold War era, while virtually all the leading women in the films remain spectacular and Bond himself heroic, by the 1990s, they also seem to be moving 'into place' *vis á vis* the male-dominated hierarchy: Bond girls become computer wizards, science geeks, and secret service agents, and Bond himself is commanded by a female 'M' and reduced to driving a Ford Focus in *Casino Royale*. Although there appears to be some equalisation of gender relations in these films, in fact the Bond women remain 'out of place' in relationship to the international security and gender orders and still need to be 'put in place' by Bond. For example, in *Casino Royale*, the now female head of MI6 (Judi Dench as M) has her authority undercut when Bond breaks into her home office and hacks her computer.[12] The other female ally of Bond, Vesper Lynd, is an official of the British Treasury ('I'm the money,' she says), but she too is revealed to be 'out of place' and possibly 'disloyal' because of her previous romantic liaison with a French Algerian who was kidnapped and ransomed by Le Chiffre's organisation. Her emerging love affair with Bond promises to reconnect her to the nation and to international security norms. Despite the spectre of women's national unreliability, the post-Cold War Bond films reassert liberal, democratic, capitalist, and state sovereignty norms via the re-stabilisation of male and female relations, and homosocial relations between Bond and his enemies in particular. These norms are inscribed through the images of Bondian bodies: to the extent that *Casino Royale* breaks with other post-Cold War era Bond films, it is through the visualisation of the body of Bond himself.

Bondian bodies are visibly and invisibly marked by these processes of national and transnational politics. As the representative of the British state, Bond's job is not only to defend the physical territory and boundaries of the nation, it is also to maintain its interests and project power *vis á vis* other actors in the international system. However, Bond recognises that Britain's security is not merely a question for the British; the British nation represents the international order, especially global capitalism. Threats to Britain are, by extension, threats to the system, and conversely, threats not directed at Britain are taken to be national security threats because they could destabilise the global order. The Bond series has always recognised what scholars of post-Cold War international relations have observed: actors can be states, but they can also be non-state entities who threaten the system, sometimes working against and through states and sometimes against and through other criminal, paramilitary, or terrorist organisations.[13] Thus, the British nation and other Western nations can come under attack in multiple ways – disruptions of its economy (*GoldenEye*), attacks on information and media networks (*Tomorrow Never Dies*), conventional, nuclear, and biological attacks (*The World Is Not Enough)*, and illicit arms transfers to terrorist groups (*Casino Royale*) – in short, a variety of actors and threats in a complicated intermestic world. Such threats require an operative who is well-armed on many levels: physically, mentally, technologically, militarily, and sexually. As Bond's body must act for the nation and the international system – engaging in combat, foiling plots, moving across state borders, and traversing the globe – it simultaneously signifies the nation and its position in the international arena.

In *Casino Royale*, the pre-title and title sequences provide a prologue by which to understand the hypermasculine world in which Bond operates. The pre-title sequence consists of the intercutting of two distinct albeit related narratives. The first, although temporally after the second, finds James Bond in Prague, Czech Republic, where he is about to kill a British double agent who has been selling secrets. The second finds Bond engaged in a gruelling, intense, hands-on struggle. The two sequences use contrasting filmic styles: Bond's detached and mechanical assassination of the agent is clearly shot in a classic shot-reverse-shot manner reminiscent of Cold War films such as *The Third Man* (1949) and *The Spy Who Came in From the Cold* (1965). The fight sequence, however, is built utilising frenetic movement and multiple disoriented camera angles – all of which suggest the postmodern condition of post-Cold War global security. The tension created by the juxtaposition of the two styles is not resolved until the killing of the double agent. With these killings, Bond achieves 00 status. The total effect is to encompass the duality of Bond: 007 must not only use his body and his physical abilities to vanquish enemies, he must discipline his body to control his emotions in order to be an effective agent for the state. His personal struggle can be seen as an attempt to resuscitate realist international relations: in order to be an effective representative of the nation-state and to protect its security, Bond – like the state – must be physically aggressive, self-reliant, logical, and sharp. The sequence then is a genesis story: 007 is born into a black and white world of men and international intrigue, one that intentionally invokes the aura of the Cold War and establishes Bond as a professional operative with a 'licence to kill' on behalf of the nation. Bond becomes a rational actor who dispassionately calculates each action and reaction in the game of international espionage.

The body politics of the pre-title sequence, particularly when linked to the familiar international security terrain of Prague and the double-agent ploy, facilitate the move into the title sequence's graphics. Here male silhouettes fight amidst floating casino images – roulette wheels and cards – which become weapons, emphasizing the need for Bond to play and win the 'game' of international politics. Unlike other Bond openings in which images of women are liberally used, objectified, and sometimes mortified, the world of *Casino Royale* is established as a male-dominated arena in which men's bodies are in motion and at risk. The only female figure that appears amid the male silhouettes is relegated to the face on a playing card, the Queen of Hearts. The graphic landscape of the title sequence is punctuated by the appearance of two human forms – one male, one female – James and Vesper, his lover. Again, though, the screen time is disproportionately male, Vesper's human face makes but a fleeting appearance, as a gun scope passes over the face of the Queen of Hearts. Bond, on the other hand, steps out of a silhouette to stare penetratingly at the audience. Taken together, then, the pre-title and title sequences establish (inter)national security as the domain of men, men who threaten stability and order, and men who respond to this threat. They also align Bond (via his body) with agency and rationality in dealing with (inter)national security threats. Thus, as the international body politic is male-dominated, Bond and his body must be manly because only a man can defeat the diverse but largely man-made threats foisted upon the post-Cold War world.

Of course, it is not only Bond's body that functions to enact contests between nation-states and often deterritorialised, supranational criminal or paramilitary organisations in the post-Cold War Bond films. Other Bondian bodies (male and female) defend or disrupt the gendered nation-state system and its security, and simultaneously echo the complicated binaries of gender and international security. Such 'embodiments' of gender and (inter)national politics play out in several ways in all of the post-Cold War filmic narratives. First, the films continue the long-standing tradition of specularising women's bodies, thus making them objects of national and international politics. However, *Casino Royale* complicates this specularisation by refocusing the gaze onto the body of Bond: it is not merely trim and handsome; it is ripped, it is desirable, and it gets comparable screen time to the Bond girls' bodies. Second, each of the post-Cold War Bond films retains the normative heterosexual ideology so necessary for the preservation of nation-state sovereignty. *Casino Royale* sharpens this ideology with/through its dependence on hypermasculinity and its displacement of sexual heterogamy. Finally, all the films preserve the connection between Bond and national security interests. As always, Bond is ready to sacrifice his body for the mission. *Casino Royale*, however, largely dispenses with the arsenal of fantastic technological devices found in other films' narratives and instead relies on technology to augment his impressive physical abilities.[14]

Body politics: image, sexuality, security

The scopic regime of Bond films has traditionally been understood as one that eroticises women and their bodies – both are the objects of desire.[15] Woollacott illustrates this point effectively in her essay, 'The James Bond Films: Conditions of Production':

> Women in the Bond films have always been conceived in terms of male desire and pleasure . . . The scenes in which Honey [Honeychile Rider, as portrayed by Ursula Andress in *Dr. No*] makes her appearance as a latter-day Venus could be read as a textbook illustration of scophophilic pleasure, whereby the manipulation of 'looks' in the film establishes the woman as the object of sexual desire for the hero and for the audience . . . [A] particular regime of pleasure is established through the 'looks' of the hero and the audience. While women are represented as erotic spectacle, the audience is led to identify with the male hero, the active performer.[16]

The post-Cold War films continue to evoke such a 'gaze': for example, in *The World Is Not Enough*, the body of Elektra (Sophie Marceau) is repeatedly shown barely covered by a sheet as the camera slowly pans her body. The repetition of such scenes throughout the series bears out Woollacott's argument about the male gaze as it raises audience expectations that each film will offer pleasurable, eroticised images of women.

In *Casino Royale*, Solange (Caterina Murino), the wife of the nefarious Alex Dimitrios, is attired in a bikini as she rides her white horse down a pristine Caribbean resort's beach. The wind blows her hair and gauzy clothing as little black children run behind in wonder and awe. Women's bodies remain specularised: both Solange's and Vesper's on-screen images are lush and voluptuous, fitting the protocol of past Bond films. However, the scene with Solange on horseback is immediately followed by a shot of James Bond rising out of the sea and walking towards the beach. The intertextual references for the scene are, of course, Ursula Andress in *Dr No* and Halle Berry in *Die Another Day*. Within this scopic logic Bond also becomes an 'object of the gaze'. Attractive and desirable, he is a fitting

11.1 James Bond (Daniel Craig) emerging from the sea in *Casino Royale*

match for the glamorous Bond women. However, the gaze here is decep-
tive: we are not permitted to luxuriate in Bond's appeal.[17]

While Bond's body may be gloriously specularised in *Casino Royale*, it
is not objectified as the bodies of many a Bond girl have been. His physical attractiveness, strength, and desirability highlight his masculinity in a
way that suggests he will never give over control and that in fact empha-
sises the close connection between Bond's maleness and his ability to
thwart threats. He cannot give over control because the narrative requires
that he resolve some pressing crisis of (inter)national security. Indeed,
if the swimsuit shots of Bond were longer they might risk undermining his dominant position and masculinity, and his efficacy. The image
of bodies within the diegesis is thus tied to the gender order and to the
(inter)national security environment.

At the same time, Bond's superiority is reinforced by the juxtaposition
of his body against the bodies of other male characters, particularly his
enemies. For example, British and American colleagues are presented
as ordinary, respectable gentlemen; his male adversaries are often unat-
tractive, scarred or marred in some way, or even disembodied. Alex
Trevelyan (Sean Bean) in *GoldenEye* has a badly scarred face; and in *Die
Another Day*, diamonds are eerily embedded in the face of Zao (Rick
Yune). *Casino Royale* heightens the effect of these intertwined gender

imaginaries by a sustained on-screen focus on Daniel Craig's rugged good looks, muscular physique, and extreme physical prowess. Repeated visualisation of Craig's superbly fit body in motion and under siege not only reinforces his position as the ultimate spy but also magnifies the significance of tough guy masculinity to national security politics. For example, in the opening, Bond literally runs down a terrorist in the protracted chase sequence – it is a high adrenaline, high testosterone, high risk scene of hot pursuit in which Bond's position is established not because of the inferiority of his opponents' bodies but because of the superiority of his own. In a later scene, Bond's physical form is once again on display as a fully naked James is tied to a chair and tortured by Le Chiffre. In case the audience had not noticed, Le Chiffre comments on 007's impressive physique.[18] Whether Bond is acting or being acted upon, his marvellous/superb body remains central to the film's imagery and the narrative of national security.

Casino Royale's specularisation of Bond underscores an understand-ing of the nation as normatively masculine and heterosexual. Feminist international relations scholar V. Spike Peterson convincingly shows that nationalism is indeed heterosexist. She states, 'heterosexism is key to nationalism because today's state-centric nationalisms . . . not only engage in sexist practices that are now well documented by feminists, but also take for granted heterosexist sex/gender identities and forms of group reproduction that underpin sexism.'[19] Throughout the series, as Jeremy Black points out, Bond is the 'visual guarantee of the maleness of the Secret Service',[20] and by extension of the nation itself. Women are objects of Bond's heterosexual desire and seemingly very willing par-ticipants in his sexual hi-jinx: Bond is irresistible to them because of his physical attractions and his legendary sexual prowess. In *Casino Royale*, Bond easily seduces a receptive Solange and eventually enters into a monogamous sexual relationship with Vesper. Heterosexuality is further normalised in this film. Even a woman who is not sexually involved with Bond is portrayed as heterosexual: for the first time we see M, played by Judi Dench, in bed with a man, presumably her husband. The audience is reassured that this female head of MI6 not only has a personal life but that it is 'normal' and 'natural'. Again, when Bond's manhood is directly threatened in the scene where Le Chiffre ties him to a chair and tortures him, Bond remains virile and sexualised. Indeed, as Vesper confirms in a later scene when she offers herself to Bond not knowing if he is impo-tent, his 'little finger' is more capable of giving sexual pleasure than other men's penises.

Bond's inherent sexual potency is further distinguished by the deficient sexualities and characters of his enemies. For example, in *GoldenEye*, Xenia Onatopp's sexual perversity is shown by her penchant to gratify her lust while simultaneously suffocating lovers with her 'killer thighs'. She may be straight, but she is hardly 'normal'. In the same film, Alex Trevelyan has similar aggressive and deviant behaviour: he threatens to rape Natalya. Bond, on the other hand, risks his life to save Natalya and to protect her from Alex's perversions. Although outlandish sexual perversity is absent from *Casino Royale*, Bond's heteronormativity and heroism are reinforced through a contrast of his body and its actions with those of the film's thugs. As Patrick O'Donnell, writing of an earlier Bond era, notes, 'Bond's body becomes the "answer" to the seeming impotence, celibacy, or gender ambiguity attributable to many of the films'. . . villains.'[21] For example, Le Chiffre looks on helplessly as an African paramilitarist threatens to cut off his girlfriend's hand. His cowardice and impotence stand in stark contrast to the courage of Bond who is repeatedly shown risking his life to defend others, even others he does not personally know (as in the scene when he battles a terrorist to stop him from blowing up an airliner at Miami International Airport).

Normative heterosexuality then helps to align masculinity with (inter)national security. Since using the body to stand in for actors in the international system necessarily involves its physical bombardment, its mutilation, even its disposability, it is necessarily *men*'s bodies that generally come under attack or threat in the films. In *Casino Royale*, Bond's body is repeatedly assaulted and brutalised. He is even poisoned by Le Chiffre during a high stakes poker game which, if won by Le Chiffre, will provide funding for international terrorists. Unlike in other films where Bond is under threat, the poisoning sequence is protracted and intimate: we see Bond as he realises he has been poisoned, drinks salty water to try to expel the poison, but ultimately suffers cardiac arrest. Had Le Chiffre succeeded in killing Bond, Britain's efforts to thwart the spread of global terrorism would have failed. Throughout the film, we see an almost literal re-inscription of masculinity onto the 'body' of Bond, as he (his body) takes the blows that are inflicted by 'terrorism' and/or 'bad' global capitalism.

Indeed, Bond is rooted in territorialised and nationalised politics, but in the twenty-first century, these politics are necessarily globalised. For example, in the same poker game, Vesper controls the Crown's purse and refuses to front Bond any more funds; however, the CIA's Felix Leiter steps in and stakes Bond in the contest (which he, of course, wins). While *Casino Royale* suggests the collusion of the nation-state in a 'cosmopolitan' international system in which Britain and its 'Western' allies have a clear interest, it simultaneously links bodies to the nation and its place in the international system: 'good' nations, as represented by a very masculine and heterosexual Bond, are sexually 'normal' just as 'good' states play by the system's rules, while opponents of the international regime or the nation-state system – such as Le Chiffre or Mr White – threaten the entire international system. In fact, Bond's enemies in many of the post-Cold War films are presented as not only morally deformed, they are de-nationalised, with interests that are intensely personal but global in reach. They signal a different and nefarious form of international politics, one that threatens the global, capitalist international security order.

The alignment of masculinity with international security, of the body politics, in *Casino Royale*, differs from earlier films also in its orientation towards the use of technology. As has been well-established in the literature, over the years the series has become increasingly technologised: the state and its opponents have more access to high tech toys and the stakes of the 'game' grow ever more frightening. The Lektor decoder in *From Russia With Love* (1963) is replaced by satellites that can trigger nuclear explosions and computer programs that can disrupt global markets. The Brosnan films retain the close relationship between Bond and MI6's gadgetry.[22] The message of these films is that Britain, in the guise of Bond, remains a competent, indeed a powerful international actor, if not through its overwhelming military might then through its mastery of technology and intelligence as well as its bravery. In these instances, technology becomes an extension of the gendered body, enhancing Bond's physical strength and prowess through the ways in which he uses it. As O'Donnell notes, 'as Bond becomes one with the car, or the mini-helicopter, or the fashion accessories concealing knives and explosives, it is as if the totality of these resources and his expertise must be deployed in order for him to achieve totality as Bond.'[23]

If technology in the Cold War era Bond films seemed to reinforce the binary gender order (insofar as male bodies usually controlled it), in the post-Cold War era, women's and men's bodies operate in a computerised and technologically sophisticated global environment in which expertise insinuates power. Women, like men, should be capable of mastering certain kinds of technology that are important to global capitalism and the international system. Indeed, *GoldenEye*'s Xenia can pilot jet planes and skilfully wield small arms; Natalya proves to be a first-rate computer specialist. However, women's knowledge and bodies are nonetheless insufficient to thwart the enemy's conspiracy. *Casino Royale* interrogates but ultimately reinforces this masculinised world of national security and technology. In its post-9/11 world, technology is democratised in that it can be used by or is familiar to virtually all the characters in the film and everyone in the audience: cell phones, computers, microchips, surveillance cameras. For example, M implants a GPS microchip into Bond's forearm in order to monitor his movements. Bond, M, Vesper, Felix, Le Chiffre – everyone – can make extensive use of cell phones to locate addresses and persons and of text-messaging to communicate critical instructions or information. And a miniature version of a stand-ard hospital defibrillator is handily available (in the glove compartment of the Aston Martin) and used by Vesper when Bond suffers digitalis poisoning. Such commonplace technology, while pervasive, is nonethe-less essential to MI6's mission and to Bond's survival. The effect of this 'democratic' technology is not only to signal the rootedness of *Casino Royale* in the 'real', it is to assert or reassert the significance of the physical body in navigating geostrategic spaces and in combating threats to global markets and (inter)national security. At the same time, such technology highlights the necessity of Bond's male body because only Bond can in fact defend Britain – that is, only he can undertake the arduous physical exertions that are required to strangle a man, to run down a terrorist, and to stop a plane from being blown-up.

(Inter)national security is also instantiated through the deployment of technology that is real-time and synchronic, able to detect threats to Britain, its allies, and agents. In a world in which forces can be rapidly deployed and information instantaneously transmitted, protection of the nation is dependent upon ability to perceive threats as they are occurring, hence, the enhanced role of electronic surveillance in intelligence organi-sations.[24] In *Casino Royale*, the use of real-time intelligence gathering is crucial to the narrative. For example, as Bond is discovered hacking M's computer by MI6, both he and M realise that it is Le Chiffre who is behind the funding of illegal arms transfers. Similarly, a phone call to a Swiss banker alerts Bond to the fact that, as they speak, Vesper is trans-ferring funds electronically without his knowledge.

This diegetic synchronicity reinforces the deterritorialised nature and rapidity of contemporary threats and the significance of intelligence and surveillance to global security. In *Casino Royale*, as in the interna-tional system, rapidity, fluidity, and simultaneity are characteristics of the security environment. At the same time, the pervasiveness of deadly if diffuse threats is evoked through cinematic repetition, as hyperreal and symbolic violence collide, inflicted on the body of Bond or enacted by him. Thus, electronic surveillance and communications technology serve to reinforce a gender binary as it is male characters that uncover these real-time threats and suffer the consequences of potentially lethal interactions. Once again, men and masculinity are linked to the fate of the international order and its stability.

Bond's got balls: or, why realists should love Casino Royale

'Wow, you've taken good care of your body. Such a waste.' Le Chiffre's loaded observation to Bond during the torture scene underscores not only 007's incredible physique but ultimately his body's importance to international security and the British nation. It suggests that Bond's body and by extension the nation-state cannot survive the nefarious threats of global terror (no matter what kind). Such threats not only mark and scar the body in that moment; they may cripple the broader potency of the nation-state. Le Chiffre continues, taunting Bond, 'It's not only the immediate agony, but the knowledge that if you do not yield soon enough, there will be little left to identify you as a man.' This dialogue performs two functions. First, it links Bond's body and his (hetero)sexuality to the nation and its vitality. Bond's genitals are emblematic of the nation's ability to reproduce and survive in the evolving post-Cold War (dis)order. Second, it connects the filmic narrative to the larger international system in two ways. It recalls a fundamental principle of political realism that all actors in the international system should comprehend – that rational actors yield to superior power or pay the consequences. This implicit invocation could hardly be lost on Bond, Britain's super agent and the West's key weapon in the struggle for its security. It is not surprising, then, that Bond refuses to yield to Le Chiffre's threats, refuses to recognise his subordinate position. He instead responds to Le Chiffre's taunting with an audacious retort: 'I've got a little itch – down there. Would you mind? . . . Now the whole world is going to know that you died scratching my balls.' On one level, Bond's cheeky response is the clever retort we have come to expect of him in such pressure-filled moments – after all, Bond always escapes. (And he does here as well: Mr White enters, shoots Le Chiffre, and leaves Bond alive to recuperate with Vesper by his side.) However, on another level, the response serves to solidify the linkage both between Bond and global security, and Bond and political realism. In fact, the scene proves political realism right: the superior force does win, as Le Chiffre is vanquished and Mr White is trapped by Bond at the end of the film.

Throughout the film, as encapsulated in the harrowing torture scene, the trope of the body ultimately supports the gender politics of international security by drawing on stock Bondian specularisation but it also presses beyond it. The hypervisibility of Bond's body works within the (in)visible logic of the nation-state system where rational actors (state as well as non-state actors) are presumed to make value-maximising choices that advance their interests and secure their position in the international system. If this logic is revealed through hypervisibility, it is also enacted through hypermasculinity. While for a moment in the torture scene it might seem that Bond's manliness is dispensable to British interests, Bond's genitals are shown to be coterminous with those interests. In fact, the film's gender politics on Bond's balls are no different than its gender politics on male–female relations. *Casino Royale*'s insistence on reconfiguring the body politics of the post-Cold War world in terms of masculinity/hypermasculinity and the real suggests gender does continue as a marker of national and 'cosmopolitan' identities and of (inter)national security.

Notes

1 Alexis Albion, 'Wanting to Be James Bond', in *Ian Fleming and James Bond: The Cultural Politics of 007*, ed. by Edward P. Comentale, Stephen Watt and Skip Willman (Bloomington: Indiana University Press, 2005), pp. 202–20; James Chapman, *Licence to Thrill: A Cultural History of the James Bond Films* (New York: Columbia University Press, 2000); Jim Leach, 'Bond in the 1990s – and Beyond?', in this book; Simon Winder, *The Man Who Saved Britain: A Personal Journey into the Disturbing World of James Bond* (New York: Farrar, Straus and Giroux, 2006).

2 Wendy Ide's *Times* commentary that this Bond is 'ruthless, reckless' and 'up with the best' was echoed by critics in the US. '*Casino Royale*', *The Times*, 4 November 2006.

3 Toby Miller, in his provocative analysis in 'James Bond's Penis', argues that the masculinity on display in the Bond series is in fact unstable, undermined by the films' self-parody and by the commodification of male beauty and desirability. See Chapter 17 in this book.

4 Bond is also subject to on-screen torture in *Die Another Day* (2002).

5 See, for example, Kenichi Ohmae, *The End of the Nation-State: The Rise of Regional Economies* (New York: Touchstone, 1996); Jan Aart Scholte, *Globalization: A Critical Introduction* (London: Palgrave Macmillan, 1999);

David Held, Anthony McGrew, David Goldblatt and Jonathan Perraton, *Global Transformations: Politics, Economics, and Culture* (Stanford University Press, 1999).

6 According to the realist tradition in the field of international relations, states became the building blocks of the international system with the peace of Westphalia (1648). Many realist scholars today are arguing that the 'Westphalian system' persists, but its foundational components (e.g., sovereignty, nationalism, and national identity) are increasingly under pressure from a range of emerging threats and from new transnational allegiances and relations of production (see Charles Kupchan, *The End of the American Empire: US Foreign Policy and the Geopolitics of the 21st Century* (New York: Vintage, 2003)); and some scholars have actually predicted the demise of the state system because of globalisation (see Kenichi Ohmae, *The End of the Nation-State: The Rise of Regional Economies* (New York: Touchstone, 1996)).

7 Many scholars have explored the complexity of Bond's identity. On Bond's racial identity, for example, see Vivian Halloran, 'Tropical Bond', in *Ian Fleming and James Bond: The Cultural Politics of 007*, ed. by Edward P. Comentale, Stephen Watt, and Skip Willman (Bloomington: Indiana University Press, 2005), pp. 158–77.

8 On the debate contrasting 'nationalism' and 'cosmopolitanism', see Pheng Cheah and Bruce Robbins, eds, *Cosmopolitics: Thinking and Feeling Beyond the Nation* (Minneapolis: University of Minnesota Press, 1998), and Daniele Archibugi, ed., *Debating Cosmopolitics* (London: Verso, 2003).

9 For discussions of gender, states, nationalism, and the international system, see Cynthia Enloe, *Bananas, Beaches and Bases: Making Feminist Sense of International Relations*, updated edn (Berkeley: University of California Press, 2001) and *Maneuvers: The International Politics of Militarizing Women's Lives* (Berkeley: University of California Press, 2000); Steve Niva, 'Tough and Tender: New World Order, Masculinity and the Gulf War', in *The Man Question in International Relations*, ed. by Jane Parpart and Marysia Zalewski (Boulder: Westview, 1998), pp. 109–28; Carole Pateman, *The Disorder of Women: Women, Democracy, Feminism and Social Theory* (Stanford: Stanford University Press, 1990); V. Spike Peterson, 'Sexing Political Identities/ Nationalism as Heterosexism', in *Women, States, and Nationalism: At Home in the Nation?*, ed. by Sita Ranchod-Nilsson and Mary Ann Tetreault (London/ New York: Routledge, 2000), pp. 54–80; Nira Yuval-Davis, *Gender and Nation* (London: Sage, 1997).

10 Janet Woollacott, 'The James Bond Films: Conditions of Production', in *The James Bond Phenomenon: A Critical Reader,* ed. by Christoph Lindner. (Manchester: Manchester University Press, 2003), pp. 99–117 (p. 110).

11 Woollacott, 'The James Bond Films', p. 110.

12 M's authority and competence are also undermined in *The World is Not*

Enough. M's misjudgment of the villainess Elektra King leads to risk for the nation and to her own imprisonment by King and her partner Renard in Maiden's Tower in Istanbul. She is, of course, saved by Bond.

13 Because the SPECTRE organisation was the main protagonist in many of the Cold War era Bond films, scholars have argued that the series presaged the coming threats from de-territorialized criminal organisations. See, for example, David C. Earnest and James N. Rosenau, 'The Spy Who Loved Globalization', *Foreign Policy*, 120 (September/October, 2000), pp. 88–90.

14 Thus, *Casino Royale* breaks with other films that, according to Jim Leach, depict worlds 'in which electronic technology both transcends the limits of the human body and makes possible a surveillance system that erodes any notion of privacy.' See Jim Leach, 'Bond in the 1990s – and Beyond?' in this book.

15 See Laura Mulvey, 'Visual Pleasure and Narrative Cinema', *Screen*, 16, no. 2 (1975), 6–18; Stephen Neale, 'Masculinity as Spectacle', *Screen*, 24, no. 6 (1983), 2–16; Mary Ann Doane, *Femme Fatales: Feminism, Film Theory and Psychoanalysis* (London/New York: Routledge, 1991); Elizabeth Cowie, *Representing the Woman: Cinema and Psychoanalysis* (London: Macmillan, 1997).

16 Woollacott, 'The James Bond Films: Conditions of Production', p. 110.

17 In fact, his attention is immediately drawn to the figure of Solange on the beach. The image is repeated a second time when a swimsuit clad Bond emerges from the ocean during a holiday with Vesper (who is, by the way, fully dressed). The first and longer image of Bond's almost naked body lasts about 14 seconds until it cuts away to Solange, in contrast to the scene in *Die Another Day* in which Berry's body is telescoped on screen in slow motion for over 40 seconds.

18 The importance of the body trope is further flagged in between these two scenes. Bond goes to Miami in pursuit of Alex Dimitrios and ends up at a museum exhibition, Bodyworlds, where human forms and cadavers are literally on display and fully exposed.

19 V. Spike Peterson, 'Sexing Political Identities/Nationalism as Heterosexism,' p. 59.

20 Jeremy Black, *The Politics of James Bond* (Lincoln: University of Nebraska Press, 2005), p. 107.

21 Patrick O'Donnell, 'James Bond, Cyborg-Aristocrat', in *Ian Fleming and James Bond: The Cultural Politics of 007*, ed. by Edward Comentale, Stephen Watt and SkipWillman (Bloomington: Indiana University Press, 2005), pp. 55–68 (p. 59).

22 For a full discussion of Bond and technology in the Brosnan films, see Martin Willis's essay in this book, 'Hard-Wear: The Millenium, Technology, and Brosnan's Bond'.

23 Patrick O'Donnell, 'James Bond, Cyborg-Aristocrat,' p. 63.
24 Indeed, both the United Kingdom and the United States initiated reviews of their intelligence systems after 9/11 and 7/7.

Part III

Re-thinking 007

Christine Bold

'Under the very skirts of Britannia': re-reading women in the James Bond novels

Never say never again. In the late 1980s and early 1990s, James Bond was back, his masculine privileges intact. In the summer of 1992, MGM/UA released a 'Limited Collector's Edition' of eight Bond films, remastered for VHS and repackaged with new covers. This initial set concentrated primarily on the early Sean Connery performances, rather than the later productions which parody Bond's phallic powers. The iconography of the covers flaunts the triumphant male: in full evening suit, gun at the ready, Bond is propelled upwards by various rocket-powered vehicles while scantily-clad women cling to him, their hands hovering suggestively around his lower parts. A similar reaffirmation of male supremacy operates, much more subtly, in Coronet Books' 1988 and 1989 reprints of the full range of Bond fiction. Each paperback volume is prefaced with the same introduction by Anthony Burgess, essentially a celebration of Bond as Fleming wrote him and a relegitimation of the novels' and short stories' representations of gender. Countering Fleming's reputation for softcore pornography, Burgess insists that only the movies, debased versions of the fiction, give grounds for that accusation: 'The girls [*sic*] in the Bond films tend . . . to be nothing more than animated centrefolds. In the books they are credible and lovable because of some humanising flaw – a broken nose, a slight limp, most of all the trauma of psychological injury or personal guilt.'[1]

Tellingly, Bond does not need to undergo physical and psychological trauma to achieve credible humanity: he is 'a fuller man' because he loves cars, vodka martinis, and women. Bond is, Burgess resoundingly concludes, 'a hero we need'. Shades of Kingsley Amis, who chortled nearly thirty years ago: 'We don't want to have Bond to dinner or go golfing with Bond or talk to Bond. We want to be Bond.'[2] The question begs to be asked: who are 'we'?

There is a more sceptical reading of Bond that recognises the patriarchal interests at work in the fiction and the attendant infantilisation and objectification of female figures. Tony Bennett and Janet Woollacott argue, for example, 'In . . . responding to the challenge posed by "the girl", putting her back into place beneath him (both literally and metaphorically), Bond functions as an agent of the patriarchal order, refurbishing its imaginarily impaired structure by quelling the source of the disturbance within it.'[3] Bennett and Woollacott sustain a highly nuanced exploration of this potent 'Bond phenomenon' as it is produced and received within a discursive field of novels, films, advertising, magazine pieces, and the intertextual resonances of other popular genres. In a more limited, but equally suggestive materialist reading, Michael Denning qualifies the argument about gender relations in Fleming's fiction. Situating the Bond novels in the particular social climate of the 1950s and 1960s, he argues that they articulate 'the new organisation of sexuality in consumer capitalism' which involves 'a reconstitution of sexuality in a fetishised mode that continues to subordinate and oppress women.'[4]

In awareness of the current cultural moment – the end-point of a trajectory that stretches from the exuberance of 1960s' 'women's lib' with its faith in the sexual revolution, to the more sober and angry gains of feminism in the 1970s and 1980s, to the troubling present of documentable 'backlash' – I propose a resistant reading that opts out of the consensual 'we' invoked by Burgess and Amis, but also avoids the logic of the more radical readings which recognise the sexism of the fiction without escaping its patriarchal priorities. However critically, the Bennett–Woollacott– Denning argument becomes complicit in Fleming's project to foreground masculine power. (A much harsher disjunction operates in Mordecai Richler's dismantling of the Bond myth: while angrily denouncing Fleming's 'sanitised' anti-Semitism, Richler happily subscribes to the sexism: 'If I find Fleming's politics distasteful . . . his occasional flirtation with ideas embarrassing, I am happy to say that I am in accord with him in admiring firm, thrusting, beautiful breasts.')[5] Reading as a woman (not an identical activity, as Jonathan Culler pointed out, to a woman reading), I have no wish to be Bond, nor does any community of which I imagine myself part need him as its hero.[6] Yet Bond is a cultural force to be reckoned with, sold to more than 45 million readers by 1966, and back now with the backlash. In the words of Bennett and Woollacott, again:

> Popular heroes are public property, not in the sense that anyone can produce a Bond film, but in the sense that their images can be reworked, inflected in different directions and to different ends. Certainly such figures

occupy too important a position within the terrain on which popular consciousness is shaped and defined, to be simply abandoned.[7]

Bond also constitutes part of the terrain on which myths of espionage,
patriotism, and masculinity are made to converge, myths that service the
'imagined community' of nationhood.[8] Given Bond's centrality to inter-
secting popular mythologies, it may be purposeful to do more than slap a
'This book offends women' notice on Fleming's work. To read against the
grain of Fleming's fiction, textually, is to recuperate Bond not as the heroic
agent of the masculinised nation but as an entry-point into the fragility of
representational ruses which depend for their cultural currency on the
unrelenting subordination of women.

One of the suggestive ironies of Fleming's fiction is that its disposition
of gender does not adhere to the conventional trajectory of spy fiction. In
the secret loop of international intrigue traced by LeQueux, Buchan,
Ambler, Greene, and le Carré, women are always the outsiders. The clandestine power of spy masters and secret agents is represented as the
proper preserve of men. Female characters who attempt clandestine
interventions in international politics suffer the fate of the real Mata Hari;
more commonly, women are represented in subservient positions outside
the sphere of secret influence. They most typically function as peripheral
romantic interest, domestic background, or ambiguously androgynous
companionship for the hero.

While Fleming reproduces that power imbalance, his novels do foreground women as the enabling mechanism of the spy's fictional universe.
In Fleming's depiction, the British secret service depends upon its female
infrastructure: women carry the files, operate the decoders, oversee the
paperwork, screen the appointments, and supply the canteen services
which keep the institution running. Headquarters hums with efficient
women: trotting along corridors, dispensing advice in outer offices, even
operating a 'powder-vine' through 'the girls' restroom', which dissemi-
nates confidential information far more efficiently than any official
communications system, 'to the impotent fury of the Security staff'.[9]

Women are equally indispensable on the front lines of international
spying. Bond frequently depends on women to guide him through the
enemy territory of his exotic locations: Honeychile Rider, who knows the
Jamaican tides and island terrain of *Dr No* (1958); Kissy Suzuki, who
steers Bond to and rescues him from Blofeld's Garden of Death in *You
Only Live Twice* (1964); and Tiffany Case, who skilfully false-deals him the
winning cards at the Spang brothers' Las Vegas casino in *Diamonds Are*

Forever (1956). As often as Bond snatches women from the jaws of death, they repay the compliment: Pussy Galore thwarts the arch-villain's plans and saves the lives of not only Bond but the entire population of Fort Knox in *Goldfinger* (1959); Domino Vitale fires the fatal spear into Emilio Largo, SPECTRE agent, just as he is about to shoot Bond in *Thunderball* (1961).

Whatever skills female characters demonstrate, however, their one great prowess – insisted on by narrative voice and Bond's own comments – resides in their bodies. It is a cardinal rule of Fleming's fiction that women who serve – and service – the British espionage forces are buxom, slim, long-legged, lightly tanned – and, more often than not, they wear their long, glossy hair curved into the nape of the neck. This physical sensuousness is evident not only in the island beauties Bond encounters in the field but in Miss Moneypenny, Mary Goodnight, and all the minions scuttling around the Ministry of Works. This effortless perfection is not offered as a sign of woman's agency. The subservient sexual service of Headquarters staff is reflected on by Loelia Ponsonby, Bond's private secretary, in *Moonraker* (1955):

> It was true that an appointment in the Secret Service was a form of peonage.
> If you were a woman there wasn't much of you left for other relationships.
> It was easier for the men. They had an excuse for fragmentary affairs ...
> But, for the women, an affair outside the Service automatically made you
> a 'security risk' and in the last analysis you had a choice of resignation
> from the Service and a normal life, or of perpetual concubinage to your
> King and country.[10]

Women's bodies are designed to pleasure others: notably, James Bond, who ritually rewards himself in the course and at the close of all his dangerous assignments by sexual intercourse with one or more of these women: 'Solitaire, the ultimate personal prize.'[11] It is no secret that Fleming's fiction ritually works to objectify and infantilise its 'girls', as these sexually mature women are routinely named; moreover, because women are often exoticised in terms of their racial and ethnic heritage, the novels mount a politics of colonisation across a broad front.

This insistent reification of women can be understood, however, within a wider trope equating 'lines of national affiliation and sexual attachment',[12] the fundamental co-ordinates of international espionage as fictionalised by Fleming. In this reading of women's bodies, women retrieve agency as the determinants of Britain's national identity. The trope attaching nationhood to sexuality is signalled by the metonymic

12.1 Bond (Sean Connery) enjoys a relaxing bath in *You Only Live Twice*

link between Britain's political potency and the sexual potency of its
heroic secret agent. If, as Michael Denning argues, 'the spy novel is . . . the
cover story of an era of decolonisation and, particularly after the debacle
at Suez in 1956, the definitive loss of Britain's role as a world power', then
the waning and waxing of Bond's sexual dominance – most explicitly in
You Only Live Twice – represent and reverse a larger cultural pattern.[13] The
efficacy lies specifically in heterosexual potency: the representatives of
lesser nations are not just sexually impotent but sexually 'deviant'. The
Bond novels promote what Adrienne Rich names 'compulsory heterosexuality' as the irrefutable sign of a healthy imperial nation; that trope is
sustainable only if at its centre exists a stream of emphatically sensuous
women desiring and desired by James Bond.[14]

The conflation of the physical and national body is most insistent in
From Russia, With Love (1957): the beautiful Tatiana Romanova, Russian
lure for Bond, is told, 'Your body belongs to the State . . . Now your body
must work for the State'; Bond recognises his own role 'as he sourly

described it to himself, of "pimping for England"'.[15] When the two discover a healthy passion for each other, the ending is foreclosed: Tatiana
ultimately discovers the perfidy of the Soviet regime and defects to
England. The essential inhumanity of the Soviet state is figured with
insistent sexuality by Rosa Klebb, head of Operations and Executions in
'the official murder organisation of the Soviet government', SMERSH –
'Smiert Spionam' or 'Death to Spies'.[16] Klebb's reputation for sadism is
underwritten by her lesbian tendencies. Klebb propositions Tatiana in
a scene that caricatures the advances of the many young women who
desire Bond:

> Colonel Klebb of SMERSH was wearing a semi-transparent nightgown in
> orange crêpe de chine. It had scallops of the same material round the low
> square neckline and scallops at the wrists of the broadly flounced sleeves.
> Underneath could be seen a brassiere consisting of two large pink satin roses.
> Below, she wore old-fashioned knickers of pink satin with elastic above the
> knees. One dimpled knee, like a yellowish coconut, appeared thrust forward
> between the half open folds of the nightgown in pink satin slippers with
> pompoms of ostrich feathers. Rosa Klebb had taken off her spectacles and
> her naked face was now thick with mascara and rouge and lipstick.
>   She looked like the oldest and ugliest whore in the world.
>   Tatiana stammered, 'It's very pretty.'
>   'Isn't it', twittered the woman. She went over to a broad couch in the
> corner of the room . . .
>   With a squeak of pleasure, Rosa Klebb threw herself down in the caricature
> of a Recamier pose. She reached up an arm and turned on a pink shaded
> table-lamp whose stem was a naked woman in sham Lalique glass. She patted
> the couch beside her.
>   'Turn out the top light, my dear. The switch is by the door. Then come and
> sit beside me. We must get to know each other better.'[17]

By heavy-handed caricature and ridicule, the scene simultaneously
polices women's clothing, bodies, and sexual desires, while exposing the
perversion of the Soviet system. While Tatiana 'ran wildly off down the
corridor with her hands over her ears', later to fall happily into bed with
Bond, Rosa ends up committing suicide with poison after attempting to
assassinate Bond by the same method.

The equation never fails: beauty, heterosexuality, and patriotism go
together; ugliness, sexual 'deviance', and criminality are linked equally irre-
sistibly. The litmus test is foreign agents' attitude to women. The bestiality
of Donovan Grant – the Irishman-turned-SMERSH agent in *From Russia,
With Love* – is signalled in the opening pages of the novel, when his
celibacy and complete lack of desire for women are revealed. The East

European Blofeld, mad master of SPECTRE, takes as his apparently amorous companion Irma Blunt, a hideously squat caricature of woman-hood 'too ugly to live', in the words of Tiger Tanaka, head of the Japanese secret service and ally of the British service.[18] Once a month, the Latvian arch-villain Goldfinger hires a woman, sprays her with gold paint, and rapes her: a conflation of desire and riches that goes beyond the acceptable objectification of women practised by British men. Pussy Galore, as a les-bian, is the leader of a lesbian gang and collaborator with Goldfinger; once seduced by Bond – who 'felt the sexual challenge all beautiful Lesbians have for men'[19] – she abandons her allegiance both to lesbianism and to the villain. In the same novel, Tilly Masterton, who refuses Bond's advances because of her emerging preference for women, dies. Bond reflects disdainfully on the political sources and consequences of Tilly's sexuality:

> Bond came to the conclusion that Tilly Masterton was one of those girls whose hormones had got mixed up. He knew the type well and thought they and their male counterparts were a direct consequence of giving votes to women and 'sex equality'. As a result of fifty years of emancipation, feminine qualities were dying out or being transferred to the males. Pansies of both sexes were everywhere, not yet completely homosexual, but confused, not knowing what they were. The result was a herd of unhappy sexual misfits – barren and full of frustrations, the women wanting to dominate and the men to be nannied. He was sorry for them, but he had no time for them.[20]

The crucial trick is to separate this alien lesbianism and homosexuality from the hearty homosociality of the British establishment. The Bond novels exhibit a high level of nervousness about 'the homosexual spies' Burgess and Maclean; this narrative obsession can be read as part of the wider Cold War hysteria that conflated homosexuality and communism, and insisted that 'perversion is synonymous with treason'.[21] Felix Leiter, Bond's CIA ally, articulates the casual, unchallenged homophobia of the spy world when he describes the villains to Bond in *Diamonds Are Forever*: 'Kidd's a pretty boy. His friends call him "Boofy". Probably shacks up with Wint. Some of these homos make the worst killers.'[22]

At the same time, Fleming's fiction represents British imperialist power as residing within intimate male relations. The homoerotics of Bond's relationship with M are suggested by Bond himself, in his explanation to Tiffany Case as to why he won't marry: 'I'm almost married already. To a man. Name begins with M. I'd have to divorce him before I tried marry-ing a woman. And I'm not sure I'd want that.'[23] The narrative voice con-firms the relationship, less flippantly: Bond 'looked across into the tranquil, lined sailor's face that he loved, honoured and obeyed'.[24] Similar intimacies are indicated by Bond's repeated links with male agents; there is even a covert homoeroticism decipherable in his confrontations with male villains who more than once concentrate their torture on Bond's genitals. It is this vein of repressed homosexuality that Cyril Connolly mined in his hilarious parody, 'Bond Strikes Camp', in which Bond is tricked into cross-dressing by a service riddled with transvestites (most flamboyantly, M and 'Lolita' Ponsonby).[25] The representational ruse that offsets these signals is the desire of women: Darko Kerim, one of Bond's sidekicks, engages in a frenzy of heterosexual activity which protests too much his sexual identity; in Bond's genealogy, he begins education at Eton, byword of upper-class homosexuality, but is removed almost immediately 'after some alleged trouble with one of the boys' maids'.[26] Yet the textual slippage continues, homoerotic pleasure surfacing in physical descriptions of women: of Tatiana Romanova, 'A purist would have disapproved of her behind, its muscles were so hardened with exercise that it had lost the smooth downward feminine sweep, and now, round at the back and flat and hard at the sides, it jutted like a man's'.[27] Bond first sees and desires Honeychile Rider from the rear: 'the behind was almost as firm and rounded as a boy's'.[28]

Thus the agency lost by women at the level of manifest narrative commentary is recovered by a strategy which positions women centrally within the formation of national identity. In my reading, the Bond novels transcode the politics of nationhood – with considerable tension and slippage – into what Judith Butler terms the 'heterosexual matrix': 'that grid of cultural intelligibility through which bodies, genders, and desires are naturalized'.[29] In the context of the homosociality of the British establishment and a libidinous hero, that heterosexuality crucially depends on women. In balancing the fine line, female figures live out the symbolism of the female body politic signified by Britannia, the symbolism evoked by the evil Hugo Drax in *Moonraker*. Masquerading as a British philanthropist, the neo-Nazi Drax threatens the cosmopolitan centre of Britain – London – with his atomic rocket. But he also threatens the central ruse of national representation. When he aims, as he says, 'under the very skirts of Britannia' with his phallic rocket – 'this great arrow of vengeance . . . the might of my fatherland' – threatens to broach the boundaries of nationality and sexuality policed by Bond, as well as state security.[30] He may expose the erotics of British nationalism ('love of country') masked by Britannia by exposing an icon in drag. In the instant of destroying the rocket with its multiple threats, Bond conveniently has at hand a female agent, over whom he adopts his familiar missionary position to protect them both from flying masonry. The symbolism is obvious; heterosexuality wins the day once more.

The dependence of the nationalist–masculinist mythology on women is suggested most emphatically when the Bond fiction articulates a need for female affirmation. In *Gender Trouble*, Judith Butler argues of representation generally: 'the radical dependency of the masculine subject on the female "Other" suddenly exposes his autonomy as illusory'.[31] This need is played out most explicitly in *The Spy Who Loved Me* (1962), a straight crime-thriller which has nothing to do with spying but everything to do with the co-option of the female reader. Singularly, for a Fleming novel, it is narrated in the first-person voice of a woman: Vivienne Michel, a twenty-three-year-old French Canadian. With the assumed authenticity of experience, Michel confirms all the sexist and racist stereotypes of the earlier Bond novels; her stories confirm that women do define themselves by their bodies, they are child-like naifs who need the guidance and protection of a man, and colonials are less complex types than their British counterparts. Above all, Michel underwrites Bond's sexual dominance over women. Immediately after being saved from a battering by a couple of American gangsters, Michel falls into bed with her *deus ex machina*:

> All women love semi-rape. They love to be taken. It was [Bond's] sweet brutality against my bruised body that had made his act of love so piercingly wonderful . . . After looking long at him, I lay back. No, he was as I had thought him to be. Yes, this was a man to love.[32]

Michel is also a reader, eager to be trained by Bond. She has read about SPECTRE and Operation Thunderball in the newspapers: 'I could hardly believe it. It was like something out of a thriller.'[33] Bond now overlays his own first-person experience on the story, situating its significance for his eager listener. Michel is even less sophisticated as a reader of consumerist messages. In the aftermath of the gun battle, she carefully selects Camay soap for Bond, explaining when he demurs at her choice, 'It's very good. It's got costly French perfume in it. It says so on the packet.'[34] Bond's farewell note to her, as he disappears mysteriously off into the night, instructs her to go up-market in her consumerism: 'Try Guerlain's "Fleur des Alpes" instead of Camay!'[35] Tony Davies argues that the regulatory operations of political thrillers are coded in dominant looking: 'Masculinity is grounded, in these texts, in the power of the gaze.'[36] *The Spy Who Loved Me* offers no reversal of the gaze, but an invitation to women to submit to the patriarchal gaze, identify with James Bond, masculinise themselves as spectators of female objectification, and thus 'other' their own womanhood, as Laura Mulvey has famously argued about women spectators of Hollywood feature films.[37]

In the same year as the publication of *The Spy Who Loved Me*, the first of the Bond films underwrote the novel's message about the inevitable rightness of gender relations within the masculine domain of the spy. In *Dr No* (1962), Honeychile Rider is played by Ursula Andress. While the female body is the more powerful in this medium for its visual representation, the possibilities for identifying female agency are much dimmer. The Andress character is a much less resourceful figure than Fleming's version: whereas, in the novel, her superior knowledge of sea life facilitates her escape from Dr No's trap, in the movie she is chained down helplessly and must be rescued by Bond. The position of powerlessness is generalised for women across class and race lines by the early scenes of the film. In the opening sequence, the viewer watches a gang of Chinese-African-Jamaican men close in on, then kill, the first female figure to be represented: the white secretary to the representative of the British Secret Service in Jamaica. (In the immediately preceding scene, her boss is killed by the same team, but without the audience's anticipation.) The scene shifts to a London casino, where an elegant, bejewelled white woman is trounced at baccarat by James Bond. Then Bond appears with Miss Moneypenny, eluding her mock advances and laughingly dubbing her 'government property'. Next a female Chinese-Jamaican photographer is caught by Bond and hurt by his African-Jamaican sidekick, Quarrel. And so on.

Generally, the early Bond films limit women's initiatives: playing down the threat of alternative sexualities, these productions reduce the nationalist symbolism of the female body, and they represent desirable women as unknowing, helpless dupes. The politics of representation are the more slippery and the more difficult to challenge in this medium because of the hints of self-mockery: the films mine what John Cawelti calls 'the edge of irony' in Fleming's fiction, in the style of their excessive violence and sex and in Connery's characteristically sardonic facial expression.[38] Only later – with the Roger Moore performances, especially – do the films become pronouncedly, indeed mechanically, self-parodic, and at that point women visibly complicate the disposition of power. In *A View to a Kill* (1985), for example, the powerful African-American woman May Day, played by Grace Jones, takes the upper hand, in bed and out, from a jowly, glassy-eyed Roger Moore. The descent into manifest self-parody suggests something about the exhaustibility of the Bond formula and the resort to women and other colonised figures to revive its energy, but filmic texts clearly demand different strategies of readerly resistance from written texts.

If Fleming could construct a fictional female voice and reader to his formula's specifications, the responses of 'real readers' were not necessarily so easily contained. We know that women read Bond novels, though specific figures are not available. Perhaps the most famous female Bond fan was Jackie Kennedy. John Kennedy ranked *From Russia, With Love* among his ten favourite books; Jackie is said to have recommended it to Allen Dulles, the Director of Central Intelligence.[39] While JFK's literary taste here seems consistent with what we know of his cultural and sexual appetites, what was in the novel for Jackie? Indeed, how did women read James Bond, and what imaginative identifications did they make? Kingsley Amis hypothesises that women read these works not as part of the spy genre but within the coordinates of the woman's genre of romance. But it is Amis who so casually effaces difference in his assumption that we all share his desire to 'be Bond', and it is not clear that his characterisation covers all the cultural competencies that women may bring to the reading situation.

My own reading luxuriates in the insistent contradictions between the manifest narrative voice, which consistently denies the centrality of female figures, and the evidence of recurrent plot patterns and spectacles. As reader, I know more than Bond, especially as the series proceeds and he and M fail, increasingly, to decipher clues and avoid traps that I have anticipated. The position of 'knowing subject' becomes powerfully gendered when it is shared with female characters: Vesper Lynd in *Casino Royale* (1953) manipulates Bond from her position as double agent; Solitaire in *Live and Let Die* (1954) has a mystical foreknowledge of the future which she hides from Bond; Gala Brand and Tatiana Romanova know more than Bond, as does, climactically, Kissy Suzuki, who trains an amnesiac Bond into a new identity for her own pleasure. As a child of 1950s and 1960s middle-class Scotland – sharing Bond's identification with Britain's 'period of prosperity' – I also bring my own cultural associations to the brand names that densely populate Fleming's fictional scene.[40] I have my own memories of the Guerlain bathcubes favoured by Dr No and the Lentheric aftershave lotion that wafts around all Bond's adventures. These products do not necessarily signal male supremacy and the containment of female self-esteem; they also smack of the homeliness and quotidian pleasures of adolescent girls beginning to enjoy our own bodies and use the vocabularies of consumerism to create our own communities. This is not the whole story of the tensions of consumerism, but

I can test my taste against Bond's and know when his choices are wrong; in my circle, Rolex watches were decidedly *de trop*.

As a Scot, I also read Bond self-consciously from the margins of the national formation that the novels demarcate. The establishment Bond serves is emphatically English, but Bond himself (like Fleming) is Scottish on his father's side (Swiss on his mother's). He is educated at Fettes in Edinburgh after his expulsion from Eton; he employs a Scottish house-keeper; and as the series proceeds he appeals more and more frequently to his distinct Scottish identity: at the close of Fleming's last novel, *The Man With The Golden Gun* (1965), Bond refuses a knighthood with the cipher message, 'EYE AM A SCOTTISH PEASANT AND EYE WILL ALWAYS FEEL AT HOME BEING A SCOTTISH PEASANT.'[41] Reading from a geo-political margin, as well as a gendered one, I note it as a further fissure in the confident carapace of cultural hierarchies that the icons of South British life – London, Parliament, Blades of Pall Mall – should depend for their survival on a figure from the periphery. The tension is played effectively by Sean Connery in the early Bond movies, his raw-boned workingman's frame barely contained within the Savile Row suits, the Scottish burr within the mid-Atlantic vowels. But the joke turned on the British establishment when Connery chose to campaign for Scottish nationalism in the 1992 election; 'James Bond Votes SNP!' the tabloids shrieked.

There has emerged, as yet, no outpouring of feminist spy fiction on the order of the feminist (sometimes lesbian feminist) detective fiction cur-rently destabilising that genre. Yet the recognition that Fleming's fiction makes desperate gestures to the woman reader suggests her power, a power that can be redeployed subversively. Fleming mounts a regulatory scheme that aligns good and bad nations with 'normal' and 'abnormal' sexual pref-erences. Under the pressing anxieties of the atomic age, articulated increas-ingly insistently as the series proceeds, sexuality operates as a normative and essentialist measure of nationhood: beautiful women demonstrate that it is 'natural' to be heterosexual; they turn their services, sooner or later, to Britain (via its agent, James Bond); hence, Britain's natural and irresistible superiority is proven. Simply recognising the fundamental reliance of this scheme on women returns to them some of the agency denied by their manifest objectification in the fictional narrative.

By exploiting textual fissures and gaps that contradict the logic of mas-culinity or patriarchy, however, the resistant reader can go further: she can destabilise the hierarchy of gender and race on which the Bond insti-tution rests, interpreting textual fissures as faultlines in the construction of patriarchal nationhood. Benedict Anderson argues that the nation is an imaginary construct, shored up in part by reading practices, particularly of mass-distributed works.[42] Catharine MacKinnon insists that 'social power shapes the way we know and . . . the way we know shapes social power in terms of the social inequality between women and men'.[43] These twin propositions suggest the urgency in challenging the conventions of spy fiction, one of the main conduits for popular images of international power relations. Reversing dominant reading practices in this case may be a step towards rewriting women's agency within the closed world of fictive clandestinity, refeminising the secret sphere of influence, and changing the rules of the 'great game' and the socio-political matrix it trails with it. We can choose to know that (fictional) women make Bond's existence possible. We can choose to supplant him by imagining a new lineage of feminist power, escape the constraints of traditional gender categories, and refuse the objectification of 'others' on which their male counterparts so precariously depend.

Notes

1 Anthony Burgess, introduction to Coronet Books' editions of Ian Fleming's James Bond novels, 1988.

2 Kingsley Amis, *The James Bond Dossier* (London: Jonathan Cape, 1965), p. 38.

3 Tony Bennett and Jane Woollacott, *Bond and Beyond: The Political Career of a Popular Hero* (New York: Methuen, 1987), p. 116.

4 Michael Denning, *Cover Stories: Narrative and Ideology in the British Spy Thriller* (London: Routledge & Kegan Paul, 1987), p. 112, p. 113.

5 Mordecai Richler, 'James Bond Unmasked', in *Mass Culture Revisited*, ed. by Bernard Rosenberg and David Manning White (New York: Van Nostrand Reinhold, 1971), pp. 341–55 (p. 343).

6 See Jonathan Culler, 'Reading as a Woman', in *On Deconstruction: Theory and Criticism After Structuralism* (Ithaca: Cornell University Press, 1982), pp. 43–64.

7 Bennett and Woollacott, *Bond and Beyond*, p. 283.

8 Benedict Anderson, *Imagined Communities: Reflections on the Origin and Spread of Nationalism* (London: Verso, 1983).

9 Ian Fleming, *Moonraker* (London: Coronet Books/Hodder and Stoughton, 1989), p. 11.

10 Fleming, *Moonraker*, p. 10.

11 Ian Fleming, *Live and Let Die* (London: Hodder and Stoughton, 1988), p. 124.

12 Andrew Parker, Mary Russo, Doris Sommer and Patricia Yaeger (eds), 'Introduction', *Nationalisms and Sexualities* (New York: Routledge, 1992), p. 2.

13 Denning, *Cover Stories*, p. 92.

14 See Adrienne Rich, 'Compulsory Heterosexuality and Lesbian Existence', in *Blood, Bread, and Poetry: Selected Prose 1979–85* (New York: W.W. Norton, 1986), pp. 23–75.

15 Ian Fleming, *From Russia, With Love* (London: Coronet Books/Hodder and Stoughton, 1988), p. 70, p. 94.

16 Fleming, *From Russia, With Love*, p. 27.

17 Fleming, *From Russia, With Love*, pp. 71–2.

18 Ian Fleming, *You Only Live Twice* (London: Coronet Books/Hodder and Stoughton, 1988), p. 114.

19 Ian Fleming, *Goldfinger* (London: Coronet Books/Hodder and Stoughton, 1989), p. 168.

20 Fleming, *Goldfinger*, p. 189.

21 Lee Edelman, 'Tearooms and Sympathy, or, The Epistemology of the Water Closet', in *Nationalisms and Sexualities*, ed. by Andrew Parker *et al.* (New York: Routledge, 1992), pp. 263–84 (p. 263, p. 268).

22 Ian Fleming, *Diamonds are Forever* (London: Coronet Books/Hodder and Stoughton, 1988), p. 99.

23 Fleming, *Diamonds are Forever*, pp. 163–4.

24 Fleming, *From Russia, With Love*, p. 85.

25 See Cyril Connolly, 'Bond Strikes Camp', in *Previous Convictions* (London: Hamish Hamilton, 1963), pp. 354–71.

26 Fleming, *You Only Live Twice*, p. 179.

27 Fleming, *From Russia, With Love*, p. 59.

28 Ian Fleming, *Dr No* (London: Coronet Books/Hodder and Stoughton, 1988), p. 69.

29 Judith Butler, *Gender Trouble: Feminism and the Subversion of Identity* (New York: Routledge, 1990), p. 151.

30 Fleming, *Moonraker*, p. 164.

31 Butler, *Gender Trouble*, p. ix.

32 Ian Fleming, *The Spy Who Loved Me* (London: Coronet Books/Hodder and Stoughton, 1989), pp. 15–45.

33 Fleming, *The Spy Who Loved Me*, p. 119.

34 Fleming, *The Spy Who Loved Me*, p. 152.

35 Fleming, *The Spy Who Loved Me,* p. 186.

36 Tony Davies, 'The Divided Gaze: Reflections on the Political Thriller', in *Gender, Genre and Narrative Pleasure*, ed. by Derek Longhurst (London: Unwin Hyman, 1989), pp. 118–35 (p. 118).

37 See Laura Mulvey, 'Visual Pleasure and Narrative Cinema', *Screen*, 16.3 (1975), 6–18; and 'Afterthoughts on "Visual Pleasure and Narrative Cinema" Inspired by *Duel in the Sun*', in *Popular Fiction: Technology, Ideology, Production, Reading*, ed. by Tony Bennett (London: Routledge, 1990), pp. 139–51.

38 John G. Cawelti and Bruce A. Rosenberg, *The Spy Story* (Chicago: University of Chicago Press, 1987), p. 150.

39 David Stafford, *The Silent Game: The Real World of Imaginary Spies* (Toronto: Lester & Orpen Dennys, 1988), p. 170.
40 Furio Columbo, 'Bond's Women', in *The Bond Affair*, ed. by Oreste Del Bueno and Umberto Eco (London: Macdonald, 1966), pp. 86–102 (p. 89).
41 Ian Fleming, *The Man With The Golden Gun* (London: Coronet Books/Hodder and Stoughton, 1989), p. 157.
42 See Anderson, *Imagined Communities*.
43 Catherine A. MacKinnon, *Toward a Feminist Theory of State* (Cambridge, Mass.: Harvard University Press, 1989), p. ix.

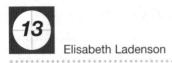

13

Elisabeth Ladenson

Pussy Galore

By the early 1970s, when I came of Bond-appreciating age, the first Bond films were being recycled as classic antecedents to the increasingly self-parodic and gadget-driven vehicles that continued, and still now continue, to appear. My own Bondophilia was a product of this early kitschification (later to become meta-kitschification) of the Bond phenomenon. I fell prey to this preoccupation in earnest in 1972 or so when my father took me to see a triple feature playing on Eighth Street in Greenwich Village. We saw, I think, *From Russia With Love* (1963), *Goldfinger* (1964), and *You Only Live Twice* (1967), all in the course of a single afternoon. These were not the first Bond films I had seen, nor was it the first time I had seen them, but this experience cemented the doubtless unhealthy passion I had already begun to exhibit, and have never ceased to harbour, for all things Bond. My mother sanely refused to participate in what she viewed as an excessive indulgence, despite her own keen appreciation of the charms of Sean Connery in particular and the Bond films in general.

I begin this essay with a foray into autobiographical reminiscence of adolescent Bond-worship not only out of sheer self-indulgence (which nonetheless has its part), but also in a desire to highlight aspects of the Bond phenomenon that are sometimes underrepresented in academic studies. It has been pointed out, for instance, no doubt accurately, that 'in the 1960s, the audience for the Bond films had consisted, in the main, of adolescents and young adults', whereas by 1979, 'the audience consisted mainly of parents with pre-adolescent children'.[1] While this may well be true, that parenthetical 'in the main' covers a multitude of exceptions. One of the many interesting aspects of the Bond phenomenon is that both the books and the films defied from the first all sorts of expectations as to the extent and identity of their audience. Just as Ian Fleming's novels had originally been written for and appreciated by what he called an '"A" readership', the earliest films, at least, held an appeal far beyond what the above-cited demographic observation suggests.² I remember listening with perplexed fascination as my parents and their friends, fully adult New Yorkers who had all seen the early Bond films, often without children in tow, discussed their relative merits. They unanimously concluded that *From Russia With Love* was the best: indeed it was, they agreed, not just the best Bond movie but an actual good film, a work of art. This finding I filed away along with all the other incomprehensible adult opinions I heard bandied about. To me, there were no two ways about it. *From Russia With Love* was an absorbing thriller, one I was to watch with pleasure several times, but my allegiance lay elsewhere. *Goldfinger* was obviously the best Bond movie; not only that, it had a certain purity that made it quite possibly the best film ever.

In the interim I have seen many films and no longer feel convinced that *Goldfinger* represents the summit of cinematographic art. Nonetheless, I continue to be struck by the purity of both novel and film: *Goldfinger*, it still seems to me, is distilled essence of the James Bond phenomenon. From the clever title of the novel's first chapter, 'Reflections in a Double Bourbon', to Shirley Bassey's unforgettable vocals, *Goldfinger*, book and film, consistently runs the gamut between high and low cultures, between urbanity and vulgarity, which vacillation being a hallmark of the Bond corpus. It resumes everything that has made the Bond phenomenon a key aspect of late twentieth-century Western civilisation. According to his biographer John Pearson, Fleming had experimented with new elements in *From Russia, With Love* (1957). Having met with somewhat hostile press as a result, he decided, 'quite consciously', to write 'the same book over and over again', starting with *Dr No* (1958).³ Fleming, who had begun writing his Bond series at forty-four and produced a book each year once he got going, hit his stride with *Goldfinger* (1959). The latter represents, I would maintain, the apogee of his formulaic art. Among the factors that make *Goldfinger* the cornerstone of the Bond oeuvre are Goldfinger himself, and, of course, Pussy Galore, the latter being perhaps the most memorable figure in the Bond periphery.

What the two have in common, and what makes them so emblematic, is that both characters function purely in relation to their names. The names of characters, especially villains and love-interests, carry a distinctive weight in the Bond oeuvre. One of the strangest features of Fleming's literary output is that, in the words of his biographer, 'the one quality the books lack is humour'.⁴ (One might well object that they lack other qualities as well, such as verisimilitude, subtlety, and psychological depth, but presumably Pearson is taking the works within the context of their own generic constraints.) Fleming himself, as anyone who has perused his correspondence with his friend Noel Coward can attest, hardly lacked a sense of humour. The fact that the Bond books do not much reflect this can perhaps be elucidated by a dedication of one of his later books to Paul Gallico: 'To Paul, who has always seen the joke.'[5] To their author, it seems, the Bond novels were one vast joke, which helps explain how a writer endowed with a sharp sense of humour managed to produce a corpus notably devoid of same. The books themselves were the joke, which allowed them to be relatively joke-free, with one salient exception: the names of some of the characters. The global-joke aspect was, of course, rendered evident and in fact writ large in the films, starting with *Goldfinger*. The films of *Dr No* (1962) and *From Russia With Love* (1963) are both straight-faced thrillers – to the extent, that is, that Sean Connery is ever entirely straight-faced – whereas with *Goldfinger* in 1964 the self-parody potential begins to be exploited. This is without a doubt due in large part to Pussy Galore. In the novels the names of villains and sexual objects are often parodically hyperbolic, such as the eponymous villain Dr No, and Bond Girl Honeychile Rider from the same work (again, the 1958 novel in which Fleming had decided to go with his formula in its most formulaic form). No name, though, figures its character quite as grotesquely as does that of Pussy Galore. Whereas this does not quite imbue the entire book with burlesque comedy, the latter effect is inescapable when the name is coupled with an actual person on screen, and pronounced with delicate incredulity by Sean Connery.

But in order fully to appreciate the importance of Pussy Galore it is important to consider her textual context in the novel. The plot itself of *Goldfinger* prepares the reader (and viewer) for Pussy Galore since the villain sports a name that is even more emblematic than that of the chief female interest. Auric Goldfinger is a walking tautology. His Christian name repeats his surname, *aurum*, of course, being Latin for gold. Lest we have missed this detail the naïve American who is losing to him at cards in the opening scenes catches it for us: 'Auric. That means golden, doesn't it? He certainly is that. Got flaming red hair', Du Pont points out helpfully, as though his gambling partner's first name and hair colour were the only gold-related aspects of his personage.[6] In fact everything about the character has to do with that metal. He is not merely red-haired, named Auric Goldfinger, and obsessed with gold itself to the exclusion of all other concerns. He also wears yellow and orange clothing; drives a yellow car (which turns out in fact to be made entirely of gold); and keeps Asian servants, who are duly referred to, in keeping with the then-familiar theme of 'yellow peril', as being themselves yellow. What is more, we learn in the book that Goldfinger comes from a long line of goldsmiths.[7] Everything related to the character is some variation on or shade of gold. If related qualifiers, such as yellow and orange, are most often used, this is not only to vary the vocabulary and avoid crashing obviousness, but also because the adjective 'golden' used for skin-tone is always positive, and almost always erotically charged, whereas these characters are meant to be repellent. The golden theme includes every detail of his entourage, from the ginger cat James Bond encounters on his property to Goldfinger's taste in literally gilded women, rendered in such memorable fashion in the film. His name motivates the character, and indeed the plot, entirely. His name resumes him: golden goldfinger, 'the man with the Midas touch', as the film soundtrack has it.

In order to make certain that even the most dim-witted reader cannot fail to grasp the point, Fleming takes the trouble to emphasise our hero's cool counterpoint to this obsession from the outset. "'I don't want it", Bond says, "wouldn't know what to do with it"', of the ten thousand dollars Du Pont gives him in gratitude for his having unmasked Goldfinger's cheating at cards.[8] Bond repeatedly gives away the money he wins from Goldfinger, thus demonstrating his own disinterest in such sordid matters. His priorities lie elsewhere: in women, and combatting the forces of evil; the order of importance is not always clear, which is another hallmark of the Bond phenomenon. The entirety of Du Pont's reward goes to Jill Masterton, the girl who is then fatally gilded by Goldfinger, in an economic – and also sexual – short-circuit that continues until Pussy Galore breaks it by changing sides. Fleming himself, it should be noted, showed himself in this sense to share the tastes of the villain rather than the hero of *Goldfinger*: in 1953 he had celebrated the first positive responses to his first book, *Casino Royale*, by having a golden typewriter custom made for him by the Royal Typewriter Company.[9]

The extent to which Auric Goldfinger's name determines his character and the plot of the book makes the text read as though it had been written as a case-study for a beginning-level textbook on structuralist semiotics.[10] *From Russia, With Love* includes an 'Author's Note' which opens with the observation 'Not that it matters, but a great deal of the background to this story is accurate', and then goes on to outline the ways in which he has not made things up.[11] Fleming thus manages simultaneously, and elegantly, to have his referential cake and eat it too: the story is based in reality, he suggests, but we need not concern ourselves with such matters. *Goldfinger* offers no such claim (or disclaimer). It could not plausibly do so, notwithstanding the research that went into the novel, which contains the requisite amount of instructive information on gold, just as *Diamonds Are Forever* (1956) does about diamonds.[12] The accurate background referred to in the 'Author's Note' is of a specific kind. *Goldfinger* too vaguely concerns the nefarious doings of SMERSH, but unlike *From Russia, With Love* in particular and most of the other books in general it contains only the most perfunctory nod to international spy networks. Instead it is a story of individual megalomania, its plot deriving almost exclusively from the name, and nominal motivating obsession, of its central villain. In its evident self-referentiality the novel perfectly enacts some of the central tenets of structuralist and post-structuralist theory: its plot and descriptive passages alike both arise from and refer back to its own linguistic givens. As we have seen, for instance, each time Goldfinger's already pleonastic name is mentioned, a descriptive system cranks into motion whereby everything around him is yellow. Lest the naive reader take this to be a mimetic effect designed to drive home the character's passion for gold, when Goldfinger plays golf with Bond the latter's black and white hound's tooth suit is described as 'yellowing'.[13] Since the condition of Bond's suit cannot referentially be a consequence of his opponent's gold fever, nor can we reasonably suppose, given everything else we know about our hero, that the adjective is there to suggest that he neglects his clothing, the yellowing coat must be read as a purely semiotic detail attesting to the linguistic power of Goldfinger's malevolent golden aura.

Pussy Galore operates on the same principle of onomastic determination, although the relation between her name and her character is a bit more complicated than is the case for Goldfinger himself. It has often been noted that the women in the Bond stories are somewhat lacking in psychological nuance, even more so than the majority of male characters (again, though, it should be remembered that Fleming is no Henry James when it comes to psychological nuance, regardless of sex). For the most part they are nothing more than animated Barbie dolls, whence the generic term 'Bond Girls'. Pussy Galore represents, strangely enough, both the rule and its exception in this regard. She represents the rule in that she is impeccably, and generically, beautiful, and her role in the narrative is successively to thwart and then to help Bond, having succumbed to his irresistible charms. Nonetheless, her part in the plot, at least in the film version, is crucial, rather than merely accessory. Her change of heart as a result of seduction by Bond is what breaks the short-circuit and

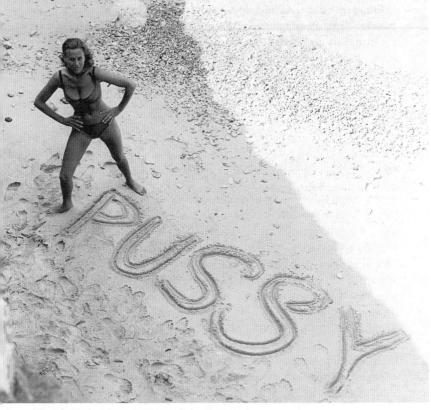

13.1 Honor Blackman, 1964 publicity shot

allows good to triumph over evil in the end. The chief manner in which she represents the exception to the rule is that she is a lesbian (or Lesbian, as Fleming would have it). Indeed, *Pussy Galore* offers one of the most arresting images of lesbianism in popular culture in the twentieth century, and this is of course also because of her name. Fleming reserves his most grandiosely tautological sex-object name for the character whom it would seem to fit the least easily, and therefore the most gratifyingly.

The representation of Pussy Galore differs in a number of ways between the book and the film, although it is in the end central to both. In the film, in which her role is more developed and important to the plot, she is Goldfinger's private pilot and leader of a phalanx of female flyers, 'Pussy Galore's Flying Circus' (possibly an inspiration for Monty Python's several years later). In the book she is introduced as one of the group of America's most important gangsters whom Goldfinger enlists to aid his nefarious plan. She is the only female gangleader in the United States, and included because Operation Grand Slam requires women to pose as nurses. The aviatrices of the film start out as a group of female acrobats in the book, 'Pussy Galore and her Abrocats'. As Goldfinger explains for Bond's benefit:

> The team was unsuccessful, so she trained them as burglars, cat burglars. It grew into a gang of outstanding ruthlessness. It is a Lesbian organization which now calls itself 'The Cement Mixers'. Even the big American gangs respect them. She is a remarkable woman.[14]

Even beyond the Abrocats and cat burglars of this history, Miss Galore's name seems to spread through the book as a whole, engendering a feline leitmotif. Just as Goldfinger's name causes everything in his vicinity including Bond's coat to turn yellow, Pussy Galore's presence produces cats in the text, a process which starts some time before she herself appears. The ginger cat mentioned earlier figures as a prop in the scene in which Bond explores Goldfinger's house. (Having served its purpose of moving the plot along, this unfortunate creature is offered to Oddjob for his dinner, and when a bit later Tilly Masterton is threatened with the same fate, it seems among other things this is meant to suggest that the barbarous henchman is interested in pussy in any form for gastronomic purposes only.[15]) Later on, as Goldfinger outlines his Operation Grand Slam plan to steal the gold from Fort Knox, Pussy Galore admiringly compares it to a fairy tale, another of the gangsters supplying *Puss in Boots* as the title.[16] Bond notices 'a treacherous purr' in Goldfinger's voice that suggests he is lying.[17] At Fort Knox it is observed that 'not a cat moved' to betray whether or not Operation Grand Slam has succeeded; and finally, in order to indicate a similar lack of activity, Felix Leiter notes that 'Not a cat's been near that warehouse'.[18]

All these cats, proverbial, folkloric, metaphorical, and literal, serve as signs indicating the paradoxical centrality to the text of a character who is not so much as mentioned before the last quarter. In the film, as previously noted, Pussy Galore takes on an importance in terms of both the plot and sheer visibility that far outstrips her presence in the book. The cat motif in the book anticipates her centrality to the ending, however, which is crucial for structural reasons. Like the book, the film contains three female characters: Jill Masterton, Tilly Masterton, and Pussy

Galore.[19] Jill, who works for Goldfinger in his card sharp capacity, is almost immediately seduced by Bond in the beginning of the story and loses no time in switching sides. The film concentrates on her visually spectacular fate, foreshadowed in the opening credit sequence. In the book we learn only after the fact that Jill died of being completely covered with gold paint as retribution for having slept with Bond. At the same time – all this is revealed to Bond by Tilly, her sister, who has come to exact vengeance – we are also told that Goldfinger's sex life regularly involves his hiring women to be covered in gold (although non-fatally as a rule: he leaves the backbone bare so as not to kill the woman). In the film, of course, we see the results.

The second woman, Tilly Masterton, plays a secondary role in both versions, with one important difference. In the film she engages in a car chase with Bond, he flirts with her, but she is single-mindedly intent on payback. Her role is to be ambiguous as to her allegiance; it is unclear for several scenes what her motivation is. Eventually we learn that she is trying to avenge her sister. She avoids either becoming or refusing to become a canonical Bond Girl by being killed by Oddjob in a skirmish. In the book Tilly Masterton is described in much the same manner as all the other generically beautiful women in the Bond books, except for a certain amount of emphasis on 'something faintly mannish and open-air about the whole of her behaviour and appearance'.[20] Bond hypothesises that she is an athlete, a skier or horsewoman. He had also appreciated her sister's muscular look: 'her arms and legs looked firm as if she might be a swimmer'.[21] In fact Bond's penchant for boyish women is emphasised in a number of novels. In *From Russia, With Love*, for instance, Tatiana Romanova, the comely spy courted both by Bond (successfully, of course) and (unsuccessfully, of course) by Rosa Klebb, the repellent, 'toad-like' SMERSH operative who represents the other face of lesbianism in the Bond oeuvre, is described as having a backside which does not quite fit the canonical expectations of Bond Girl femininity: 'Its muscles were so hardened with exercise that it had lost the smooth downward feminine sweep, and now, round at the back and hard at the sides, it jutted like a man's.'[22] A similar description in *Dr No* elicited the following comment from Noel Coward: 'I was also slightly shocked by the lascivious announcement that Honeychile's bottom was like a boy's. I know that we are all becoming progressively more broadminded nowadays but really old chap what *could* you have been thinking of?' In his reply Fleming responds quite irascibly to his friend's other objections to the novel, but fails to defend or explain Honeychile's backside.[23]

Tilly's muscularity, however, turns out to signify more than just a titillating pederastic note in an otherwise impeccably heterosexual story. As the description progresses, two things become clear: there is something a bit strange about Tilly Masterton, and that strangeness, which turns out to be nothing more or less than a lack of sexual responsiveness to Bond, at first only serves to make her more attractive to him:

> Although she was a very beautiful girl she was the kind who leaves her beauty alone. She had made no attempt to pat her hair into place. As a result, it looked as a girl's hair should look – untidy, with bits that strayed and a rather crooked parting.[24]

Continuing along the same lines, we learn that she has 'an air of determination and self-reliance' in both face and figure, her breasts are 'outthrown and unashamed under the taut silk', and her stance is 'a mixture of provocation and challenge'.[25]

Structurally, Tilly Masterton acts as an intermediary between her sister Jill and Pussy Galore. What is remarkable about Bond's relations with her is the uncharacteristic obtuseness he exhibits in trying to figure out what is so peculiar about her. Indeed it seems that he would never grasp the point were it not, bizarrely enough, for Goldfinger's superior powers of psychosexual penetration. When showing Bond the adjoining cells he has rigged up for his two prisoners, Goldfinger specifies: 'Here you will live and work and possibly, though personally I have doubts about Miss Masterton's inclinations in that respect, make love.'[26] Bond's sole response is to ask him about what the work will consist of, but a few pages later we find him pondering the rest of the sentence:

> Why had Goldfinger made that cryptic remark about her 'inclinations'? What was there about her that that he himself felt – something withdrawn, inimical. She was beautiful – physically desirable. But there was a cold hard centre to her that Bond couldn't understand or define.[27]

Her strangeness consists in the fact that, although desirable, she does not desire him. We can only conclude that she is the first woman he has ever met who has not instantly fallen for him. And yet ten pages later we learn that Bond has in fact heard of lesbianism, as he meets Pussy Galore for the first time: 'Bond liked the look of her' – she looks, in fact, much like Tilly Masterton, only more so: both have an athletic build and a masculine *je ne sais quoi*, except that in Miss Galore's case Bond knows what, because Goldfinger has already dotted the i's. Both, moreover, have black hair and blue eyes, in Pussy's case uniquely so: they are blue-violet, 'the only violet eyes Bond had ever seen'.[28] Bond himself has black hair and grey-blue eyes, whereas Jill Masterton had been blonde: black hair and blue eyes appear to be a sign of attractive masculinity, in whichever sex, in the novel, whereas blonde hair in women is an accoutrement of femininity.[29] In the film, all the women, including not just Jill, Tilly, and Pussy, but every single member of the Flying Circus, are blonde. The sole exception is the quaint old woman who pulls out a machine gun at the guard-post to Goldfinger's factory compound; her hair is the requisite grey. This is, clearly, the film's answer to the book's gilding descriptive contagion.

In the novel, in any case, faced with Pussy Galore, 'Bond felt the sexual challenge all beautiful Lesbians have for men.'[30] Things become more complicatedly explicit a few lines later: 'Bond thought she was superb and so, he noticed, did Tilly Masterton who was gazing at Miss Galore with worshipping eyes and lips that yearned. Bond decided that all was now clear to him about Tilly Masterton.'[31] Much of this is lost in the film. It is fairly obvious, for anyone who cares to notice such things, that Pussy Galore is a lesbian, who is then converted by Bond. We are tipped off by Honor Blackman's brusque butch manner, her team of all-girl aviatrices and also, certainly, by her initial resistance to Bond's charms. The mainstream cinematic mores of the era made it impossible for the film to be as explicit as the book on this score. The film-makers, faced with this problem as well as the constraints of time and action, decided to do away with the Tilly Masterton–Pussy Galore subplot, and to make Tilly a mere vehicle of familial revenge. She is offed before Pussy enters the picture. As a result, part of the book's structural unity is lost, as Fleming has Tilly serve as an example of what happens to a girl who persists in preferring other girls. In the book Tilly continues to worship Miss Galore, and perishes for her pains. Bond tries to save her, but she remains convinced that Pussy will see her through, and she is proved wrong by a single blow from Oddjob's fatal bowler hat.

The book therefore showcases a trio of women who, taken as a group, tell a cautionary tale, albeit a somewhat incoherent one. Woman no. 1 mixes with the wrong sort of man, who has her killed because she then mixes with the right sort of man. Woman no. 2 refuses the right sort of man because she prefers women, and is killed by the wrong sort of man because she places her faith in women. Woman no. 3 mixes with the wrong sort of man because she prefers women, but is then converted by the right sort of man. She not only lives, but lives to tell the tale of how it was that she had come to make her initial mistake. At the end of the book, when Pussy Galore has fully changed her mind, Bond tells her that he had heard she only liked women. She says she had 'never met a man before',[32] and further explains that she is from the American South, where incest is apparently the rule, and therefore was raped by an uncle at the age of twelve. It is this that accounts for her former heterophobia. What is particularly remarkable about this explanation is that while her sexual history is accounted for, even if in a fairly cursory manner, her name is left entirely unglossed.

Her name taxes verisimilitude if anything even more than that of Goldfinger himself: after all, Auric is at least a phonetically plausible first name, resembling an exotic variation on Eric, and its etymology may not immediately be obvious (in the novel, again, it is helpfully explained). Goldfinger, moreover, is a real, even if unusual, surname. Given the character's lineage of goldsmiths, his obsession with gold, along with his Christian name, can be ascribed to a particularly zealous family preoccupation. No such explanation may be devised for Pussy Galore's name, which operates along different linguistic principles from Goldfinger's. Where his name is tautological, merely repeating itself, hers is a noun followed by an intensifier: the last name modifies the first, which precludes the sort of pleonasm inherent in Goldfinger's name. According to the onomastic logic of the book, anyone with the name Goldfinger might reasonably be interested in gold, whereas anyone named Galore would simply be hyperbolic. Although an explanation, however perfunctory, of her previous sexual preference is offered, no explanatory mention is made of her name, for the very good reason that her name is inexplicable. It introduces a different note into the story, even though its outrageousness is prepared by the name of the villain. Goldfinger's obsession evidently springs from and is determined by his name, prior to the plot, which is in some sense its culmination, but Pussy Galore's exists as a sort of evolving undercurrent to the vagaries of the story. In sexual terms it *is* the story. *Goldfinger* contains two distinct though parallel and intertwined plots, each determined by a name: the politico-economic Auric Goldfinger story, which establishes the central problem, and the Pussy Galore story, which provides its resolution. In sexual terms, for Bond, in the beginning there is pussy, in the brief form of Jill Masterton; then pussy fatally withheld, with Tilly; then finally, with the third female character, pussy withheld and then galore. All the rest is icing, as it were. The name of this character represents, in the form of the three successive female figures, a conquest (Jill); an unsurpassable challenge (Tilly); another interdiction (Pussy I); and finally, a reward (Pussy II). Goldfinger himself, in this structure, is a mere obstacle, the dragon to be got rid of before the worthy knight can make off with the duly conquered lady.

Pussy Galore, however, it is clear in the book, is no lady. One of the many changes made between the novel and film is that in the former Miss Galore expresses herself in terms that designate her as vulgarly lower-class. This is hardly surprising, given her professional history as well as her name, but it is not the case in the film. Honor Blackman plays the role with as much dignity as she can muster given the circumstances, and what is more she is clearly not from the American South. Although she only appears in the American part of the film and her Flying Circus is based in Kentucky, her accent suggests she is British, and her demeanour is coolly neutral. In the book, despite the Southern upbringing she announces in the closing passage, Pussy Galore is not just vulgar but lower-class in a way entirely foreign to representations of the American South. She holds her linguistic own, for instance, with the gangsters in the scene in which Operation Grand Slam is outlined. Her objection to her neighbour's foul-smelling cigar is presented in the following terms:

> Next to him Miss Pussy Galore sucked her teeth sharply with the incisiveness of a parrot spitting. She said, 'Go buy yourself some better smokes, Jacko. That thing smells like burning wrestlers' trunks.'[33]

Pronouncements of this sort, which issue forth each time she opens her mouth in the scenes in the novel in which she is first presented, bespeak not merely unfemininity, but American criminal-class idiom of the 'hardboiled' variety, a type associated with the North East, Chicago, or California, as in gangster films and the novels of Raymond Chandler or Dashiell Hammett. A Southern character, even a 'white trash' Southern character, would normally never be depicted speaking in this manner. (Of course, it is quite possible that no one has ever actually spoken in this manner, but we are in the realm of generic expectations, not reality.) It seems unlikely that this inconsistency stems from a lack of familiarity on Fleming's part with the nuances of American dialects, especially since what is at issue is not the nuances of American dialects so much as their mythology as represented in books and movies. Since Fleming had presumably seen both *The Big Sleep* (1946) and *Gone with the Wind* (1939), we may confidently assume that he did not imagine himself to have created in Pussy Galore a plausible Southern belle gone bad. Nor, surely, was he striving to hit a Faulknerian note. It is more likely that the origin announced by Pussy Galore in the final pages is due to the plot-driven necessity of accounting at once for her previously unswerving sexual orientation and for its sudden renunciation. In the novel, the stunning vulgarity of Pussy Galore's name is matched by that of her character, whereas in the film the name can only be read as ironic counterpoint on all levels.

Pussy Galore's sexual about-face does, in any case, present a problem, one that Fleming solves in the book by the absurd device of suddenly slapping a Southern background on her, the South serving in this context as the equivalent in American mythology to Sardinia for the Italians or Corsica for the French, a sort of internal colony where barbarous clannishness has its way, incest and bestiality are the rule, and no holds are barred. This Southern origin is invoked to account single-handedly for her abrupt turnaround. She never really liked women, but had unknowingly been waiting all her life for a real man, i.e. one at once virile and civilised, to come along. What is particularly striking in all this is the fact that an explanation is necessary at all: James Bond's charms alone are apparently not enough. In the film, no motivation is offered: the most we get along these lines is an arch 'I must have appealed to her maternal instinct' pronounced by Bond when he is asked about Pussy's change of heart. The background is left out of the film because the film obligatorily avoids all explicit reference to sexual orientation. As a result, not only is no overt explanation possible, it is also unnecessary, since the film by the same token does away with the Tilly Masterton lesbian subplot.

In the book an alternative account of homosexuality had already been advanced. When Tilly Masterton goes off to her doom as a result of her obstinate preference of Pussy over Bond, the latter draws the following conclusion: 'Tilly Masterton was one of those girls whose hormones had got mixed up. He knew the type well and thought they and their male counterparts were a direct consequence of giving votes to women and "sex equality"'.[34] This explanation cannot do service for Pussy Galore as well, because a political discussion leading to an antifeminist epiphany on her part, with consequent hormonal realignment, would hardly provide an appropriate ending to the novel. Also, of course, it is necessary for the Bond legend that he convert her to heterosexuality not through ideological but sexual persuasiveness. She abandons both criminality (Goldfinger) and homosexuality (Tilly) not because she sees the error of her ways but because in Bond she finds the Real Man she hadn't known she was looking for.

In this sense Bond acts in terms of Pussy Galore as a sort of Derridean supplement: his phallic power at once completes what is therefore revealed to be incomplete and adds an extra element to what had been presented as an integral whole. But this ambiguity is already resumed in her name itself, especially as its shifting valences animate the sexual plot. As already mentioned, the name changes meaning over the course of the story in that it represents successively a challenge, an interdiction, a promise withheld and then finally delivered. More specifically, Pussy Galore as signifier means, first, a self-sufficient proliferation of pussy, as in the all-female team, be they cat burglars or aviatrices, or simply lesbians. (It is true that Pussy does not prove sufficient to save Tilly Masterton, but that is at least on the literal level of the text because the former has already, after a brief period of indifference, fallen prey to Bond's real-man charms and therefore forgotten all about Tilly.)[35] One of Goldfinger's gangsters even warns Bond of Miss Galore's sexual efficacy as competition: 'Mister, if that's your doll, you better watch her', he says of Tilly. 'Pussy gets the girls she wants. She consumes them in bunches – like grapes, if you follow me'.[36] 'Pussy Galore', according to this initial logic, means a multiplication of women not only inaccessible to men but encroaching on their territory. Lesbianism is therefore not a second-best option in the absence of 'real men' but a powerful alternative, sufficient to itself. By the end of the book, though, the Galore remains as an intensifier, rather than a multiplier, and what it now intensifies is no longer inaccessibility but lack. Pussy Galore has by this time been de-clawed, domesticated into the requisite recipient waiting to be filled. The whole has become a hole.

Goldfinger is therefore, among other things, a perfect exemplar of the appeal of lesbianism in popular culture. Pussy Galore incarnates everything that male heterosexuality seems to demand of representations of female homosexuality, neatly resumed in Bond's reaction to her: 'Bond liked the look of her. He felt the sexual challenge all beautiful Lesbians have for men'.[37] Bond's appeal too is explained here, as he is the only man fully able to rise to this challenge. Pussy Galore is in a sense to Bond as Fort Knox is to Goldfinger, and his conquest of her is a recapitulation of Operation Grand Slam, except that in his case the plot succeeds. This is because, unlike Goldfinger, Bond is accessorily rather than exclusively obsessed with the object of his desire. It is also, though, because her name exemplifies her function differently from Goldfinger's. The latter's name determines his character in that he is what he seeks. Gold is at once what he is, because of his name and description; what he has, because of his relentless pursuit of it; and what he wants, because his quest is endless. Goldfinger is among other things an exemplary representation of capitalist consumerism: he insists on defining himself by what he has, and always wants more. Operation Grand Slam may appear to represent the ultimate goal of his search for gold, but it is clear that even if the plan were to succeed, it would only give rise to further plans. His desire for gold is insatiable, and we can hardly imagine someone so singularly obsessed retiring quietly off somewhere, content to fondle his extant stock, however vast.

Pussy Galore appears at first to obey a similar logic. She both is and desires pussy galore, a beautiful woman herself who consumes women, as Jed Midnight puts it, 'in bunches – like grapes'. But with her change of heart her name changes value in the story, so that she becomes no longer, as in the case of Goldfinger, identical with her object of desire. Instead she herself becomes the object of desire: she becomes the object of consumption, no longer the consumer. (In Lacanian terms, she is now doomed to be rather than to have the phallus.) Goldfinger himself is never, it is clear, an object of desire. He may figure that which he desires, in the ways that have been outlined, but he himself is always repellent, even especially so because of his resemblance to the object of his acquisitive obsession. That his sexuality itself is subsumed in his desire for gold only serves to render him all the more disgusting. It is also, presumably, what allows him to discern Tilly Masterton's sexual preference in the book where Bond himself is blind to it until it is pointed out to him. Goldfinger has no stake in the matter, being interested in gold rather than pussy, and he engages Pussy Galore on her own original terms because she is useful to him in her capacity as concomitant with her name as he is with his own.

It is when she ceases to be one with her name (in order to assume it as object rather than subject) that she switches sides and betrays him, and James Bond and heterosexuality are able to carry the day. When she realises that what she has been seeking all along is James Bond, she ceases to be 'priceless', taking on instead the banal, replaceable value of the generic Bond Girl. After all, the Bond Girls are only that, pussy galore, and this character is able to carry that status as her name only because its valence is initially different in her case. Once she has accepted Bond's terms, she incarnates merely the generic object, the hole that Bond briefly fills, as he does with Jill Masterton and as he does with all the other girls in all the other stories.

In the film, it seems, this key aspect of *Goldfinger* came close to being suppressed. Several sources note that Pussy Galore's name was almost changed to Kitty Galore, in order to avoid possible censorship problems. There are at least two different versions of this story, although they agree as to Prince Philip's inadvertent part in the affair. One account of the story maintains that Eon Productions' publicity agent arranged for Honor Blackman to be photographed with the Prince Consort at a charity ball shortly before release of the film, granting an exclusive with the proviso that the picture be captioned 'Pussy and the Prince'. When this met with no objection, the character name was maintained.[38] Another grants less prescience to the film-makers, suggesting that American censors had initially refused to allow the film to go forward with the character named as planned, but, when the 'Pussy and the Prince' photograph was published, changed their minds.[39] In any case, what is certain is that if the name of Pussy Galore had been changed, the James Bond phenomenon would have lost one of its most emblematic features.

As I conclude the writing of this essay the third Austin Powers film has just come out: *Goldmember* (2002). This imbecilic satire is hardly the first exploitation of the *Goldfinger* phenomenon. *The Man With The Golden Gun* (1974) and *GoldenEye* (1995) already served as internal proof that *Goldfinger* occupies a privileged place at the very centre of the Bond legend, while *Octopussy* (1983) suggests that gold alone does not explain its centrality. Even if innumerable changes can be rung on the golden theme, though, the appeal of Pussy Galore is more difficult to reproduce, for the reason outlined above. All the Bond girls respond generically to this name, which in the case of its actual bearer is exemplary only to the extent that it seems at first to represent its character antonymically rather than accurately. The Austin Powers films, which of course have their work cut out for them satirising a phenomenon which had long been doing a fine job of satirising itself, deal with this problem by reproducing the name in inverted form, with a character named Alotta Fagina. To my knowledge, the sole instance of another character actually named Pussy belongs to the television series *The Sopranos*, in the form of a corpulent male gangster who meets an unfortunate end during the show's second season (and whose verbal style resembles that of Fleming's character much more closely than does her counterpart in the film). Pussy Galore is, oddly enough, unique in the annals of popular culture for the very reason that she is so tremendously generic. At first she is the 'beautiful Lesbian' familiar from *Penthouse* spreads, the faux-unattainable precursor of such characters as Sharon Stone's in *Basic Instinct* (1992). The dénouement of *Goldfinger* makes her live out her onomastic fate as the vacuous sum of all Bond Girls. Because she is precisely concomitant with her name, she is at once more and less than what she appears to be: proof that all that glitters is not pussy.

Notes

1 Tony Bennett and Janet Woollacott, *Bond and Beyond: The Political Career of a Popular Hero* (London: Macmillan, 1987), p. 38.

2   See Fleming's letter to CBS when they were planning a James Bond television series: 'In hard covers my books are written for and appeal principally to an "A" readership, but they have all been reprinted in paperbacks, both in England and America and it appears that the "B" and "C" classes find them equally readable, although one might have thought that the sophistication of the background and detail would be outside their experience and in part incomprehensible.' Quoted in John Pearson, *The Life of Ian Fleming* (London: Jonathan Cape, 1966), p. 320.

3   Pearson, *The Life of Ian Fleming*, p. 307.

4   Pearson, *The Life of Ian Fleming*, p. 206.

5   Quoted in Pearson, *The Life of Ian Fleming*, p. 206.

6   Ian Fleming, *Goldfinger* (London: Penguin, 2002), p. 25.

7   Fleming, *Goldfinger*, p. 81.

8   Fleming, *Goldfinger*, p. 62.

9   Pearson, *The Life of Ian Fleming*, p. 223.

10 It is, of course, no accident that Umberto Eco devotes an essay to the morphology of the Bond oeuvre: see Eco, 'Narrative Structures in Fleming', in *The Role of the Reader: Explorations in the Semiotics of Texts* (Bloomington: Indiana University Press, 1984), pp. 144–72. Reprinted in this volume.

11 Ian Fleming, *From Russia, With Love* (London: Penguin, 2002).

12 See Pearson, *The Life of Ian Fleming*, p. 302.

13 Fleming, *Goldfinger*, p. 111.

14 Fleming, *Goldfinger*, p. 261.

15 See Fleming, *Goldfinger*, p. 232. The relation between evil and sexlessness in the Bond stories is a subject that merits its own essay.

16 Fleming *Goldfinger*, p. 281.

17 Fleming, *Goldfinger*, p. 283.

18 Fleming, *Goldfinger*, p. 320, p. 328.

19 The Masterton sisters' name is changed to Masterson in the film, doubtless for phonetic reasons.

20 Fleming, *Goldfinger*, p. 197.

21 Fleming, *Goldfinger*, p. 48.

22 Fleming, *From Russia, With Love*, p. 125. For a discussion of Pussy Galore and Rosa Klebb in the context of representations of lesbianism in popular culture in general, see my 'Lovely Lesbians, or Pussy Galore', in *GLQ* 7.3 (2001), 714–23.

23 Pearson, p. 326.

24 Fleming, *Goldfinger*, p. 197.

25 Fleming, *Goldfinger*, p. 197.

26 Fleming, *Goldfinger*, p. 247.

27 Fleming, *Goldfinger*, pp. 254–5.

28 Fleming, *Goldfinger*, p. 266.

29 Relatedly, in men fair hair is often a mark of asexuality or perverse sexuality: see, for example, the description of Donovan Grant in *From Russia, With Love*, as well, of course, as that of Goldfinger himself.

30 Fleming, *Goldfinger*, p. 265.
31 Fleming, *Goldfinger*, p. 266.
32 Fleming, *Goldfinger*, p. 353.
33 Fleming, *Goldfinger*, p. 272.
34 Feming, *Goldfinger*, pp. 299–300.
35 See, for example, *Goldfinger*, p. 308: 'Miss Pussy Galore strolled by. She ignored the upturned face of Tilly Masterton but gave Bond the usual searching glance.'
36 Fleming, *Goldfinger*, p. 293.
37 Fleming, *Goldfinger*, p. 265.
38 Steven Jay Rubin, *The Complete James Bond Movie Encyclopedia* (Chicago: Contemporary Books, 1995), p. 125.
39 Graham Rye, *The James Bond Girls* (Secaucus: Citadel Press, 1998), p. 11.

14

Tara Brabazon

Britain's last line of defence: Miss Moneypenny and the desperations of filmic feminism

I'm a bitch
I'm a lover
I'm a child
I'm a mother
I'm a sinner
I'm a saint
I do not feel ashamed
I'm your hell
I'm your dream
I'm nothing in between
You know you wouldn't want it any other way. (Meredith Brooks, *Bitch*,
1997)

'Good old Moneypenny. Britain's last line of defence.' (James Bond, *On Her Majesty's Secret Service*, 1969)

The fracturing of femininity is a strength of, as well as a problem for, contemporary feminism. No political label can encompass the plurality of women. The representational politics of subjectivity has been a central topic for gender theorists since suffragettes chained themselves to the gate of Number 10 Downing Street. Without a metaphoric Boadicea to embody strength, the political objectives of contemporary feminism seem tenuous and ambivalent.[1] Texts such as Catharine Lumby's *Bad Girls* assert the existence of a generation gap dividing feminism.[2] She argues that only by reconnecting feminism and the media can political and theoretical objectives be aligned. Discussion of waves, clashes, and culture wars bubble with rhetorical juice, but leave a nasty political aftertaste. There is value in swimming through popular cultural sites that have rarely been noticed by either feminist or screen theorists. From Bewitching

Samantha to Scary Spice, humorous, quirky, and bitchy women permeate film and television, and are far more than a footnote to feminist history. In response to these larger concerns, this chapter explores a minor character from a long-running film series and demonstrates that even in the midst of saturating sexism, a voice of social justice and responsibility can speak. With the release of Brosnan's last Bond film, ironically titled *Die Another Day*, it is timely to evaluate a superspy's supersecretary.

Miss Moneypenny has been featured in more James Bond films than any figure except the title role.[3] She is the assistant to M, head of the British secret service. All agents, administrators, technicians, and scientists must pass through the Moneypenny office and ante-chamber to reach the Imperial core. She is, as the Lazenby-Bond described her, 'Britain's last line of defence'. The character has been played by three actors: Lois Maxwell, Caroline Bliss (in *The Living Daylights* (1987) and *Licence to Kill* (1989)), and Samantha Bond (in *GoldenEye* (1995), *Tomorrow Never Dies* (1997), and *Die Another Day* (2002)).[4] Moneypenny's scenes with James Bond have become a generic characteristic of the series. The gender politics enacted through these semiotic snippets of text provide an insight into the desperations of filmic feminism. This chapter introduces the character of Moneypenny, following the changes to her ideological configuration from 1962 to 1995, and concludes with an exploration of *textual* harassment and seduction.

Filmic feminism may seem a clumsy or awkward phrase, yet it acknowledges a political framework that stands for and against specific discourses, world-views, and values. Recognition is made of a representational field while maintaining a politically astute identification of who speaks, who is spoken for, and how subjectivity is constituted. As Judith Butler has stated:

> Politics and representation are controversial terms. On the one hand, representation serves as the operative term within a political process that seeks to extend visibility and legitimacy to women as political subjects; on the other hand, representation is the normative function of a language which is said either to reveal or to distort what is assumed to be true about the category of women.[5]

The relationship between feminist theory and politics is particularly convoluted and ambiguous when invoking desires for social justice in the cinema. There is a necessity to concede that the label of 'woman' is a signifier of contestation and anxiety. While statements about the fragmentation of the sisterhood are common, it is rare to watch the workings of desperation within a film's frame. Very few historical or semiotic spheres have survived like the Bond phenomenon. The character of Moneypenny reveals the crevices in patriarchy and normative categories.

Feminist readings of Bond films are frequently negative and generalised. As Lindsey has (over)stated:

> The James Bond films ... depict women enjoying rape, especially since Bond is the 'good guy' and the supposed fantasy of every woman. Once raped they are then ignored by the male star. Rapes and murders are likely alternatives to women in token roles.[6]

Although Moneypenny is the token woman in the masculinist, colonial project of the British secret service, she has never been raped or murdered. Instead, the muffled eroticism of Moneypenny and Bond has survived for over thirty years, forming the longest unconsummated screen relationship. Wearing suggested that 'women need to be depicted in situations in which they are active and autonomous, assertive and able'.[7] Miss Moneypenny performs a mode of femininity outside of marriage, fidelity, and the private sphere. Certainly the character is framed by her attachment to men. Yet all forms of gender organisation are historically specific and mobile, particularly in film. When strong binaries are presented, like an aggressive, powerful, financially secure heterosexual man or a woman who is a home-maker, wife, and mother, the ideologies of these formations are subsumed: they have become normalised. Only through the presence of anxious or contradictory binaries, such as a woman active in the public domain or a politically active gay man, can the oppressive structures that determine the limits of acceptable behaviour be revealed. Moneypenny is liminally placed: as a white woman, she evokes a tenuous position in the colonial framework. While not holding power, she handles its signifiers at all times. She is complicit in the oppression and colonisation of others. Moneypenny's office is encased not only by the proverbial glass ceiling, but also glass walls. She can view power, but wields little. Moneypenny remains the woman behind the man (M) behind the legend (Bond).

Moneypenny is not a static figure: sexual politics and Bond films have changed markedly since 1962. Yet the workings of ideologies are difficult to trace and document without analysing the behaviours, institutions, and texts that circulate in society. Bennett and Woollacott described Bond as 'a moving sign of the times', yet this description is far more appropriately applied to the superspy's supersecretary.[8] As Bennett and Woollacott have suggested,

14.1 Miss Moneypenny (Lois Maxwell) and Bond (Sean Connery) in *Thunderball*

'The Bond girl' of the 1960s disconnected female sexuality from traditional female gender identities, reserving the latter virtually intact . . . whilst articulating the former in male defined norms of genital sexuality.[9]

The obvious rupture in this reinscribed femininity is Moneypenny. She is neither a safely sexual or predictably patriarchal performer. She remains a bitch, a demanding woman who cannot be trusted.

From the first Bond film, *Dr No* (1962), Moneypenny and Bond displayed a flirtatious but good-willed attachment.

> *Bond:* Moneypenny, what gives?
> *Moneypenny:* Me, given an ounce of encouragement. You never take me to dinner looking like this James. You never take me to dinner period.
> *Bond:* I would you know, but M would have me court marshalled for illegal use of government property.
> *Moneypenny:* Flattery will get you nowhere, but don't stop trying.

The acknowledgment of flattery, rather than sexual harassment, renders Bond's comments benign and banal. In 1962, terming Moneypenny 'government property' was cheeky, perhaps flirtatious, but not framed as offensive. The consensual nature of the liaison allows for the negotiation of (in)dependencies. Pivotally, James Bond has a flexibility and freedom not possible within the limits of Moneypenny's office. In *From Russia With Love* (1963), Bond is sent to fetch an encryption device. Moneypenny supplies his transportation arrangements.

> *Moneypenny:* One plane ticket. Lucky man, I've never been to Istanbul.
> *Bond:* You've never been to Istanbul? Well, the moonlight on the Bosphorous is irresistible.
> *Moneypenny:* Maybe I should get you to take me there some day. I've tried everything else.
> *Bond:* Darling Moneypenny, you know I've never even looked at another woman.
> *Moneypenny:* Really, James?

Here, in the second Bond film, the representation of Moneypenny starts to change. The humour from this scene is generated because the filmic viewer knows that Bond looks at (and touches) many other women. However, Moneypenny is aware of the joke and doubts his intentions. By *Goldfinger* (1964), Bond is more open to Moneypenny's advances.

> *Bond:* And what do you know about gold, Moneypenny?
> *Moneypenny:* The only gold I know about is the kind you wear on the third finger of your left hand.
> *Bond:* One of these days we really must look in to that.
> *Moneypenny:* You could come around for dinner and I'll cook you a beautiful angel cake.
> *Bond:* Nothing would give me greater pleasure, but unfortunately I do have a business appointment.
> *Moneypenny:* That's the flimsiest excuse you've ever given me. Well some girls have all the luck. Who is she James?

M: She is me, Miss Moneypenny, and kindly omit the customary byplay with 007. He's dining with me and I don't want him to be late.

The *Miss* in Miss Moneypenny is significant. Operating outside of the roles of wife and mother, the character challenges gender roles. Still, her desperation for a golden wedding ring is clear. Doyle and Paludi described marriage as 'a rite de passage, an entrance into the world of adults'.[10] Yet Moneypenny maintains a job with considerable responsibility. Operating in the liminal social space between youth and old age, without the ideologically saturated adjective of 'married', is a complex semiotic site for women. The spectre of the 'old maid', although never mentioned in the films, hovers uncomfortably around her desk. By maintaining her singleness, Moneypenny does not allow the male/female, active/passive binary to stand. While she is helplessly romantic, she also actively pursues her quarry.

The ambivalence of the Bond/Moneypenny relationship not only adds raillery to their scenes, but inserts soap opera elements into the action film series. The banter continues in the next Bond film, *You Only Live Twice* (1967).

M: Moneypenny, give 007 the password we've fixed up with SIS.
Moneypenny: We tried to think of something you wouldn't forget.
Bond: And that is?
Moneypenny: 'I love you.' Please repeat it to make sure you've got it.
Bond: Don't worry. I've got it.

The 'romance' between Moneypenny and 007 in these early Bond films was humorous, but relatively innocuous. This reading was inculcated through the choice of actors: Sean Connery and Lois Maxwell were the same age and therefore able to engage in a more equitable exchange of ideologies and innuendoes. Moneypenny remained a semiotic suffragette: probing and questioning the limits of women's sexual and societal roles. Like the suffragettes, however, the political effectiveness of her words in the long term is difficult to assess.

From *On Her Majesty's Secret Service* (1969), George Lazenby replaced Connery in the role, making Moneypenny's part even more pivotal to the survival of Bond. Moneypenny, along with M and Q, allowed for a continuity of plot and character development.

Moneypenny: Where have you been?
Bond: Much too far from you, darling?
Moneypenny: Same old James, only more so. Heartless brute, letting me pine away without even a postcard.

> *Bond:* Pine no more. Cocktails at my place – just the two of us.
> *Moneypenny:* Oh, I'd adore that, if only I could trust myself.
> *Bond:* Same old Moneypenny. Britain's last line of defence.

This new Bond, who was the 'same old James, only more so', claimed both a similarity and difference with the past by maintaining the Moneypenny moment. Significantly, on this occasion it was Moneypenny who rejected Bond's advances. Once more, an equitable jousting was established. However, as Roger Moore assumed the role, major changes in the gender order took place.

During *Live and Let Die* (1973), the relationship became iniquitous. Moneypenny complicitly withheld from M the details of a sexual encounter between Bond and an Italian spy hiding in his closet.

> *M:* Now come along Miss Moneypenny. Morning Bond
> *Bond:* Sir. Thank you. (*to Moneypenny*)
> *Moneypenny:* Goodbye James, or should I say Ciao bello.

Similarly, in *The Man With The Golden Gun* (1974), Moneypenny is de-eroticised, while Bond mocks her knowledge and ability.

> *Bond:* Moneypenny you are better than a computer.
> *Moneypenny:* In all sorts of ways, but you never take advantage of them.

Through the Moore years, Moneypenny's role was reduced. She became an instrument of the plot. This tendency was clearly shown in *Moonraker* (1979).

> *Bond:* Good morning Moneypenny.
> *Moneypenny:* But why are you so late?
> *Bond:* I fell out of an aeroplane without a parachute. Who's in there?
> *Moneypenny:* Q and the Minister for Defence.
> *Bond:* You don't believe me.
> *Moneypenny:* No, and you should go right in.
> *Bond:* Yes, Moneypenny.

From this banality, the framing of Moneypenny became twisted and negative. Although Maxwell was the same age as Moore, she was aged through makeup and costuming. The Moneypenny scene is at its most destructive in *For Your Eyes Only* (1981).

> *Moneypenny:* James . . .
> *Bond:* A feast for my eyes.
> *Moneypenny:* What about the rest of you?
> *Bond:* I was just going to get around to that.

Her facade is ragged, over-painted and old, compared to a youthful, muscular, and tanned Bond. The age difference, rendered through performance rather than chronology, makes Moneypenny a figure of ridicule. Her vanity is confirmed through the on-screen application of makeup. Her 'weakness', judged by the value of face rather than face value, allowed a fatiguing Roger Moore to be propped up as an ideal man. This archetype permits the ambivalent but disturbing proto-feminism of Moneypenny to be rendered desperate and a visual joke.

By *Octopussy* (1983), the aging Moneypenny no longer had control over her own office. A younger, blonder woman was hired as her assistant.

Bond: Well I must say you've become more beautiful every day.
Moneypenny: I'm over here.
Bond: Well of course you are.
Moneypenny: And this is my assistant, Penelope Smallbone.
Bond: What can I say Moneypenny, except that she is as beautiful and charming.
Moneypenny: As I used to be.
Bond: I didn't say that.
Moneypenny: You're such a flatterer, James.
Bond: You know there never has been and never will be anyone but you.
Moneypenny: So you've told me.

The indignity and condescension by which the older Moneypenny is represented is to the detriment of the character and the films. Germaine Greer stated that 'the sight of women talking together has always made men uneasy'.[11] Such discomfort is not witnessed by Bond, as he attempts to instigate competition between Smallbone and Moneypenny. By the final Moore motion picture, *A View to a Kill* (1986), she is adorned in a floral frock for a day at the races. In response, Bond simply asks, 'Don't you think it's a little bit over the top for the office?' As an excessive site, she becomes a camp figure, an aged aunt, rather than sexualised partner to Bond. Through her clothing, Moneypenny, like all women, suggests how her body is to be read and treated. Negrin realised that 'one of the primary functions of women's clothing was to enhance a woman's erotic appeal to prospective suitors'.[12] By making fashion a site for humour and ridicule, her sexuality is muffled or perhaps even extinguished.

It is significant that when the feminist movement was radical and active in the public domain, the representations of Moneypenny were at their most repressive and disapproving. Framing Moneypenny as the tortured spinster who no longer had a right to pine for the dashing hero, transformed the supersecretary into a warning beacon for aging women.

The commencement of what Susan Faludi termed a '*Backlash*' is clearly witnessed in these Bond films from the 1970s and 1980s.[13] Second wave feminism aimed to formulate connections between women, but during this era, Moneypenny remained isolated in her office.

Not surprisingly, when the Bond role moved from Roger Moore to Timothy Dalton, Lois Maxwell was replaced by a younger, blonder version, more suited to a Duran Duran video than a 007 film. She arrives as Q is briefing 007 for his next assignment in *The Living Daylights* (1987).

> *Q:* Her methods of killing include strangulation between the thighs.
> *Moneypenny:* Just your type, James.
> *Bond:* No Moneypenny, you are.
> *Moneypenny:* I'll file that with the other secret information around here.

As during the Connery years, humour re-entered the relationship. However, for 'equality' to be constructed, Moneypenny had to be young and beautiful. The decline of Moneypenny's role signalled a loss of the plural representation of femininity within the Bond discourse. Through the Roger Moore and Timothy Dalton years, the Bond gender order became rigid and binarised.

Only with the arrival of Pierce Brosnan (and *GoldenEye*, 1995) was the Moneypenny character revived.

> *Bond:* Good evening Moneypenny.
> *Moneypenny:* Good evening James. M will meet you in the situation room. I'm to take you straight in.
> *Bond:* I've never seen you after hours, Moneypenny. Lovely.
> *Moneypenny:* Thank you, James.
> *Bond:* Out on some professional assignment – dressed to kill.
> *Moneypenny:* I know you find this crushing 007, but I don't wait home every night waiting for some international incident, so I can rush down here to impress James Bond. I was on a date, if you must know, with a gentleman. We went to the theatre together.
> *Bond:* Moneypenny, I'm devastated. What would I do without you?
> *Moneypenny:* As far as I can remember, James, you've never had me.
> *Bond:* Hope springs eternal.
> *Moneypenny:* You know, this sort of behaviour could qualify as sexual harassment.
> *Bond:* Really? What's the penalty for that?
> *Moneypenny:* Some day, you will have to make good on your innuendo.

This film was significant to the Bond series for many reasons. Firstly, Brosnan's performance of masculinity maintained a knowing display of codes and narratives. Importantly, the new Moneypenny was attractive, bright, and efficient. Her clothes once more signify a desiring and desirable woman, who is able to demand rights in the workplace. Her availability, yet distance from Bond, is reinforced by Moneypenny's recognition that she has never been 'had'. By rendering Moneypenny sexual yet unattainable, the tension, conflict, and humour of their relationship continues with a sharper edge. The power imbalance between them is narrowing. It is Moneypenny who enters the security code into the situation room, not Bond. The importance of hearing the phrase 'sexual harassment' in a Bond discourse must not be underestimated. As Doyle and Paludi have suggested, 'we need to think of sexual harassment as being not the act of a disturbed man, but rather an act of an over-conforming man'.[14] Bond is framed by a hyper-heteronormative masculinity. By Moneypenny reminding Bond of his responsibilities and limitations, the textual harassment of the character is brought to an end.

The gender order of the Bond discourse was changed radically through *GoldenEye* (1995). Not only was Moneypenny renewed, but a remarkable inversion was enacted: M was played by a woman. The office dynamics changed radically. Suddenly, Moneypenny was no longer isolated in her office, but part of a feminist stronghold. M became an ally, a powerful boss who made her displeasure (and feminism) clear.

> *M:* You don't like me, Bond. You don't like my methods. You think I am an accountant, more interested in my numbers than your instincts.
> *Bond:* The thought had crossed my mind.
> *M:* Good, because I think you're a sexist, misogynist dinosaur, a relic of the cold war, whose boyish charms although wasted on me obviously appealed to that young woman I sent to evaluate you.
> *Bond:* Point taken.

Margaret Thatcher's chickens continue to roast, rather than roost. The presentation of a female head of the British secret service radically reframed the Bond character. A subordinated masculinity, particularly if the character is heterosexual, Anglo-Celtic, educated, and able-bodied, is a rare and unusual vision in a patriarchal culture. It shakes (rather than just stirring) what Tolson has termed 'a masculine aura of competence'.[15] A successful masculine performance means that superiority to women must be affirmed in a myriad contexts. With Bond possessing 'a female boss' and an assistant discussing 'sexual harassment', filmic feminism does mark the textual frame.

By viewing the Bond films in chronological order, it is clear that feminism has had an impact on filmic representations. The backlash may continue, but the hegemonic reconfiguration of masculinity and femininity in *GoldenEye* (1995) and *Tomorrow Never Dies* (1997) demonstrates that significant changes are being made. Bond has even been labelled a 'sexist, misogynist dinosaur'. Such a categorisation is completely appropriate, and a justifiable payback for the ideological wars fought over Moneypenny during the Roger Moore years (1973–84). It seems that the point has been taken.

Patriarchal structures have the capacity to silence alternative stories, enacting an active and passive subordination of women and homosexual men in the workplace, leisure spaces, the home, and streets. All these oppressions are made possible by evading discussion of men's power and domination. The feminist potentials from the past require an attention to popular cultural texts, such as film, television, and fashion. Clearly, Moneypenny's representation during the Roger Moore years configured aging women as invisible and inept. Yet the potential of the character to move and build on this weakness permits the remaking of an unmarried woman. Instead of the doting, embarrassing, spinster, Moneypenny is an active, intelligent, and demanding woman, claiming her rights and reminding Bond that he is accountable for his actions.

The final component of this chapter evaluates the politics of seduction for men and women. Jean Baudrillard was clear in his assessment: 'in my view the strategy of seduction is a happy, liberating power for women'.[16] The desperation of seduction remains absent from his analysis. The repeated textual embrace of Bond and Moneypenny raises specific questions about politics and sexuality. Yet as Ellen Willis stated, 'without contradiction there can be no change, only impotent moralising'.[17] It would be too straightforward to saturate Moneypenny with the excesses of patriarchy. Actually the role has demonstrated much alteration, subtlety, and disquiet. Importantly, she has served to re-shape and refocus the limitations of Bond's power. Women who seduce men summon the spectre of the shrew, who is independent, demanding, and wilful. However, unlike bad women from daytime soap opera, Moneypenny has not been punished for her autonomy. Instead, the language of feminism ('sexual harassment') and the changes to societal structures (M is currently a female), have altered both her demands and rights. Sexual experience means knowing the rules of sexuality, subjectivity, and normality.

Sex remains a regulated discursive site. Sexual pleasure possesses contradictory social functions: it is not an end in itself, but linked to

punishment or duty. To be normalised and naturalised, sexual intercourse must be situated in 'relationships'. Yet as Julie Burchill has stated,
'people who have relationships put the kettle on, talk things out and
"grow"', while 'sex was meant to be dirty, dangerous, and disturbing'.[18]
Neither Bond nor Moneypenny is committed to the other: no rings have
been exchanged and they never consummated their conversations. As
with the Nescafé couple, talking substitutes for sex.[19] Their desires permit
the competent performance of gender differences. At times, these
exchanges are dirty, dangerous, and disturbing. Seduction opens out the
potential for pleasure, yet is continually trailed by ambiguity and contradiction. Cinematic representations of seduction are what Sharon Willis
has termed 'part of film's allure: as we read it, it also reads us'.[20] Film is
a highly evocative ideological sphere. It does not reflect its time or
society: instead it reinforces, moulds, twists, and subverts the many truths
of a culture.

Moneypenny moved beyond the home and lived outside marriage
throughout much of the post-war period. She remains a figure of
strength and commitment during an era of changing social and political
structures. Lindsey stated that 'Movies are creations of male fantasies.
Women need to invent their own fantasies and portray these as well.'[21]
Such a statement undermines feminist theorists' recycling and reworking
of filmic texts from the past. Even the most repressive of sites, like the
action adventures of James Bond, offer a Moneypenny moment of
humour, discomfort, and rejection for 007. She provides a transgressive
reinscription of the masculine, colonising project while allowing the
superspy to maintain a heterosexual performance. As the bitch, rather
than the love, of Bond's life, she is not only Britain's last line of defence,
but feminism's first foothold for attack.

Notes

1 The contradictory and camp elements of strong female personas in film and
   television are discussed by Thomas Andrae in 'Television's First Feminist: The
   Avengers and Female Spectatorship', *Discourse*, 18 (1996), 112–36.
2 See Catherine Lumby, *Bad Girls* (St. Leonards: Allen and Unwin, 1997), p. 171.
3 The character of Q, played by Demond Llewelyn, was featured in all the
   films up to *The World is Not Enough* (1999), except *Dr No* (1962) and *Live and
   Let Die* (1973).
4 Lois Maxwell appeared in the fourteen films following *Dr No*. Her last screen
   appearance was in the last Roger Moore Bond film, *A View to a Kill* (1986).
5 Judith Butler, *Gender Trouble* (New York: Routledge, 1990), p. 1.

6 Linda L. Lindsey, *Gender Roles: A Sociological Perspective* (Englewood Cliffs, NJ: Prentice-Hall, 1994), pp. 312–13.

7 Barbara Wearing, *Gender: The Pain and Pleasure of Difference* (Melbourne: Addison Wesley Longman, 1996), p. 109.

8 Tony Bennett and Janet Woollacott, *Bond and Beyond: The Political Career of a Popular Hero* (London: Macmillan, 1987), p. 19.

9 Bennett and Woollacott, *Bond and Beyond*, p. 242.

10 James Doyle and Michele Paludi, *Sex and Gender* (Madison, WI: Brown and Benchmark, 1995), p. 95.

11 Germaine Greer, *The Female Eunuch* (London: Paladin, 1971), p. 13.

12 Llewellyn Negrin, 'The Meaning of Dress', *Arena Journal*, 7 (1996), 131–46 (p. 138).

13 Susan Faludi, *Backlash: The Undeclared War Against Women* (London: Chatto and Windus, 1991), p. 103.

14 Doyle and Paludi, *Sex and Gender*, p. 172.

15 Andrew Tolson, *The Limits of Masculinity* (New York: Simon and Schuster, 1985), p. 7.

16 Jean Baudrillard, 'Politics of Seduction', *Marxism Today*, 33 (1989), 54–5 (p. 54).

17 Ellen Willis, *No More Nice Girls* (Hanover: Wesleyan University Press, 1992), p. 18.

18 Julie Burchill, *Sex and Sensibility* (London: Grafton, 1992), p. 45, p. 46.

19 A series of commercials in Australia and New Zealand for Nescafé coffee feature the saga of a man and woman in the rural Antipodes 'moving on' from their past lives and trying to establish a relationship. The couple have never been intimate, but persist in talking through their problems, always accompanied by a cup of black Nescafé coffee. The significance of that dialogue should not be underestimated. As Chris Weedon, in *Feminist Practice and Poststructuralist Theory* (Oxford: Blackwell, 1987), has stated 'language is the place where actual and possible norms of social organisation and their likely social and political consequences are defined and contested' (p. 21).

20 Sharon Willis, 'Disputed Territories: Masculinity and Social Space', *Camera Obscura*, 18 (1989), 1–8 (p. 8).

21 Lindsey, *Gender Roles*, p. 315.

Paul Stock

Dial 'M' for metonym: Universal Exports, M's office space and empire

Perched on top of one of Miss Moneypenny's filing cabinets, in an early scene from *Dr No*, was a tray of teacups and saucers accompanied by a pot and associated implements. Perhaps props are easily overlooked, but flowing from this a clear distinction can be drawn between Moneypenny's and M's workspaces when Moneypenny's secretarial role, and the corresponding functions of the offices are identified in the scene. Cups and saucers are not stored in M's office. Domestic duties obviously aren't his forte. After engaging in the usual flirtatious banter with the 'supersecretary',[1] upon entering M's office, Bond is quickly briefed on the crises at hand, and rapidly sent off to Jamaica, Istanbul, or Nassau. While yet to formally pay his respects to the Antipodes, Bond explores the margins and protects the national interest on the edge of an Empire. The real business of keeping the nation-state safe is engaged behind the soundproofed doors of M's office, the administrative core of the British secret service.

For Bond, Britishness is most often realised outside the British Isles, or within the confines of an old Empire. As far as the cinematic narrative that we are familiar with is concerned, whenever physically located in Britain proper, he is most likely to be found in the offices of *Universal Exports* – Ian Fleming's original home for the secret service. In this essay I argue that M's office is a metonym for England. It is a stable point of departure for Bond's adventures. It is also a site from which to theorise the relationship between M as the iconic representative of England and Englishness, and Bond as Britain and Britishness incarnate. It is a place where ideology, iconography, and office fittings converge; where changes and challenges to that 'office space' are juxtaposed; and where cognitive maps and the resonance of a British signifier on the margins of Empire can be examined.

M's office space

Until 1995 M's spacious office had polished wooden walls, one or two windows, and a number of small tables on either side of the entrance. A large antique desk faced the door, and his guests would sit in leather arm-chairs with their backs to the same egress. From the outset, M's office was stable, conservative, and dependable. For thirty-three years it remained true to the formula set out in 1962 with *Dr No*. The items collected in M's office included at that point:

- numerous framed paintings of tall sailing ships;
- a scale model of a ship, contained in a glass cabinet;
- tiny replica cannons;
- busts of reputable historical figures;
- luxurious green curtains;
- and an antiquated world globe, with Britain's Imperial conquests pretty in pink.

An old telescope was later added to the personal collection of memora-bilia of a naval career, as were a number of antique maps, but the fittings remained consistent over the period of nearly three and a half decades.

Raphael Samuel described history and memory as both 'inherently revisionist and never more chameleon than when (they appear) to stay the same'.[2] This office that remains remarkably unchanged over such a long period of time is engaged in the process of protecting more than just official state secrets. M's office is a museum that stands in memorial to itself, and a superseded empire. In the film *On Her Majesty's Secret Service* (1969) Bond even goes as far as to identify M himself as the 'monument'. It is a site that hails recollections and fabricated memories of a past, retaining its stability through mooring to a bygone period of Imperial ascendancy. David Lowenthal's 'tangible and secure' past ensures that this stability is actualised and represented in some tactile form.[3] Samuel's, David Harvey's, and Robert Hewison's observations that one museum opens every one or two weeks in Britain, perhaps underestimates the danger of Britain becoming 'museumified'.[4] The private and personal museums created for the self are innumerable and unaccounted for, hiding in un-catalogued collections of ephemera.

Just like Bond, M – when played by Bernard Lee (1962–79) and Robert Brown (through to 1989) – longs for the moment of Empire. While protecting what remains, he aligns himself with what Fredric Jameson has called 'nostalgia for the present'.[5] Following Jameson,

Samuel describes such nostalgic tendencies as a 'desperate desire to hold on to disappearing worlds'.[6] This disappearing world is that of a pre-eminent Great Britain, a nation-state in a position of dominance and international influence. Britain's imperial growth was through its naval world prowess. When James Thompson in 1740 heralded a Britain that ruled the waves – in 'Rule Britannia' – 'it scarcely seems to matter', Linda Colley observes, 'that it is Britain's supremacy *offshore* that is being celebrated, not its internal unity'.[7] M, as the head of the secret service, represents the core in an adapted version of Michael Hechter's 'internal colonisation' model. This office is the administrative centre where resources are allocated, priorities are assessed and where risks are calculated. The office offers M a secure base for his secret service, and as a consequence he seldom moves his operations to locations outside his immediate sphere of influence. M seldom leaves his office, but when he does, his office moves with him.

In *You Only Live Twice*, released in 1967, M meets Bond on board a nuclear submarine in the Sea of Japan. Certain adornments have necessarily changed, but M has brought his bookshelves with him, and a model ship retains its presence in a glass cabinet. The office is cramped, partially because the majority of the fittings and adornments from his land-locked original are retained. M remains at the centre wherever he might be physically located, and the world of his operatives revolves around him. M is the administrator, as comfortable at home in the ocean as he is in London, as if the sea is a natural extension of an island nation.

Removed from the trappings of his office, M is unsettled, and confusion gains the ascendancy. He has lost his hold on the signifiers of a stable working environment. In *You Only Live Twice* he had his pipes and his model ships, and remained in a position of control. The balance of power is clearly upset in *The Spy Who Loved Me* (1977) when M meets Bond in the ancient Egyptian ruins of what might have been a temple or a mausoleum. At this point M shares his office with his 'opposite number' in the KGB, General Gogol. There are few additions to the existing decorations that had survived thousands of years, and for the first time M was without his model ships. M and Gogol concede that each needs the other's assistance in the operation of global proportions. Encircled by the remains of one of the first 'civilisations', M is confronted with the fact that he needs the help of an obvious enemy, and arrives at a conclusion similar to John Gaddis's realisation, that:

If history demonstrates anything at all, it is that the condition of being a great power is a transitory one: sooner or later, the effects of exhaustion, overextension, and lack of imagination take their toll among nations, just as surely as does old age itself among individuals.[8]

M remains at the core, but only when he is surrounded by the signifiers of Imperialism and former naval superiority. Outside the office, and without his paintings, M is at a disadvantage. His sense of loss is so much that he risks losing his control over Bond, such as in *Licence to Kill* (1989). When in Key West to instruct his agent to cease his private vendetta against a Colombian drug baron, Bond informs M of his intended resignation on the shaded veranda of an urban estate. M warns Bond that the secret service is 'not a country club', then instructs Bond to hand over his Walther PPK. Fortunately Bond manages to escape attempts made by M's speechless, American, and ill-suited assistants. Away from his office, M has diminished powers. It is clear that M's advantage lies in his administrative space (which, in this particular case, remains in London), and at the iconic representation of 'centre'. Even when M is on leave the office remains as the point where Bond is briefed and sent to accomplish his tasks. The Chief of Staff performs M's duties surrounded by the same objects M collected to reassure himself, and they (to butcher Lowenthal) 'promise immortality . . . to undo errors or right wrongs' and to 'escape from the weight and woes of the present'.[9] They aid as a mnemonic device to assist the recollection of eighteenth- and nineteenth-century expansionism.

The super-spy turns super-salesman

An important part of being British in the eighteenth century was the increasing significance of what Colley calls 'a cult of commerce'.[10] As Paul Langford argues in *A Polite and Commercial People*, 'commerce did not merely signify trade. Rather it suggested a definitive stage in the progress of mankind, as evidence in the leadership of western Europe, and the manifold social and cultural consequences thereof'.[11] The marketing of Bond, and Bond's own salesmanship, is focused on the marketing of Western Europe. Swiss watches, German motor vehicles, and mobile phones from Sweden, were granted an elevated status in *Tomorrow Never Dies*. But, the 'off the shelf' product is altered and improved by Q Branch, providing superior British amendments to top-of-the-line European technology. As an aside, beneath the Euro-friendly exterior, Bond remains British. Tony Bennett and Janet Woollacott argue that when Bond is

required to vindicate a myth of Englishness which has been put into question by the tide of history (as represented by the allusions to Britain's declining power and status), he does so not by sheer force of personality or by
means of naturally acquired aptitudes; instead, he relies on the assistance of
technological gadgetry, does regular target practice and trains for physical
fitness, especially when an arduous task awaits him.[12]

Significantly in *Tomorrow Never Dies*, Bond looks to Continental Europe,
and not the United States or Japan for a technological advantage. This
Eurocentric pitch has shifted over the past three or four decades, from
Britain (in the form of the Aston Martin DB5 and the Bentley), towards
the Continent (with the BMW Z3 roadster). Is this all part of being a good
European in a new Europe?

Bond's sales technique is quintessentially jingoistic, functioning as an
'exemplary representative of the virtues of Western capitalism triumphing over the evils of Eastern communism'.[13] Bond demonstrates his own
superiority over enemy agents of varying origins, with the assistance of
many of these implements. The endorsed products are aligned with his
successes, and with the debonair image of the super-spy. In the 1960s the
figure of Bond became 'the condensed expression of a new style and
image of Englishness around which the clock of the nation was made to
run imaginarily ahead of itself, a pointer to a brighter and better future'.[14]
Bond became a technologically progressive icon, the object of neophilic
desire, and the commercial allegiances formulated through product tie-
ins and placements were suitably beneficial to both parties. But it was not
an inexpensive enterprise to solicit Bond's approval. Product placements
in *Tomorrow Never Dies* were worth £20 million to the producers, consti-
tuting over one quarter of the production costs of the movie. Product
placement is not new to the film industry, nor is it unique to the Bond
franchise. J.D. Reed observed Joan Crawford's fondness for Jack Daniel's
in *Mildred Pierce* (1945), and in *Auntie Mame* (1958) Rosalind Russell
'dabbed on' Charles of the Ritz perfume.[15] But *GoldenEye*, *Tomorrow
Never Dies*, and *The World Is Not Enough*, have set new standards for the
practice. The revenue-raising practices of the movie-making industry
were in these cases intimately linked to the salesmanship of Bond, and
what Bond has come to represent.

In Australia during December 1997 and January 1998, Ericsson held a
competition tied in with the cinematic release of *Tomorrow Never Dies*.
The winner of the competition would be awarded a new BMW Z3 roadster. But missing from the bulk of the publicity surrounding the competition were two critical images: the first was the notable exclusion of a

mobile phone, and the second was the absence of the prize motor car. The central figure in the promotion was that of Pierce Brosnan as 007, with a raised Walther pistol, the film's logo, and the caption: 'Ericsson Made/Bond Approved'. The distinction between Brosnan's and Bond's product endorsements were at some points non-existent.[16] Bond was the embodiment of the desired, modern, civil, and stylish masculine form. Bond's value as a discerning customer is measured by the success of the promotions. At the time of their alliance with the producers of the Bond series, Omega experienced an increase in sales of their Seamaster model of over 100 per cent.[17] And BMW received 10,000 advance orders for the Z3 roadster when *GoldenEye* was released.[18]

In his varying incarnations, James Bond has for the most part been portrayed as a connoisseur with expensive tastes. His hard life in the service of Queen and Country is rewarded with a lifestyle of excess and overindulgence. He drinks the best vodka, champagne, and bourbon; he drives the flashiest of performance motor vehicles; he wears the best shoes, and finest vestments. He selects the best because he is reputedly 'the best', and he is British.[19] In spite of worried complaints that he has compromised his principles, Bond has become the super-salesman, and used in the marketing of everything from IBM computers to Perrier mineral water. But Bond has been selling from the outset, and his product is a rendering of Britishness that is characterised by a consistently suave, but conservative, style.

Linda Colley writes in *Britons* that 'trade followed the flag . . . but it also helped to keep the flag flying'.[20] It is no coincidence that Fleming housed his secret service in the offices of an import/export company, and that Bond often travelled under the guise of a salesman. Britain's colonial empire was extended by creating colonies as dependencies, both on what Hechter has called the Celtic fringe, and further afield. Hechter writes that 'commerce and trade among members of the periphery tend to be monopolised by members of the core . . . The peripheral economy is forced into complementary development with the core, and thus becomes dependent on external markets.'[21] This is necessarily extended to the colonies in the Americas (at one point), the Caribbean, and the Antipodes. There was of course greater interdependence than this model allows, but it is this export industry that justifies Bond's preoccupation with 'the rest of the world' rather than the internal divisions and local allegiances.

Bond's Britishness is made distinct through juxtaposition with post-colonial subjects: loud and white North Americans and servile Asians are common stereotypes. Bond is framed as civil and superior. While he is the agent of Imperialism, he is also the embodiment of Britishness abroad. It is here that the clichés are realised, and the excesses become banal. Bond's public school refinements and conservative stylings are often considered typical of both English and British identities. In assessing the value of James Bond in the marketing of the company, Paul Andrews of BMW explained that Bond was 'quintessential British'.[22] Bond was also considered by another company spokesperson to be 'the epitome of English elegance'.[23] These conflated national identities demonstrate the contradictions of Britishness, without challenging British hegemony, demonstrating the ability of British nationalism to 'absorb internal national units'.[24] The pronoun 'British' is a name prescribed by the English for the non-English components of the 'internal' colonies. The salesmanship of Bond is so thorough, that it does not matter that a Scot, an Irishman, or even an Australian can portray 'the epitome of English elegance'. In fact these inconsistencies only serve to support the thesis.

The figure of Bond is a signifier that crosses national boundaries. Reading strategies are as diverse as the discursive fields of operation within the films and across audiences. What makes Bond interesting is that national identities are not produced exclusively for domestic markets. Unlike Australian beer commercials, where state- and national-based affiliations and idiosyncrasies are played upon to encourage domestic consumption, the Bond franchise has an international market. Bond is performed for global consumption. Following this, Bond remains a capitalist commodity, and one that has the advantage of a globalising economy, and a global commercial media system. Pinewood Studios in England remains central to the production of the films, but the United Artists series is notorious for the amount of work conducted 'on location'. Filming in the United States, Jamaica, and Thailand is critical in the plot development and central to the characterisation of Bond as the 'blunt instrument' of British policy, and a figure of colonialism. David Harvey writes that when 'even imaginary and vicarious', travel 'is supposed to broaden the mind, but it just as frequently ends up confirming prejudices'.[25] Whether identified as a British or English tourist, Bond performs these converging identities for the export film market. This is not to suggest that each and every trait expected of such an identity is fully catered to. Resistive readings are seldom circumvented, but the clichés and commonalties between possible readings are portrayed to excess.

Bond is the hero of corporate capitalism, and the endorser of fetishised commodities. His current preferences for Omega watches and BMW motor cars are noted, and notable examples. The modern film industry plays an important part in advertising goods within an increasingly glob-alised economy. As Edward S. Herman and Robert McChesney write in *The Global Media*:

> The global media's news and entertainment provide an informational and ideological environment that helps sustain the political, economic, and moral basis for marketing goods and for having a profit-driven social order. In short, the global media are a necessary component of global capitalism and one of its defining features.[26]

Herman and McChesney stipulate that 'the film industry was the first media industry to serve a truly global market'.[27] The sway of the motion picture industry developed along with the increasing sphere of influence of the United States, and the 'imperial legacy of Britain, which effectively made English the global "second language"'.[28] For much of the twentieth century Hollywood dominated this market (both in terms of production and box office receipts) but it has become less and less American-owned.[29] Amongst the most prolific and longest running series of films, the James Bond franchise retains its Britishness, despite all the contradictions of financing the enterprise and meeting the demands of an international audience that includes the United States. National identities have finally become commodified, and acquired not through a citizenship ceremony, but through performance and the acquisition of goods and participation in events.

Colonialism begins at home

To simultaneously poach and coin a phrase, colonialism begins at home, and this is why 'Britishness' is such a diverse conceptualised identity. No one person or character can embody all that it means to be British, but a national identity affiliated with the nation state of course displaces other identities when granted primacy. Linda Colley argues that 'Great Britain in 1707 was much less a trinity of three self-contained and self-conscious nations than a patchwork in which uncertain areas of Welshness, Scottish-ness and Englishness were cut across by strong regional attachments, and scored over again by loyalties to village, town, family and landscape.'[30] Nationalism unsettles these regional and local allegiances, and re-deploys such sentiments in the aid of acknowledging wider commonalities across broader geographical spaces. These commonalities, whether based on reli-gious, racial, or geo-political grounds, establish a clear – and vulgar – binary opposition between those described as 'Us' and those labelled as

'Them'. These same commonalities are more pronounced when surrounded by the 'other' in the binary. Scots and English, when re-categorised as British, seemingly had more in common with each other than they did with Native Americans, Australian Aboriginals, or New Zealand Maori.

When removed from the setting of local patronage and obligation, 'Britishness' gains primacy, and the basis for new alliances, and reflexivity. The commonalities become clichés, and the cultural traits are performed to excess within their given parameters. As Simon Gikandi argues in *Maps of Englishness*, colonial 'others' were 'a constitutive element in the invention of Britishness; that it was in writing about it that the metropolis could be drawn into the sites of what it assumed to be colonial difference and turn them into indispensable spaces of self reflection'.[31] Flowing from this, it is my argument that 'Britishness' is best portrayed abroad, which is why the character of James Bond is such an evocative textual site. Surrounded by Americans with less than credible reputations, pursued by an entourage of Continental European women, Bond's identification as British is never more apparent. He is the refined, civilised and competent agent of colonialism.

Bennett and Woollacott argue that Bond was 'first and foremost an English hero', and his actions in the service of protecting and vindicating Western values and interests, placed England 'imaginarily at the centre of the world stage'.[32] Bennett and Woollacott argue that the 'myth of Englishness' is personified in Bond, and that he is its most virulent defender:

> That myth is none the less conspicuously on trial, to be validated or exposed as, indeed, a myth depending on the way in which Bond conducts himself. In *From Russia, With Love*, SMERSH's aim is to secure a propaganda victory over England – and, thereby, over the West as a whole – by discrediting Bond, selected as a target because it is judged that he most consummately incarnates the myth upon which the alleged strength of the Secret Service – and, thereby, of England – depends.[33]

But it is important to remember that Bond isn't actually 'English'. As banal as it sounds, Bond is a Scot, rather than one of the 'effete arseholes' of Mark Renton's colonial experience in *Trainspotting*.[34] This of course suggests that Bond was the most successfully colonised of Scots, and that the most that the figure could aspire to become was a cog in the works of an Imperial machine. This corresponds with Fleming's conceptualisation of Bond. Fleming originally envisioned 007 as a mechanical device to be used in the implementation of British foreign policy and defence. Jack Fishman recounts that Fleming's 'brief-word picture of his super-spy creation' was 'a blunt instrument wielded by a Government department. Hard, ruthless, sardonic, fatalistic. He likes gambling, golf, fast motor cars. All his movements are relaxed and economical.'[35] There are parallels between such a conceptualisation, the 'biographical' details of the fictional character, and the history of Scotland's role in establishing the foundations of the British Empire. William Pitt, the Elder, concluded in Parliament that Highland Scots were 'a hardy and intrepid race of men' who 'conquered for you in every part of the world', and as Marshall writes, 'Highlanders became the flower of the British army.'[36] Scotland was, as Colley succinctly puts it, 'the arsenal of empire' and following this, Bond is the coloniser to M's administrative England.[37] London might have been hesitant to maintain a stranglehold on the affairs of the colonies, but as David Fieldhouse has argued, 'although many new colonies lacked self government, the tradition that London would not interfere continued almost unchanged' until the nineteenth century.[38] But once most of the colonies had evolved into Dominions, and the protectorates ceased to exist in such a capacity, the decline of an empire became a point of concern. M clings to a past where an empire was at its height, by surrounding himself with Imperial and nautical artefacts. His administration is a reprise of expansionism during a long period of contraction.

It is because of these iconic references that it is M who is a more useful signifier of Englishness than Bond. As an ex-Admiral 'embodying the strength of England's naval traditions' M's role is to delegate responsibility, and oversee the completion of the task of ensuring national security. The portrayal of M as a 'fuddy-duddy Establishment figure' by both Lee and Brown, assists to distinguish between the administrative and instrumental roles of M and Bond, and the national identities associated with each.[39] This is not to suggest that either offers a precise or authentic rendering of Englishness or Britishness (if such a singular incarnation exists). But within the discursive frame-work of the narrative, the two roles, functions, and corresponding national identities, are made distinct from one another.

By comparison, Bond is encircled by the colonised, the losers in battles over British imperial and naval superiority. His dominant position is performed through his own refined precision, style, and bloody-mindedness. In *The Spy Who Loved Me* he epitomises the Eurocentrism characteristic of the series, defying the heat of an Egyptian sun by marching through a desert in his dinner suit. The dismissive way in which he admits to being awarded a first in Oriental languages at Cambridge University, in *You Only Live Twice*, either betrays his unsavoury disposition towards Asian languages, Cambridge, or academia broadly defined. Bond's presence on the margins of empire is an attempt to retain a paternalistic and empowered position in a 'post-colonial' era. But the resonance of that rendering of Britishness hints at a new age of colonialism. As Stuart Hall writes: 'Empires come and go. But the imagery of the British Empire seems destined to go on forever. The imperial flag has been hauled down in a hundred different corners of the globe. But it is still flying in the collective unconscious.'[40] The sun might just have set on the British Empire, but the ideologies are pervasive, and the traces maintain a resonance in the former colonies. It is an Empire that exists in the traces of outposts, rather than inhabited fortresses.

The Union Jack designates geo-political areas of historical significance to the United Kingdom, identifying remaining protectorates, dependencies, and in many cases former colonies. Its presence marks out regional affiliations, and designated geographical regions of political domination and subversion. The place of the Union Flag in the corner of both Australian and New Zealand ensigns (as only two examples) recognises the significance of Britain in their history of the past two centuries, and the contradiction of their primacy in the present. But it remains as a monument and a marker in the 'cognitive mapping' of relations between nation-states. Jameson describes an 'aesthetic of cognitive mapping' as 'a pedagogical political culture which seeks to endow the individual subject with some heightened sense of its place in the global system'.[41] In spite of the familiar rhetoric concerning the collected identities of grown-up nations (as distinct from former convict settlements and colonies with unplanned metropolitan centres), the hesitancy involved in abandoning the Jack betrays its modern significance in those places. As Jameson writes, 'cognitive mapping in the broader sense comes to require the coordination of existential data (the empirical position of the subject) with unlived, abstract conceptions of the geographic totality'.[42] The persistence of the Jack betrays the significance of Britishness in the Antipodes, and the regard held for their necessary inverse. Britishness remains a highly evocative and value-laden identity on the margins of empire. Representations of this aggregated national identity remain resonant in the former colonies, and such signifiers of Britishness serve as 'ideological shorthand' for identifiable traits, mannerisms, and styles. The figure of James Bond may function, as Bennett and Woollacott have argued, as a 'moving sign of the times',[43] but Bond remains a resonant signifier, asserting the value and paternalistic superiority of the United Kingdom in particular, but the West in more general terms.

Reassignment

The return of 007 in 1995 in *GoldenEye*, saw M return to the office after the disaster of *Licence to Kill*. M retreated to the sphere of the position's influence, and returned as a woman. But M's gender reassignment was not the most staggering thing to happen to the head of the secret service: while the shift in gender is of course significant, it was M's office that underwent the most dramatic change. Bond still drove to work in an Aston Martin, but he didn't park it near the offices of Universal Exports. Instead he had to find a space close to a plush new headquarters besides the Thames, and M's new office was not as self-indulgent as her predecessor's. There are no large portraits of war heroes or naval figures. There are no models of ships or cannon, no busts, and no globes to speak of. The office has black leather swivel chairs and M now drinks bourbon instead of cognac. Fashionable vertical blinds adorn the windows, and a few small but heavily framed images dot the walls. It is a stark contrast to the cluttered antique shop, and heart of Empire, of her predecessor's M. The trimmings are minimal, and without the trophy-like quality of a model in a glass cabinet. M's office ceases to be a monument to an old Empire. Instead it is the subtle administrator of a new. The Admiral had been replaced by an accountant.

By the end of the eighteenth century the British had arrived at the conclusion, and had come, as Marshall describes 'to define themselves as a people who ruled over other peoples'.[44] The M who is preparing to lead the service into the twenty-first century might be at a considerable advantage to that of her predecessors to explain what has occurred since then. The current M seems more in touch with the 'realities' of espionage in the modern era. In a memorable scene from *GoldenEye*, she describes Bond as 'a sexist misogynist dinosaur' and as 'a relic of the Cold War'. She recognises that the moment of empire has long since passed, and that Britain's role in the world has changed dramatically in the period since the formal conclusion of the Second World War. But M is not alone in her realisation that Britain's position in the context of global politics has changed. Bond himself has a moment of clarity, amidst his defence of Britain's national interest.

The realisation that Britain's role in world affairs had greatly diminished, was not the invention of an accountant, but also the observation of a novelist. In Fleming's novel *You Only Live Twice*, Tiger Tanaka (of the Japanese secret service) observed that the British had thrown away a 'great Empire', bungled the Suez crisis, and lost control of the trade unions. In reply Bond vehemently asserts himself, in stating:

15.1 Bond (Pierce Brosnan) and M (Judi Dench) in *The World Is Not Enough*

> Balls to you, Tiger! and balls again! . . . Let me tell you this, my fine friend.
> England may have been bled pretty thin by a couple of World Wars, our Wel-
> fare State politics may have made us expect too much for free, and the lib-
> eration of our Colonies may have gone too fast, but we still climb Everest
> and beat plenty of the world at plenty of sports and win Nobel prizes. Our
> politicians may be a feather pated bunch, and I expect yours are too. All
> politicians are. But there's nothing wrong with the British people – even
> though there are only 50 million of them.[45]

Britain's altered state of affairs was not lost on Fleming. While he seemingly
welcomed the reputed 'moral' decline of England, he resented the apparent enforced retrenchment of the nation's influence in affairs foreign.
Fleming's response to the evidence of global and political decline of Britain
was to reassert and to revive 'those competitive, tough, masculine qualities
which he and his generation had learned in public school'.[46] The objective
of such regenerated values was, as Fleming stipulated, to rekindle the 'spirit

of adventure' and to 'steam out and off across the world *again*'.[47] Fleming endorsed the reassertion and restoration of British Imperialism, and while acknowledging 'decline' his novels, according to David Cannadine 'try to pretend that in reality everything is still the same as it always was'.[48] In this way Bond served to both reassert imperialist values, and as compensatory mechanism for apparent degradation.

Outro

Simultaneously the super-spy and super-salesman, James Bond is securing Britain's national interest within the filmic narrative, and selling national identities through its performance. Bond promotes the virtues of Western capitalism with British refinements along with the watches, suits, and mineral water. The figure remains marketable, and retains a resonance on the margins of Empire, shaping the cognitive maps of international affiliations, and global relations. This is not to suggest that 007 is a cheap and effective substitute for the diplomatic corps, but that the successful commodification of national identity ensures that an international presence is felt, without starting any wars. Of course, James Bond is not the only example of this. The retailing of Irishness in films like *The Commitments*; the music of The Corrs; and the sometimes embarrassing phenomenon of *Riverdance*, is as pronounced as the loud invocation of Guinness whenever entering an 'Irish theme' pub in Wellington, Boston, or Perth. Selling difference is a critical component in this most recent stage of global capitalism. Product differentiation has been extended to citizenship and ethnic identification. This attempt to acquire difference within the capitalist mode of mass production is understandable in the context of the search for some sort of authentic individuality, and the growth of the increasingly inappropriately entitled 'alternative music' section in music stores.

Amidst the rise of global economies, and marketing territories that treat vast regions as homogeneous wholes, *difference* has been re-valued as a precious commodity. Despite the post-war marginal marginality of Britain (to paraphrase Stuart Hall), or perhaps because of this transition, their popular culture has increasingly become important in the world market.[49] Fredric Jameson argues that there is a 'frantic economic urgency of producing fresh waves of ever more novel-seeming goods . . . at ever greater rates of turnover'.[50] In the search to find something new, consumers, audiences, and media citizens have resorted to something very old, reverting to the security of the past, and the authenticity of 'the original'.

The vast influence of the British Empire is recalled via the traces (or ruins) of Imperial monuments, governmental structures, and immigration histories. These representations may aid in the recollection of painful memories and histories for some, but are a source of stability for others. This point returns us to 'the core': that is the old M, England, and his museum of an office. In spite of the changing world around him, M managed to manufacture some sort of personalised, stable centre.

The celebration of the 'greatness' of the British Empire is a convenient way of forgetting the atrocities associated with its policies of acquisition. The differences effaced in an attempt to 'make the world England' are stark, and contradictory in contrast with current discourses encircling the appropriation of a 'marginal', 'authentic', and 'credible' status within current popular cultural trends. The popularity of Brit-Pop, British film, and Britishness within the geographical spaces of former colonies and protectorates (the sites of both genocide and resistance) is symptomatic of the maintenance of a hegemonic order, and evidence that the taste of colonisation cannot be washed away with a dry martini, cognac, or French mineral water. If the popular heroes on the edges of empires, are figureheads of oppressive regimes, then it seems a little askew to be talking about an era of 'post-colonialism'. Nostalgia for colonialism betrays 'colonialism by other means', as does the culture of globalisation, exploiting the networks established by British naval prowess.

James Bond always returns to the centre while in the employ of Her Majesty's Secret Service, and will always be bound by the Official Secrets Act. While he may retire to Nassau, Miami Beach, the Gold Coast, or wherever Mr Connery is living at present, Bond will always be a tourist, in his observations of the quaint practices of the locals, and the charming characteristics of the women. James Bond will always be bound to the service of his Queen, and his country, and the ideologies that marinate within and beyond his textual incarnations. But while 'The World is Not Enough' for Robert Carlyle's Renard, perhaps the same is true for Bond as well.

Notes

1 Tara Brabazon, 'Britain's Last Line of Defence: Miss Moneypenny and the Desperations of Filmic Feminism', *Women's Studies International Forum*, 24.1 (1998), 489–96 (p. 493). Reprinted in this volume.
2 Raphael Samuel, *Theatres of Memory: Volume 1. Past and Present in Contemporary Culture* (London: Verso, 1996), p. x.
3 David Lowenthal, *The Past is a Foreign Country* (Cambridge: Cambridge University Press, 1985), p. 4.

4 Samuel, *Theatres of Memory*, p. 139; David Harvey, *The Condition of Post-modernity: An Enquiry into the Origins of Cultural Change* (Oxford: Basil Blackwell, 1989), p. 62; Robert Hewison, *The Heritage Industry: Britain in a Climate of Decline* (London: Methuen, 1987), p. 9.

5 Fredric Jameson, *Postmodernism, or, The Cultural Logic of Late Capitalism* (London: Verso, 1991), pp. 279–96.

6 Samuel, *Theatres of Memory*, p. 140.

7 Linda Colley, *Britons: Forging a Nation, 1707–1837* (New Haven, CT: Yale University Press, 1992), p. 11.

8 John Gaddis, *The Long Peace* (New York: Routledge, 1987), p. 244.

9 Lowenthal, *The Past is a Foreign Country*, p. xx.

10 Colley, *Britons*, p. 56.

11 Paul Langford, *A Polite and Commercial People: England, 1727–1783* (Oxford: Clarendon Press, 1989), p. 2.

12 Tony Bennett and Janet Woollacott, *Bond and Beyond: The Political Career of a Popular Hero* (London: Macmillan, 1987), pp. 110–11.

13 Bennett and Woollacott, *Bond and Beyond*, p. 25.

14 Bennett and Woollacott, *Bond and Beyond*, p. 34.

15 J.D. Reed, 'Plugging away in Hollywood: companies push hard to get their products on the silver screen', *Time*, 2 January 1998, 103.

16 Wayne Friedman and Jean Halliday, 'BMW's MGM promotion puts 007 in Z8 driver's seat: $20 mil backs sleek roadster involved in new James Bond film', *Advertising Age*, 1 March 1999, 8.

17 'Bond: Nobody sells it better', *BBC News* (4 December 1997).

18 Guy Whittell, 'James Bond falls into the clutches of marketing men's $100m plot', *The Times*, 13 December 1997, 13.

19 If Carly Simon can be trusted in her theme song for *The Spy Who Loved Me* (1977).

20 Colley, *Britons*, pp. 99–100.

21 Michael Hechter, *Internal Colonialism. The Celtic Fringe in British National Development, 1536–1966* (Berkeley: University of California Press, 1975), p. 33.

22 'Bond: Nobody sells it better', *BBC News* (4 December 1997).

23 Paul Majendie, 'James Bond Saves The World With Mobile Phone', *Reuters News Agency*, 25 November 1997.

24 Iain Chambers, *Border Dialogues* (London: Routledge, 1990), p. 15.

25 Harvey, *The Condition of Postmodernity*, p. 351.

26 Edward Herman and Robert McChesney, *The Global Media: The New Missionaries of Global Capitalism* (London: Cassell, 1997), p. 10.

27 Herman and McChesney, *The Global Media*, p. 13

28 Herman and McChesney, *The Global Media*, p. 18.

29 Tunstall and Palmer, cited in Herman and McChesney, *The Global Media*, p. 40.

30 Colley, *Britons*, p. 17.

31 Simon Gikandi, *Maps of Englishness: Writing Identity in the Culture of Colonialism* (New York: Columbia University Press, 1996), p. xviii.

32 Bennett and Woollacott, *Bond and Beyond*, pp. 99–100.

33 Bennett and Woollacott, *Bond and Beyond*, pp. 107–8.

34 Irvine Welsh, *Trainspotting* (London: Minerva, 1996), p. 78.

35 Jack Fishman, 'Jack Fishman presents 007 and Me by Ian Fleming', in *For Bond Lovers Only*, ed. by Sheldon Lane (London: Panther Books, 1996), pp. 9–12 (p. 10).

36 Quoted in Colley, *Britons*, p. 103; Peter Marshall, 'A Nation Defined by Empire, 1755–1776', in *Uniting the Kingdom?: The Making of British History*, ed. by Alexander Grant and Keith Stringer (London: Routledge, 1995), pp. 208–22 (p. 209).

37 Colley, *Britons*, p. 120.

38 David Fieldhouse, *The Colonial Empires: A Comparative Survey from the Eighteenth Century* (London: Weidenfeld & Nicolson, 1971), p. 74.

39 Bennett and Woollacott, *Bond and Beyond*, p. 106, p. 34.

40 Stuart Hall, *The Hard Road to Renewal* (London: Verso, 1988), p. 68.

41 Jameson, *Postmodernism*, p. 54.

42 Jameson, *Postmodernism*, p. 52.

43 Bennett and Woollacott, *Bond and Beyond*, p. 35, p. 19.

44 Marshall, 'A Nation Defined', p. 221.

45 Ian Fleming, *You Only Live Twice* (London: Jonathan Cape, 1964), pp. 77–8.

46 David Cannadine, 'James Bond & the Decline of England', *Encounter*, 53.3 (1979), 46–55 (pp. 50–1).

47 Fleming quoted in Cannadine, 'James Bond', p. 50.

48 Cannadine, 'James Bond', p. 52.

49 Stuart Hall, 'Minimal Selves', in *Black British Cultural Studies*, ed. by Houston Baker, Manthia Diawara, and Ruth Lindeborg (Chicago: University of Chicago Press, 1996), pp. 114–19 (p. 119).

50 Jameson, *Postmodernism*, p. 4.

Ajay Gehlawat

Kamasutra Bond-ing

It has been said that Bond is 'the ultimate Orientalist',[1] yet precisely what does that entail? To be sure, Bond frequently travels to points East, including Japan (*You Only Live Twice*, 1967); Macao, Hong Kong, Thailand (*The Man with the Golden Gun*, 1974); Egypt (*The Spy Who Loved Me*, 1977); India (*Octopussy*, 1983); and Vietnam (*Tomorrow Never Dies*, 1997). Yet is it his 'Oriental' itinerary alone that makes him an 'Orientalist'? Could one, to paraphrase Disraeli, go even further and posit Bond as an Oriental 'expert', for whom the East is, more often than not, 'a career'?[2] If so, is Bond's relationship with the East, to invoke the words of Edward Said, one of 'power, of domination, of varying degrees of a complex hegemony'?[3] A cursory glance at, say, Bond's interactions with Kissy Suzuki in *You Only Live Twice* certainly seems to present the sort of classic 'Orientalising' framework that Said critiques in his treatise on the subject, with Kissy conforming, a la Puccini, to the 'Butterfly' model of the subservient Oriental woman who essentially serves an erotic function for the European colonialist (in this case, Bond). Frequently clad in a skimpy white bikini, Kissy is framed in *plongée* shots, providing glimpses of her ample bosom and generally adhering to what Laura Mulvey and other psychoanalytic film theorists have described as the objectification of woman via the voyeuristic male gaze.[4] In this sense, via the metonymic Kissy, the 'East' may be said to serve as a figure to be dominated, and this early Bond film as one which depends in a quite constant way on what Said has described as a 'flexible *positional* superiority', in which the Westerner is placed 'in a whole series of possible relationships with the Orient without ever losing . . . the relative upper hand'.[5] Indeed, it is Bond who initiates and suspends lovemaking sessions with his female Asian comprador, and Kissy, subsequently, who is perpetually at hand to service Bond.

16.1 James Bond (Roger Moore) posing with the *Octopussy* women

Compare this earlier, decidedly 'Orientalised' picture of Bond travelling East with a later outing – this time by Roger Moore in *Octopussy*. This time around Bond visits India and, invariably, the secluded island of the title character, a *sari*-clad Western woman (Maud Adams) who maintains an aura of mystery about her. Naturally Bond's curiosity is aroused when his male Indian comprador, Vijay (played by the Indian tennis star Vijay Amritraj), tells him, 'I hear the island's full of beautiful women. No men allowed.' Raising his eyebrows while continuing to receive his back massage, Bond replies, 'Really? Sexual discrimination. I'll definitely have to pay a visit.' And so he does, slipping onto the island via stealth crocodile under cover of night. Peering through the bushes Bond glimpses Octopussy from behind, emerging nude from a pool, surrounded by her female cohorts who giggle as they wrap her in a towel. In this depiction, we see both the previously noted voyeurism and Orientalism intact: Bond gazes at the (naked) woman in secret and the camera parodies his gaze. The ambience meanwhile invokes Frantz Fanon's description of the male coloniser's fantasy of the veiled native woman – 'the dream content' of the European coloniser, in which the latter figure always imagines 'a group of women . . ., suggestive of the gynaeceum, the harem – exotic themes deeply rooted in the unconscious.'[6]

At first glance, then, it appears that *Octopussy* functions along the same Orientalist 'grid' informing *You Only Live Twice*. Yet it is when Bond attempts to penetrate this exotic setting that an interesting development unfolds: even as he moves with stealth, he is secretly watched, via television monitors, by an unknown presence. As Bond navigates his way through the various corridors of Octopussy's lair, the camera simulates the gaze of the unknown figure, so that when Bond finally arrives, with gun drawn, in Octopussy's chamber, the element of surprise has already been destroyed, and a smiling Octopussy greets him by name before turning, catching Bond off-guard.

I would like to begin with this moment of displacement, in which the tables are turned and a basic component of Bond's imperialist power – his ability to remain 'monarch-of-all-he-surveys'[7] – is interrupted by Octopussy's technologically savvy gaze, in order to chart both the Orientalist logic underlying the Bond film and how this logic is reshaped via the Bond-ing experience between 007 and the *Octopussy* women. Before examining this relationship further – leaving Bond in freeze-frame facing the mysterious Octopussy – let us flash back to an earlier point in the narrative, as well as to an important preliminary question, namely, why Bond comes to India.

The property of a lady: Bond in India

After Agent 009 literally crashes into the British Embassy in Berlin in a clown suit with a Fabergé egg in his dead, outstretched hand, 007 is brought in to investigate, or, to continue 009's investigation (into stolen eggs). Bond follows the egg – named 'The Property of a Lady' – and attends an auction at Sotheby's to spot the buyer, who turns out be one Kamal Khan (Louis Jourdan), an exiled Afghan prince.[8] Bond swaps eggs surreptitiously, substituting the real with a fake, then follows Kamal Khan (who purchased the egg for £500,000) to India. Arriving by helicopter at the scenic Lake Pichola in Udaipur, Bond checks in to the Shiv Niwas Hotel. Later that evening he plays a game of loaded backgammon with Khan, pulling out the swapped Fabergé egg as collateral while Khan's glaring, turbaned henchman, Gobinda (Kabir Bedi), looks on. Having won the game and retained the egg, Bond is invited to dinner in the Shiv Niwas courtyard by the blonde who accompanied Khan to the auction, Magda (Kristina Wayborn).

Wearing a *sari* and levelling double entendres, Magda accompanies Bond up to his room and proceeds to sleep with him. Later, as they lie in bed sipping champagne, Bond spots a strange tattoo on Magda's back-side. Curiosity aroused, he pulls back the bed sheet to get a better look.

> *Bond*: Forgive my curiosity, but what is that?
> *Magda*: That's my little Octopussy.

Magda rises to leave, wrapping her discarded *sari* around her and sur-reptitiously slipping the Fabergé egg out of Bond's coat pocket. As Bond approaches her, gazing at her reflection in the mirror before them, Magda turns around, hiding the egg behind her and kissing James, who looks up and sees the egg in the mirror even as he reciprocates her overtures. Walking towards the balcony, she slips the egg into her blouse and pro-ceeds to tie the end of her *sari* to the railing, again turning just as Bond approaches her from behind.

> *Magda*: I don't know how to say goodnight.
> *Bond*: Actions speak louder than words.
> *Magda*: You're so right.

Even as Bond leans forward to kiss her, Madga leans back and casually flips off the balcony, twirling gracefully to the ground by her *sari* while Bond looks on. Arriving at ground level wearing only her colourful underwear, she is met by Kamal Khan, who slips a fur coat over her shoulders and escorts her to the waiting car. As she hands him the egg, he looks up at Bond, who returns his gaze with a bemused expression just before being karate-chopped by Gobinda from behind.

Bond is taken to Kamal Khan's palace (the Monsoon Palace), high upon a hill overlooking Udaipur and Lake Pichola, where he is held prisoner. Breaking out of his room using one of Q's latest pens, he uses the transmitter in this latter device to listen in (via the previously planted bug in the egg) on Khan's conversation with the renegade Communist General Orlov (Steven Berkoff), whose red helicopter Bond noticed arriving before. Bond listens to the men discussing a giant explosion at Karl Marx Stadt just before the bug is discovered. Khan tells Gobinda to 'get Bond', while the latter escapes from Khan's palace via a colourful jungle romp featuring tigers, elephants, snakes, and spiders. Returning to Indian HQ, Bond discusses Octopussy with his Indian compradors, Sadhruddin and Vijay, while the latter gives him a massage. Sadhruddin holds up his notepad on which is written, 'Tattoo: sign of an old secret order of female bandits and smugglers', below which appears a colour rendering of the tattoo Bond glimpsed on Magda's backside, identified as 'Blue Ringed Octopus'. '*Genus hapalochlaena*', states Bond in his towel.

'Produces a venom that's invariably fatal in seconds.' Vijay informs Bond about Octopussy's island and, naturally, Bond's curiosity is aroused, leading to the point arrived at earlier.

One hour into the film, then, the mysterious title character finally appears, welcoming Bond to her exotic island and informing Kamal Khan, who arrives to tell of Bond's escape, that she will take care of the secret agent personally. Smiling as Khan leaves, she faces Bond. After assuring him that she had nothing to do with 009's death, Octopussy turns the discussion in a different direction.

> *Octopussy*: Mr. Bond, smuggling is no concern of the Secret Service. I've violated no British law. You're free to leave but I would prefer if you'd stay as my guest for a few days.
> *Bond*: I'd like that.
> *Octopussy*: Gwendolyn, show Mr. Bond to his room. [Pausing, smiling] Goodnight, Mr. Bond.
> *Bond*: Till the morning then.

The following day, while giving Bond a tour of her island and wearing what will become her signature blue *sari*, Octopussy explains her operation to the secret agent.

> *Bond*: So you went into business for yourself?
> *Octopussy*: Yes, but I needed an organization, so I revived the old Octopus cult.
> *Bond*: Well then, where did you . . . recruit all these lovelies?
> *Octopussy*: There are many of them, all over Southeast Asia, looking for a guru, a spiritual discipline, who knows what. I train them, give them a purpose, a sisterhood, and a way of life.
> *Bond*: In crime?
> *Octopussy*: In business.

Later that evening Octopussy comes, again in a blue *sari*, to Bond's chambers and propositions him, even as the theme song begins. She starts by announcing that she will be gone for a week but insists that he stay as her guest, promising to 'discuss matters further' upon her return.

> *Bond*: Well . . . I can't guarantee that I'll be here when you return.
> *Octopussy*: Oh, James, we're two of a kind. There are vast rewards for a man of your talents willing to take risks.
> *Bond*: [Pausing] I'm not for hire.
> *Octopussy*: Oh, a man of principle [smiling], with a price on his head.

Naturally you'll do it for Queen and country. [Getting up and walking out angrily, then stopping at the door to look back] I have no country, I have no price on my head. I don't have to apologise to you, a paid assassin, for what I am!

Turning and walking out, Octopussy slams the door behind her, entering another room – the bedroom. Bond follows her in, walking up from behind as she turns and kissing her, embracing her roughly.[9] At first Octopussy resists, saying, 'No!' Then, as he persists, she relents as Bond says, 'You're right, we *are* two of a kind', again kissing her while Octopussy whimpers, 'Oh, James. . .' and the theme music swells as they sink to the bed.

Following a fade-out through a blurring chandelier, Bond gazes, frowning, out the window. Octopussy approaches him, asking him to return to bed, where he is subsequently ambushed – one of Kamal Khan's men, having snuck on to Octopussy's island with others, thrusts a razor-tipped discus down at the couple, cutting short their commingling. Bond manages to escape via the same crocodile he arrived in and resurfaces in Berlin, where he chases down Orlov and successfully defuses the latter's nuclear bomb just one second before it detonates.

It is at this moment that 'a structural flaw' in the film becomes apparent. Though, as James Chapman notes, it is Orlov who 'fulfills the more important ideological role' as villain, and though he has been killed (by the Russians) and his bomb defused, the film is not over. For the climax, Bond returns to India. In other words, though ostensibly dealing with a Cold War scenario involving renegade Russian generals and nuclear weapons, more time is spent – approximately seventy of 125 minutes – in India, a place that essentially has nothing to do with the plot. Yet I would like to suggest that the reason for this 'Oriental preoccupation' lies not so much in a contemporary 'fascination with India', *per se*, as it does with the latter's metonymic signifier in this instance, one Octopussy. Just as Bond originally arrives in India in search of the 'Lady' whose property he carries, he returns out of concern for her, thus displaying what Chapman, in his cultural history of the James Bond films, describes as an increased focus on 'the relationship between Bond and the heroine rather than Bond and the villains'.[10]

This narrative shift underscores both the importance of the title character in the film and what Chapman refers to as 'the ideological potency of the Bond/Octopussy relationship' (the Octopussy-Bond, as it were).[11] Given that Bond's ostensible mission is over with Orlov's death (and the bomb's defusion), the return of the secret agent – and the film – to India belies Bond's earlier rejection of Octopussy's proposition and, ultimately, illuminates the bond that has developed between the two. Contrary to the predominant reading of their earlier encounter (ending in bed), in which Octopussy is reduced to 'a simpering sex kitten',[12] it is possible to see Octopussy as playing Bond, that is, enticing him in order to make use of his services. Given that Bond has previously described himself as 'pimping for England', and has been described by *Time* as early as *Dr No* (1962) as 'a used-up gigolo', such a reading is not a stretch.[13] Only, in this instance, Bond follows his penis not for 'Queen and country' but for Octopussy. The question, then, is: who is this figure who so effectively guides Bond's libido or, to invoke an Orientalist palaver, so entrances Bond?

'White men saving brown women from brown men'

While I will claim that the ultimate reason Bond visits (and returns to) India has more to do with Octopussy, the question still remains: Why India? In this sense, it is important to see *Octopussy* in the larger context – one which, as Chapman and others have noted, saw an increase in 'fascination with India', or 'a comeback' of the era of the British Raj in British cinema, signified by such films as *Gandhi* (1982) and *A Passage to India* (1984).[14] Yet while *Octopussy* differs from these films in that it is set in the present (as opposed to the colonial past), these other films – or, specifically, one of their central strategies – do provide for interesting insight into *Octopussy*. I am specifically addressing here the use of 'brownface' in Attenborough's and Lean's respective films.[15] It is via this contemporary trope, then, that we may examine, in Gayatri Spivak's words, 'how the third-world subject is represented within Western discourse' and how, indeed, this representation potentially complicates said racialisation (and its reception by film audiences).[16]

I shall argue, via Spivak's post-colonial strategy for reading the third-world figure – what she labels 'productive catachresis', or a deliberately paradoxical or improper use of a word or phrase – that Octopussy may be seen, following the previously noted instances of 'brownface', as donning native costume or, indeed, as a costumed native.[17] To productively re-appropriate Spivak's words, such a transfiguration would illuminate how 'the relationship between the imperialist subject [Bond] and the subject of imperialism [Octopussy] is at least ambiguous.'[18] Reading *Octopussy* along Spivak's formulation of the (gendered) colonial encounter – 'white

men saving brown women from brown men'[19] – immediately complicates a facile reading of Bond's relationship with Octopussy, even as it
perhaps suggests strategies for resisting the oft-noted colonialist/impe-
rialist discourse of Bond movies. While, as Christine Bold has noted, in
the original Fleming novels and in other Bond films (e.g., *You Only Live
Twice*), 'women are often exoticised in terms of their racial and ethnic
heritage,'[20] Octopussy is only superficially exoticised and, furthermore,
one might say it is a self-exoticisation (after all, it is Octopussy who
revives the Octopus cult and dons a *sari*). On a superficial level, then, one
might apply Spivak's formulation to the film as Bond (white man) saving
brown woman (Octopussy) from brown man (Kamal Khan). Yet ultimately both the 'brown' man and woman are white (i.e., played by white
actors, respectively, the French Louis Jourdan and the Swedish Maud
Adams). Thus whereas in its superficial application one might detect a
colonial paradigm in Bond's return/visit to India (to 'save' Octopussy), in
fact, such a reading is false in a double sense: not only is Octopussy not a
'brown woman' (re: racial and ethnic heritage) but also Bond (the white
man) is not saving her.

After Bond successfully defuses Orlov's bomb in Berlin, the camera
cuts to Octopussy, who demands to know where Kamal is. In returning
to India to pursue Khan – her onetime business partner whose nuclear
plot with Orlov would have sacrificed her as well – Octopussy is moti-
vated to 'change sides', as Chapman notes, not 'due to the force of Bond's
sexual charisma . . . but rather due to her own feelings of betrayal and
desire for vengeance.'[21] From Germany the film abruptly shifts to India,
where Kamal and Gobinda are preparing their departure at the Monsoon
Palace. Upon hearing the sound of music, the latter looks out the window
and, following his gaze, the camera presents Indian and white women,
in Indian outfits, dancing to Indian music at the gates of Khan's compound.

Kamal Khan: What is that?
Gobinda: Girls, selling themselves.
Kamal Khan: Good. It will keep the men occupied.

The camera then cuts to the women while Indian music (i.e., flutes and
tablas) plays on the soundtrack. While some of the (white) women
dance seductively with veils and musical instruments for Khan's (brown)
guards, others take advantage of this diversion and employ their gymnas-
tic skills to vault, climb, and otherwise infiltrate Khan's compound. The
camera cuts back and forth from one set of women 'seducing' the native

guards to another, ascending Khan's walls. Then, as Octopussy (again wearing her blue *sari*) gives the signal, the women 'seducing' the native guards immediately lash out, knocking out the guards for a second time with their objects of seduction.

A battle ensues between Khan's male Indian compradors and Octopussy's hybrid followers, some, including Octopussy, wearing Indian garb. The women outwit and overwhelm the men and are in the process of defeating them when Bond arrives with Q (Desmond Llewelyn) in a hot air balloon bearing the insignia of the Union Jack. Q's comment is telling: 'They [the women] seem to be doing all right.' And so they are. Rather than, as Cynthia Baron asserts, the climactic battle 'begin[ning] with Bond and Q',[22] the men are latecomers and, *pace* Q's comment, rather unnecessary. If, following Paul Stock's analysis, one sees the Union Jack metonymically, then what is signified in this instance, rather than the continued geopolitical significance of Great Britain, is its utter irrelevance to the battle at hand. Rather than the flag functioning as what Stock labels a 'resonant signifier' of 'the value and paternalistic superiority of the United Kingdom', it is their mode of arrival that serves as the more relevant icon at this moment: a hot-air balloon adrift in the night, manned by a quivering septuagenarian.[23]

Thus, to turn to Fanon's analysis of the anti-colonial struggle, we see how incorporating women as 'essential elements' modifies the very conception of combat and how, particularly in the context of the Bond genre, this constitutes 'a whole revolutionary step'.[24] By utilising what Fanon describes as 'the cult of the veil', the 'Octopussy Girls' paradoxically adopt 'an absolutely unbelievable offensive tactic' that relies for its very effectiveness on the misassumptions of the male figures ('What is that?'/ 'Girls, selling themselves').[25] In the process Octopussy, though superficially clothed in the garb of a 'native' woman, deviates from Said's description of 'the model of the Oriental woman': she speaks and acts for herself (rather than being spoken for and acted upon by Bond).[26] What at first glance appears to be an instance of the typical colonial intervention is in fact an instantiation of the essentially secondary role of the 'white man' (the colonial agent in Spivak's formulation) in the operation at hand. While, according to Baron, 007's 'humour and "masterful" style' may have 'consistently reassured the First World of its hegemonic position', *Octopussy* does not exactly provide reassurance, or 'a nostalgic bandage', for 'England's wounded pride in the 'post-colonial' era'.[27] If anything, following Salman Rushdie's description of the jingoistic foreign policy of the UK at this time as 'the phantom twitchings of an amputated limb',

Octopussy reveals a transparent attempt to revive such a position.[28] To say otherwise, at least regarding *Octopussy* – or, by the time of *Octopussy* (both in terms of British and Bond history) – is to overlook the actual inner-workings of the film and its problematic signifiers, i.e., making *Octopussy* fit the Procrustean bed of the hegemonic view of Bond.[29]

Bond's exploits in *Octopussy* remain only superficially 'steeped in the discourse of Orientalism' (i.e., an Orientalism in quotation) and, because superficially, ineffectively.[30] That is to say, the film's so-called 'Orientalist' discourse reveals its own fissures or, as Said describes it, 'representations *as representations*'.[31] It is in this way that, rather than Bond being defined through tropes of Orientalism '*in an entirely unmediated way*',[32] one finds in *Octopussy* an instance of what Bold calls 'myths . . . made to converge' but not fitting; the Bondian tropes are mediated.[33] Yet contrary to Bold's claim, saying this is not entirely 'reading Bond against the grain'.[34] For instance, whereas women may have been 'commonly . . . represented in subservient positions' (in the Fleming novels), functioning as 'peripheral romantic interest, domestic background, or ambiguously androgynous companionship for the hero',[35] in the case of *Octopussy*, it is the title figure who has Bond entangled in her tentacles. To say this is not to 'read against the grain' but rather to precisely see the plot for what it is.

If, as Baron notes, the established 'racial and imperial discourses . . . over-determine every aspect' of Bond's encounters with others/ the Other, then, in *Octopussy*, this over-determination produces the effect of bracketing these discourses (as discourses) or, rather, bracketing these encounters.[36] In the process, a space for resistance is indeed provided and, more to the point, this space is internally produced – that is, it emanates from within the film itself. This may be described, to paraphrase Homi Bhabha, as the profoundly ambivalent nature of negotiating Bond/ the Bond film where, 'in the very act of mediation or representation there is a necessary threat' to the work of art's 'originary or essentialising presence'.[37] As has been oft-noted, the Bond films remain popular, or ensure their survival, by consistently adapting. To again invoke Bhabha's terms, one might say, paradoxically, that in order to ensure its continuation, the 'authenticity' of the Bond film has to (consistently) be 'partially erased'.[38] Thus, in the case of *Octopussy* (or, indeed, by the time of *Octopussy*), in the place of a 'blazing Bond', one begins to glimpse what Stephen Greenblatt, in a differing context, describes as 'something that seems at first far less spectacular: a subtle, elusive set of exchanges, a network of trades and trade-offs, a jostling of competing representations, a negotiation between'.[39]

Interpreting the Bond film – in this case, *Octopussy* – in this way thus functions '*as intervention*' but not, as has been previously noted, within the film's signifying system but, rather, within the hegemonic discourse surrounding the Bond film(s).[40] Such an 'adjudication' of an aesthetic, while indeed 'problematic', serves to re-enact the Bond film via cultural translation, i.e., opening up 007 with Octopussy pincers. Nothing '*at first sight*', as Bhabha notes, is either 'less negotiable than rapture', or 'less rapturous than negotiation'.[41] Yet, upon closer examination (cf. 'resistant reading'), it is precisely such 'rapturous negotiation' that *Octopussy* can be seen as engaging in. The crucial paradox is that such negotiation presumes an already existing network of signification, i.e., familiarity with the Bond persona/corpus. Indeed, it is such a pre-existing network that allows for a narrative voice that 'speaks between', or questions the very premise underlying such signification; the enunciation of the 'failing' of a heretofore (mechanically) infallible system. As Toby Miller states, 'the point is that viewers can see all this', i.e., all this artifice or, to paraphrase Said, this highly artificial enactment.[42] The question then becomes: who are these viewers?

Ars erotica *or* scientia sexualis?

James Chapman has noted that 'despite their political incorrectness – or perhaps even because of it – the Bond films have been enormously popular with cinema-goers around the world, suggesting either that audiences do not pay as much heed to the ideological content of the films as do academics, or that the films provide a particular sort of pleasure which mediates their sexist and racist overtones.'[43] It is precisely this latter option that I would like to explore here in relation to the profoundly ambivalent nature of negotiating Bond/films. If, as Chapman notes, 'the evidence of the international popularity of the Bond films is overwhelming' and, indeed, if it is in overseas markets that Bond performs best, then we must ask: how does a global (and, specifically, non-Western) audience mediate Bond/films?[44]

In their study of the Bond phenomenon, *Bond and Beyond*, Tony Bennett and Janet Woollacott examine the films comprising this oeuvre through the Gramscian notion of hegemony, arguing that, rather than being 'reducible to a particular ideology or a simple meaning', Bond films 'can mean different things to different people at different moments'.[45] Flash back to the context of the earlier-noted 'British Raj revival' of the early 1980s, in which one gets the India of *Octopussy*, one of 'colorful bazaars, luxurious hotels', and white women in Indian clothing.[46] This 'tourist's view of India', as Chapman notes, has frequently been denigrated for its 'Orientalism' and linked, subsequently, to the cycle of British films comprising the 'Raj revival'.[47] Salman Rushdie, for instance, claims, regarding *Octopussy*, that 'one can only say that its portrait of modern India was as grittily and uncompromisingly realistic as its depiction of the skill, integrity and sophistication of the British secret services.'[48] Yet Rushdie has also acknowledged that it is 'undeniable that Indian urban culture . . . is full of fakery and gaudiness and superficiality.'[49] Perhaps the most vivid instance of such 'superficial' representation can be found in the Indian popular cinema, or Bollywood, as it is more commonly known. Sumita Chakravarty has described the predominant aesthetic of this cinema (the most prolific in the world) as one of 'imperso-nation':

> Concentrated within this metaphor are the notions of changeability and metamorphosis, tension and contradiction, recognition and alienation, surface and depth: dualities that have long plagued the Indian psyche and constitute the self-questionings of Indian nationhood. Indian cinema, caught in the cross-currents of this national dialogue and contributing to it, has made impersonation its distinctive signature. This is more than a matter of reinforcing truisms that films impersonate life; characters impersonate real men and women; the film-viewing experience impersonates dream. Impersonation subsumes a process of externalization, the play of/on surfaces, the disavowal of fixed identity.[50]

An Indian audience of *Octopussy*, then, would be quite familiar with 'superficiality and gaudiness' (specifically in terms of representing 'India') and, indeed, based on the immense popularity of Bollywood, be receptive to such an aesthetic (many budget restaurants in Udaipur are reported to have nightly screenings of *Octopussy*).[51] Yet a Kiplingesque tendency remains in the theorisation of Bollywood (in relation to its implied Other, Hollywood), charting a difference in film composition linked to an attendant assumption of irreducible cultural difference ('East is East, West is West').[52]

Such attempts at cultural differentiation become acute in the sexual arena. In the first volume of his *History of Sexuality*, Michel Foucault claims that 'historically, there have been two great procedures for producing the truth of sex', namely, an *ars erotica* and a *scientia sexualis*.[53] Along with other 'Eastern civilizations', Foucault includes India in the societies 'which endowed themselves with an *ars erotica*', which he then goes on to describe in detail:

In the erotic art, truth is drawn from pleasure itself, understood as a practice and accumulated as experience; pleasure is not considered in relation
to an absolute law of the permitted and the forbidden, nor by a reference to
a criterion of utility, but first and foremost in relation to itself; it is experienced as pleasure, evaluated in terms of its intensity, its specific quality, its
duration, its reverberations in the body and the soul.[54]

'On the face of it', Foucault declares, 'our [Western] civilization possesses no *ars erotica*', but rather a *scientia sexualis* in which 'procedures
for telling the truth of sex . . . are geared to a form of knowledge-power
strictly opposed to the [*ars erotica*].'[55] In describing the 'making of a
complex machinery for producing the true discourses on sex', then,
Foucault clings to this binarism of 'Eastern' and 'Western' sexualities. Yet
in *Octopussy* one sees the *scientia sexualis* functioning, or masquerading,
as a form of *ars erotica* – *sari*-clad white women in harem-like settings
whose 'seduction' is a joke the audience is in on, a form of 'discrepant awareness' providing precisely the sort of pleasure, perhaps, that
Chapman was previously alluding to.[56]

These delicate inner-workings of 'Kamasutra Bond-ing' have grown
even more culturally complex in light of rumours in 2004 that Bollywood
superstar and former Ms. World, Aishwarya Rai, would play the next
'Bond girl'. In interviews with the British press, Rai claimed she would
consider the role if a body double were used for sex scenes.[57] Additionally,
Rai was asked, again and again, if she would share an on-screen kiss with
Bond (at the time, Pierce Brosnan). Rai demurred in her reply, making
note of her strict upbringing and invoking Indian tradition.[58] Yet while
actual kissing has been rare for Bollywood films in the past, as with the
Bond films, this genre continues to change with the times and, interestingly enough, Rai is one of the actresses currently breaking this alleged
taboo. In the recent Bollywood blockbuster, *Dhoom 2* (2006), for instance,
Rai's character, Sunehiri, shares an extended on-screen kiss with her love
interest in the film, Aryan Singh, played by fellow Bollywood superstar,
Hrithik Roshan. Furthermore, in the film's frequent song and dance
numbers, Rai appears in what could be mistaken as stereotypical Bond
girl apparel, including micro-mini-skirts, day-glo halter-tops, and not
much else.

Given such on-screen antics in Bollywood, Rai's request for a body
double in a Bond film seems doubly perplexing, to say the least. One may
surmise that the truly troubling issue posed by Rai acting in a Bond film
is not sexuality *per se* but, rather, the age-old issue of miscegenation. Yet

Rai is one of the few crossover stars of Bollywood and has recently made two popular English-language films with Gurinder Chadha and Paul Mayeda Berges, *Bride and Prejudice* (2004) and *The Mistress of Spices* (2005), both of which feature her in romantic relationships with white men.[59] While it remains unclear whether the ultimate decision not to cast an Indian woman in the twenty-first Bond film had more to do with Rai or the Raj, *Octopussy* provides a primer in how to engage 'the ultimate Orientalist' in 'Kamasutra bond-ing' without sacrificing one's honour (and without a body double).

To return to the earlier freeze-frame beginning this inquiry, we see that the colonial encounter as described by Said, Fanon, and Spivak, is figuratively inverted in the lair of *Octopussy*. The title figure inhabits the subjective position of power previously occupied by Bond, watching (along with viewers) his stealthy entrance and anticipating it with pleasure. Rather than the camera remaining over Bond's shoulder, it reduces him to a series of tiny figures trapped within a larger frame – Octopussy's surveillance screen. To read the ensuing exchange of gazes along a post-colonial grid, one could say Octopussy displaces Bond from his positional superiority at the moment of climax, a displacement that serves as a prototype for the rest of the film. Smiling at Bond, the title figure mirrors the audience's pleasure at seeing the normally staid secret agent shaken, if not stirred.

Notes

I would like to thank Special Agents Julia Goesser and Neil Gehlawat for their assistance in preparing this dossier.

1 See Cynthia Baron, '*Dr No*: Bonding Britishness to Racial Sovereignty', in this book.
2 Quoted in Edward Said, *Orientalism* (New York: Vintage, 1994), p. 71.
3 Said, *Orientalism*, p. 72.
4 See Laura Mulvey, 'Visual Pleasure and Narrative Cinema', *Screen*, 16 (1975), 6–18; and Christian Metz, *The Imaginary Signifier: Psychoanalysis and the Cinema*, trans. by Celia Britton *et al.* (Bloomington: Indiana University Press, 1982).
5 Said, *Orientalism*, p. 73.
6 Frantz Fanon, 'Algeria Unveiled', in *A Dying Colonialism*, trans. by Haakon Chevalier (New York: Grove, 1965), p. 46.
7 See Mary Louise Pratt, *Imperial Eyes: Travel Writing and Transculturation* (New York: Routledge, 1992), pp. 201–6.

8 This initial aspect of the story – attending the auction at Sotheby's to spot the buyer of the egg – adheres to Fleming's original story, 'The Property of a Lady,' one of the two tales serving as the literary basis for *Octopussy*. Kamal Khan's character, however, is a new element introduced in the film.

9 Moore later said, 'I remember this, uh, this scene. As we broke away, Maude turned, and it was a rather violent turn, and her knee made contact with my nether-regions, which is very painful as any man will tell you' (*Octopussy* Ultimate Edition DVD commentary track, 2006).

10 James Chapman, *Licence to Thrill: A Cultural History of the James Bond Films* (New York: Columbia University Press, 2000), pp. 211–13.

11 Chapman, *Licence to Thrill*, p. 215.

12 Chapman, *Licence to Thrill*, p. 215.

13 Ian Fleming, *From Russia, With Love* (London: Jonathan Cape, 1957), p. 94; and quoted in Alan Barnes and Marcus Hearn, *Kiss Kiss Bang! Bang! The Unofficial James Bond Film Companion* (Woodstock: Overlook Press, 1998), p. 16.

14 See Chapman, *Licence to Thrill*, p. 212; and Salman Rushdie, *Imaginary Homelands* (London: Granta Books, 1991), p. 87.

15 Brownface is employed, respectively, for the title character in *Gandhi*, played by Ben Kingsley, and for Professor Godbole, played by Alec Guinness, in *A Passage to India*.

16 Gayatri Chakravorty Spivak, 'Can the Subaltern Speak?' in *Marxism and the Interpretation of Culture*, ed. by Lawrence Grossberg and Cary Nelson (Urbana: University of Illinois Press, 1988), p. 271.

17 Spivak, 'Can the Subaltern Speak?', p. 297. For more on the concept of catachresis, see Spivak, *The Post-Colonial Critic: Interviews, Strategies, Dialogues*, ed. by Sarah Harasym (New York: Routledge, 1990), p. 125; and Homi K. Bhabha, *The Location of Culture* (London: Routledge, 1994), p. 183.

18 Spivak, 'Can the Subaltern Speak?', p. 297.

19 Spivak, 'Can the Subaltern Speak?', p. 296.

20 Christine Bold, '"Under the Very Skirts of Britannia": Re-Reading Women in the James Bond Novels', in this book.

21 Chapman, *Licence to Thrill*, p. 227.

22 Baron, 'Dr No', in this book.

23 Paul Stock, 'Dial "M" for metonym: Universal Exports, M's office space and empire', in this book. Technically, at the time of filming, Q was sixty-nine and Moore, fifty-four.

24 Fanon, 'Algeria Unveiled', pp. 48–9.

25 Fanon, 'Algeria Unveiled', p. 47, p. 51.

26 Said, *Orientalism*, p. 72.

27 Baron, 'Dr No', in this book.

28 Rushdie, *Imaginary Homelands*, p. 92. One may, indeed, posit *Bond* (or, more to the point, his penis) as being such an 'amputated, twitching limb'.

29 As Toby Miller notes in his chapter in this book, 'The James Bond films are *routinely* held up as a significant contributor to, and symptom of, imperialism, sexism, Orientalism, class hierarchy, and jingoism' ('James Bond's Penis', in this book, emphasis mine).

30 Baron, '*Dr No*', in this book.

31 Said, *Orientalism*, p. 87, emphasis in original. As Baron has noted, Bond 'announces' his role (as imperial hero) and locations *are presented* as '"natural" site[s] for colonial adventures' ('*Dr. No*', in this book).

32 Baron, '*Dr No*', in this book, emphasis in original.

33 Bold, 'Under the Very Skirts of Britannia', in this book.

34 Bold, 'Under the Very Skirts of Britannia', in this book.

35 Bold, 'Under the Very Skirts of Britannia', in this book.

36 Baron, '*Dr No*', in this book. Regarding the concept of 'bracketing', see Robert Stam, *Reflexivity in Film and Literature: From Don Quixote to Jean-Luc Godard* (Ann Arbor: UMI Research Press, 1985).

37 Homi K. Bhabha, 'Aura and Agora: On Negotiating Rapture and Speaking Between', in *Negotiating Rapture: The Power of Art to Transform Lives*, ed. by Sue Taylor (Chicago: Museum of Contemporary Art, 1996), p. 10, p. 12.

38 Bhabha, 'Aura and Agora', p. 12.

39 Stephen J. Greenblatt quoted in Bhabha, 'Aura and Agora', p. 12.

40 Bhabha, 'Aura and Agora', p. 13, emphasis in original.

41 Bhabha, 'Aura and Agora', p. 8, emphasis in original.

42 Miller, 'James Bond's Penis', in this book; Said, *Orientalism*, p. 87.

43 Chapman, *Licence to Thrill*, p. 13.

44 Chapman, *Licence to Thrill*, p. 13, p. 201.

45 Quoted in Chapman, *Licence to Thrill*, p. 15.

46 Chapman, *Licence to Thrill*, p. 212.

47 Chapman, *Licence to Thrill*, p. 212.

48 Rushdie, *Imaginary Homelands*, p. 87.

49 Rushdie, *Imaginary Homelands*, p. 110.

50 Sumita Chakravarty, *National Identity in Indian Popular Cinema, 1947–1987* (Austin: University of Texas Press, 1993), p. 4.

51 *Lonely Planet India*, 10th edn. (Melbourne: Lonely Planet Publications, 2003), p. 607. Vijay Amritraj recalls *Octopussy* being the #1 Bond film in India until the later [Pierce] Brosnan films. Released under its original title, in English, and without any scenes or elements censored or otherwise changed, the film was 'an absolute box-office success' in India, as it was worldwide (Telephone interview, 16 August 2007).

52 For a discussion of this trend, see Ajay Gehlawat, 'The Bollywood Song and Dance, or Making a Culinary Theatre from Dung-Cakes and Dust', *Quarterly Review of Film and Video* 23.4 (2006), 331–40.

53 Michel Foucault, *The History of Sexuality, Volume 1: An Introduction*, trans. by Robert Hurley (New York: Vintage Books, 1980), p. 57.

54 Foucault, *History of Sexuality*, p. 57.

55 Foucault, *History of Sexuality*, p. 58.

56 See Chapman, *Licence to Thrill*, p. 13. Regarding the concept of 'discrepant awareness', see Manfred Pfister, *The Theory and Analysis of Drama*, trans. by John Halliday (Cambridge: Cambridge University Press, 1988).

57 Siddharth Srivastava, 'What kissing James Bond means to India', *Asia Times*, 9 January 2004.

58 Srivastava, 'What kissing James Bond means'.

59 Indeed, the poster for *The Mistress of Spices* – in a cultural twist on *American Beauty* (1999) – features Rai lying naked on a bed of red chili peppers with her co-star, Dylan McDermott, with only a red blanket covering their mid-sections.

Toby Miller

James Bond's penis

Jane, 17, was quite indignant when I asked her if she found the films sexist. She replied sharply: 'I think a lot of women would love Bond to have his wicked way with them, don't you?' It was a rhetorical question, so I didn't answer. (Maria Manning)[1]

The most successful saga in postwar popular culture got off to a start after breakfast on a tropical morning in Jamaica on January 16, 1952. Ian Fleming ... knocked out about two thousand words on his Imperial portable ... two months later, he was done, with Commander James Bond recovering from a near lethal attack on his balls and Vesper Lynd dead by her own hand. A major addition to the world's cultural and political furniture was under way. (Alexander Cockburn)[2]

You've caught me with more than my hands up. (James Bond, *Diamonds Are Forever* (Guy Hamilton, 1971))

It's almost as if Bond was written for the purpose of being read for his ideological incorrectness by angsty academics who felt decidedly uncomfortable that they actually enjoyed these unsound films. Where could you find a better example of xenophobic, chauvinistic behaviour? Whether as a fantasy of post-colonial or masculine power, James Bond films are rampantly reactionary. So how do you explain their popularity? (Suzanne Moores)[3]

Admiral Roebuck: With all due respect, M, sometimes I don't think you have the balls for this job.
M: Perhaps. The advantage is that I don't have to think with them all the time. (*Tomorrow Never Dies* (Roger Spottiswoode, 1997))

The James Bond books and films are routinely held up as a significant contributor to, and symptom of, imperialism, sexism, Orientalism, class hierarchy, and jingoism – even as the first form of mass pornography.[4] And so they are. But frequently in a chaotic manner that is more complex and contradictory than teleological accounts of a phallic, hegemonic hero will allow. In this chapter, I follow up some previous work on men and culture, using methods that are comparatively rare in screen studies but are available in both popular culture and social theory.[5] These methods are not beholden to the unsaid, the repressed, or the hermeneutic turn. Instead, they are mundane, positive knowledges that work with conventional public truths as commonsense ways of making meaning. I will contend that (a) far from being the alpha of the latter-day Hollywood *macho* man, as per Sylvester Stallone, Bruce Willis, Arnold Schwarzenegger, and Wesley Snipes, Bond was in the *avant garde* of weak, commodified male beauty; (b) we can see this in the history of his penis; and (c) psychoanalysis doesn't help us to do so.

Bond's penis is a threat to him – a means of being known and of losing authority, a site of the potentially abject that must instead be objectified as an index of self-control and autotelic satisfaction. In the character's first film incarnation, Sean Connery's Bond was very much a spectator to his own, publicly shared penis, its stark movements between patriarchal power and limp failure anticipating the long, slow move that has gradually made the male body the object of routine speculation for commercial and governmental purposes, in a very conscious, highly unimaginary series of material encounters. Governmentality, the refinement of human bodies as part of rationalisation and utilitarianism, connects to capital accumulation in a network of power dispersed across the conditioned and consuming body. The male body references these complexities of contemporary capitalism, played out over the public bodies of headlined workers. Bond's gender politics are far from a functionalist world of total domination by straight, orthodox masculinity. Excoriating evaluations of women's bodies have long been a pivotal node of consumer capitalism. Now, slowly in many cases but rapidly in others, the process of bodily commodification through niche targeting has identified men's bodies as objects of desire, and gay men and straight women as consumers, while there are even signs of lesbian desire as a target. Masculinity is no longer the exclusive province of men, either as spectators, consumers, or agents of power. And Bond was an unlikely harbinger of this trend.

Why not use the nineteenth-century metanarrative that claims to deal with repression and displacement? After all, the hermeneutics of spotting hidden genitals may be the most enduring Freudian legacy. People 'effortlessly and unembarrassedly identify the phallus in dream objects, domestic objects, and civil objects', its real nature mystified by a metaphor that has distanced it from sex.[6] Psychoanalysis holds that the phallus represents power. The phallus itself lacks a universal material sign. The closest signifier is the penis, given male social dominance (and Freudianism's dependency on sex as the epicentre of life and analysis). The penis fails to live up to this responsibility, however – it is not as powerful as the phallus. At the same time, its unsuitability as a signifier, and the taboo on its public emergence, is said to metaphorise phallic power. Suppression of penile representations is generally attributed in psychoanalytic cultural theory to castration anxiety and the formation of the superego. When the penis appears, foregrounding its sex, it becomes paradoxically difficult to know in this discourse, because it fails to conceal its true nature. Hence the problem of the filmic penis. What is to be done when the penis is encountered as an overt textual sign: not secreted behind phallic signifiers or sedimented psychic narratives, but straightforwardly present on-screen?

Psychoanalysis is a factor in what follows to the extent and on the occasions when Freudianism and its kind are invoked intratextually as systems of thought, but not as an extra-textual truth to be used as a metacode. The position enunciated in *The Well-Tempered Self* and repeated here is that the human sciences (linguistics, psychoanalysis, and so on) divide the person into discrete entities that are set up as in need of amendment, reconciliation, and renewal because they are ethically incomplete. This search is asymptotic – it never reveals or creates that person's supposed expressive totality – but also productive, in that its legacy is a set of cultural norms that construct inadequacy. Such endeavours should be displaced by an historicised use of social theory to assist in the generation of new selves derived from the detritus of our present past. The penis is always already located in a symbolic order: distinctions between the imaginary and the symbolic, or the phallic and the penile, are distinctions of discourse. They reside in sometimes parallel, sometimes overlapping formations, with different material effects depending on their mobilisation at specific moments and places.

In this chapter, I present myself as a vulgar sexual materialist concerned to comprehend man-as-commodity. Because Bond is such a complex series of social texts, his film *persona* needs to be understood across sites, starting with the originary novels. Their trace was significant to film reviewers of the day and also provides an abstraction from contemporary viewing positions in order to get at 'the affective structure' of Bond.[7] This structure spoke to eight-year-old Jay McInerney when *Dr No* (Terence Young, 1962) was released. Bond had come 'to save America, and not incidentally to liberate me from my crew cut and help me to meet girls'.

McInerney's parents forbade him to see the film because it was said to be 'racy' and because the father's domestic mastery was attested by the son's hairstyle.[8] Now that's a male affective structure.

The novel Bond

Many British critics of the mid-1960s interpreted Bond as a symptom of imperial decline, evidenced by his lack of moral fibre and an open sexuality that assumed the legitimacy of strong women desiring heterosexual sex outside marriage.[9] This aspect made Bernard Bergonzi deride Bond as not 'an ideal example for the young', because women are 'only too eager to make love to him'.[10] The Salvation Army's *War Cry* journal objected to the same tendency.[11] Bond represented the casual pleasures that derived from a perverse intermingling of American consumer culture with European social welfare – what the *New Statesman*, in a celebrated essay on Bond, referred to as 'our curious post-war society'.[12] Connery stood for the right and the space – for men *and* women, albeit in unequally gendered ways – to be sexual without being 'committed', and he also symbolised polymorphous sexuality.[13] In *Dr No*, Fleming describes Honeychile Rider's buttocks as 'almost as firm and rounded as a boy's'. This drew a rebuke from Noel Coward: 'Really, old chap, what could you have been thinking of?'[14] Any scan of the popular sociology and literary criticism of the time indicates how threatening this was to the right, which drew analogies between the decline of empire and the rise of personal libertarianism.[15]

For all the supposed association with fast living, high-octane sex, and a dazzling life, Bond basically runs away from fucking in the novels, leaving the desiring women who surround him in a state of great anxiety. Attempts to match Bond with other literary-historical figures, notably via claims that the novels are based on either *Beowulf* or *Sir Gawain and the Green Knight*, explain this rejection of women as Fleming's 'medieval blueprint' of chaste valour.[16] But it's more than that:

> God, it was turning towards his groin! Bond set his teeth. Supposing it liked the warmth there! Supposing it tried to crawl into the crevices! Could he stand it? Supposing it chose that place to bite? Bond could feel it questing amongst the first hairs.[17]

Of course, 'it' is a centipede heading for 'that place'. Everyone recalls the spider doing the same in the film – after which, Connery runs to the bathroom and is violently ill. But the steadfast way with which Bond eschews sex in the original stories might as well have made it a human being that 'liked the warmth there', for all the horror of intimacy.

Bond's terror about 'that place' is also evident in *Casino Royale*. Le Chiffre tortures him with 'a three-foot-long carpet-beater in twisted cane'. The details are fetishistically enumerated in three pages of purple Fleming prose that describe the evil mastermind making his way across what he calls Bond's 'sensitive part', while the latter awaits 'a wonderful period of warmth and languor leading into a sort of sexual twilight where pain turned to pleasure and where hatred and fear of the torturers turned to a masochistic infatuation'.[18]

In *Dr No*, Bond is confronted with his desire for Honeychile Rider, her 'left breast . . . hard with passion. Her stomach pressed against his'. In response he 'must stay cold as ice . . . Later! Later! Don't be weak'.[19] Bond risks being taken down by desire, the threat of woman exhausting man's capacity to control his environs. This refusal draws a mocking retort when Honey addresses him in the third person: 'His arms and his chest look strong enough. I haven't seen the rest yet. Perhaps it's weak. Yes, that must be it. That's why he doesn't dare take his clothes off in front of me'.[20] Bond's struggle with the attraction he feels for women stands in contrast to Scaramanga, the villain of *The Man With The Golden Gun*, an assassin who 'has sexual intercourse shortly before a killing in the belief that it improves his "eye"', according to a briefing provided by the British secret service.[21]

The screen Bond

Ayn Rand, who adored the 007 books for what she saw as their unabashed romanticism and heroic transcendence, was appalled by the films because they were laced with 'the sort of humour intended to undercut Bond's stature, to make him ridiculous'.[22] These qualities of self-parody are key aspects to the unstable masculinity on display. The technology of the penis is mockingly troped again and again in details and stories from the series. The film of *Dr No* featured condoms as special-effects devices. Loaded with explosives, they blow up the sand in puffs when Bond and Honeychile are shot at.[23] The producers, keen from the first to defray costs through product placement and merchandising, refused permission, however, for a line of 007 condoms, despite pressure from the Salvation Army to refer in the film to the use of prophylactics.[24]

Elsewhere in the movies, however, the penis comes out of this protective sheath, just as the literary Bond's ambivalence about commodities bursts onto the screen as joy through consumption. Connery's Bondian sex is fairly progressive for its day, with the sadomasochistic aspects, predictably, too much for US critics: *Newsweek* condemned Connery in *Dr No* as of interest solely to 'cultivated sadomasochists'.[25] Identical critiques came from the Communist Party youth paper *Junge Welt* in the German Democratic Republic, and from the Vatican City's *L'Osservatore Romano*.[26] Britain's *Daily Worker* found an 'appeal to the filmgoer's basest instincts' and 'perversion', while on the other side of politics, the *Spectator* deemed the film 'pernicious'. *Films and Filming* called the 'sex and sadism' a 'brutally potent intoxicant' and identified Bond on-screen as a 'monstrously overblown sex fantasy of nightmarish proportions'. He was 'morally . . . indefensible' and liable to produce 'kinky families'.[27] But for Susan Douglas growing up, the film of *Dr No*, for example, was a sign that 'sex for single women [could be] glamorous and satisfying'.[28]

The producers cast Connery knowing full well that he was not the ruling-class figure of the novels, in the hope that he would appeal to women sexually and encourage cross-class identification by men.[29] Co-producer Albert Broccoli called this 'sadism for the family'.[30] Connery as Bond was frequently criticised as a 'wuss' during the 1960s, in keeping with the notion that his s/m style embodied·the weak-kneed and decadent cosseting that was losing an empire. *Time* labelled him a 'used-up gigolo' after *Dr No*,[31] while many US magazines objectified him mercilessly by listing his bodily measurements. (Connery's successor, George Lazenby, was criticised by the producers for being too *macho* by contrast with the first film incarnation: 'one could wish he had less *cojones* and more charm'.)[32]

In *Dr No*, Bond hands his card to a woman he meets in a club and invites her to come up and see him some time. This is an invitation for the woman, Sylvia Trench, to exercise her desire – which she does, astonishing him by breaking into his apartment within the hour. He encounters her practising golf in his rooms, attired in just a business shirt. *Thunderball* (Terence Young, 1965) finds Bond chided by Fiona Volpe:

> I forgot your ego, Mister Bond. James Bond, who only has to make love to a woman and she starts to hear heavenly choirs singing. She repents, then immediately returns to the side of right and virtue. But not this one. What a blow it must have been – you, having a failure.

The equal legitimacy of male and female extra-marital desire lives contradictorily within Bond's violent patriarchal attitudes. So it should be no surprise to find that the first *Sunday Times* magazine colour supplement (1962) features Mary Quant clothing, worn by Jean Shrimpton and photographed by David Bailey; a state-of-the-nation essay on Britain; and a James Bond short story. Or that the inaugural *Observer* equivalent includes fashions from France and stills from the forthcoming Bond movie.[33]

This is the all-powerful brute at work, with women cowering defensively?

Connery's prior careers as Scottish Mr Universe, Carnaby Street model, and Royal Court Shakespearean background the intersection of body, style, action, and performance perfectly. In gesturing against McInerney's father's crew-cut, Connery showed that the look of a man could transcend his class background and *politesse*. This was a postmodern figure of beautiful male commodification *avant la lettre*, exquisitely attractive to many women and men who either shared or read through his sexism and racism to enjoy goodness, excitement, and parody.[34]

From the first, Connery was the object of the gaze, posing in 1966 besuited for *GQ* and bare-cleavaged for *Life*, making it clear that sexiness did not have to be associated with a choice between ruggedness and style – the harbinger of a new male body on display.[35] The style has become increasingly familiar across the 1980s and 1990s. Consider male striptease shows performed for female audiences. This fairly recent phenomenon references not only changes in the direction of power and money, but also a public site where 'women have come to see exposed male genitalia; they have come to treat male bodies as objects only'.[36] Something similar is happening in feminist 'slash lit' fanzines that recode male bonding from TV action series as explicitly sexual, depicting hyperstylised, hugely tumescent cocks at play in sadomasochistically inflected pleasure.[37] Such texts trope Cyril Connolly's 1963 spoof 'Bond Strikes Camp', which finds M coming out as gay and 007 a transvestite.

Thirty years on, Connery's remains the style, the way to be. The *London Review of Books* published poetry about his Bond three decades after the fact.[38] And when CNN devoted ten minutes to the summer 1995 release of a new book on the culture of the martini, the story was divided in two. The principal diegesis was the launch in a Manhattan bar. Increasingly unappealing-looking yuppies were interviewed after their first, second, and third martinis. As hair went askew, ashtrays overflowed, words slurred, and mascara ran, the viewer was offered another diegesis: Connery's martini order from each of his Bond films, lovingly edited together by the network.

Connery goes gold/twenty years after

The Bond films make much play of the penis, spectacularly in *Goldfinger* (Guy Hamilton, 1964) and *Never Say Never Again* (Irvin Kershner, 1983). They do so parodically. Janet Thumim reads *Goldfinger* as a paean to 'personal liberation . . . privileging the young and the new' through the blurring of espionage with comedy, where the unpacking of secrets is less important than the work of spectacle: luxury Miami hotel life, a personal jet plane, gold bullion holdings, private laser weaponry, and regal sports. The real 'secret' is the capacities of Bond's Aston Martin.[39] She is so right. Bond offers transcendence from the bonds of origin via a form of life that uses commodities and sex to go beyond, to another place, and then moves on, without any drive toward accumulating power and authority. He is the drifter in a tux whose body bears the signs of social stratification, but who never stays in one place long enough to adopt the mantle of patriarchy through its trappings of soil, blood, and home. 'Why do you always wear that thing?' inquires a woman of Connery's shoulder holster in the pre-credits diegesis of *Goldfinger*. His reply – 'I have a slight inferiority complex' – short-circuits the critique. Narratively, this exchange bespeaks a gratuitous self-confidence: he lets go of the gun and is subsequently exposed to peril. For alongside all his dexterity, the Connery body is on display as ever, notably in a terry-cloth jumpsuit that he dons in a subsequent scene. This is 'major beefcake'. A sequence in bed with Jill Masterson is initially characterised by smart-ass conduct during a phone call where he tells a CIA agent that they cannot meet immediately because 'something big's come up'. But this is followed by defeat: he is knocked senseless and Eaton is drowned in gold paint. Back in Britain, Connery beats his adversary in a round of golf. But then Oddjob squashes a golf-ball in front of his nose in reprisal. Bond's reaction is registered via a medium close-up on a very anxious face. For Anthony Burgess, it shows Bond disconcerted rather than imperturbable. This quality of being 'ironic, but never facetious', where 'he knows the world, but he is not knowing', makes Connery not only a star but a strangely esteemed public figure.[40]

Bond is more directly at risk in the laser-castration scene, sensationalised on the poster advertising the film. Strapped to a table, Bond is taunted by Auric Goldfinger as an industrial laser cuts through wood and metal between his spread legs. As 007's muscles visibly tense, the two men engage in some badinage, and a close-up on Bond's face evidences further concern. He looks between his legs and across the room in a series of reverse shots with Frobe. As Bond is spread-eagled before the

17.1 Bond (Sean Connery) and Goldfinger (Gert Frobe) in the 'laser-castration' scene in *Goldfinger*

beam, John Barry's three-minute musical sequence 'begins by simply sustaining and repeating, with characteristic punctuation from the xylophone, an F-minor added-second chord'. As the beam heads for 007's wedding tackle, violins offer 'an eight-note motif, harmonised by the same chord'. It repeats in crescendo a dozen times, then returns to the opening two notes of the previous motif, which also repeats twelve times. Throughout, harmonies are sustained, with volume providing the chief dynamic.[41] Throwing out a last suggestion that he knows something about 'Operation Grand-Slam', Connery persuades his adversaries to turn off the band of light as it is about to reach his crotch. The segment illustrates Michel Chion's concept of 'added value', the mix of information and expressivity with which sound enriches pictures. It is fully achieved at moments of 'synchresis', when there seems to be 'an immediate and necessary relationship' between what is seen and heard, an organic one-on-one correspondence of visual and aural signs that produces empirical faith in the listener-watcher.[42]

Stunned by a tranquillising dart, Bond awakens (as do we through subjective camera) to the face of Pussy Galore, as if to complete the point. His weakness is certainly signalled by the fortunes of his penis – a sign of lacking control. Caught up earlier by strong feelings over Jill Masterson's killing, he had failed to manicure his conduct as per the technologies of the self that should mark him out as an effective agent. He has risked reassignment away from the mission, faced a gendered death, and then confronted the eponymous Other. We receive some telling lessons in the management of nuclearity toward the climax of the text. The sure and certain hand of a nameless, speechless bureaucrat brushes confidently past 007's clammy paws to disarm the bomb that threatens both them and Fort Knox. Smooth and direct, entirely free of the panic revealed on Connery's face via a series of cuts from ticking timer to sweating spy, this sober and anonymous administrative intellectual simply cuts off the device. For New York critics at the time of the release, this 007 was just too much of a failure for the film to appeal.[43]

Never Say Never Again marks Connery's return to the role, some two decades after *Goldfinger*. It contrasts Bond with his colleague Nigel Small-Fawcett (Rowan Atkinson), an ineffectual bureaucrat abroad who represents the unearned decadence of the English ruling class. His name alone establishes this ineffectualness through a penile slight. Yet, throughout, Bond's own penis is a vehicle for investigation and doubt. Dispatched to a health farm for a thorough purgation and makeover, as per the shared storyline of *Thunderball*, 007 is required to provide a urine sample. He makes a joke of this to the nurse, but the text then cuts to a worm's-eye view from the stiletto heels of the villainous Fatima Blush (Barbara Carrera). And Bond's line 'I was up all night', a knowing remark to his doctor made to be heard by the woman he has just slept with, is countered with the prescription of a herbal enema. Each triumphal moment is followed by a letdown. Even defeat of a muscle-bound enemy is only achieved by blinding the assailant with what turns out to be Bond's urine sample from the first morning. Breathlessly talking to Small-Fawcett over the phone while having sex, he quips: 'Just be brief; I don't have too much time.' As a woman moves astride Bond, Small-Fawcett offers: 'Just want you to know that I'm on top of things.' In their final confrontation, Blush orders 007 to 'spread your legs' and sign a testament to her superior sexual skill before being shot ('Guess where you get the first one'). But he overcomes.

This mythic imbrication of sex, secrets, and the slide from an Empire to the Commonwealth of Nations, drawn across the body of Bond and his others, is quite overtly a 'postimperial fantasy life'.[44] Being dispatched to a health farm in search of renewal is an intervention, not a symptom.[45] It's the fantasy life that saw huge public support in Britain for the folly of the Suez Canal in 1956, a folly that ended when Eisenhower told Prime Minister Anthony Eden to stop, and for the Falklands/Malvinas War of 1982, a farce that continued because Reagan told Thatcher to keep going. Bizarre sexual activities by politicians at home helped to bring down both British administrations, even as this desperate staging of global authority played out antediluvian hegemony.

The point is that viewers can see all this: there are no suppressed psyches here, clinging on to a lost world. Rather, Bond is the first screen action hero to embody and address the new, fragile pleasure of the commodity, where both his own form and the object he encounters are 'mundane objects of desire'.[46] What Michel Foucault called in the mid-1970s 'the grey morning of tolerance' that seemed to be dawning for a diversity of sexual practice could never be wholly welcomed or welcoming. It was necessarily marked by anxieties over sudden change and the inevitability of cheapened commodification through a 'movement of growth-consumption-tolerance'.[47]

Encoded psychoanalysis and the bodily commodity

Psychoanalysis has certainly been the preferred system of inscribing ethical incompleteness onto James Bond, Ian Fleming, and their male readers. Mythological and psychological criticisms of the series have been prominent for almost four decades now, stretching from Lacanian interrogations of woman and her lack to an object-relations account that says the gold in *Goldfinger* is faeces, Goldfinger himself the father's cock, and spying a regressive primal-scene pastime that makes men gay. Such approaches have made their way so successfully into the language of Bond that *GoldenEye* (Martin Campbell, 1995) finds Pierce Brosnan alluding to the issue. Conversely, alternatives to Jungian and Freudian methods have generally involved either genre thematisation or ideology critique. Here the penis disappears beneath a welter of spy-story precedents, class politics, or international relations.[48] Or does it? The gun as phallus is encoded in the textuality of Bond. It does not await the amateur-hour psychoanalytic textual analyst to uncover this fact. Rather, the symbolism is played with deliberately. In Fleming's *The Man With The Golden Gun*, a report is read that says 'the pistol . . . has significance for the owner as a symbol of virility – an extension of the male organ – and that excessive interest in guns . . . is a form of fetishism'.[49] Critics of the time recognised this. Sydney Harris regarded *Goldfinger* as giving permission 'to eat our Freudian cake and keep our All-American frosting at the same time' and the *London Magazine* pointed to the 'consciously Freudian structure of the fictions', evident in the father–son conflicts that Bond has with M and the master villains.[50] *Newsweek*'s *Goldfinger* review was titled 'Oedipus Wrecks', referring to Bond's relations with his boss M and the title character. And Vincent Canby looked forward to a moment when writers would use these symbols as an alibi to uncover 'some anxious, fundamental truth about our time'.[51] Where to now for the psy-complex hermeneut ablaze within us?

Instead, let us consider Joseph Maguire's four-part social typology of the body as a site of discipline, mirroring, domination, and communication. The *disciplined* penis is trained to be obedient, to transcend but also operate alongside biology – to be under control in a satisfactorily self-policed body, as per today's penile prostheses and Bond's time spent at the health farm recovering from his various excesses in *Never Say Never Again* and *Thunderball*. The *mirroring* penis is a desirable icon, used in the Bond saga to represent and produce excitement, anxiety, and failure, as per the bedroom triumph and decline of *Goldfinger*. The *dominating* penis is a physical sign and technique for exerting force over others, especially women – Bond's instant attraction to those he meets on the street or anywhere else, in all the films. And the *communicative* penis stands for a combination of the aesthetic and the sublime, as in the complex relations of size, race, sexual activity, and the Bondian organ's wry history – Bond sickened by desire and terror in the *Dr No* spider sequence.

Commercial and historical shifts in the protocols of producing and viewing James Bond's penis seem to heed, however unconsciously, Félix Guattari's call to bring down the binary that divides people by sex. Guattari seeks to 'destroy notions which are far too inclusive, like woman, homosexual'. He argues that when these are 'reduced to black-white, male-female categories, it's because there's an ulterior motive, a binary-reductionist operation to subjugate them'.[52] This is not to suggest the prospect of transcendence through the discovery of an authentic self: that search is an unending one given the power of ethical incompleteness over the human sciences. Rather, it is to call for an engagement with the sometimes murky, sometimes clear, often unworthy, and frequently insignificant historicism of man and his penis, their thick and thin past – in a practical encounter with occasions of masculinity. The nature of these occasions will be decided by differential forms and uptakes of a text, based on the social formation and the reading protocol disposed at the time: 007 is decoded by different audiences as sadistic snobbery, modern transcendence, libertine promise, amateurish dash, organisational obedience, new technological heroism, and outmoded imperial folly – and all through the lens of commodified male beauty.[53] James Bond's penis comes in many sizes.

Notes

1 Maria Manning, 'Futile Attraction', *New Statesman and Society*, 3.122 (1990), 12–13 (p. 13).

2 Alexander Cockburn, 'James Bond at 25', *American Film*, 12.9 (1987), 26–31 (p. 27).

3 Suzanne Moores, 'Britain's Macho Man', *New Statesman and Society*, 2.55 (1989), 44–6 (p. 44).

4 See Cynthia Baron, '*Dr No*: Bonding Britishness to Racial Sovereignty', *Spectator*, 14.2 (1994), 68–81; Christine Bold, '"Under the Very Skirts of Britannia": Re-Reading Women in the Bond Novels', *Queen's Quarterly*, 100.2 (1993), 310–27; Lee Drummond, 'The Story of Bond', in *Symbolizing America*, ed. by Hervé Varenne (Lincoln: University of Nebraska Press, 1986), pp. 66–89; Drew Moniot, 'James Bond and America in the Sixties: An Investigation of the Formula Film in Popular Culture', *Journal of the University Film Association*, 28.3 (1976), 25–33; and Michael Denning, 'Licensed to Look: James Bond and the Heroism of Consumption', in *Contemporary Marxist Literary Criticism*, ed. by Francis Mulhern (London: Longman, 1992), pp. 211–29.

5 For popular culture, see Joseph Cohen, *The Penis Book* (Cologne: Könemann, 1999); and Maggie Paley, *The Book of the Penis* (New York: Grove Press, 1999). For social theory, see Toby Miller, 'A Short History of the Penis', *Social Text*, 43 (Autumn 1995), 1–26; Toby Miller, *Technologies of Truth: Cultural Citizenship and the Popular Media* (Minneapolis: University of Minnesota Press, 1998), pp. 101–40; and Toby Miller, *The Well-Tempered Self: Citizenship, Culture, and the Postmodern Subject* (London: The John Hopkins University Press, 1993), pp. 49–94. For anthropology, see T.O. Beidelman, *The Cool Knife: Imagery of Gender, Sexuality, and Moral Education in Kaguru Initiation Ritual* (Washington, D. C.: Smithsonian Institution Press, 1997). For film, see Peter Lehman, 'In an Imperfect World, Men with Small Penises are Unforgiven', *Men and Masculinities*, 1.2 (1998), 123–37; and Peter Lehman and Susan Hunt, 'From Casual to Melodramatic: Changing Representations of the Penis in the 70s and 90s', *Framework*, 40 (April 1999), 69–84.

6 Elaine Scarry, *The Body in Pain: The Making and Unmaking of the World* (New York: Oxford University Press, 1985), p. 282.

7 Bernard Bergonzi, 'The Case of Mr Fleming', *Twentieth Century* (March 1958), 220–8 (p. 221).

8 Jay McInerney, 'How Bond Saved America – And Me', in *Dressed to Kill: James Bond the Suited Hero*, ed. by Jay McInerney, Nick Forllas, Neil Norman, and Nick Sullivan (Paris: Flammarian, 1996), pp. 13–37 (p. 13).

9 See Denning, 'Licensed to Look', p. 223; and David Cannadine, 'James Bond and the Decline of England', *Encounter*, 53 (1979), 46–55 (pp. 49–50).

10 Bergonzi, 'The Case of Mr Fleming', p. 222, p. 225.

11 See Michael Woolf, 'Ian Fleming's Enigmas and Variations', in *Spy Thrillers: From Buchan to le Carré*, ed. by Clive Bloom (New York: St Martin's Press, 1990), pp. 86–99 (p. 86).

12 Paul Johnson, 'Sex, Snobbery, and Sadism', *New Statesman*, 5 April 1958, pp. 430–2.

13 Bold, 'Under the Very Skirts of Britannia', p. 320.

14 Quoted in Mordecai Richler, 'James Bond Unmasked', in *Mass Culture Revisited*, ed. by Bernard Rosenberg and David Manning White (New York: Van Nostrand Reinhold, 1971), pp. 341–55 (p. 343).

15 See Cannadine, 'James Bond and the Decline of England', p. 46, pp. 49–50; Christopher Booker, *The Neophiliacs: A Study of the Revolution in English Life in the Fifties and Sixties* (London: Collins, 1969), pp. 42–3; and Penelope Houston, '007', *Sight and Sound*, 34.1 (1964–5), 14–16.

16 See Bernice Larson Webb, 'James Bond as Literary Descendant of Beowulf', *South Atlantic Quarterly*, 67.1 (1968), 1–12; and H.R. Harris, 'New Light on James Bond', *Contemporary Review*, 256 (1990), 30–4 (pp. 30–1).

17 Ian Fleming, *Dr No* (New York: Berkeley, 1990), p. 65.

18 Ian Fleming, *Casino Royale* (London: Pan, 1966), pp. 119–22.

19 Fleming, *Dr No*, p. 142.

20 Fleming, *Dr No*, p. 144.

21 Ian Fleming, *The Man With The Golden Gun* (New York: Signet, 1966), p. 30.

22 Ayn Rand, *The Romantic Manifesto: A Philosophy of Literature* (New York: Signet, 1971), p. 138.

23 See Alan Barnes and Marcus Hearn, *Kiss Kiss Bang! Bang! The Unofficial James Bond Film Companion* (Woodstock: Overlook Press, 1998), p. 13.

24 See Lee Pfeiffer and Philip Lisa, *The Incredible World of 007* (New York: Citadel Press, 1995), pp. 218–19.

25 Quoted in Nicholas Anez, 'James Bond', *Films in Review*, 43.9–10 (1992), 310–19 (p. 314).

26 See Paul Sann, *Fads, Follies and Delusions of the American People* (New York: Crown, 1967), p. 34.

27 Quoted in Alan Barnes and Marcus Hearn, *Kiss Kiss Bang! Bang!*, pp. 16–17, pp. 26–7.

28 Susan J. Douglas, *Where the Girls Are: Growing Up Female with the Mass Media* (New York: Times Books, 1994), p. 72.

29 See Albert Broccoli, with Donald Zec, *When the Snow Melts: The Autobiography of Cubby Broccoli* (London: Boxtree, 1998), p. 171.

30 Quoted in Barnes and Hearn, *Kiss Kiss Bang! Bang!*, p. 20.

31 Quoted in Barnes and Hearn, *Kiss Kiss Bang! Bang!*, p. 16.

32 Quoted in Barnes and Hearn, *Kiss Kiss Bang! Bang!*, p. 93.

33 See Booker, *The Neophiliacs*, p. 49, p. 238.

34 See Anthony Synnott, 'The Beauty Mystique: Ethics and Aesthetics in the Bond Genre', *International Journal of Politics, Culture, and Society*, 3.3 (1990), 407–26; Maria Manning, 'Futile Attraction', p. 13; and Bold, 'Under the Very Skirts of Britannia'.

35 McInerney, 'How Bond Saved America', p. 26, p. 32.

36 Susan Baggett Barham, 'The Phallus and the Man: An Analysis of Male Striptease', in *Australian Ways: Anthropological Studies of an Industrialized Society*, ed. by Lenore Manderson (Sydney: Allen & Unwin, 1985), pp. 51–65 (p. 62).

37 See Constance Penley, 'Feminism, Psychoanalysis, and the Study of Popular Culture', in *Cultural Studies*, ed. by Lawrence Grossberg, Cary Nelson, and Paula A. Treichler (New York: Routledge, 1992), pp. 479–94; and Constance Penley, *NASA/TREK: Popular Science and Sex in America* (London: Verso, 1997).

38 Robert Crawford, 'Male Infertility', *London Review of Books*, 17.16 (1995), p. 22.

39 Janet Thumim, *Celluloid Sisters: Women and Popular Cinema* (New York: St Martin's Press, 1992), pp. 73–6.

40 Anthony Burgess, 'Oh, James, Don't Stop', *Life*, 10.4 (1987), 114–20 (p. 117).

41 Royal S. Brown, *Overtones and Undertones: Reading Film Music* (Berkeley: University of California Press, 1994), pp. 46–7; also see Jeff Smith, *The Sounds of Commerce: Marketing Popular Film Music* (New York: Columbia University Press, 1998), pp. 115–30.

42 Michel Chion, *Audio-Vision: Sound on Screen*, trans. and ed. by Claudia Gorbman (New York: Columbia University Press, 1994), p. 5.

43 Anez, 'James Bond', p. 317.

44 Cockburn, 'James Bond at 25', p. 30.

45 Ralph Harper, *The World of the Thriller* (Cleveland: The Press of Case Western Reserve University, 1969), pp. 83–4.

46 Cockburn, 'James Bond at 25', p. 31.

47 Michel Foucault, 'Grey Mornings of Tolerance', trans. by Danielle Kormos, *Stanford Italian Review*, 2.2 (1982), 72–4 (pp. 73–4).

48 See David Holbrook, *The Masks of Hate: The Problem of False Solutions in the Culture of an Acquisitive Society* (Oxford: Pergamon Press, 1972); John G. Cawelti and Bruce A. Rosenberg, *The Spy Story* (Chicago: University of Chicago Press, 1987), pp. 126–55; and Tony Bennett and Jane Woollacott, *Bond and Beyond: The Political Career of a Popular Hero* (Basingstoke: Macmillan, 1987).

49 Fleming, *The Man With The Golden Gun*, p. 35.
50 Sydney Harris, 'Embarrassed, but He Did Like the Movie', *Citizen-News*, 29 March 1965; David Ormerod and David Ward, 'The Bond Game', *London Magazine*, 5.2 (1965), 41–55 (pp. 42–3).
51 Vincent Canby, 'United Artist's Fort Knox', *Variety*, 31 (March 1965), p. 3.
52 Félix Guattari, 'Becoming-Woman', *Semiotext(e)*, 4.1 (1981), 86–8 (pp. 86–7).
53 Denning, 'Licensed to Look', p. 213.

Jim Leach

'The world has changed': Bond in the 1990s – and beyond?

The future of the Bond phenomenon must be in some doubt after the terrorist attacks of 11 September 2001. In the days following the attack, many commentators drew attention to the disturbing resemblance between the televised images of mass destruction and the spectacular explosions generated by special effects in numerous action movies. The experience of watching television on that day involved feelings of fear and awe at the traumatic eruption of the 'Real', in Jacques Lacan's sense of the term as '"the impossible thing" that turns our symbolic universe upside down'.[1] At the same time, however, the images of the plane flying into the World Trade Center towers and their eventual collapse produced a disturbing sense of the 'hyperreal', defined by Jean Baudrillard as a state in which the real is 'that which is always already reproduced'.[2]

Baudrillard indeed argued that an understanding of the 'symbolic dimension' of the events of September 11 requires an awareness that 'it was they who did it but we who wished it' through our participation in the fantasies enacted in 'countless disaster films'.[3] Slavoj Zizek also felt that 'the shots we saw of the collapsing towers could not but remind us of the most breathtaking scenes of the catastrophe in major film productions', and he too argued that 'the unthinkable which happened was the object of fantasy, so that, in a way, America got what it fantasised about, and this was the greatest surprise'. The effect was that the 'violence directed at the threatening Outside' in such films was 'directed back at us'.[4]

The films that came most readily to mind in this context were not usually the Bond films but spectacular blockbusters, like *Independence Day* (Roland Emmerich, 1996) and *Armageddon* (Michael Bay, 1998), whose appeal depended on the spectacular destruction of many familiar landmarks. However, similar explosions, on a smaller scale, occur frequently in the Bond films, and Zizek used them as an example of the paranoid fantasies that shaped perception of the events and influenced responses to them. He suggested that Osama Bin Laden had become 'the real-life counterpart of Ernst Stavro Blofeld', the 'master-criminal' whose plans for 'global destruction' were foiled by Bond's 'fireworks'.[5]

In these circumstances, Zizek asked, 'will single hero movies like James Bond survive?'[6] It is not, of course, the first time that this question has been asked during the fifty years since the character of James Bond first appeared in Ian Fleming's novels. The question of Bond's survival was probably not uppermost in most people's minds, but it was part of the larger question of the extent to which the world had changed after September 11. While it became a commonplace to declare that the world would never be the same, Zizek's invocation of Blofeld suggested that the new situation would be explained and addressed according to the old scenarios.

A few years earlier, when Pierce Brosnan took over as Bond, a publicity release for *GoldenEye* (Martin Campbell, 1995) had already raised the question of whether the series could maintain its appeal at a time when 'the world has changed'. The answer, of course, was that the film-makers had responded to the challenge by producing 'a *contemporary* action film reflecting the world in which we live'.[7] Its commercial success suggests that audiences were convinced, and the next films – *Tomorrow Never Dies* (Roger Spottiswoode, 1997) and *The World Is Not Enough* (Michael Apted, 1999) – proved equally popular.

The specific world-changing event referred to in the press release was the dismantling of the Berlin Wall which, as seen on television, became a powerful visual emblem marking the end of the Cold War. It soon became clear, however, that, even if the world had changed, the new situation was not going to produce a new world order in which secret agents would be declared redundant. The bloody civil wars that followed the withdrawal of the Soviet Union from Eastern Europe, the Gulf War, the growth of global terrorism, and even the vague anxieties about the coming millennium created a sense of political instability that could challenge the abilities of any 'single hero'. In the circumstances, it was not difficult for the makers of *GoldenEye* to convey 'the idea of a world as dangerous as ever'.[8]

When the first Bond films appeared in the 1960s, critics were impressed by their 'non-stop action and fast cutting'.[9] These films now seem very slow to young viewers who watch them after seeing the more recent films and other contemporary action films. The new Bond films had to capture the imagination of audiences used to high-speed communications technology and living in a 'hyperreal' culture in which, according to Baudrillard, the 'contradiction between the real and the imaginary is effaced'.[10] They were thus under pressure to move even faster than their predecessors and, in so doing, they recycled images from the past, both the historical past and the fictional past of the Bond phenomenon, in frenetic complicated plots that often seem on the verge of implosion.

Bond's credibility as a 'single hero' depends on a conflation of the real and the imaginary. The world in which he operates must bear some relation to reality, and the films thus always include topical allusions, location shooting, and convincing special effects. On the other hand, each Bond film is judged by its variations on a well-established formula that provides its own terms of reference. In his review of the first Brosnan film, José Arroyo suggested that it succeeded in keeping the Bond phenomenon alive after the fall of the Soviet Union because 'we've seen the Bond films so often and for so long that we understand *GoldenEye* more in relation to the history of Bond films rather than feel the need to relate it to a broader history through some notion of realism'.[11] Arroyo was less enthusiastic about *The World Is Not Enough* which, he thought, depicted 'all-too-fleshy characters who desire, lack and feel' in a realist style that 'acts as an explosive and unsettling expulsion from the fantasies Bond films invite us to'.[12]

As we shall see, the tension between realism and formula takes on a new meaning in a cultural context in which reality itself is hard to define. In their elaborate pre-title sequences, as required by the formula, the new Bond films set the tone by using highly 'realistic' special effects to present actions that are clearly impossible. These openings contain 'enough explosions and spectacular destruction to provide the climax to most action movies', but they also establish the 'mood of good-humoured complicity' that Penelope Houston found in the early Bond films, although the 'good humour' is a little more strained than it used to be.[13]

The pre-title sequence in *GoldenEye* encourages complicity through an effect that is also rather unsettling. As James Chapman points out, the film 'straddles the end of the Cold War by setting its pre-title sequence in the past', but it does not clearly signal that it is beginning with a flashback.[14] Our first view of Brosnan as Bond shows him running across a hydro-electric dam from which he bungee jumps, as a rather improbable means of breaking into a military establishment identified by a caption as 'Arkangel Weapons Facility USSR'. Although the reference to the Soviet Union suggests that the action is indeed set in the past, the Bond films have always operated very much in the present, and we may be tempted to ignore this evidence. Perhaps the new Bond is operating in a fantasy world in which Glasnost never took place?

The credits sequence that follows includes toppled Soviet statues as a setting for its scantily-clad female dancers, lending topicality to the formula and confirming that the film-makers knew that the world had changed. In the first post-title sequence, we see the familiar sight of Bond driving a fast car with a female passenger, and a caption tells us that it is 'nine years later'. The precision about the time that has passed seems odd since we were not given a date in the previous caption but, while the world may have changed in the meantime, we are now in territory familiar from previous Bond films, even though we are not told the location of the mountain road or the casino at which the car eventually arrives.

The momentary uncertainty encourages us to fill in the gaps and thus draws us into the film's processes of narration. We are also invited to share the film's ironic perspective on the formula that it is using. When Bond enters the Soviet armoury, he meets his colleague, agent 006 Alec Trevelyan (Sean Bean), who cheerfully greets him by asking if he is 'ready to save the world again' and declaring that their mission is 'for England'. While the latter remark draws attention to the restoration of 'the patriotic code' that Chapman finds in the Brosnan films, the main effect is to establish a knowing awareness of the unrealistic claims that the Bond series makes for its hero and his country.[15]

The pre-title sequence in *Tomorrow Never Dies* seems much more up-to-date. It introduces the 'theme of cooperation with former enemies' but also demonstrates that the problem is now 'freelance menace rather than Cold War rivalry'.[16] Bond has infiltrated a 'terrorist arms bazaar somewhere on the Russian border'. Using satellite technology, he transmits images back to Britain where they are viewed by M and other members of the secret service, but also by a British Admiral and a Russian General. The weapons come from various sources (including the US), and the sequence plays on fears that the new weapons technology (celebrated during the Gulf War) will get into the 'wrong hands' (as was the case with a former Soviet weapon in *GoldenEye*).

The arms dealers are a threat because they contribute to 'techno-terrorism'. Yet they are simply applying free enterprise methods, and there is a sense that the officials who observe them are equally out of control. Against M's advice, the Admiral orders the firing of a long-range missile and then discovers that there are nuclear devices among the arsenal offered for sale. When it proves impossible to abort the missile attack, Bond saves himself and a large part of the world by taking off in the nuclear-equipped plane, after eliminating many of the dealers with their own weapons and just in time to escape the fireball that destroys the site.

18.1 Filming a boat stunt on the river Thames in London for *The World Is Not Enough*

Unlike in *GoldenEye*, this pre-title sequence has no direct connection to Bond's assignment in the rest of the film, but its linkage of business, technology, and politics recurs in the plot by which media mogul Elliot Carver (Jonathan Pryce) seeks to create a war that will be good for his business. He uses modern weapons technology to build a 'stealth ship', which cannot be detected by radar, and uses it to sink a British frigate and to place the blame on the Chinese. With the aid of satellite communications, he is then able to publish stories in his newspapers before the event to which they refer has taken place. As in the pre-title sequence, Bond has to prevent disaster before a trigger-happy government, under pressure from the media, can send the navy to attack China.

The long pre-title sequence in *The World Is Not Enough* begins with Bond in Bilbao where he retrieves a suitcase of money, apparently paid as ransom to kidnappers. He narrowly escapes an ambush, but the real action only begins back in London, where he delivers the money to Sir Robert King, an oil magnate whose daughter was the kidnap victim. After the suitcase explodes, killing King, Bond commandeers a speedboat and chases a woman he suspects of being involved along the Thames. When he is blocked by a wall of fire, Bond takes a short-cut by turning into a narrow canal, driving along a street, crashing through a restaurant, and landing back in the river, causing panic and mayhem as he goes.

King was a personal friend of the new female M (Judi Dench), introduced in *GoldenEye*, and both she and Bond feel responsible for his death. They both want to protect his daughter Elektra (Sophie Marceau), who takes over his company which is constructing an oil pipeline across the Caucasus Mountains. Their personal concern gives the narrative a more emotional charge than in most Bond films, but the opening also uses irony to draw attention to our complicity in Bond's exploits. When King offers Bond a job, he replies that 'construction is not my speciality', and M sardonically adds, 'quite the opposite, in fact'. The subsequent chase reminds us that our pleasure depends on Bond's capacity for destructive effects that he (and the film-makers) shares with the villains he is fighting.

There is also some more direct criticism of Bond and his methods in these films. On her first appearance, the new M denounces him as 'a sexist, misogynist dinosaur' and, later in *GoldenEye*, Alec Trevelyan, now unmasked as a traitor, asks Bond if 'all the vodka martinis ever silence the screams of all the men you killed'. He also wonders if Bond finds 'forgiveness in the arms of all those willing women for all the dead ones you failed to protect'. These are awkward questions, even if they are posed by a villain but, like M's feminist attack, they are easily caught up in the rapid flow of action and irony. There are similar moments in the other films, but the main effect is to defuse possible objections by showing that the film-makers are aware of them.

The absorption of critical arguments against Bond into the formula parallels the way in which the films handle their political references. Like the earlier films, they use topical allusions to link their narratives to actuality: *GoldenEye* refers to the break-up of the Soviet Union, *Tomorrow Never Dies* appeals to concerns about the spread of terrorism and about the power of the mass media, and the politics of oil provides the framework for *The World Is Not Enough*.[17] There are also casual allusions that connect the plots to historical events, as when Bond tells M in *GoldenEye* that the Janus Group, who are suspected of stealing the weapon that gives the film its title, were the first to restock Iraq during the Gulf War.

As in Ian Fleming's novels, references to actual events and institutions help to make the fantasy more convincing. Fleming also often used brand names to provide 'realistic' detail and to define the social status and personal tastes of the characters. The Bond films fairly quickly became willing participants in the culture of product placements that became a major feature of commercial film production. Brand names can still serve a realist function – and this, in effect, becomes the alibi for their presence – but the choice of product is now determined largely by the advertiser. In the latest Bond films, familiar products function less as a means of relating the action to external reality than as another component of the network of reflexivity and intertextuality generated by the formulaic style, which itself increasingly resembles contemporary cultural experience in which advertising and media imagery dominate many aspects of our personal and public lives.

One highly visible example of product placement occurs in *Golden-Eye*, when Bond drives a tank through the streets of St Petersburg and demolishes a truck loaded with cases of Perrier water, a striking image that functions both as an advertisement and as an ironic comment on post-Communist Russia. According to the terrorist Renard (Robert Carlyle) in *The World Is Not Enough*, Bond is himself an agent dedicated to 'the preservation of capital', and the films are very much aware of their own role in the cultural logic of the new economic and technological environment.

In their 1987 study of the Bond phenomenon, Tony Bennett and Janet Woollacott noted that, 'although Bond's success with women . . . continues unabated, the sexual attractiveness of the Bond character is no longer played straight' because 'Bond's sexuality has become fetished on to machinery, cars, guns, motorcycles, and what have you'.[18] Bond's long association with gadgets continues in the latest films, all of which include the obligatory sequence in which Q (Desmond Llewelyn) equips Bond for his mission.[19] He provides a perfect illustration of Bennett and Woollacott's argument in *Tomorrow Never Dies* when he provides Bond with a car that he can operate by remote control, like a toy, but whose computer speaks to him with a female voice.

In the earlier films, sexuality may be projected on to machines, but organic bodies are also a major attraction. With the emergence of electronic technology, the gadgets are now only a part of a much larger cultural process in which bodily experience is caught up in the (con)fusion of image and reality. According to Jeremy Black, the Brosnan films adapted Bond's character to make him more socially responsible, reducing the sexual content in response to the AIDS crisis and feminist discourses. He suggests that 'in place of sex . . . there is massive violence'.[20] It is not so much that violence replaces sex, however, but that violence and sexuality are both projected on to technology.

Bond's sexual relations have not changed as much as Black suggests. The most radical change is the substitution of a female M for the father-figure of the earlier films. In an ironic reversal of gender stereotypes, her subordinates regard her as a 'bean counter', and her analytic approach contrasts with Bond's trust in his 'instincts'. She regards him as 'a relic of the Cold War', but he is usually right, and her status is undermined in *The World Is Not Enough*, when Bond has to rescue her after she walks into a trap (nothing like this ever happened to her male predecessors). There is also a new Miss Moneypenny who accuses Bond of 'sexual harassment' (in *GoldenEye*), but the punishment she suggests is that some day he must make good on his 'innuendos'.

In all three films, Bond is (as so often in the past) attracted to and/or makes love to a woman who turns out to be a villain and/or dies, before he teams up with another woman who assists him in saving the world. He also still has casual affairs: in *Tomorrow Never Dies*, Moneypenny phones him when he is 'brushing up on a little Danish' in bed with a blonde pro-fessor at Oxford, and he seduces the psychiatrist M sends to assess him in *GoldenEye* and the doctor who must declare him fit for service in *The World Is Not Enough*. Women also continue to have suggestive names, like Xenia Onatopp (Famke Janssen) in *GoldenEye* and Christmas Jones (Denise Richards) in *The World Is Not Enough*.

The difference is that these affairs now take place in a world in which electronic technology both transcends the limits of the human body and makes possible a surveillance system that erodes any notion of privacy. There are two recurring images in these films that become icons of the new Bond: the fireballs that punctuate the films and from which Bond or others desperately try to escape, and groups of officials gathered around video screens watching action transmitted from elsewhere (as at the beginning of *Tomorrow Never Dies*).

The technology can be used both for destruction and surveillance on a global or more intimate scale. In *GoldenEye* the destruction of a Russian tracking station by a satellite weapon is intercut with shots of M and Bond watching the events via satellite. In *Tomorrow Never Dies*, when Bond attends the opening of Carver's television network, he discovers that Carver's wife, Paris (Teri Hatcher), is a woman he had an affair with in the past, and they renew their relationship at the crowded reception during a conversation that Carver observes but cannot hear. Carver dis-covers the truth when one of his employees shows him a video recorded by a surveillance camera and uses sophisticated audio equipment to filter out the ambient noise.

The interplay of sexuality, violence, and technology is handled in different ways in each film, but the films all draw attention to the formula to acknowledge their (and our) complicity in the technological culture that they depict. The range of possibilities can be illustrated by comparing the depiction of Bond's relationships with two very different women: Wai Lin in *Tomorrow Never Dies* and Elektra King in *The World Is Not Enough.*

Wai Lin was widely regarded as 'the most progressive heroine of the series to date'.[21] Played by Hong Kong movie star Michelle Yeoh, Wai Lin works for the Chinese government and is given plenty of opportunity to display her martial arts skills. Yet even she has to be rescued from drowning after the final battle, and the film ends with the inevitable embrace with Bond. The formula makes this ending necessary, but the effect is undercut by its parodic tone. Bond's refusal of help from the ship that comes to their rescue is reminiscent of the end of *Dr No*, the first Bond film, in which Bond and Honey Ryder are left drifting in their sail boat, but Bond and Wai Lin are on the smouldering wreck of a stealth boat.

Bond's affair with Elektra King is more complicated and 'realistic'. As they lie in bed, she tells Bond that she used her body to survive when she was kidnapped and asks him what he does to survive. He replies that he takes 'pleasure in great beauty' but later discovers that she has used her beauty to manipulate him as well as Renard, the terrorist who kidnapped her. Her belief that 'there's no point in living if you can't feel alive' initially affirms bodily experience in the uncertain world she and Bond inhabit, but Bond becomes suspicious when Renard uses exactly the same words. He thinks that Elektra may be suffering from Stockholm Syndrome, in which a kidnap victim comes to identify with the captor, but it seems that she controls Renard, who is gradually losing the use of his senses because of a bullet lodged in his brain.

Bond never really discovers who first used the words, but the effect is not so much to endow the characters with the 'depth' expected of realist films as to suggest that, in a world in which everything is open to surveillance, there are areas of human experience that cannot be known. In the end it matters little whether Elektra was a victim before she became a villain because Bond kills her anyway, after transferring his affections to Christmas Jones, a rather unlikely nuclear scientist who helps to defuse the nuclear device stolen by Renard. At the end of the film, M and her colleagues use satellite images that respond to body heat to locate Bond and discover him enjoying Christmas (Bond, too, cannot resist Christmas jokes).

This use of surveillance technology updates the endings of other Bond films in which observers are shocked to find Bond in a compromising situation with the latest 'girl'. Through such devices, the series has always played with the voyeurism inherent in spying, but now the experience of watching a Bond film becomes one in which the real and the imaginary are inextricably entangled. As José Arroyo suggests, *Tomorrow Never Dies* is 'a photocopy of a collage of previous Bonds', and so are the other recent Bond films, not to mention the DVD Special Editions and video games to which they give rise.[22] The formula precedes the experience, but then this is what happens so often in (hyper)reality.

At the end of *Tomorrow Never Dies*, Bond tells Carver that his efforts to use the media to achieve world domination have failed because he forgot 'the first law of mass media: give the people what they want'. The people, of course, want an ending in which Bond defeats the villain and saves the world, and the Brosnan films, like all the Bond films before them, provide this satisfaction. While Bond's enduring popularity depends on the appeal of imaginary solutions to real problems, the terrorist attacks of September 11, and the subsequent critical and political responses, expose the complexity of the relations between the imaginary and the real in the contemporary cultural environment. The future of the Bond phenomenon will help to show if the world has really changed.

In the September 2002 issue of *Vanity Fair*, a brief article previewed the release of the new Bond film, *Die Another Day*, directed by Lee Tamahori and starring Brosnan and Halle Berry. The article is placed immediately after a long photo-essay commemorating the first anniversary of the September 11 attacks. The reader thus turns the page from images of New York enveloped in smoke from the collapse of the WTC towers to images of the production of the latest film in which Bond saves the world. Tamahori is quoted as saying that he will be disappointed 'if it turns out the same old Bond film', but one of the photos shows Halle Berry emerging from the sea 'wearing an homage to Ursula Andress's bikini/hunting knife from the first Bond feature'. The more things change . . .

Notes

1 Alenka Zupancic, *Ethics of the Real: Kant, Lacan* (London: Verso, 2000), p. 235.
2 Jean Baudrillard, *Simulations*, trans. by Paul Foss, Paul Patton, and Philip Beitchman (New York: Semiotext(e), 1983), p. 146.
3 Jean Baudrillard, 'L'Esprit du terrorisme', trans. Donovan Hohn, *Harper's*, 304.1821, February 2002, 13–18 (p. 13).
4 Slavoj Zizek, *Welcome to the Desert of the Real* (New York: The Wooster Press, 2001), pp. 16–7, p. 21.
5 Zizek, *Welcome to the Desert*, p. 21.

6 Zizek, *Welcome to the Desert*, p. 39.

7 Quoted in James Chapman, *Licence to Thrill: A Cultural History of the Bond Films* (New York: Columbia University Press, 2000), p. 252.

8 Jeremy Black, *The Politics of James Bond: From Fleming's Novels to the Big Screen* (Westport: Praeger, 2001), p. 164.

9 John Brosnan, *James Bond in the Cinema* (London: Tantivy Press, 1972), p. 11.

10 Baudrillard, *Simulations*, p. 142.

11 José Arroyo, 'GoldenEye', *Sight and Sound*, 6.1 (1996), 39–40 (p. 40).

12 José Arroyo, '*The World Is Not Enough*', *Sight and Sound*, 10.1 (2000), 62–3 (p. 63).

13 Chapman, *Licence to Thrill*, p. 265; Penelope Houston, '007', *Sight and Sound*, 34.1 (1964–65), 14–6 (p. 16).

14 Chapman, *Licence to Thrill*, p. 253.

15 Chapman, *Licence to Thrill*, p. 248.

16 Black, *The Politics of James Bond*, p. 166.

17 *Tomorrow Never Dies* was originally going to deal with the impending transfer of Hong Kong from Britain to China, but the producers felt that this issue was too sensitive. It still lurks behind the film and contributes to the topicality of its plot; see Chapman, *Licence to Thrill*, p. 260.

18 Tony Bennett and Janet Woollacott, *Bond and Beyond: The Political Career of a Popular Hero* (New York: Methuen, 1987), p. 203.

19 John Cleese is introduced as Q's successor in *The World Is Not Enough*.

20 Black, *The Politics of James Bond*, p. 168.

21 Chapman, *Licence to Thrill*, p. 262.

22 José Arroyo, '*Tomorrow Never Dies*', *Sight and Sound*, 8.2 (1998), 52–3 (p. 53).

Stefan Hall

Shaken, stirred, pixellated: video gaming as Bond

In their introduction to *Ian Fleming & James Bond: The Cultural Politics of 007*, Edward Comentale, Stephen Watt, and Skip Willman ask, 'Where does Bond begin and end – in Fleming's mind, in the British spy novel tradition, in the many fan pages and websites devoted to his cult status? Does the cultural franchise of Bond rest on the novels or the films?'[1] To this list, one must add video games. Beginning with the earliest adaptations for the home console market and moving through the rise of home computer gaming in the 1980s to modern console releases beginning in the 1990s (including *GoldenEye 007*, *James Bond 007: Everything or Nothing*, and most recently *From Russia with Love*), over twenty video game titles feature Bond. Over their shared history, the Bond franchise and the video game industry have intersected in many ways, sometimes fruitfully and at other times unevenly. If we accept the premise that 'while James Bond is very much a human being, 007 is a technological construction,'[2] what does 007 as a gaming character share with his cinematic and print brethren?

There are three primary relationships between Bond's incarnations in literature, cinema, and video games. The first connection has to do with the consideration of the Fleming stories as games, both in their form and content. The narrative structure as set up in novels is a type of invitation by Fleming to play in Bond's universe as much as to play Bond himself. One can find origins of this premise in some of the earliest critical analysis of Fleming's novels, such as in Umberto Eco's influential essay (reprinted in this book) on their game-like narrative structure. From the beginning, there is something fundamentally part of Bond and his world that invites film, and subsequently video game, adaptations into the 'play situations' that Eco identifies in the novels.

The second association has to do with the development of Bond as cultural and consumer icon (both as one who consumes and one to be consumed), ultimately becoming a brand unto himself. Translating Bond as a 'trademark which, having established a certain degree of brand loyalty among certain sections of the cinema-going public, remains a viable investment' to the medium of video games has met with a great deal of success and occasional disappointment.[3] In the April 2007 issue of *Game Informer*, James Bond was ranked fifteenth in a listing of the top twenty best-selling video game properties, moving 30 million units in the life of the franchise, and ninth on a list of the top ten intellectual properties derived from a non-gaming source (selling seven million units during the last console generation alone).[4] In a field dominated by gaming icons such as Mario and Pokémon, successful series like *Grand Theft Auto* and *The Sims*, and lucrative film franchises from *Star Wars* and *Spider-Man*, James Bond has managed to hold his own over the past quarter century.

The third correlation has to do with Bond as technological body, first as a user of technology and second in his very presence being mediated by technology itself (through print, cinema, and video games). This creates an interesting series of questions, ranging from 'what can James Bond tell us about our own relationship to technology?' to 'what does (Bond's relationship to machinery in a particular way) say about humanity, and how we should use our own machines?' to 'what does it mean that Bond is defined by technology?'[5] The Bond aesthetic in video games must negotiate the influence of its visual presentation in cinema, and its derivations from that of its literary source, as well as the technical capabilities of the hardware and genre styles in the video game industry. The drive for visual spectacle in the Bond films is replicated in the video games; the cinema of attraction is mirrored in the attract modes of the games themselves. As a mixture of action, adventure, and stealth, the Bond films offer lucrative gaming potential in terms of genre adaptation. As a character inhabiting a world of increasing technological sophistication, the transfer of involvement in technology issues also affords a connection between certain aspects of cinematic content and gaming possibilities for players as technophiles.

This chase at first to suggest and then to wholly replicate a cinematic aesthetic within the construct of the games is a move which parallels greater trends in the video game industry to achieve a sense of immersion, photorealism (as defined by cinema, which itself is already an approximation of non-filmic reality), and verisimilitude in the Bond universe. As a '"mobile signifier", a floating cultural icon who is continually reconfigured and repositioned in the face of social change,'[6] Bond undergoes numerous transformations in his move to video games as both he and the industry change over time.[7] This then is his most difficult assignment ever: the agent in pursuit of himself.

A blunt instrument wielded by gamers: Bond in the 80s

The video game market in the United States had been in existence a full decade before Bond's emergence into the industry. Expanding its board game properties, Parker Brothers had found success in 1978 with their electronic handheld game *Merlin* and was thinking about video games. In 1981, at the Consumer Electronics Show in Las Vegas, the head of Atari's home computer division approached the senior vice president of research and development at Parker Brothers to ask if Atari could license some Parker Brothers board games for video game conversion. Parker Brothers decided Atari's interest, as the most powerful video game company at the time, was evidence enough that they should develop their own games. In a move that would have made Q himself proud, Parker Brothers was able to reverse-engineer Atari's hardware, which enabled them to go independently into cartridge production.[8] In-house development of their own games coupled with the licensing of easily identifiable properties would be the key to the company's success, and for their first title they turned to film and *Star Wars: The Empire Strikes Back*.

With the stunning success of their first set of releases, the next wave of games by Parker Brothers in 1983 would include more titles based on the *Star Wars* license and the addition of another lucrative film franchise with *James Bond 007*. Due to an ambitious production schedule, Parker Brothers had to subcontract production of *James Bond 007* to an external company, Western Technologies. While Western Technologies was working on the game, Parker Brothers had already announced the title and its concept in a 1983 game catalogue:

> Based on the daring train sequence from the James Bond adventure, 'Octopussy'. Take the train ride of your life with Agent 007 in this fast-moving action video adventure. A deadly knife-thrower and some trigger happy gunmen are on your heels as you battle across the top of a speeding train. Think fast – and act even faster – as you try to avoid their attacks without being knocked off the train.

Parker Brothers even went so far as to create promotional display boxes for the unreleased game. The first advertised the title of the game as

'James Bond 007 as seen in *Octopussy*', complete with the film's stylised, tentacled logo from the theatrical poster. The picture on the front of the box replicated the famous view of Bond seen through the barrel of a gun used in the cinematic introduction sequence. The second display box removed the 'as seen in *Octopussy*' tag line and replaced the graphic with a close-up drawing of a very recognisable Roger Moore, clad in tuxedo and brandishing a handgun.

The change in concept art was a reflection of a growing problem with the production of the game and a harbinger of Bond's often complicated adaptation to video games. According to Joe Gaucher, lead designer and programmer for the Atari 2600 version, Parker Brothers approached his company, On Time Software, because Western Technologies was behind schedule on releasing a Bond game. The 'Octopussy' version apparently existed in some form, although it was never completed. Internally at Parker Brothers, Charlie Heath, a programmer with the company from June to November 1982, programmed a short Bond demo based on *Moonraker* where the player was 'in space orbiting earth in the space shuttle, chasing bio-terrorist pods to shoot them down before they break up in the atmosphere, while [the] shuttle and the pod are being buffeted about by reentry.'[9] Gaucher remarked that Parker Brothers stipulated that the game 'had to have the James Bond 007 opening, correct music and proper James Bond action,' but left everything else open to interpretation.[10] In the game that was eventually released for the Atari 2600, players guided Bond through an oil rig raid based on *Diamonds Are Forever* (1971), an attack on Stromberg's undersea hideaway from *The Spy Who Loved Me* (1977), and a space sequence from *Moonraker* (1979). The box art returned to the first display version, again with 'as seen in *Octopussy*' removed, with 007 now returned to a fairly generic looking, tuxedo-clad man. The Atari 5200 and Colecovision versions began with a new underwater level based on *For Your Eyes Only* (1981).[11]

Despite the technical limitations of the hardware, the game did begin with a very recognisable version of the signature James Bond theme song even if the titular hero was reduced to a blocky graphic approximation. Since the game player controlled Bond as he was driving a rather advanced car – in a manner reminiscent of other popular side-scrolling games such as *Scramble* (1981) and *Moon Patrol* (1982) – the association was not so much with the character as with the sophisticated technology frequently at Bond's command. To make up for any deficiencies in identification with the character, the game manual begins by directly telling the player, 'In this game, you are Bond. James Bond, 007, the world's most famous secret agent. Renowned for your cool and confidence (not to mention your biting wit), you've been selected by the British Secret Service for four clandestine, utterly critical, and nearly impossible missions.' The manual continues to address the player in second person narration as each movie-themed mission is explained. Because of hardware limitations, the first Bond adaptations had to choose particularly iconic moments from Bond films to approximate and hope that the existing cinematic property would fill in not only visual but also narrative components that were missing in the games.

With the video game crash of 1984, the console market was effectively abandoned by game developers looking to utilise the Bond franchise, despite the introduction of the Nintendo Entertainment System to North America and Europe in 1985. Instead, that year saw the release of *A View to a Kill* in dual incarnations, with two different companies seeking to capitalise on a direct tie-in with the film being released at the same time. The first game, released by British software company Domark Group Ltd., was produced for a variety of home computer systems, including the Amstrad CPC, Commodore 64, MSX, and ZX Spectrum. Taking three scenes from the film – the chase in Paris, the escape from City Hall, and the race around the Silicon Valley mine – Domark utilised a mixture of side-scrolling game play and rudimentary 3D graphics, essentially crafting three mini-games under the umbrella of the overall narrative. The game box used the theatrical poster for its cover image, while the back displayed three stills taken directly from the film. Also that year, the US company Mindscape Inc. would release *James Bond 007: A View to a Kill* for the Apple II and DOS-based computers. Whereas Domark's release was a graphically based game, Mindscape's production was actually a text-based adventure where players were invited to 'experience all the action, excitement, and romance of James Bond in this interactive fiction adventure.'[12] Since text-based adventures are a type of game with text-based input and output instead of imagery produced by graphics, this move by Mindscape actually recalled Fleming's prose as much as the Roger Moore film and allowed Mindscape to diverge from the film's narrative in several places. Text-based adventure games were popular at the time also because the prose could suggest far more than the technology could actually represent visually on screen. Mindscape did well enough with this approach that they released *James Bond 007: Goldfinger* the following year, again for the Apple II and DOS-based computers.

For the remainder of the 1980s, however, it would be Domark who would produce all the games based on the Bond franchise. Their next release was *The Living Daylights* (1987), again solely for computer gaming. Using the theatrical poster again as the game box art, this title was released the same year as its film counterpart. A side-scroller featuring eight levels of game play, *The Living Daylights* began with a training mission in Gibraltar, had Bond assist General Koskov's defection to the West, rescue a Bond Girl, fight off henchmen, and finally confront an evil weapons dealer. In between Bond releases, Domark published *Live and Let Die* (1988). This game actually began as a completely different production called *Aquablast* being developed by Elite Systems International. Seeing the connection between the game play of controlling a boat and fighting enemies and the speedboat chase from the film *Live and Let Die*, Domark acquired the rights to distribute the game and swiftly rebranded it as an 007 product, complete with new title. With the 1989 release of *007: Licence to Kill*, Domark started a trend in naming the games by beginning with the 007 association. Continuing the practice of using the theatrical poster as the box art and being released the same year as the film, Domark published a vertical scroller where the player has to fly, drive, or walk through the various levels while dispatching enemies employed by Franz Sanchez and avenging the death of Felix Leiter.

The Bond games of the 1980s were primarily about representing some exciting action for the player, providing lots of shoot-em-up destruction, and what amounted to an unlimited license to kill. While providing some entertainment, at times stimulating and thoughtful, it is important to consider that these games were meant to be played on home systems in a reasonably private environment. This meant that the user had an intimate relationship with the title character more akin to personal consumption of printed texts (and later, home videos) instead of public consumption in theatres. Sales of Bond games showed solid performance, and even though there had not yet been a breakout hit, Bond was far from 'Game Over'.

Wear and tear out in the field: gaming as Bond in the early 90s

After the release of *Licence to Kill*, while the Bond film franchise took several years off, the video game industry kept the secret agent busy. Interplay Productions, Inc. would release *James Bond: The Stealth Affair* (1990) for home computers. This game employed another popular genre of game design, the interactive point-and-click, a graphic user interface (GUI) where the player uses the mouse to move a cursor across objects on the screen and manipulate them. This style of game typically focuses on puzzle-solving, and so *James Bond: The Stealth Affair* ultimately is in more of a detective/mystery style with regard to narrative, and closer to Mindscape's Bond releases, although Interplay did mix in a few arcade sequences to bolster the game's action.

Domark would continue their line of Bond adaptations into the 1990s, first with *The Spy Who Loved Me* (1990) for the home computing market. Surprisingly, the cover art on the box was not the theatrical poster for the film, as with previous releases, but instead featured a generic tuxedo-clad man brandishing a Walther-style handgun. The reason for this departure is most likely due to legal problems. The game itself is only very loosely based on the 1977 film; according to *The Bond Files: An Unofficial Guide to the World's Greatest Secret Agent*, aside from the title, the game was prohibited from using anything of the plot elements from the original Fleming novel. This certainly helps to explain why the game itself was basically a revamped shooter similar to Domark's own *Live and Let Die*.

Here, the player controls the Lotus Esprit, which can transform into a boat and a submarine, to destroy targets with lasers, missiles, and the typical Bond gadgetry. Following the trend to be further distanced from the source material, Domark would abandon home computer games with *James Bond: The Duel* (1993) and turn to home consoles, specifically Sega's Master System and Genesis.[13] Although the game box featured Timothy Dalton, the narrative created around this side-scrolling shoot-em-up involved a 'crazy professor' who is bent on world domination. Bond has to infiltrate his Caribbean island base, using Q's newest gadgets to dispatch the madman and his minions while also rescuing hostages. Since the market was already flooded with platform action games, *James Bond: The Duel* did not make a noticeable splash in the industry.

Reflections in a GoldenEye

Even with eleven titles, across ten different hardware platforms, produced over a decade, the popularity of the James Bond video game had yet to reach the level of success of the films on which they were based. After a run in the early 1990s, the game industry followed the hiatus of the films, waiting to see what was next. With the arrival of *GoldenEye* in 1995, the smash success of the film reawakened the franchise potential for Bond video games. Unlike the handful of titles in the 1980s that had been released in the same year as the films from which they were derived, the *GoldenEye 007* game was not released until well after the original release of the film, but in advance of *Tomorrow Never Dies*. Designed by the British company Rare, Ltd. for the Nintendo 64 (N64) system, *GoldenEye 007* is a first-person shooter (FPS) that not only includes explicit elements from the film (characters, locations, narrative) but also expands on what was originally seen in the film. As a game genre, FPS titles merge first-person action with cinematic sequences (first done as cut scenes and then later rendered in-game using the game engine, further erasing the line between scripted scenes and player agency).

Since *GoldenEye 007* was originally announced for the Super Nintendo Entertainment System (SNES), transitioning the title to the greater processing power of the N64 meant that the developers would have more opportunity, and more pressure, to showcase the features of the system. The long development cycle also gave the designers time to adjust much of the game engine and visual representation as well as to improve the enemy artificial intelligence (AI) and give the player more sophisticated adversaries worthy of a character with Bond's reputation. Finally, even though Bond is a global phenomenon, his roots are thoroughly British, and allocating the project to a British company helped to validate the line of succession for the publisher, Nintendo of America, itself a subsidiary of Nintendo Co., Ltd. in Japan.[14]

In the same manner that *GoldenEye* was to (re)present Bond for the 1990s – 'the new Bond was to be technological rather than physical'[15] – the game was considered to be a crucial development for consoles, which had been lagging behind home computer systems in gaming prowess. For several years prior to *GoldenEye 007*, primarily PC gamers had been enjoying titles such as *Doom* (1993) and *Quake* (1996). These not only demonstrated the processing power of home computers over home consoles but moreover showcased an increased interrelation between game story and game design. Initially, the design for *GoldenEye 007* was to be a rail shooter similar to Sega's *Virtua Cop* (1994). While a rail shooter does provide a first-person perspective on the action, the player has little or no control over the character's movement and instead only directs the targeting reticle of a weapon, typically a light gun controller used by the game player, in dispatching enemies, destroying the game environment, and sometimes rescuing hostages and other non-lethal targets. While the idea of stopping hostile forces and saving innocents seems completely in line with the Bond ethos, the limited style of interaction was not a radical departure when compared to the shoot-em-ups of previous games. Only after several months of development was the initial design modified to turn the game into an FPS. The success of replicating this genre of game on the N64, and advancing the gaming possibilities inherent in the world and narrative, established *GoldenEye 007* as an important title in the development of the overall FPS genre. Moreover, as it was an exclusive title for the N64 system, the popularity of the game – both in terms of critical praise and entertainment value – caused many consumers to buy the N64 system solely to play *GoldenEye 007* resulting in it becoming the first killer application for the console and giving it a solid foundation in the gaming market.[16]

While *GoldenEye 007* was the first title where actors from the film were visually recognisable secondary characters within the game, since the game is an FPS, all the action takes place from Bond's first-person perspective, so his 'body' is strangely absent. For such an iconic character, it is particularly striking that the Bond body – which has received considerable attention over its cinematic history – instead becomes an interface upon which several associations may be written. Accepting Bond's 'body as an instrument of perception', then in the case of *GoldenEye 007* this perceiving apparatus becomes quite literal in the way it stands in as the means by which the game is played or enacted.[17] Fleming's description of Bond, in *Casino Royale*, to be both 'an actor and a spectator . . . in other men's dramas and decisions' seems especially prescient given how he functions in the game.[18] Players feel engagement with the game while simultaneously forming an identification with the character they are playing much greater than with the earlier game adaptations. With *GoldenEye 007,* for the first time in the history of the Bond franchise, the game player actually had the chance to finally be Bond, a desire Kingsley Amis had identified long before in *The Bond Dossier* (1965).

Players of this game system, particularly younger ones who had little knowledge of Bond aside from his status as a cultural reference, did not fall into the target demographic of the established Bond fan, and thus might have had difficulty knowing 'the purpose of an object with which [they] have no familiarity. Philosophers of technology refer to this phenomenon as "technological embodiment."'[19] One of the main objectives of *GoldenEye 007*, aside from delivering a fun and marketable game, was in some way to reconfigure the franchise for an inexperienced audience. Even though the 'modern world knows James Bond through the films, not the novels . . . it is this very plasticity of the Bond persona that has permitted his adaptation to different contexts,' and thus the game provided a reference point for exposing a new generation to Bond, first to cinema and then to print.[20] Conversely, this plasticity worked in the other direction, as more mature Bond devotees could see the game as an access point to the entire world of video gaming, and certainly the association with Bond and technology makes the premise of video gaming a much more acceptable pastime. For Nintendo, the addition of *GoldenEye 007* to its roster of games definitely expanded its appeal. While being famous for Mario and other whimsical characters set in bright, cartoon-like settings, the Nintendo aesthetic definitely skewed towards the young player, and so *GoldenEye 007* gave Nintendo a level of credibility with the older demographic in the video gaming market in search of more serious play.

Interestingly, the game was based upon both the *GoldenEye* film and the novelisation of the screenplay by John Gardner, who had previously turned the *Licence to Kill* screenplay into a book. The combination of both texts allowed the game designers to extend or modify many of the mission sequences, which enables the game player, as Bond, to participate in an expanded capacity both in terms of narrative role and virtual environment. The original sets created for the film were first replicated within the game world as playable environments easily identifiable for users who had seen the film. As the gaming technology developed over time, the capacity to manufacture greater recreations of films became possible, including expansions of the cinematic worlds, thus extending the narrative past the original boundaries of its presentation. Much in the same way that the films had to negotiate the translation of their sources from print to cinema, the video games based on Bond constantly had to figure out ways to approximate the visual referents and refine this approach as gaming technology improved in what it could actually represent on the screen.

After the basic *mise-en-scène* was established, designers then added characters who linked the various game elements to objectives for the gamer. Not all of the missions were based on overt tactical offence. Many harkened back to Bond's role as a spy and incorporated stealth components. Others had variable goals that might change as the player progressed through the missions or became increasingly complex as the player selected harder difficulty levels, moving from 'Agent' to 'Secret Agent' to '00–Agent'. To further enhance the feel of being an agent on assignment, the game's menu system is represented onscreen as an MI6 dossier, with M, Q, and Miss Moneypenny providing background information on the mission and its objectives, increasing the realness of Bond 'primarily in the relation between the individual subject and the technological bodies that surround and interpenetrate him' within the game world.[21] Once a mission is completed, the player may continue to the next one, in essence advancing the narrative, or choose to replay a previously completed level. The incentive here is not to foster a greater understanding of the story but to complete missions within particular target times and unlock bonus options which can be used to modify various game elements such as graphics and action. Becoming adept at the mechanics of play, 'the self-reflective prostheses of [Bond's] profession, signifies mastery itself' over the game as much as Bond himself for the game player.[22]

Like its cinematic counterpart, *GoldenEye 007* begins in the same time and place, the mid-1980s in the Soviet city of Arkhangelsk. Following the opening sequence, *GoldenEye 007* deviates from the narrative of the film to include new missions in Severnaya and Kirghizstan. The game's narrative returns to that of the film, with Bond travelling to Monte Carlo, but then goes on to constantly alter the narrative of the film by rearranging, expanding, or adding plot elements. For players with no familiarity with the film, these changes are undetectable. For those who have seen the film and/or read the novelisation, this expansion of the narrative boundaries can be both confusing and enticing in that playing the game creates another read of the narrative, and so competing versions can engage in a sort of textual competition, while at the same time providing something unexpected. Furthermore, the surprising quality of the narrative can be changed several times by selecting the various difficulty levels, essentially creating new permutations on a previously played and understood part of the game. Of course, multiple versions of a text open up questions of authenticity, an issue which has continually underscored the entire Bond franchise, from fidelity to the Bond canon by continuation authors writing after Fleming's death to legal issues over ownership of film rights to the much-debated topic of which actor is the 'true' Bond.

'World domination. The same old dream.'

Following the success of *GoldenEye 007*, many publishers aggressively lobbied for the rights to the franchise, and in 1999 the James Bond game license was acquired by Electronic Arts. Electronic Arts tried to capitalise on the renewed interest in both the films and video games, releasing the adaptation for *Tomorrow Never Dies* in 1999 and *The World Is Not Enough* in 2000. *Tomorrow Never Dies* abandoned the FPS style of *GoldenEye 007* in favour of a third-person, or chase, perspective, but the game failed to achieve the same measure of success as *GoldenEye 007*. Electronic Arts decided to return back to the FPS format with *007: The World Is Not Enough*. Electronic Arts made the odd decision of farming out the game to two different developers: Eurocom, who would work on the N64 version, and Black Ops, who would code for the Sony PlayStation (PS). This strategy resulted in two games that, while similar in game play, were programmed at different levels of quality. The N64 version sold well, although still not up to *GoldenEye 007* level, while the PS version noticeably underperformed. Where had the *GoldenEye 007* magic gone?

Like many video game characters, '007 doesn't die, he just regenerates.'[23] Seeking to change their fortune, Electronic Arts tried a different tactic and for their next Bond game, *007: Agent Under Fire* (2001), Electronic Arts developed the game themselves (licensing the *Quake III* engine from id Software) and took the unusual step of creating a completely original storyline based on no previously existing Bond films or books.[24] This story involves Bond infiltrating a Swiss biotechnology company to stop a plan to replace the world leaders of the G8 summit with clones. Additionally, Electronic Arts fashioned a completely new look for Bond, based neither on then-current actor Pierce Brosnan nor any previous Bond actors. Various narrative moments in the story necessitated departing from the FPS format and using driving segments in addition to rail shooter sequences. This mixture of gaming genres, coupled with a derivative narrative, failed to deliver the much sought-after *GoldenEye 007* success.

Electronic Arts released their next Bond title, *007: Nightfire*, in 2002. Like, *007: Agent Under Fire*, *007: Nightfire* was based on an original story where Bond must investigate Raphael Drake, the president of Phoenix International, a green-industrialist behind the 'Nightfire' project, a secret operation that will allow him to take control of all global corporations and thus the world. This time, Electronic Arts licensed the likeness of Pierce Brosnan for use in the actual game and featured him prominently on the game box. To further enhance its cinematic relationship, *007: Nightfire* had an original theme song written for it in the same manner as the Bond films. As they did with *007: The World Is Not Enough*, Electronic Arts employed two different developers for different hardware platforms of the game, creating a similar situation as before where one version (for consoles) was considered a better produced product and sold better than the other (for home computers).

Frustrated by their inability to deliver a hit Bond game, Electronic Arts decided to take their time with the next Bond title, working on the game in-house and taking several years for development.[25] Completely eschewing the chance to make a game based on *Die Another Day* (2002), in 2004 Electronic Arts released both *007: Everything or Nothing* and

GoldenEye: Rogue Agent.[26] Electronic Arts appeared to have carefully thought through the game design process in order to emulate a particular Bondian experience, beginning with Bond himself. While the technical ability had been available for several years, *007: Everything or Nothing* marked the first time that a Bond actor (Pierce Brosnan) provided both his licensed appearance and his voice talent to a Bond title's in-game content. The drive to replicate Bond as a fully realised character as seen in the films had finally been achieved. Since *007: Everything or Nothing* returned to using a third-person perspective for its game play, the visual representation of Pierce Brosnan as Bond was strongly accentuated throughout the entirety of the game.

Moreover, the game was populated by additional actors, and their voices, reprising their roles from Bond films including Judi Dench, John Cleese, and Richard Kiel. The Bond Girl roster was populated with famous celebrities such as Shannon Elizabeth and Heidi Klum, and master actor Willem Dafoe was cast as the main villain and Bond adversary, Nikolai Diavolo, an ex-KGB officer and former business protégé of Max Zorin, who has a weapon capable of destroying all metals, except for platinum (he is as obsessed with it as Goldfinger was with gold). As with *007: Nightfire*, Electronic Arts opted for an original Bond story, but this time they hired Bruce Feirstein, who had written *Tomorrow Never Dies* and received screenplay credit on both *GoldenEye* and *The World Is Not Enough*. Finally, Electronic Arts chose to have an original theme song written for *007: Everything or Nothing*, but commissioned established pop artist Mya, who appears in the game as Bond Girl Mya Starling, to provide the vocal arrangements.

007: Everything or Nothing did enjoy improved success over previous Bond titles by Electronic Arts, but still not to the same extent as *GoldenEye 007*. The high production values of the game, from script to acting to design, actually helped distinguish it from *GoldenEye 007*. With the game being an original Bond story, and the lack of any Bond films after *Die Another Day*, some reviewers actually referred to the game as essentially being the Bond film for 2004. Certainly with Brosnan's departure from 007 status, it is a video game that marks his final performance as Bond. For a Bond so closely associated with technology, it seems like a fitting conclusion as the focus moved from 'Brosnan's Bond . . . onto the hardware itself'.[27]

With *GoldenEye: Rogue Agent*, Electronic Arts hoped to cash in on the popularity of the original *GoldenEye 007* release and offer a chance for gamers to engage in a little anti-hero identification. Returning to the FPS format, instead of Bond, a player controlled Jonathan Hunter, an 00–agent who loses an eye in an encounter with Dr No. After failing a holographic training mission (the opening level of the game, which serves to both acquaint the player with the mechanics of the game as well as advance the narrative), Hunter is recruited by Auric Goldfinger. As an incentive, Hunter is given a gold-hued cybernetic eye, created by Francisco Scaramanga (voiced by Christopher Lee, reprising his role from *The Man with the Golden Gun*), that gives him various technical powers. Rechristened 'GoldenEye' by Goldfinger, Hunter is sent to thwart various operations of Dr No around the world, and many of these settings are taken directly from the Bond films and novels.

Unfortunately, *GoldenEye: Rogue Agent* suffered from both a mediocre reception and outright derision for attempting to exploit the *GoldenEye* name. Coming after *007: Everything or Nothing*, *Rogue Agent* appeared to be lacking in many areas of what made the preceding title a solid game. Perhaps it was true that 'the very dependence of this cyborg subject-formation upon technology' revealed a vulnerability in that the 'right stuff' for a Bond game only really worked 'when it is properly connected to the right technological stuff'.[28] The ability to play an augmented super-agent somehow violated the humanity that underlies Bond no matter what the trappings of his role.

'Go on about the mechanism'

If 'Pierce Brosnan's portrayal of Bond in *GoldenEye, Tomorrow Never Dies*, and *The World Is Not Enough* simultaneously refreshes Bond's place in contemporary culture and reconnects him with the Bond of the 1960s,'[29] then it seems fitting that the next incarnation of Bond in video games after Brosnan's departure would be precisely from that era. Since *007: Everything or Nothing* was a completely original production, *From Russia with Love* marks the first adaptation of a previously existing film title to feature both the likeness and voice of the Bond actor (Sean Connery), although in this case the living actor is providing newly recorded voice work that is matched up with a different image of how he now looks, so that the Bond seen in the game is how Connery appeared in 1963. How curious, then, that the realisation of the cinema-to-game transition finally occurs in 2005 from a film property originally made over forty years ago, set during the now-defunct apparatus of the Cold War:

That the Bond of the millennium should revert to the Bond of the 1960s is due in some degree to the various interlinking themes – including global conflict and technological advancement – that bind the two periods together. It is also, of course, a recognition of Connery's esteemed position in the Bond canon.[30]

It certainly helped that *From Russia, With Love* remains the best received of all Bond novels and lends itself quite readily to game adaptation in how its 'game-like structure comes to a sort of narrative self-consciousness.'[31] Its film adaptation is held in equally high regard, not only as an exemplary Bond film but also as a genuinely artistic piece of cinema.

Various other actors that originally appeared in *From Russia With Love* had their likenesses, but not voices, adapted from archival film footage for use in the game, including Bernard Lee, Desmond Llewelyn, Robert Shaw, Pedro Armendáriz, Gert Fröbe, Lotte Lenya, and Daniela Bianchi (of these, only Bianchi is not deceased). Joseph Wiseman's likeness from *Dr No* was also used in the game. While primarily based on its namesake film, to strengthen the pedigree of the game Electronic Arts again hired Bruce Feirstein to write the script and make changes or updates as necessary. One of the most obvious in the game is the absence of SPECTRE, present in the film version but not in the novel. Most likely due to legal issues surrounding the Bond films, Feirstein rechristened the organisation OCTOPUS and removed Ernst Stavro Blofeld as the Bond antagonist.[32]

The game opens with the type of pre-title sequence that has become standard in Bond films. While attending a party, Elizabeth Stark, the British Prime Minister's daughter, is kidnapped by OCTOPUS. Fortunately, Bond was covertly assigned to protect Stark and he rescues her. In the game, Bond's primary antagonist is Rosa Klebb, here a KGB agent; in both the novel and film, Klebb was an agent of SMERSH. Klebb has secretly defected to OCTOPUS, and she uses Grant, her immediate subordinate, to track Bond. In the first half of the game, Grant protects Bond, but then turns into an attacker for the second half. The game ends with an assault sequence on OCTOPUS headquarters that is reminiscent of the finale from *You Only Live Twice*.

The most advanced gaming technology for *From Russia With Love* was used in the service of 'the image of Bond manufactured by the early films . . . bound over to the human as its own anachrony, to use the Derridean term for the historical subject originating in and haunted by its own displacement in time.'[33] Perhaps it was this displacement that caused the game, despite a good deal of advance interest, to fail to find an audience.

Certainly from a marketing perspective, the ability to play the Connery Bond was touted in the early press releases but not capitalised on in the commercial campaign for the game. Much like Fleming's later novels marked Bond's Scots background as a nod to Connery's cinematic success, here too the run of Electronic Arts ends with, for many, the quintessential Bond as far as the films are concerned. The idea of essentially rebooting the franchise for video game consumers was, at the core, a solid one, and certainly a similar move in the cinema with *Casino Royale* (2006) proved effective. Although *From Russia With Love* had extremely high production values for a game, the design was given higher priority over actual game play, which resulted in a lacklustre game. For video game players, however, *GoldenEye 007* remains the definitive Bond experience.

James Bond will reload

In 2006, Electronic Arts lost the Bond video game rights to Activision, the first independent developer of video games and a company whose origins date back to the era of the Atari 2600, where James Bond made his first video game appearance.[34] At the time of writing this chapter, Activision is working with one of its subsidiary companies, Treyarch Invention, LLC, on its first Bond game, a tie-in with 2008 film release. Since Treyarch has received much praise for many of its games – including *Die By the Sword* (1998), entries in the WWII *Call of Duty* (2003) series, and most importantly with the film adaptations of all three recent *Spider-Man* movies – and Activision has a well-established reputation, the hopes are high for an engaging Bond experience, utilising the most recent version of gaming technology available, including the game engine developed for the *Call of Duty 4: Modern Warfare* (2007) title.

While virtually every Bond video game since *GoldenEye 007* has attempted to replicate that game's degree of success, designers looking to the future of gaming and Bond need to be extremely cognisant of the history of the character, now spread across the media trifecta of novels, films, and video games. Bond will continue to be a site and a source for power and control. No matter what form he may take, his avatar speaks to images of affluence, fashion, modernity, and even class. Of all the issues raised by Bond in video gaming, however, programmers and players would do well to remember a core tenet underlying the action and entertainment of his endless adventures: 'Through Bond we are confronted with humanity's intersection with technology: how we create it and it creates us.'[35]

Notes

1 Edward Comentale, Stephen Watt, and Skip Willman, 'Introduction', in
   Ian Fleming & James Bond: The Cultural Politics of 007, ed. by Edward
   P. Comentale, Stephen Watt, and Skip Willman (Bloomington: Indiana
   University Press, 2005), pp. xi–xxiii (p. xiii).

2 William McKinney, 'James Bond and the Philosophy of Technology: It's More
   than Just the Gadgets of Q Branch', in *James Bond and Philosophy: Questions
   are Forever*, ed. by James B. South and Jacob M. Held (Chicago: Open Court.
   2006), pp. 187–97 (p. 187).

3 Tony Bennett and Janet Woollacott, *Bond and Beyond: The Political Career of
   a Popular Hero* (London: Macmillan, 1987), p. 294.

4 'Video Gaming's Moneymakers', *Game Informer*, 17.4 (2007), 18–42 (30).

5 Steven Zani, 'James Bond and Q: Heidegger's Technology, or "You're Not a
   Sportsman, Mr. Bond"', in *James Bond and Philosophy: Questions are Forever*,
   ed. by James B. South and Jacob M. Held (Chicago: Open Court, 2006),
   pp.173–86 (p. 174).

6 Christoph Lindner 'Introduction', in this book.

7 Christoph Lindner, 'Introduction', in this book.

8 Sydney Ladensohn Stern and Ted Schoenhaus, *Toyland: The High-Stakes
   Game of the Toy Industry* (Chicago: Contemporary Books, 1990), p. 259.

9 Matt Reichert, 'James Bond: Moonraker Demo', <http://www.atariprotos.
   com/rumormill/2600/2600rumor.htm#J> [accessed 15 November 2007].

10 'Octopussy – Some of the mystery solved?', <http://www.atariage.com/
    forums/index.php?showtopic=88086> [accessed 15 November 2007].

11 While James Bond did appear as a pinball game – 'Licenced to Thrill' – in
    1980, no licensed games were manufactured for the video game arcades that
    were so popular in the 1980s. Unlicensed appropriations of Bond, however,
    did appear, including titles such as *005* (1982), *Agent Super-Bond* (1982), *Spy
    Agent* (1983), *Spy Hunter* (1983), and *Sly Spy* (1989). Bond would reappear
    once more as a pinball with *GoldenEye* (1996) with the caveat, 'Be warned,
    after playing this game you may develop an uncanny desire for a Brioni
    tuxedo and a martini . . . shaken, not stirred.'

12 *James Bond 007: A View to a Kill*, <http://www.mobygames.com/game/
    james-bond-007-a-view-to-a-kill> [Accessed 15 November 2007].

13 James Bond's reappearance on consoles technically had occurred indirectly
    the year before, with the release of *James Bond Jr.* by THQ, Inc. for the NES
    and SNES. Based on a 1991 cartoon series by the same name, the player con-
    trolled James Bond's teenage nephew on a mission to find missing scientists
    and save the world in a manner of side-scrolling action similar to the arcade
    game *Contra* (1987).

14 Rare would be awarded the Best UK Developer Award by the British
    Academy of Film and Television Arts (BAFTA) during the 1998 Interactive

Entertainment Awards, while *GoldenEye 007* earned the Best Game award in the same year.

15 Martin Willis, 'Hard-Wear: the Millennium, Technology, and Brosnan's Bond', in this book.

16 Eventually, five of the top 20 all-time-best-selling N64 titles were developed by Rare, including *GoldenEye 007*, which became the second-best-selling game in North America and eventually moved over 8 million units in worldwide sales. In a move to further legitimise its Xbox system, Microsoft eventually acquired complete rights to the company in 2002 at a total cost of $377 million.

17 Suzie Gibson, 'Bond and Phenomenology: Shaken, not Stirred', in *James Bond and Philosophy: Questions are Forever*, ed. by James B. South and Jacob M. Held (Chicago: Open Court, 2006), pp. 46–62 (p. 59).

18 Ian Fleming, *Casino Royale* (London: Pan Books, 1955), p. 48.

19 McKinney, 'James Bond and the Philosophy of Technology', p. 189.

20 Jeremy Black, *The Politics of James Bond: From Fleming's Novels to the Big Screen*, (Westport: Praeger, 2001), p. 91.

21 Patrick O'Donnell, 'James Bond, Cyborg-Aristocrat', in *Ian Fleming & James Bond: The Cultural Politics of 007*, ed. by Edward P. Comentale, Stephen Watt, and Skip Willman (Bloomington: Indiana University Press, 2005), pp. 55–68 (p. 67).

22 Judith Roof, 'Living the James Bond Lifestyle', in *Ian Fleming & James Bond: The Cultural Politics of 007*, ed. by Edward P. Comentale, Stephen Watt, and Skip Willman (Bloomington: Indiana University Press, 2005), pp. 71–86 (p. 71).

23 Lindner, 'Introduction', in this book.

24 In 2000, Electronic Arts had released a second Bond game for that year, *007: Racing*, which was not based on any pre-existing Bond story but instead was essentially a reworked version of the classic arcade game *Spy Hunter*, a vertical scrolling shooter where the player guided a specially outfitted car – clearly inspired by the Bond films – that could fire machine guns and missiles, deploy oil slicks and smoke screens, and transform into a boat. In *007: Racing*, players could choose among different cars, including the BMW Z3, Aston Martin DB5, or Lotus Esprit, to complete the missions. This game did license Pierce Brosnan's likeness and featured both Q and R modifying the vehicles.

25 In 2002, In-Fusio released *007: Ice Racer*, a game designed for mobile phones using the ExEn system (now defunct). Based on *Die Another Day*, the player drove the modified Aston Martin in pursuit of Zao and Jinx en route to the Ice Palace.

26 In late 2003, Electronic Arts actually released a version of *Everything or Nothing* for the Nintendo Game Boy Advance (GBA). While this version was drastically altered due to the processing power of the GBA, it featured isometric game play, as Bond and while driving his car, over more than 20 levels,

and a multiplayer mode that unlocked once the single-player campaign was completed. Additionally, when players connected the game to a Nintendo GameCube, bonus content to the game was activated.

27 Willis, 'Hard-Wear', in this book.

28 O'Donnell, 'James Bond, Cyborg-Aristocrat', p. 56.

29 Lindner, 'Introduction', in this book.

30 Willis, 'Hard-Wear', in this book.

31 Denning, 'Licensed to Look', in this book.

32 This is a fairly curious situation, particularly since this game requires Bond to use the jet pack from *Thunderball* (1965), which is the film that caused the rights dispute in the first place.

33 O'Donnell, 'James Bond, Cyborg-Aristocrat', p. 60.

34 Since 1999, Electronic Arts held the exclusive rights to develop games based on the official James Bond films. In 2003, MGM Interactive extended those rights until 2010; however, this deal was terminated in September 2007 due to the publicly expressed desire of Electronic Arts to move away from movie franchise games and develop original intellectual properties. Privately, some sources claimed that the lack of a tie-in game for *Casino Royale*, which cost MGM millions of dollars in lost revenue, resulted in the two companies terminating their deal.

35 Jacob Held, 'Tell me, Commander, how far does your expertise extend into the field of philosophy?', in *James Bond and Philosophy: Questions are Forever*, ed. by James B. South and Jacob M. Held (Chicago: Open Court. 2006), pp. xiii–xv (p. xv).

Select bibliography

Amis, Kingsley, *The James Bond Dossier* (New York: New American Library, 1965).

Balio, Tino, *United Artists: The Company That Changed the Film Industry* (Madison: University of Wisconsin Press, 1987).

Banner, Deborah, 'Why Don't They Just Shoot Him? The Bond Villains and Cold War Heroism', in *The Devil Himself: Villainy in Detective Fiction and Film*, ed. by Stacy Gillis and Philippa Gates (Westport, CT: Greenwood, 2002).

Barnes, Alan and Marcus Hearn, *Kiss Kiss Bang! Bang! The Unofficial James Bond Film Companion* (Woodstock: Overlook Press, 1998).

Bear, Andrew, 'Intellectuals and 007: High Comedy and Total Stimulation', *Dissent*, Winter (1966), 23–7.

Bennett, Tony, 'James Bond as Popular Hero', *U203 Popular Culture: Unit 21* (Milton Keynes: Open University Press, 1982).

——, 'Text and Social Process: the Case of James Bond', *Screen Education*, 41 (1982), 3–14.

——, 'The Bond Phenomenon: Theorising a Popular Hero', *Southern Review*, 16.2 (1983), 195–225.

——, 'James Bond in the 1980s', *Marxism Today*, 27.6 (1983), 37–9.

Bennett, Tony and Janet Woollacott, *Bond and Beyond: The Political Career of a Popular Hero* (London: Macmillan, 1987).

Benson, Raymond, *The James Bond Bedside Companion* (New York: Dodd, Mead, and Co., 1984).

Black, Jeremy, *The Politics of James Bond: From Fleming's Novels to the Big Screen* (Westport: Praeger, 2001).

——, 'The Geopolitics of James Bond', *Intelligence and National Security*, 19.2 (2004), 290–303.

Booker, Christopher, *The Neophiliacs: A Case Study of the Revolution in English Life in the Fifties and Sixties* (London: Collins, 1969).

Boyd, Ann, *The Devil With James Bond* (Richmond: John Knox Press, 1967).

Brabazon, Tara, *Ladies who Lunge: Celebrating Difficult Women* (University of New South Wales Press, 2002).

Britton, Wesley A., *Beyond Bond: Spies in Fiction and Film* (Oxford: Harcourt, 2005).

Broccoli, Albert with Donald Zec, *When the Snow Melts: The Autobiography of Cubby Broccoli* (London: Boxtree, 1998).

Brosnan, John, *James Bond in the Cinema* (London: Tantivy, 1981).

Cannadine, David, 'James Bond & the Decline of England', *Encounter*, 53.3 (1979), 46–55.

Carpenter, Rebecca, 'Male Failure and Male Fantasy: British Masculine Mythologies of the 1950s, or Jimmy, Jim, and Bond, James Bond', *Minnesota Review* 55–7 (2002), 187–201.

Chapman, James, *Licence To Thrill: A Cultural History of the James Bond Films* (London: I.B. Tauris, 2000).

Chirico, Robert, 'From Baker Street with Love: Being a Study of James Bond and His Illustrious Predecessor', *The Baker Street Journal*, 38.4 (1988), 199–203.

Comentale, Edward P., Stephen Watt, and Skip Willman (eds), *Ian Fleming & James Bond: The Cultural Politics of 007* (Bloomington and Indianapolis: Indiana University Press, 2005).

Curran, James and Vincent Porter (eds), *British Cinema History* (London: Weidenfeld and Nicolson, 1983).

Del Bueno, Oreste and Umberto Eco (eds), *The Bond Affair*, trans. by R. A. Downie (London: Macdonald, 1966).

Denning, Michael, *Cover Stories: Narrative and Ideology in the British Spy Thriller* (London: Routledge and Kegan Paul, 1987).

Dodds, Klaus, 'Licensed to Stereotype: Popular Geopolitics, James Bond, and the Spectre of Balkanism', *Geopolitics* 8 (2002): 125–56.

——, 'Screening Geopolitics: James Bond and the Early Cold War Films' *Geopolitics* 10 (2005), 266–89.

Douglas, Andy, 'Bond Never Dies', *British Film and Television Facilities Journal*, 9 (1998), 46–55.

Dow, Richard R., 'Bond Films; Exploits of a Culture Hero', *Screen Education*, 41 (1967), 104–17.

Drummond, Lee, 'The Story of Bond', in *Symbolizing America*, ed. by Hervé Varenne (Lincoln: University of Nebraska Press, 1986), pp. 66–89.

——, *American Dreamtime: A Cultural Analysis of Popular Movies and their Implications for a Science of Humanity* (London: Littlefield Adams, 1996).

Early, Gerald, 'Jungle Fever: Ian Fleming's James Bond Novels, the Cold War, and Jamaica', *New Letters*, 66.1 (1999), 139–63.

Earnest, David C. and James N. Rosenau, 'The Spy Who Loved Globalization', *Foreign Policy*, 120 (September/October, 2000), pp. 88–90.

Eco, Umberto, *The Role of the Reader: Explorations in the Semiotics of Texts* (Bloomington: Indiana University Press, 1979).

Edgren, Gretchen, *The Playboy Book: Fifty Years* (London: Taschen, 2005).

Fiegel, Eddi and John Barry, *A Sixties Theme: From James Bond to Midnight Cowboy* (London: Constable, 1998).

Gant, Richard, *Ian Fleming: The Man with the Golden Pen* (London: Mayflower-Dell, 1966).

Hibbin, Sally, *The Official James Bond 007 Movie Book* (London: Hamlyn, 1987).

Hoberman, J., 'When Dr No Met Dr Strangelove', *Sight and Sound*, 3.12 (1993), 16–21.

Jenkins, Tricia, 'James Bond's "Pussy" and Anglo-American Cold War Sexuality', *Journal of American Culture*, 28.3 (2005), 309–17.

Ladenson, Elisabeth, 'Lovely Lesbians; or Pussy Galore', *GLQ: A Journal of Lesbian and Gay Studies*, 7.3 (2001), 417–23.

Lane, Andy and Paul Simpson, *The Bond Files: The Unofficial Guide to the World's Greatest Secret Agent* (London: Virgin, 1998).

Lane, Sheldon (ed.), *For Bond Lovers Only* (London: Panther Books, 1996).

Lehman, Peter (ed.), *Masculinity: Bodies, Movies, Culture* (Routledge, 2001).

Lukk, Tiiu, *Movie Marketing: Opening the Picture and Giving It Legs* (Los Angeles: Silman-James, 1997).

Lycett, Andrew, *Ian Fleming: The Man Behind James Bond* (London: Weidenfeld & Nicolson, 1995).

McInerney, Jay, Nick Foulkes, Neil Norman, and Nick Sullivan, *Dressed to Kill: James Bond the Suited Hero* (Paris: Flammarion, 1996).

Mellen, Joan, *Big, Bad Wolves: Masculinity in the American Film* (New York: Pantheon Books, 1977).

Merry, Bruce, *Anatomy of the Spy Thriller* (Dublin: Gill and Macmillan, 1977).

Miller, Toby, *Spyscreen: Espionage on Film and TV from the 1930s to the 1960s* (New York: Oxford University Press, 2003).

Moniot, Drew, 'James Bond and America in the Sixties: An Investigation of Formula Film in Popular Culture', *Journal of the University Film Association*, 28.3 (1976), 25–35.

Morgan, Kenneth, *The People's Peace: British History 1945–1990* (Oxford: Oxford University Press, 1990).

Mosley, Rachel (ed.), *Fashioning Film Stars: Dress, Culture, Identity*, (London: BFI, 2005).

Murphy, Robert, *Sixties British Cinema* (London: British Film Institute, 1992).

Murray, Scott, 'The Bond Age', *Cinema Papers*, 66 (1987), 20–5.

——, 'Bond Age Women', *Cinema Papers*, 67 (1988), 32–7.

Neale, Stephen, 'Masculinity as Spectacle', *Screen*, 24.6 (1983), 2–16.

Osgerby, Bill, *Playboys in Paradise: Masculinity, Youth and Leisure-style in Modern America* (Oxford: Berg, 2001).

Pearson, John, *The Life of Ian Fleming* (London: Jonathan Cape, 1966).

——, *James Bond: The Authorised Biography of 007* (London: Sidgwick and Jackson, 1973).

Pfeiffer, Lee and Philip Lisa, *The Incredible World of 007* (New York: Citadel, 1992).

Pfeiffer, Lee and Dave Worrall, *The Essential Bond: The Authorized Guide to the World of 007* (London: Boxtree, 1998).

Price, Thomas J. 'The Changing Image of the Soviets in the Bond Saga: From Bond-Villains to Acceptable Role Partners', *Journal of Popular Culture*, 26.1 (1992), 17–37.

Rissik, Andrew, *The James Bond Man: The Films of Sean Connery* (London: Elm Tree, 1983).

Rosenberg, Bruce A., *The Spy Story* (Chicago: University of Chicago Press, 1987).

Rubin, Steven Jay, *The James Bond Films* (Norwalk: Arlington House, 1981).

——, *The Complete James Bond Movie Encyclopedia* (Chicago: Contemporary Books, 1995).

Rye, Graham, *The James Bond Girls* (Secaucus: Citadel Press, 1998).

Sauerberg, Lars Ole, *Secret Agents in Fiction: Ian Fleming, John le Carré, and Len Deighton* (London: Macmillan, 1984).

South, James B., and Jacob M. Held (eds), *James Bond and Philosophy: Questions are Forever* (Chicago: Open Court, 2006).

Smith, Jeff, *The Sounds of Commerce: Marketing Popular Film Music* (New York: Columbia University Press, 1998).

Smith, Jim and Stephen Lavington, *Bond Films* (London: Virgin Books, 2002).

Snelling, O. F., *James Bond: A Report* (London: Panther, 1965).

Stafford, David, *The Silent Game: The Real World of Imaginary Spies* (Toronto: Lester & Orpen Dennys, 1988).

Sutherland, John, *Fiction and the Fiction Industry* (London: Athlone Press, 1978).

Synnott, Anthony, 'The Beauty Mystique: Ethics and Aesthetics in the Bond Genre', *International Journal of Politics, Culture, and Society*, 3.3 (1990), 407–26.

Walker, Alexander, *Hollywood England: the British Film Industry in the Sixties* (London: Michael Joseph, 1974).

Wark, Wesley K. (ed.), *Spy Fiction, Spy Films, and Real Intelligence* (London: Frank Cass, 1991).

Webb, Bernice Larson, 'James Bond as Literary Descendant of Beowulf', *South Atlantic Quarterly*, 67.1 (1968), 1–12.

Winder, Simon, *The Man Who Saved Britain: A Personal Journey into the Disturbing World of James Bond* (New York: Farrar, Straus and Giroux, 2006).

Woodward, Stephen, 'The Arch Archenemies of James Bond', in *Bad: Infamy,*

Darkness, Evil, and Slime on Screen, ed. by Murray Pomerance (Albany: State University of New York Press, 2004), pp. 173–86.

Worrall, Dave, *The Most Famous Car in the World: The Complete History of the James Bond Aston Martin DB5* (Christchurch: Solo, 1991).

Index